The Right to Development

# Chinese Perspectives on Human Rights and Good Governance

*Editor-in-Chief*

Zhang Wei

*Executive Editors*

Li Ruoyu, Zhang Chong and Shi Hui

*Editorial Board*

Bai Guimei – Ban Wenzhan – Chang Jian – Chen Shiqiu – Duan Qinghong – Han Dayuan – Li Buyun – Li Weiwei – Liu Hainian – Luo Yanhua – Shu Guoying – Sun Xiaoxia – Wei Mei – Xia Yinlan – Zhang Aining – Zhang Xiaoling – Zou Xiaoqiao

*Chairman of the International Advisory Board*

Gudmundur Alfredsson

*Members of the International Advisory Board*

Florence Benoit-Rohmer – Brian Burdekin – Andrew Clapham – Barry Craig – Felipe Gomez-Isa – Jonas Grimheden – Zdzislaw Kedzia – Wayne Mackay – Peter Malanczuk – Fabrizio Marrela – Ineta Ziemele – Tom Zwart

VOLUME 3

The titles published in this series are listed at *brill.com/cphr*

# The Right to Development

*Sustainable Development and the Practice of Good Governance*

*Special Editor*

Wang Xigen

BRILL
NIJHOFF

LEIDEN | BOSTON

Library of Congress Cataloging-in-Publication Data

Names: Wang, Xigen, 1965- author.
Title: The right to development : sustainable development and the practice of good governance / Xigen Wang ; special editor, Wang Xigen.
Description: Boston : Brill, [2019] | Series: Chinese perspectives on human rights and good governance ; Volume 3 | Includes bibliographical references and index.
Identifiers: LCCN 2019016264 (print) | LCCN 2019017985 (ebook) | ISBN 9789004364455 (ebook) | ISBN 9789004364448 (hardback : alk. paper)
Subjects: LCSH: Sustainable development. | Human rights. | Corporate governance.
Classification: LCC HC79.E5 (ebook) | LCC HC79.E5 W3566 2019 (print) | DDC 338.9/27--dc23
LC record available at https://lccn.loc.gov/2019016264

Typeface for the Latin, Greek, and Cyrillic scripts: "Brill". See and download: brill.com/brill-typeface.

ISSN 2352-2593
ISBN 978-90-04-36444-8 (hardback)
ISBN 978-90-04-36445-5 (e-book)

Copyright 2019 by Koninklijke Brill NV, Leiden, The Netherlands.
Koninklijke Brill NV incorporates the imprints Brill, Brill Hes & De Graaf, Brill Nijhoff, Brill Rodopi, Brill Sense, Hotei Publishing, mentis Verlag, Verlag Ferdinand Schöningh and Wilhelm Fink Verlag.
All rights reserved. No part of this publication may be reproduced, translated, stored in a retrieval system, or transmitted in any form or by any means, electronic, mechanical, photocopying, recording or otherwise, without prior written permission from the publisher.
Authorization to photocopy items for internal or personal use is granted by Koninklijke Brill NV provided that the appropriate fees are paid directly to The Copyright Clearance Center, 222 Rosewood Drive, Suite 910, Danvers, MA 01923, USA. Fees are subject to change.

This book is printed on acid-free paper and produced in a sustainable manner.

# Contents

Preface    IX
*Zhang Wei and Gudmundur Alfredsson*

Brief Introduction    1
*Wang Xigen*

**PART 1**
*General Theory*

1   Relationship between the Human Right to Development and Core Elements of the Sustainable Development Goals    11
    *Zamir Akram*

2   The Right to Development from a Human Rights Approach: Conceptual Bases and Contemporary Challenges    27
    *Flavia Piovesan*

3   The Development Approach of Human Rights    48
    *He Zhipeng*

4   The Relationship between Human Rights and Development: An Analysis of Chinese Scholars' Perspectives and the Practice of the Chinese Government    57
    *Zhang Wei and Zhang Aitong*

**PART 2**
*Environmental Perspective*

5   On the Realization of the Right to Development under the Context of Environmental Rights    75
    *Zhang Aining*

6   Role of Rural Regulations in Environmental Protection and Green Development. *Findings from Wendou Village in Qiandongnan Miao and*

　　　　　Dong Minority Autonomous Prefecture Pinghe County Hekou Township in
　　　　　Guizhou Province　　94
　　　　　　　*Gao Qicai*

7　　　The Development and the Environment: The Conflict and Balance
　　　　in the View of Human Rights Law. *Perspective and Reflection Based on
　　　　China*　　105
　　　　　　*Li Hongbo*

8　　　Legal Research on Carbon Emission Rights from the Perspective of a
　　　　Right to Development　　117
　　　　　　*He Miao*

### PART 3
## *Empirical Analysis*

9　　　Guidance from the Ground up: Lessons from South Asia for Realizing
　　　　the Sustainable Development Goals　　141
　　　　　　*Sumudu Atapattu and Shyami Puvimanasinghe*

10　　China's Theoretical Innovation and Practical Contribution to the Right
　　　　to Development. *In Commemoration of the Thirtieth Anniversary of the
　　　　United Nations Declaration on the Right to Development*　　168
　　　　　　*Wang Xigen*

11　　Practices for Realization of the Right to Development and Experience
　　　　Sharing in Peru　　197
　　　　　　*Carlos Alberto Aquino Rodriguez*

12　　"Ubuntu-ism" as the Arbiter between Cultural Relativism and
　　　　Universalism in the Context of the Right to Development　　207
　　　　　　*Mofihli Teleki*

13　　The Contribution of the Belt and Road Initiative to the Global Right to
　　　　Development　　229
　　　　　　*Li Erping and Yao Yunsong*

14　　Basic Principles of the Legal System of the Right to Regional
　　　　Development　　241
　　　　　　*Lyu Ning and Wang Xigen*

## PART 4
*Global Order*

15  The Declaration on the Right to Development as a First Step towards a Comprehensive Southern Vision on Human Rights    257
   *Tom Zwart*

16  A Comprehensive and Multidimensional Survey of Law and Development in the 21st Century. *Taking Stock of the New Right to Development*    271
   *Zhu Liyu*

17  Implementation of the Right to Development by Optimizing WTO Regulations. *From the Perspective of the Doha Development Agenda*    288
   *Wang Bei*

   Index    303

# Preface

*Zhang Wei\* and Gudmundur Alfredsson\*\**

As pointed out by Professor Wang Xigen of Huazhong University of Science and Technology in his Introduction to this book, more than 30 years after the adoption of the UN *Declaration on the Right to Development* (DRD), the meaning of the right is still subject to different views and a lively debate. As a result, States are not implementing it and international organizations are by and large not monitoring State compliance with the right. In this preface, we look at some of the reasons and raise some of the same questions as Professor Wang. If the DRD is to succeed, responses to these questions are necessary.

Several schools of thought have emerged over the years about the international contents of the 1986 *Declaration on the Right to Development*. One school is about the right of developing peoples and countries to be developed, including the transfers of funding and technology from developed to developing countries. A second school is about respect for human rights in the development process, or a human rights-based approach to development, similar to what UNDP and other multilateral and bilateral development agencies have been pursuing, and a third related school is about the elevation of economic, social and cultural rights to the level of protection available for civil and political rights. All three schools of thought appear explicitly or implicitly among the UN 2030 Sustainable Development Goals[1] which presumably helps explain the broad agreement to the Goals.

There are significant overlaps between the three schools. For example, all of them can play a role in poverty reduction—but there are also differences. Under the first school of thought as listed above, if it is a right, the transfers would constitute legal obligations. If the bar is set high, the implementation of the DRD could be costly both at home and abroad. Rich countries of the North and West have resisted this approach. With trillions of dollars in the bank, with a space program and so on, would China be willing, now or later, to come up with the resources necessary for her part? And how would the transfers

---

\* Zhang Wei, Professor at China University of Political Science and Law (CUPL), Co-Director of the Institute for Human Rights at CUPL, and Editor-in-Chief of the present book series on Chinese Perspectives on Human Rights and Good Governance.
\*\* Gudmundur Alfredsson, Law Professor at the Institute for Human Rights at CUPL and Chairman of the Advisory Board of the present book series.
1 For the UN Sustainable Development Goals, please see http://www.un.org/ga/search/view_doc.asp?symbol=A/RES/70/1&Lang=E.

be defined; would cost contributions to the Belt and Road Initiative qualify as such? Still, this school of thought is closest to the original intention of the DRD, it expands on Article 2 of the *International Covenant on Economic, Social and Cultural Rights*, and it is the only option adding value to the existing international standards.

Furthermore, with regard to the second school of thought, it can be argued that it is unnecessary, as a series of existing international human rights instruments already demand respect for human rights in the development process by both recipient and donor countries as well as the organizations involved. And the third school of thought can also be seen as unnecessary if one looks at the 1993 *Vienna Declaration and Programme of Action*[2] and at the subsequent steps taken to elevate and strengthen economic, social and cultural rights. These steps include the creation of new special procedures and the adoption of an *Optional Protocol to the Covenant on Economic, Social and Cultural Rights* opening the door to complaints.

Peoples are one of the chief beneficiaries of the right to development. The term "peoples" usually stands for the entire population of a country, irrespective of ethnic and religious composition. The peoples are presumably represented by governments, but the same governments represent the States which hold the obligations of respecting, fulfilling and protecting the DRD. How do the two carry out meaningful and effective communications? Is that type of process credible? In addition to governments, who else can represent the people, communities, minorities and/or non-governmental organizations?

Still further questions arise in connection with the right to development, be it the first school or any other interpretations. Does the DRD have both international and domestic applications? The international dimension is obvious, but should the DRD also be part of domestic law? After all, the Vienna Declaration in paragraph 10.5 spells out that "Lasting progress towards the implementation of the right to development requires effective development policies at the national level, as well as equitable economic relations and a favorable economic environment at the international level." Notwithstanding repeated attempts at bringing about national implementation and international monitoring, little or no progress has been made.

How should the national dimension be accomplished? Why have so few countries expressly addressed this issue in domestic legislation? Lessons can be learned from the instances where the African Commission and the African Court of Human Rights and Peoples' Rights have made use of the DRD under Article 22 of the *African Charter on Human and Peoples' Rights*: "1. All peoples

---

2   *Vienna Declaration and Programme of Action*, paragraphs 1, 5, 10.

shall have the right to their economic, social and cultural development with due regard to their freedom and identity and in the equal enjoyment of the common heritage of mankind. 2. States shall have the duty, individually or collectively, to ensure the exercise of the right to development."

Most notably, the African courts have employed the DRD to protect the culture and way of life of indigenous and tribal peoples.[3] We therefore particularly like Professor Wang's comments on vulnerable groups in his introduction to the present book: "In order to eliminate the developmental differences, it is imperative to safeguard the right to development of vulnerable groups, for instance people living in rural areas, mountain areas, ethnic minority areas, protected areas. Therefore, it is necessary to propose ... the right to regional development and establish a legal system to implement this right." He adds that among these would be the principles of balanced interests and social justice.

When governments or other actors use funds and technology received through the DRD, how does one ensure that the benefits actually reach the people, like the elimination of (extreme) poverty and an adequate standard of living? Could or should the good governance guidelines concerning transparency, accountability, responsiveness and non-corruption, as initially developed by the international financial institutions and development agencies, play a role in order to make sure that people benefit? Resolutions of the UN Commission on Human Rights and the UN Human Rights Council[4] and publications of the Office of the UN High Commissioner for Human Rights[5] now expressly acknowledge the links between human rights, good governance and development.

In light of these and other questions concerning the meaning and use of the right to development, additional elaboration and even the setting of new standards is likely to continue in the years ahead. The chapters in this book demonstrate and elaborate on many of the issues and approaches that will influence and shape this process. The Institute for Human Rights at China

---

3   See for example, the case affecting the Ogiek Community and other settlers of the Mau Forest in Kenya, *African Commission on Human and Peoples' Rights v. Republic of Kenya*, Judgement by the Court of May 27, 2017, paras. 207–211, available at http://www.african-court.org/en/images/Cases/Judgment/Application%20006-2012%20-%20African%20Commission%20on%20Human%20and%20Peoples'%20Rights%20v.%20the%20Republic%20of%20Kenya.pdf.

4   See for example, HRC Resolutions 7/11 and 19/20 entitled "The Role of Good Governance in the Promotion and Protection of Human Rights."

5   See *Good Governance Practices for the Protection of Human Rights*, UN publication HR/PUB/07/4, sales no. E.07.XIV.10, 2007, and *The Human Rights Case Against Corruption*, UN publication HR/NONE/2013/120, 2013. See also http://www.ohchr.org/EN/Issues/Development/GoodGovernance/Pages/Publications.aspx.

University of Political Science and Law (CUPL) is grateful to the China Society for Human Rights Studies for the opportunity to publish these materials originating in conferences organized by the Society. The chapters reflect the current thinking in official circles in China, as to both law and policy, on the right to development and thus serve as good indications of up-and-coming positive and proactive Chinese positions in future drafting debates.

# Brief Introduction

*Wang Xigen**

This book is a collection of articles on the right to development as a new generation of human rights in the context of the 2030 Agenda for Sustainable Development. The authors include top scholars and insightful officials from Europe, Asia, America and Africa as well as the United Nations. The main ideas of this book are as follows:

As for the relationship between human rights and development, three major viewpoints are reflected in this book. Firstly, development is the premise of human rights; secondly, human rights are the basis of development; and thirdly, human rights and development involve interaction and mutual promotion. Actually, the fourth viewpoint was formed by inspiring, rethinking and criticizing the above three viewpoints: a right to development is an independent human right rather than a method or a simple patchwork of development and right. The importance of the right to development (RD) should be clearly recognized. When we use the developing approach to treat human rights, we increase tolerance among human beings, widen the spectrum of human rights, and increase the probability that human rights are more widely accepted and endorsed in the cross-cultural communication. This will definitely lead to a healthier and smoother development of human rights in global and domestic politics.

The *Declaration on the Right to Development*, adopted by the United Nations in 1986, establishes the RD as an inalienable human right. Nevertheless, despite a lapse of 30 years, the RD has not been implemented due to international systematic obstacles and ideological divergences between the developed and developing states. As one of the significant frameworks concerning development adopted by the United Nations in 2015, *Transforming Our World: The 2030 Agenda for Sustainable Development* recognizes "peaceful, just and inclusive societies … are based on respect for human rights (including the right to development)".[1] The consensus adoption of the Sustainable Development

---

\* Wang Xigen, Yangtze Scholar Distinguished Professor and Dean of Law School of Huazhong University of Science and Technology; The Ph.D. Supervisor of "2011 Plan of China" - Collaborative Innovation Center of Judicial Civilization; Director of the Institute of Human Rights Law in Huazhong University of Science and Technology in China; The Chair of Academic Board of the Institute of Human Rights in Wuhan University. Email: fxywxg@whu.edu.cn.

1 The United Nations, *Transforming Our World: The 2030 Agenda for Sustainable Development*, A/RES/70/1.

Goals (SDGS) contained in the 2030 Agenda has raised hopes that it would now be possible to realize the RD. Since the 2030 Agenda is grounded in human rights including the RD and seeks to pursue the same development goals included in the *Declaration on the Right to Development*, the Agenda is only a general framework. Therefore, a new idea and an effective method on how to insert the RD into the Agenda and to stimulate every indicator in the 17 SDGS could contribute to the realization of the RD.

The realization of the RD depends on common efforts at national and international levels. At the international level, the conceptual bases and legal framework of the RD could be laid and constructed by the following aspects: social justice; participation, accountability and transparency; and international cooperation. The implementation of the RD involves challenges of a legal, cultural, political and economic nature. In order to meet the challenges, the scope of national obligations should be expanded. The obligations to respect, protect and implement the RD should be fulfilled in the following seven dimensions: development of indicators to measure the implementation of the RD; adoption of an international treaty for the protection of the RD; ratification of the *Optional Protocol to the International Covenant on Economic, Social and Cultural Rights*; reform of international financial institutions; promotion of international cooperation; stimulating action by private actors in the promotion of human rights; and best practice consolidation.

At the national level, states should undertake all necessary measures for the realization of the right to development. The Chinese theoretical system and practical model on the RD are worth sharing. Over the three decades since the adoption of the UN *Declaration on the Right to Development*, China has developed an innovative discourse system for the RD and contributed a series of original concepts and propositions to this right, which may be generally summarized as ten major aspects: in terms of orientation, the RD is taken as a primary fundamental human right; in terms of nature, the RD is an essential requirement of socialism; in terms of strategy, the RD is gradually implemented by the "development is the primary task" and "development is the top priority" strategy; in terms of concept, people's equal right for participation and development proposed by Chinese government; in terms of contents, the RD is integrated into the comprehensive process of construction of economy, politics, culture, society and ecological conservation; in terms of principle, people-centered orientation of development is a core principle to guide the practice of the RD; in terms of roadmap, the RD has been put into the context of the "Chinese dream" for the great revitalization of the Chinese Nation; in terms of focus, the RD can be promoted by distributive justice, in particular a fair social security and wealth distribution system; in terms of methodology, the rule of law is the most compulsory measure to implement the RD; in terms of ideas, the practice of the RD is guided by an innovative, coordinated, green, open and sharing outlook on development.

The relationship balance between economic development and environment protection is an eternal topic on the RD. Although the *Declaration on the Right to Development* did not directly address sustainable development, the RD should contain the five dimensions—sustainable development, economic development, political development, social development and cultural development, in the context that sustainable development is becoming an international hot topic. Therefore, it is necessary to establish a new definition: the right to sustainable development. As for the developing countries, does protection of the environment mean the economy will slow down? Regarding climate change and carbon emissions, is it possible to recognize the carbon emissions as a RD? How can we clarify the relationship between carbon emissions and the RD from a legal perspective? What kind of rule of law model could be promoted to disclose the relationship between carbon emissions and the RD, and safeguard the interests of the developing countries? This book aims to answer these questions and proposes some possible basic principles and a possible route for rule of law on their relationship.

Developed and developing countries should cooperate with each other in good faith in some economic activities and major environmental issues that are of fundamental interest to human beings, particularly in those economic activities with potentially significant threats to the environment, such as international trade, international investment, the transboundary movement of toxic or hazardous wastes and extremely hazardous activities or significant technological risks. In this regard, the principle of common but differentiated responsibility is a practical model of international cooperation between developed and developing countries to ensure implementation and realization of the RD in the perspective of sustainable development. Whether or not insisting on common but differentiated responsibilities principle is key, however, the key question is how to explore a specific legal rule or method to make this principle elaborate, easy to operate, widely recognized and implemented. This book discusses in detail the role of rural regulations in environmental protection and green development from the perspective of analytical positivism by a field investigation in typical ethnic minority villages.

Wisely choosing a practical model for the RD is a central issue on the realization of this right. This book proposes several practical models for the RD by comparative analysis:

(1) "The Belt and Road Initiative" (B&R) model. The Chinese concept of "Building a Community of Shared Future for Humankind" was incorporated

into a UN resolution for the first time in 2016, resulting in a substantial Chinese contribution to global RD. In order to establish "Fate, Responsibility and Interest Communities" and to promote the countries and regions along the B&R to together realize the RD, China proposes a B&R strategy by strengthening possible cooperation among these countries and regions in several aspects, for instance investment, trade, finance, tax, and infrastructure construction. Based on the principle of win-win cooperation, this strategy regards the idea of joint discussion, joint construction and sharing as a method to realize the people's RD of the countries along B&R, "the Community of Shared Future for Humankind" as a supporter of the RD. All of this not only enriches the philosophical connotation of the RD in the theoretical aspect, but also broadens the practical path of the right.

(2) Regional development mode at domestic level. Eliminating developmental differences is a core concern for the RD. In order to eliminate developmental differences, it is imperative to safeguard the RD of the vulnerable groups, for instance people living in rural areas, mountain areas, ethnic minority areas, or protected areas. Therefore, it is necessary to propose a new definition of the right to regional development and establish a legal system to implement this right. Among these, the basic principles of the legal system of implementing the right to regional development should include the interest balancing principle, the principle of social justice, the principle of double standards, and the power active principle. According to China's regional developmental strategy, based on the different developmental levels and a natural environment, a series of regional developmental strategies were implemented, including setting up the east coast "special economic zone", promoting "central rise", "Western exploitation", "the revitalization of northeast old industrial base", "the coordinated development of Beijing-Tianjin-Hebei", targeted poverty alleviation strategy for rural areas and free trade areas, and so on.

(3) Poverty reduction model in Peru and China. Poverty reduction is the foremost target in the 2030 Agenda. Poverty reduction plays a vital role in realizing the RD. A comparative study on the realization of this right by poverty reduction in Peru and China could help to share the models. China realized poverty reduction in three stages: "blood-transfusion" poverty alleviation, "blood-making" poverty alleviation and "targeted" poverty alleviation by providing funding, project, skills, education and human resources. In four decades of reform and opening up, China contributed 75% of the poverty reduction in the world. China realized the poverty reduction target set by the UN *Millennium Declaration*. Peru has been successful in reducing poverty, as shown by the fact that the poverty rate has decreased from a rate of 54.7% in 2001 to

22.7% in 2014. This have been achieved through four models which include more access to health, social security, education and conditional cash transfers ("Programa Juntos") for the poor, especially children, pregnant woman, the aged and other vulnerable groups.

(4) "Ubuntu-ism" model in Africa. The means for implementing the *Declaration on the Right to Development* often become irrelevant due to the conflict between universalism and cultural relativism. Ubuntu-ism, as an African philosophy, could become an arbiter between these two frames of thought and provide a theoretical basis to justify the RD. Although Ubuntu-ism is an ethic and philosophy, it has been used in various settings in the post-independent era of the African continent. Legal practices in South Africa show that Ubuntu-ism could be institutionalized in order for it to become a source of law which is conducive to the realization of the RD.

(5) International trade model. From the perspective of the Doha Development Agenda, implementation of the RD must optimize WTO regulations related to special and differential treatment, and make best efforts to overcome the three shortcomings of the regulations which are the lack of precision, effectiveness and operability. While efforts are made to reach consensus toward amendment of the regulations, some alternative approaches can be utilized in the short term. Both the Dispute Settlement Body and arbitrators should consider the interests and difficulties of less-developed countries when giving authoritative interpretation of the provisions guided by Article 3.2 of the *Understanding on Rules and Procedures Governing the Settlement of Disputes*. Moreover, improving the Monitoring Mechanism set forth during the Bali Ministerial Conference will alleviate the problem regarding poor implementation. All solutions to the problems above should be based on the theoretical consensus concerning the asymmetrical justice between the developed and less-developed countries.

Rule of law is the fundamental method to realize the RD. This book focuses on the establishment of the legal system of the RD from new perspectives. The first is making intercultural communication on the issues of the RD between the East and the West in the line of the theory of law and development. A comprehensive and multidimensional survey of law and development in the 21st century will help to take stock of the new RD and supply practical models. As a global jurisprudential movement rooted in the US policy circle and legal academia, there is growing evidence that law and development in the 21st century is beginning to transform from "movement" to "field", which can be divided into four sub-fields as follows: aid-funded law and development policy as an applied field, intellectual styles of law and development movement as a scholarly field, interdisciplinary-based law and development studies as an academic field, fact-based law and development research as a scientific field. It is necessary to bring the RD into the analytical framework of law and development, this framework provides a new idea for establishing a legal system for safeguarding the RD. Law and development scholars in the Global South should join hands and make efforts to explore context-sensitive local legal knowledge, by first concentrating on the new RD under the policy support of the UN 2030 Agenda for Sustainable Development. The second perspective is discussing the new ideas on establishing legal norms for the RD based on international human rights. What type of normative document on the RD shall we establish? Different scholars could provide different answers to this question. Some scholars suggest formulating an international convention on the RD to empower the effectiveness of international hard law to this new right; some scholars suggest that policies or action plans should be used to realize this right, not merely depending on law; some scholars advise drawing up a *Comprehensive Southern Vision on Human Rights*. As the first successful joint action undertaken by the Global South at the international level in the area of human rights, the *Declaration on the Right to Development* can serve as a source of inspiration for drafting the *Comprehensive Southern Vision on Human Rights*. The drafters will have the *Universal Declaration of Human Rights* to fall back on. The following elements could be included in the document: the need to rely on culture, customary law, and morality; the need to respect subsidiarity and non-interference; the importance of collective rights; the recognition that the right to subsistence and development are paramount rights; the acknowledgement that rights and duties complement each other; and the acceptance that human rights must be implemented within their local political, social and cultural context.

Many thanks should be given to the contributors to this volume—Zamir Akram, the Chair-Rapporteur of the UN Open Ended Working Group on the Right to Development, and the Former Ambassador and Permanent Representative of Pakistan to the United Nations in Geneva, who holds a master's degree in international relations from the London School of Economics and Political Science. Tom Zwart, Professor of Human Rights at Utrecht University and Director of the Cross-Cultural Human Rights Center of Netherland. Flavia Piovesan, Professor of Constitutional Law and Human Rights at the Catholic University of São Paulo and in the Human Rights post-graduate programs of the Catholic University of São Paulo, the Catholic University of Paraná and the Human Rights and Development Programme of Pablo de Olavide University (Spain). Zhu Liyu, Professor of Law at the School of Law at Renmin University of China, and the Executive Director of Renmin University's Centre for Human Rights Studies. Zhang Wei, Co-Director of Institute for Human Rights at China

University of Political Science and Law. Zhang Aitong, a postgraduate student of Institute for Human Rights at China University of Political Science and Law. He Zhipeng, Professor of International Human Rights Law at Jilin University of China. Sumudu Atapattu, Director of Research Centers and International Programs at University of Wisconsin Law School, Lead Counsel for Human Rights, Center for International Sustainable Development Law, Montreal; and affiliated faculty, Raoul Wallenberg Institute for Human Rights, Sweden. Shyami Puvimanasinghe, Human Rights Officer, Office of the United Nations High Commissioner for Human Rights. Wang Xigen, Yangtze Scholar Distinguished Professor, Dean of Law School at Huazhong University of Science and Technology, Director of the Institute of Human Rights Law at Huazhong University of Science and Technology in China. Mofihli Teleki, Head of Communications at the Commission for Gender Equality (South Africa) and a scholar in the right to development and human rights. Carlos Alberto Aquino Rodriguez, Professor at the Faculty of Economics at San Marcos National University of Peru. His area of research includes International Trade Theory and Policy, East Asia Economies, Comparative Economic Development of East Asia and Latin America, etc. Gao Qicai, Professor of Jurisprudence at Tsinghua University Law School. Zhang Aining, Professor of International Human Rights Law and Director of Center for Human Rights Studies at China Foreign Affairs University. Li Hongbo, Professor of Jurisprudence and Deputy Director of Center for Human Rights Studies at China Foreign Affairs University. Li Erping, Professor of International Human Rights Law at Kunming University of Technology and Science. Lyu Ning, Associate Professor at Hunan Normal University, S.J.D. of Wuhan University. He Miao, Lecturer and Post-Doctorate Researcher of Law School at Wuhan University of China, who holds Ph.D. on international human rights law in Ghent University of Belgium. Wang Bei, Ph.D. candidate at Law School of Peking University.

# PART 1

*General Theory*

CHAPTER 1

# Relationship between the Human Right to Development and Core Elements of the Sustainable Development Goals

*Zamir Akram**

It can be argued that there is a symbiotic relationship between human rights and human development. Human rights cannot be fully realized without meeting human needs. The 2030 Agenda for Sustainable Development, as it is officially termed by the UN General Assembly,[1] acknowledges this fact. While pledging that "no one will be left behind" in the collective journey towards sustainable development, the Preamble of this Agenda maintains that the 17 Sustainable Development Goals (SDGs) "seek to realize the human rights of all". This "human rights"-centered approach of the SDGs is further elaborated in paragraph 3 where it is resolved to "end poverty and hunger everywhere; to combat inequalities within and among countries; to build peaceful, just and inclusive societies; to protect human rights and promote gender equality and the empowerment of women and girls …".[2] Moreover, the Resolution goes in paragraph 10 to maintain that the "Agenda is guided by the purposes and principles of the *Charter of the United Nations*, including full respect for international law", and that "it is grounded in the *Universal Declaration of Human Rights*, international human rights treaties, the *Millennium Declaration* and the 2005 World Summit Outcome". Most importantly, the Resolution goes on to state that "it is informed by other instruments such as the *Declaration on the*

---

* Zamir Akram, served as Ambassador and Permanent Representative of Pakistan to the United Nations in Geneva for seven years. He joined the Foreign Service of Pakistan in 1978 and held assignments in Moscow, Geneva, New Delhi, and Washington. At the Ministry of Foreign Affairs in Islamabad, he dealt with the (former) Soviet Union, Afghanistan, South Asia, Disarmament and Arms Control and the UN. He was also Additional Secretary for Foreign Affairs in the Prime Minister's Office. In 2015, Ambassador Akram was unanimously elected as the Chair-Rapporteur of the UN Open Ended Working Group on the Right to Development, a position to which he has been re-elected twice. He holds a Master's degree in International Relations from the London School of Economics and Political Science.
1 UN General Assembly Resolution A/RES/70/1 on Sustainable Development Agenda, http://www.un.org/en/development/desa/population/migration/generalassembly/docs/globalcompact/A_RES_70_1_E.pdf.
2 Ibid., paragraph 3.

*Right to Development*".[3] Again in paragraph 35, the Resolution states that "the new Agenda recognizes the need to build peaceful, just and inclusive societies that provide equal access to justice and that are based on respect for human rights (including the right to development)".[4]

The repeated references in the Resolution to the SDGs clearly establishes the fact that progress towards and ultimate realization of sustainable development is not possible without the protection and promotion of all human rights and includes, most importantly from the perspective of this chapter, the concept of the right to development "as a fundamental human right, equal and an indivisible part of all human rights".

This is a central aspect of the 2030 Agenda, especially for developing countries, because the right to development as a universal and inalienable human right, as set out in the *Declaration on the Right to Development* of 1986,[5] has for decades been a controversial issue between developing and developed countries. However, the consensus adoption of the 2030 Agenda should ideally resolve this controversy and open up avenues for international cooperation as well as national efforts to implement the right to development as an integral part of the SDGs. Moreover, the right to development is not only now an integral part of the SDGs, but also intrinsically linked to all the universal declarations, conventions and consensual UN resolutions relating to human rights. Indeed, the right to development is a vehicle for the protection and promotion of all human rights. The objective of this chapter is therefore to establish that the right to development, as an integral part of all human rights, is consistent with and related to the 2030 Agenda which provides a road-map for its ultimate realization.

## 1   Antecedents of the Human Right to Development

### 1.1   *UN Charter*

While the *Declaration on the Right to Development* was adopted in 1986, its antecedents can be traced to the post-war and post-colonial international order sanctioned by the *Charter of the United Nations* in 1945. The Preamble of the Charter maintains in paragraph 3 "to establish conditions under which justice and respect for the obligations arising from treaties and other sources of international law can be maintained, and to promote social progress and better

---

3   Ibid., paragraph 10.
4   Ibid., paragraph 35.
5   UN General Assembly Resolution A/Res/41/128 dated December 4, 1986 on *Declaration on the Right to Development*, http://www.un.org/documents/ga/res/41/a41r128.htm.

standards of life in larger freedom".⁶ To achieve its ends, the Charter goes on to commit "to employ international machinery for the promotion of the economic and social advancement of all peoples".⁷

Moreover, Chapter 1 Article 1(3) of the Charter, maintains that among the purposes of the UN are "to achieve international cooperation in solving international problems of an economic, social, cultural or humanitarian character, and in promoting and encouraging respect for human rights and for fundamental freedoms for all without distinction as to race, sex, language, or religion".⁸

More specifically in Chapter 9, relating to economic and social cooperation, the Charter maintains in Article 55(a) that the United Nations shall promote "higher standards of living, full employment, and conditions of economic and social progress and development".⁹ In paragraph (c) of the same Article, the Charter calls for "universal respect for, and observance of, human rights and fundamental freedoms for all without distinction as to race, sex, language or religion".¹⁰

Article 62 in Chapter 10 on the Economic and Social Council stipulates that "The Economic and Social Council may make or initiate studies and reports with respect to international economic, social, cultural, educational, health, and related matters and may make recommendations with respect to any such matters to the General Assembly, to the Members of the United Nations and to the specialized agencies concerned".¹¹ Furthermore in Article 62(2), the Charter states that the Economic and Social Council "may make recommendations for the purpose of promoting respect for, and observance of, human rights and fundamental freedoms for all".¹²

Clearly, the UN Charter establishes the fundamental purposes that not only link human rights and fundamental freedoms to "social progress and better standards of life" i.e. human development; but also calls for international cooperation in solving international problems of an economic and social nature as well as in promoting and encouraging respect for human rights. The link between human rights and development in the Charter is, therefore, inescapable.

---

6   *Charter of the United Nations*, Preamble, http://www.un.org/en/sections/un-charter/preamble/index.html.
7   Ibid.
8   Ibid., Article 1(3) of the UN Charter.
9   Ibid., Article 55(a).
10  Ibid., Article 55(c).
11  Ibid., Article 62(1).
12  Ibid., Article 62(2).

## 1.2  Universal Declaration of Human Rights

Like the UN Charter, the *Universal Declaration of Human Rights* recognizes the relationship between human rights and satisfying human needs, stating in its Preamble that "the advent of a world in which human beings shall enjoy freedom of speech and belief and freedom from fear and want has been proclaimed as the highest aspiration of the common people".[13]

Also consistent with the Charter, the Declaration maintains the link between "fundamental human rights" and "social progress and better standards of life in larger freedom".[14]

In Article 22, the Declaration states that "Everyone, as a member of society, has the right to social security and is entitled to realization, through national effort and international cooperation and in accordance with the organization and resources of each State, of the economic, social and cultural rights indispensable for his dignity and the free development of his personality".[15]

Articles 25 and 26 identify some of the core or fundamental human rights which are also basic development goals, stating that "Everyone has a right to a standard of living adequate for the health and well-being of himself and of his family, including food, clothing, housing and medical care and necessary social services" (Article 25); and that "Everyone has the right to education" (Article 26). As such the Declaration equates the civil and political rights of freedom of speech, belief, equality, etc., to economic and social rights and identifies some of these core rights as the rights to health, food, clothing, housing, medical care, and education. Once again, the link between human rights and human development is very clear.

## 1.3  Conventions on Civil and Political Rights and Economic, Social and Cultural Rights

Two of the fundamental documents on human rights, the *International Covenant on Civil and Political Rights*[16] and *International Covenant on Economic, Social and Cultural Rights*,[17] both recognize the goal of human development as part of universal and inalienable human rights. Both Covenants maintain that "the ideal of free human beings enjoying freedom from fear and want can only be achieved if conditions are created whereby everyone may enjoy his economic,

---

13  *Universal Declaration of Human Rights*, Preamble, https://www.un.org/en/universal-declaration-human-rights.
14  Ibid., Preamble.
15  Ibid., Article 22.
16  *International Covenant on Civil and Political Rights*, https://treaties.un.org/doc/publication/unts/volume%20999/volume-999-i-14668-english.pdf..
17  *International Covenant on Economic, Social and Cultural Rights*, https://treaties.un.org/doc/treaties/1976/01/19760103%2009-57%20pm/ch_iv_03.pdf.

social and cultural rights, as well as his civil and political rights".[18] Hence a clear relationship is established between freedom from "want" and the entire spectrum of inalienable human rights which can only be achieved through economic and social development that will ensure the freedom from want.

## 1.4 International Convention on the Elimination of All Forms of Racial Discrimination

Similarly, another basic document on human rights, the *International Convention on the Elimination of All Forms of Racial Discrimination*,[19] not only identifies the basic principles on which human development is based, including non-discrimination, equality and social justice, but in its Article 5(e)[20] establishes the rights as the right to work, the right to housing, and the right to public health, medical care, social security and social services as well as the right to education and training. Again, the attainment of human rights is intrinsically linked to the goal of human development.

## 1.5 Other International Instruments Relating to Human Development

Apart from the foregoing core international instruments on human rights which clearly include human development objectives, there are several other ancillary international instruments with a focus on development. While these are too numerous to be considered here in full owing to limitations of space, some of the major instruments with a direct bearing on development that can be mentioned here are: (a) the *Declaration of Philadelphia* (1944) on the aims and purposes of the International Labor Organization;[21] (b) the *International Development Strategies for the First, Second and Third United Nations Development Decades* (1961, 1970 and 1980);[22] (c) the *Declaration on Social Progress and Development* (1969);[23] and (d) the *Declaration on the Establishment of a New International Economic Order* (1974).[24]

Moreover, from the perspective of this chapter, it is also relevant to take account of the mandates of several international and regional organizations

---

18　Ibid., paragraph 3.
19　*International Convention on the Elimination of All Forms of Racial Discrimination*, https://www.ohchr.org/en/professionalinterest/pages/cerd.aspx.
20　Ibid.
21　*Declaration of Philadelphia*, http://www.ilo.org/legacy/english/inwork/cb-policy-guide/declarationofPhiladelphia1944.pdf.
22　*Development Strategies of the First, Second and Third Development Decades*, https://www.un-documents.net.
23　*Declaration on Social Progress and Development* (1969), https://www.ohchr.org/Documents/ProfessionalInterest/progress.pdf.
24　*Declaration on the Establishment of a New International Economic Order*, http://www.un-documents.net/s6r3201.htm.

that are entrusted by the international community with the task of promoting human development in areas established as essential for the realization of human rights. These include UN organs such as UNDP, UNCTAD, UNESCO, UNIDO and UNIP among others, as well as specialized agencies such as WHO, FAO, ILO and the international financial institutions such as the World Bank and IMF. Among regional organizations the Asian Development Bank and even the EU can be included as development partners of people living in developing countries.

## 2  Declaration on the Right to Development

Based on the UN Charter, the *Universal Declaration of Human Rights* and various conventions, resolutions and agreements on human rights as well as the mandates of different development agencies, the single most important document establishing the linkage between human rights and development is the UN *Declaration on the Right to Development*, adopted by the UN General Assembly in 1986.[25] The Declaration maintains in Article 1 that "The right to development is an inalienable human right by virtue of which every human person and all peoples are entitled to participate in, contribute to and enjoy economic, social, cultural and political development, in which all human rights and fundamental freedoms can be fully realized".[26] This right is contextualized with development by the second Preamble paragraph which recognizes that: "development is a comprehensive economic, social, cultural and political process, which aims at the constant improvement of the well-being of the entire population and of all individuals on the basis of their active, free and meaningful participation in development and in the fair distribution of benefits resulting therefrom".[27]

In Article 2, the Declaration stipulates that the "human person is the central subject of development and should be the active participant and beneficiary of the right to development"[28] while Article 3 maintains that "States have the primary responsibility for the creation of national and international conditions favorable to the realization of the right to development".[29] But the Declaration also emphasizes the need for international cooperation for promoting the right to development by stating in Article 3(2) that "The realization

---

25   *Declaration on the Right to Development*, op. cit.
26   Ibid.
27   Ibid., 2nd Preamble paragraph.
28   Ibid., Article 2.
29   Ibid., Article 3.

of the right to development requires full respect for the principles of international law concerning friendly relations and cooperation among States in accordance with the *Charter of the United Nations*";[30] as well as in Article 3(3) that "States have the duty to cooperate with each other in ensuring development and eliminating obstacles to development";[31] and in Article 4 that "States have the duty to take steps, individually and collectively, to formulate international development policies with a view to facilitating the full realization of the right to development".[32] Perhaps the most important aspect of international cooperation is contained in Article 4(2) that "Sustained action is required to promote more rapid development of developing countries. As a complement to the efforts of developing countries, effective international cooperation is essential in providing these countries with appropriate means and facilities to foster their comprehensive development".[33]

With regard to specific development goals, the Declaration maintains in Article 8 that "States should undertake, at the national level, all necessary measures for the realization of the right to development and shall ensure, inter alia, equality of opportunity for all in their access to basic resources, education, health services, food, housing, employment and the fair distribution of income".[34] The Declaration further elaborates in Article 9 that "All aspects of the right to development set forth in the present Declaration are inalienable and interdependent and each of them should be considered in the context of the whole".[35] Moreover, to emphasize that the right to development is an inherent part of all human rights, the Declaration maintains in its Preamble that "all human rights and fundamental freedoms are indivisible and interdependent and that, in order to promote development, equal attention and urgent consideration should be given to the implementation, promotion, and protection of civil, political, economic, social and cultural rights ... and that respect for and enjoyment of certain human rights and fundamental freedoms cannot justify the denial of other human rights and fundamental freedoms".[36]

It is also worth noting that by basing the right to development on the UN Charter, the *Universal Declaration of Human Rights*, the *International Covenant on Civil and Political Rights*, the *International Covenant on Economic, Social and Cultural Rights* as well as the *International Convention on the Elimination of All Forms of Racial Discrimination*, the Declaration also emphasizes that the

---

30  Ibid.
31  Ibid.
32  Ibid., Article 4.
33  Ibid.
34  Ibid., Article 8.
35  Ibid., Article 9.
36  Ibid., Preamble paragraph 10.

right to development is dependent on the realization of the principles and purposes of these instruments. They are identified as the right of peoples to self-determination; exercise by people of their full and complete sovereignty over all their national wealth and resources, elimination of situations resulting from colonialism, neo-colonialism, apartheid, and all forms of racism and racial discrimination; foreign domination and occupation, aggression and threats against national sovereignty, national unity and territorial integrity and threats of war; international peace and security as essential elements for the realization of the right to development; and the close relationship between disarmament and development since the resources released through disarmament measures should be devoted to economic and social development and well-being of all peoples and, in particular, those of the developing countries.[37]

## 3  Obstacles to the Realization of the Right to Development

The adoption of the *Declaration on the Right to Development* in 1986 embodied the progression by the international community towards the recognition, based on existing international instruments relating to human rights, that human development is also an inalienable human right that is indivisible and interdependent on all human rights. In the political and economic milieu at the time, with the emphasis on a New Economic Order and the recognition of the geographic North–South divide in terms of human development, there was broad acceptance of the right to development as a human right. Hence the overwhelming support for the *Declaration on the Right to Development* in 1986.

Unfortunately, however, the hopes and aspirations raised by this Declaration have not yet been realized and the Declaration remains yet to be fully implemented. The reasons for this lack of progress are diverse, ranging from global systemic issues to divergence in the approach of states. At the heart of the problem, of course, lies the lack of political will. These factors need to be understood in order to find a way forward.

Among the systemic issues, the major obstacle has been the absence of international peace and security, a necessary condition for development recognized by the Declaration itself. As Pope John Paul once said "development is the new name for peace".[38] Similar views were also expressed by the then UN Secretary General Ban Ki-moon that "There will be no peace without development, no

---

37  Ibid., Preamble paragraphs 6 to 12 and Articles 5, 7.
38  Pope John Paul, http://w2.vatican.va/content/paul-vi/en/encyclicals/documents/hf_p-vi_enc_26031967_populorum.html.

development without peace, and neither without respect for human rights".[39] Inter-State and intra-State conflicts, tensions and competition have, therefore, retarded development and ensured denial of human rights at the national and international levels. In this negative environment, full realization of objectives such as self-determination, end to foreign domination and occupation, respect for sovereignty, especially over national wealth and resources, disarmament, fair and equal trading relations, an equitable international financial system, and non-preferential system of international assistance, have all proved to be elusive. On the contrary, use of force, military build-ups, terrorism, unilateral coercive measures, selective and conditional assistance have prevented the emergence of an enabling environment for development.

At the national level as well, lack of good governance, denial of human rights and fundamental freedoms, and lack of equality in sharing of resources, equitable distribution of income and wealth, and non-discrimination, especially relating to women and vulnerable groups, have all contributed to inadequate development within States, especially among developing countries.

Due to the absence of peace and resultant lack of development at the national and international levels, new daunting challenges to human rights and development have emerged. These include adverse climate change which poses an environmental constraint on development, especially due to water, food and energy scarcity. Increase in population, particularly within developing countries, has also increased the pressure on resources and, therefore, on development. Increasing occurrences of pandemics, exorbitant costs of medicines and drugs, and growing antibiotic resistance, are contributing to falling health standards. Migration and movement of refugees especially from conflict zones, are also posing major problems for sustained development and as a result, increasing violations of human rights.

The recent financial crises of 2008 together with sluggish growth in developed countries, some of which are also experiencing the rise of xenophobic tendencies against foreigners on the basis of race and religion, have also contributed to the lack of development and human rights abuses. A related major consequence has been a steady decline in development funds from these countries for overseas development assistance programmes (ODAs) as well as within their own economies for the vulnerable groups.

The global economic slowdown has also affected the functioning and outreach of the international and national donor agencies for development assistance with the result that development programmes in developing countries have been either reduced or shut down.

---

39   Secretary General Ban Ki-moon, https://www.facebook.com/un.geneva.posts.

Apart from these systemic factors, differences have emerged among developing and developed states over the very recognition of the right to development as a human right. Whereas developing states continue to strongly advocate the right to development as a human right that is an integral part of all human rights, developed countries have questioned this approach, albeit in varying degrees.

Some powerful developed countries have taken the extreme position that the right to development is not a human right at all and reject the very basis of the *Declaration on the Right to Development*.[40] Other developed countries have taken a more nuanced position, maintaining essentially that the right to development is an "individual" right and not a "collective" right. Moreover, they maintain that implementation of the right to development is the responsibility of states and not an international obligation.[41]

Another bone of contention between developed and developing countries is over the advocacy by the developing world for the adoption of an international convention which would be a binding legal instrument on the right to development.

As a consequence of the entire range of these factors, the implementation and realization of the right to development as a human right is at best a work in progress. At the heart of the problem is, of course, the lack of political will, at the national and international levels, which has failed to create the enabling environment to implement the right to development, even though there has been considerable emphasis, especially by the developed countries, to enforce other aspects of human rights, particularly civil and political rights.

An effort to bridge these gaps and to reiterate the right to development as a human right was made in the *Vienna Declaration and Programme of Action* (VDPA) adopted in 1993. In paragraph 10, this Declaration reaffirmed the right to development as "universal and inalienable" and an "integral part of fundamental human rights".[42] It also called upon "States to cooperate with each other in ensuring development and eliminating obstacles to development". Despite the consensus adoption of this Declaration, not much progress has been made towards implementing the right to development.

## 4 International Efforts to Promote the Right to Development

The lack of progress to implement the right to development has not been due to lack of trying. Even before and since the adoption of the *Declaration on*

---

40  US Explanation of Vote, https://geneva.unmission.gov.
41  EU Position, https://eu-un.europa.eu.
42  *Vienna Declaration and Programme of Action*, paragraph 10, https://www.ohchr.org/en/professionalinterest/pages/vienna.aspx.

*the Right to Development,* various UN mechanisms have been used to operationalize this right. The primary role and responsibility has been that of the UN High Commissioner for Human Rights with the support of the Office of the High Commissioner for Human Rights (OHCHR). This role is mandated in General Assembly Resolution 48/141 which is to "promote and protect the realization of the right to development and to enhance support from relevant bodies of the UN system for this purpose".[43] The General Assembly and the Human Rights Council also call upon the UN Secretary General and the High Commissioner to report annually on progress in the implementation of the right to development including activities aimed at strengthening the global partnership for development between States, development agencies and international financial and trade institutions.

Another important mechanism for implementing the right to development is the Open-Ended Working Group on the Right to Development set up in 1998. It was preceded by similar Working Groups of government representatives and/or experts which worked from 1981 to 1989, 1993 to 1995 and 1996 to 1997. In 1999 an independent expert was also appointed who proposed a "Concept Note" for realizing the right to development. Thereafter, the Human Rights Council set up a High Level Task Force of five independent experts to advise the Working Groups. This Task Force proposed a set of criteria and operational sub-criteria on the implementation of the right to development. However, owing to divergent views among Member States, there has been only marginal agreement on these proposals. In 2015, the Chair-Rapporteur of the Working Group prepared a set of standards for implementing the right to development as mandated by the Working Group. Most recently, in September 2016, the Council appointed a Special Rapporteur with the mandate to contribute to the work of the Working Group.

However, despite the several mechanisms and their efforts to operationalize the right to development very little progress if any has been made so far. The underlying problem remains the absence of political will to agree on a way forward. These divergent positions between developed and developing countries, therefore, continue to stymie progress.

## 5   The Human Right to Development and the 2030 Agenda

With the consensus adoption of the 2030 Agenda on SDGs there is now some light at the end of this long tunnel. This is due to the emphasis of the 2030 Agenda on a human-rights based approach to development which clearly incorporates the *Declaration on the Right to Development,* implicitly recognizing the right to development as an inalienable human right that is indivisible from

---

43   UNGA Resolution 48/141, http://www.un.org/documents/ga/res/48/a48r141.htm.

all human rights—civil, political, economic, social and cultural. A closer look at the 2030 Agenda establishes this fact.

At the beginning of this chapter, brief references were made to the relationship between human rights and the SDGs contained in the Preamble and the operative parts of the 2030 Agenda. These are now considered in more detail. This document sets the vision of sustainable development grounded in international human rights standards. In paragraph 10 it states that the Agenda "is guided by the purposes and principles of the UN Charter including full respect of international law" and that "it is grounded in the *Universal Declaration of Human Rights*, international human rights treaties", and, moreover, that "it is informed by other instruments such as the *Declaration on the Right to Development*". Moreover, in paragraph 35, it states that "sustainable development cannot be realized without peace and security" and that the "new Agenda recognizes the need to build peaceful, just and inclusive societies that provide equal access to justice and that are based on respect for human rights (including the right to development)".[44] Paragraph 18 reaffirms that "every State has, and shall truly exercise full permanent sovereignty over all its wealth, natural resources and economic activity".[45] In paragraph 19, it again reaffirms "the importance of the *Universal Declaration of Human Rights*, as well as other international instruments relating to human rights and international law" and it goes on to emphasize the "responsibilities of all States, in conformity with the *Charter of the United Nations*, to respect, protect and promote human rights and fundamental freedoms for all, without distinction of any kind as to race, color, sex, language, religion, political or other opinion, national or social origin, property, birth, disability or other status".[46] In paragraph 67 the Agenda expresses a commitment to "foster a dynamic and well-functioning business sector, while protecting labor rights and environmental and health standards in accordance with relevant standards and agreements ... such as the *Guiding Principles on Business and Human Rights* and the *Labor Standards* of the International Labor Organization, the *Convention on the Rights of the Child*".[47] In paragraph 74, relating to the follow-up and review of the SDGs, sub-paragraph (e) states that these "will be people-centered, gender sensitive, respect human rights and have a particular focus on the poorest, most vulnerable and those furthest behind".[48]

---

44   2030 Agenda for Sustainable Development, paragraphs 10 and 35, op. cit.
45   Ibid., paragraph 18.
46   Ibid., paragraph 19.
47   Ibid., paragraph 67.
48   Ibid., paragraph 74 Sub-paragraph (e).

The 2030 Agenda, furthermore, puts key human rights principles such as equality and non-discrimination at the center of its goals. This is reflected in paragraph 3 that resolves "to end poverty and hunger everywhere; to combat inequalities within and among countries; to build peaceful, just and inclusive societies; to protect human rights and promote gender equality and the empowerment of women and girls; and to ensure the lasting protection of the planet and its natural resources".[49] Most significantly it states in paragraph 4 that "no one will be left behind" in the development process and that the endeavor will be "to reach the furthest behind first".[50] This is reemphasized in paragraph 48, relating to measurement of progress in implementing the 2030 Agenda, by stating that such a measurement will "ensure that no one is left behind".[51]

The 2030 Agenda, which encompasses all human rights—civil, political, economic, social and cultural including the right to development—also stipulates in paragraph 13 that "sustainable development recognizes that eradicating poverty in all its forms and dimensions, combating inequality within and among countries, preserving the planet, creating sustained, inclusive and sustainable economic growth and fostering social inclusion are linked to each other and are inter-dependent".[52]

It is also very important to note that the Agenda places specific emphasis on international cooperation and partnership for achieving development needs, especially of the poorest and most vulnerable. It maintains in its Preamble that the international community is "determined to mobilize the means required to implement this Agenda through revitalized Global Partnership for Sustainable Development, based on a spirit of strengthened global solidarity, focused on the needs of the poorest and most vulnerable and with the participation of all countries, all stakeholders and all peoples".[53] It goes on to state in operative paragraphs 40 and 41 that "The Agenda ... can be met within the framework of a revitalized Global Partnership for Sustainable Development, supported by concrete policies and actions"; and that these "will include the mobilization of financial resources as well as capacity building and the transfer of environmentally sound technologies to developing countries on favorable terms".[54]

From the foregoing it is clear that the vision, principles, and commitments of the 2030 Agenda are inspired by and converge with the human rights principles and obligations set out by the UN Charter, the *Universal Declaration of Human Rights* and other human rights-related conventions,

---

49  Ibid., paragraph 3.
50  Ibid., paragraph 4.
51  Ibid., paragraph 48.
52  Ibid., paragraph 13.
53  Ibid., Preambles.
54  Ibid., paragraphs 40 and 41.

declarations and resolutions of the UN including the *Declaration on the Right to Development*. As a consequence, the specific Goals and targets of the 2030 Agenda also converge with the specific human rights objectives upheld by these international instruments. The 2030 Agenda enumerates these SDGS as: End poverty in all its forms everywhere (Goal 1); End hunger, achieve food security (Goal 2); Ensure healthy lives (Goal 3); Ensure inclusive and equitable quality education (Goal 4); Achieve gender equality and empower all women and girls (Goal 5); Ensure availability and sustainable management of water and sanitation for all (Goal 6); Ensure access to affordable, reliable, sustainable and modern energy for all (Goal 7); Promote sustained, inclusive and sustainable economic growth, full and productive employment and decent work for all (Goal 8); Build resilient infrastructure, promote inclusive and sustainable industrialization and foster innovation (Goal 9); Reduce inequality within and among countries (Goal 10); Make cities and human settlements inclusive, safe, resilient and sustainable (Goal 11); Ensure sustainable consumption and production patterns (Goal 12); Take urgent action to combat climate change and its impacts (Goal 13); Conserve and sustainably use the oceans, seas and marine resources for sustainable development (Goal 14); Protect, restore and promote sustainable use of terrestrial ecosystems, sustainably manage forests, combat desertification, and halt and reverse land degradation and halt biodiversity loss (Goal 15); Promote peaceful and inclusive societies for sustainable development, provide access to justice for all and build effective, accountable and inclusive institutions at all levels (Goal 16); and Strengthen the means of implementation and revitalize the Global Partnership for Sustainable Development (Goal 17). This underscores the intrinsic and symbiotic relationship between the 2030 Agenda on SDGs and the promotion and protection of all human rights.

The matrix attached on human rights and development illustrates that almost all of the specific development goals of the various human rights instruments and the 2030 Agenda are common and hence so is the relationship between them.

These Goals are further elaborated in the 2030 Agenda by specific targets and actions for their achievement within a set time line so that all are achieved by 2030. This detailed approach to the realization of the SDGs also provides a road-map for the implementation of the *Declaration on the Right to Development*, covering all human rights.

## 6 Conclusion

The foregoing considerations amply demonstrate that there is a symbiotic relationship between the human right to development and the SDGs as outlined in the 2030 Agenda. Not only are the principles and purposes, the vision and the Goals of the 2030 Agenda grounded in the core human rights instruments and the *Declaration on the Right to Development*, but the 2030 Agenda also highlights some obstacles to development as well as the requirements for an enabling environment for development as mentioned in these instruments. Moreover, the 2030 Agenda specifically recognizes that the *Declaration on the Right to Development* informs and contributes to the SDGs.

In the more than 30 years since the adoption of the *Declaration on the Right to Development* in 1986, differences between the developed and developing countries have retarded the implementation of this fundamental human right. The international mechanisms set up by the international community have, therefore, been unable to make progress. But now with the consensus adoption of the 2030 Agenda, the international community has, implicitly if not explicitly, endorsed the right to development as a human right. Moreover, the 2030 Agenda provides a specific time-bound road-map for the realization of the right to development. The time is ripe, therefore, to move forward on the implementation of the right to development as a human right in a manner consistent with the 2030 Agenda.

There will also be a need for realism and practicality on the part of States as well as the other stake-holders in their efforts to implement the right to development. Clearly, given the forces of "Realpolitik", not all aspects of the enabling environment would be possible to achieve in the foreseeable future, such as international peace and security, disarmament, or equitable trading and financial systems. Also, not all goals and objectives would be achieved over the next 15 years in equal measure, given the growth in population, diminishing resources and slowdown in different economies. For these reasons it would be prudent for the international community to combine their efforts and focus on achieving the core development goals so as to reach the furthest behind first, as the 2030 Agenda stipulates. This requires prioritizing achievement of fundamental development goals such as food, health, drinking water and sanitation, housing and women's empowerment. Realization of these goals can lay the foundations for the achievement of the other remaining goals.

Clearly the achievement of all human rights depends upon meeting these core human needs.

## Human rights and development matrix

| International instruments | Health/ sanitation | Education | Employment | Housing | Food | Women rights | Non-discrimination | Intl coop | Standard of living | Clothing | Water | Energy | Climate Justice |
|---|---|---|---|---|---|---|---|---|---|---|---|---|---|
| UN Charter | ✓ | ✓ | ✓ | | | ✓ | ✓ | ✓ | ✓ | | | | ✓ |
| Universal Declaration of Human Rights | ✓ | ✓ | | ✓ | ✓ | ✓ | ✓ | ✓ | ✓ | ✓ | | | ✓ |
| Convention on Elimination of Racial Discrimination | ✓ | ✓ | ✓ | ✓ | | ✓ | ✓ | ✓ | | | | | ✓ |
| Declaration on RD | ✓ | ✓ | ✓ | ✓ | ✓ | ✓ | ✓ | ✓ | ✓ | | | | ✓ |
| 2030 Agenda | ✓ | ✓ | ✓ | ✓ | ✓ | ✓ | ✓ | ✓ | ✓ | | ✓ | ✓ | ✓ |

CHAPTER 2

# The Right to Development from a Human Rights Approach: Conceptual Bases and Contemporary Challenges

*Flavia Piovesan**

## 1  Introduction

The right to development is the right of individuals and peoples to an enabling environment for development that is equitable, sustainable, participatory and in accordance with the full range of human rights and fundamental freedoms. Such an environment is free from structural and unfair obstacles to development domestically as well as globally.[1]

The current scale and severity of global poverty provides a jarring contrast and adds urgency to efforts to attain the sought-for enabling environment. In light of this, this chapter discusses the key attributes of the right to development from a human rights perspective, considering its conceptual and legal bases. As such, it particularly examines social justice; participation, accountability and transparency; and international cooperation. It gives special emphasis to the legal framework of the right to development, examining the extent of the State's duties to respect, protect and fulfill the right to development at a national and international level.

Considering the 1986 *Declaration on the Right to Development* as a dynamic, living instrument of enduring value in addressing current and emerging challenges central to development, this chapter concludes by highlighting the contemporary challenges and perspectives of the implementation of the right to development, inspired by a human rights-based approach to development and by a development approach to human rights.

---

\* Flavia Piovesan, Professor of Constitutional Law and Human Rights at the Catholic University of São Paulo and in the Human Rights post-graduate programs of the Catholic University of São Paulo, the Catholic University of Paraná and the Human Rights and Development Programme of Pablo de Olavide University (Spain).
1  See the report by the UN High Level Task Force on the implementation of the right to development—A/HRC/15/WG.2/TF/2. Add 2.

## 2    Conceptual Bases and Legal Framework of the Right to Development

Among the extraordinary achievements of the 1986 UN *Declaration on the Right to Development* is the advancement of a human rights-based approach to development. This approach integrates the norms, standards and principles of the international human rights system into the plans, policies and processes of development. Although the topic of development has traditionally been monopolized by economists with an exclusive emphasis on the GDP achieved by each State, the meaning of development has been revised since the 1980s, and has come to be guided by the human dimension. Article 2 of the Declaration recognizes that "The human person is the central subject of development and should be the active participant and beneficiary of the right to development".

To Stephen P. Marks "the Declaration takes a holistic, human-centered approach to development. It sees development as a comprehensive process aiming to improve the well-being of the entire population and of all individuals on the basis of their active, free, and meaningful participation and in the fair distribution of the resulting process. In other words, recognizing development as a human right empowers all people to claim their active participation in decisions that affect them—rather than merely being beneficiaries of charity—and to claim an equitable share of the benefits resulting from the development gains".[2]

To adopt Amartya Sen's conception, development has to be conceived of as a process of expansion of the true freedoms that people can benefit from.[3]

---

[2]  Stephen P. Marks, *The Politics of the Possible: The Way Ahead for the Right to Development* (Friedrich Ebert Stiftung, June 2011), 2.

[3]  In conceiving of development as freedom, Amartya Sen states that "In this sense, the expansion of liberties is seen both as (1) an end in itself and (2) the main meaning of development. Such ends may be respectively termed the constitutive and the instrumental function of liberty with regard to development. The constitutive function of liberty is related to the importance of substantive liberty for the elevation of human life. Substantive liberties include elementary capacities such as avoiding privation due to hunger, malnutrition, avoidable mortality, premature death and liberties associated with education, political participation, prohibition of censorship, etc. From this constitutive perspective, development involves the expansion of human liberties", Amartya Sen, *Development as Freedom* (New York: Alfred A. Knopf, 1999), 35–36, 297. On the right to development, see also Karel Vasak, *For Third Generation of Human Rights: The Rights of Solidarity*, International Institute of Human Rights, 1979.

Thinking along similar lines, Arjun K. Sengupta, states that the right to development is the "right to a process that expands the capabilities or freedom of individuals to improve their well-being and to realize what they value".[4]

Development from a human rights perspective embraces three key attributes:
(a) social justice (through inclusion, equality and non-discrimination, taking the human person as the central subject of development and paying special attention to the most deprived and excluded);
(b) participation, accountability and transparency (through free, meaningful and active participation, focusing on empowerment); and
(c) international cooperation (as the right to development is a solidarity-based right).

## 2.1 *Social Justice*

According to Article 28 of the *Universal Declaration of Human Rights*: "Everyone is entitled to a social and international order in which the rights and freedoms set forth in this Declaration can be fully realized".

Social justice is a central component of the conception of the right to development. The realization of the right to development, inspired by the value of solidarity, must provide equal opportunity to all in the access to basic resources, education, healthcare, food, housing, work and wealth distribution.[5]

For the *Declaration on the Right to Development*, development comprises an economic, social, cultural and political process, aimed at ensuring the constant improvement of the well-being of the population and of individuals, based on their active, free and significant participation in this process, guided by the fair distribution of the benefits resulting from it.

In promoting development, equal consideration must be given to the implementation, promotion and protection of civil, political, economic, social and cultural rights.

Effective measures must also be adopted so as to provide women with an active role in the process of development. In the contemporary world order poverty is "feminized", as women constitute 70% of the people who live in poverty. Guaranteeing the empowerment of women is a condition essential to the furthering of development. Statistics show that the countries with the highest

---

4 Report by the Independent Expert on the Right to Development, Arjun Sengupta, A/55/306, August 17, 2000, paragraph 22.
5 Allan Rosas, "The Right to Development", in *Economic, Social and Cultural Rights*, eds. Asbjørn Eide, Catarina Krause and Allan Rosas (Dordrecht, Boston and London: Martinus Nijhoff Publishers, 1995), 254–255.

HDI (Human Development Index, which measures a population's quality of life, access to healthcare, education and work) are precisely those with the smallest "gender gap", that is, the smallest difference between men and women in the exercise of human rights.[6] In the words of Amartya Sen: "nothing is as important today in the political economy of development as an adequate recognition of political, economic and social participation and leadership of women. This is indeed a crucial aspect of 'development as freedom'".[7]

In addressing the right to development from a human rights approach, Mary Robinson states that "The great merit of the human rights approach is that it draws attention to discrimination and exclusion. It permits policy makers and observers to identify those who do not benefit from development. ... so many development programmes have caused misery and impoverishment—planners only looked for macro-scale outcomes and did not consider the consequences for particular communities or groups of people".[8]

According to the 1986 Declaration, States have the primary responsibility for the creation of national and international conditions conducive to the realization of the right to development and the duty to cooperate in ensuring development and eliminating obstacles to development (Article 3).

About 80% of the world's population lives in developing countries, marked by low incomes and educational levels, and high rates of poverty and unemployment.[9] Roughly 85% of the world's income goes to the richest 20% of the world's population, whilst 6% goes to the poorest 60%.[10] The World Health Organization emphasizes that "poverty is the world's greatest killer. Poverty

---

[6] Note that Arab countries (such as Morocco, Saudi Arabia and Yemen) have the worst performance in gender disparities and inequalities. In these countries, disadvantages facing women and girls are the source of high inequality levels. See *The Global Gender Gap Report—2014*, Harvard University, University of California—Berkeley and World Economic Forum, 2015.

[7] Amartya Sen, *Development as Freedom* (New York: Alfred A. Knopf, 1999).

[8] Mary Robinson, "What Rights Can Add to Good Development Practice", in *Human Rights and Development: Towards Mutual Reinforcement*, eds. Philip Alston and Mary Robinson (Oxford: Oxford University Press, 2005), 36. To Mary Robinson, "Lawyers Should Not Be the Only Voice in Human Rights and, Equally, Economists Should Not Be the Only Voice in Development" (op. cit.).

[9] Jeffrey Sachs states that: "Eight million people around the world die each year because they are too poor to stay alive", Jeffrey Sachs, *The End of Poverty: Economic Possibilities for Our Time* (New York: The Penguin Press, 2005), 1. He adds that: "One sixth of the world remains trapped in extreme poverty unrelieved by global economic growth and the poverty trap poses tragic hardships for the poor themselves and great risks for the rest of the world", Jeffrey Sachs, *Common Wealth: Economics for a Crowed Planet* (London: Penguin Books, 2008), 6.

[10] Andrew Hurrell, *On Global Order: Power, Values and the Constitution of International Society* (Oxford: Oxford University Press, 2009), 11.

wields its destructive influence at every stage of human life, from the moment of conception to the grave. It conspires with the most deadly and painful diseases to bring a wretched existence to all those who suffer from it".[11]

For Andrew Hurrell "it is highly implausible to believe that the 20% of the world's population living in the high-income countries can insulate itself from the instability and insecurity of the rest and from revisionist demands for change".[12]

The Declaration urges that appropriate economic and social reforms should be carried out with a view to eradicating all social injustices. It also adds that States should encourage people's participation in all spheres as an important factor in development and in the full realization of all human rights (Article 8).

Development from a human rights perspective was also endorsed by the 1993 *Vienna Declaration and Programme of Action* which stresses that democracy, development and respect for human rights and fundamental freedoms are interdependent and mutually reinforcing, adding that the international community should support the strengthening and promoting of democracy, development and respect for human rights in the entire world.

## 2.2   *Participation, Accountability and Transparency*

The principle of participation and the principle of accountability are central to the right to development. According to the 1986 Declaration: "The human person is the central subject of development and should be the active participant and beneficiary of the right to development.... States have the duty to formulate appropriate national development policies that aim at the constant improvement of the well-being of the entire population and of all individuals, on the basis of their active, free and meaningful participation in development and in the fair distribution of the benefits resulting therefrom". The 1986 Declaration is the only international instrument that makes the nature of participation in development so explicit, emphasizing that States should encourage, promote and ensure free, meaningful and active participation of all individuals and groups in the design, implementation and monitoring of development policies.

Political liberties and democratic rights are among the constituent components of development, as spelt out by Amartya Sen.[13] Democracy demands access to information, alternative sources of information, freedom

---

11  See Paul Farmer, *Pathologies of Power* (Berkeley: University of California Press, 2003), 50.
12  Andrew Hurrell, *On Global Order: Power, Values and the Constitution of International Society* (Oxford: Oxford University Press, 2009), 296.
13  Amartya Sen, *The Idea of Justice* (Cambridge: Harvard University Press, 2009), 347. "Democracy is assessed in terms of public reasoning, which leads to an understanding of democracy as 'government by discussion'" (Amartya Sen, op. cit., XIII).

of expression, freedom of association, political participation, dialogue and public interaction.[14] Based on public reasoning, democracy is conditioned not just by the institutions that formally exist but by the extent to which different voices can be heard. The concept of participation and its relevance as a core element to a rights-based approach to development requires that democracy be addressed at both a procedural and a substantive level. At a procedural level, there are diverse forms of participation by populations in development through mechanisms such as public consultation, information and decision making, with special consideration given to the participation of vulnerable groups, and particularly gender, race and ethnicity perspectives, thus giving voice to the deprived and the vulnerable.

Civil and political rights are cornerstones of empowerment, strengthening democracy and improving accountability. Democracy enriches reasoned engagement through the enhancement of informational availability and the feasibility of interactive discussions. The fact that "no famine has ever taken place in the history of the world in a functioning democracy"[15] is revealing of the protective power of political liberty. Having an effective voice requires material capacities and the material conditions on which meaningful political participation depends.[16]

In the light of the principle of participation,[17] it is essential to promote participatory rights in national-level policy making, as well as in the decision-making processes of global institutions.

At a national level, the right to free, active and meaningful participation demands, on the one hand, the expansion of the universe of those entitled to

---

14  Every kind of democracy should meet a few basic requirements. To Robert Dahl, democracy will meet seven such requirements: (1) elected authorities; (2) free and fair elections; (3) inclusive suffrage; (4) the right to be elected; (5) freedom of expression; (6) alternative sources of information; and (7) freedom of association, Robert Dahl, *Democracy and Its Critics* (New Haven: Yale University Press, 1989). See also Robert Dahl, Ian Shapiro, and José Antonio Cheibub, eds., *The Democracy Sourcebook* (Cambridge, Massachusetts, London, England: The MIT Press, 2003); Robert Dahl, "What Political Institutions Does Large-scale Democracy Require?", *Political Science Quarterly* 120, no. 2 (Summer, 2005): 187–197; Robert Dahl, "A Democratic Paradox?", *Political Science Quarterly* 115, no. 1 (Spring, 2000): 35–40(6).

15  Amartya Sen, *The Idea of Justice* (Cambridge: Harvard University Press, 2009), 343.

16  Andrew Hurrell, *On Global Order: Power, Values and the Constitution of International Society* (Oxford: Oxford University Press, 2009), 316.

17  Participatory rights are also enshrined by international human rights instruments that give universal protection to political rights, including Article 21 of the *Universal Declaration of Human Rights*, Article 25 of the *International Covenant on Civil and Political Rights* and Article 7 of the *Convention on the Elimination of All Forms of Discrimination Against Women*, among others.

participate in the democratic game, inspired by the clause of equality and non-discrimination based on gender,[18] race, ethnicity and other criteria, and paying special attention to the most vulnerable.[19]

On the other hand, it demands the expansion of participatory arenas, strengthening democratic density—which can no longer be limited to *who* participates in the democratic game, but must also include *how* to participate[20]— based on the principles of transparency and accountability, highlighting human beings as agents for democracy. The rise of local participatory processes has taken different forms, fostering citizen participation. People should be active participants in development and implement development projects rather than being treated as passive beneficiaries. Every democracy entails agents and their consequent dignity as moral beings who deserve to be treated with full consideration and respect.

In addition to being active and free, participation should be meaningful as an effective expression of popular sovereignty in the adoption of development programs and policies. Meaningful participation and empowerment are reflected by the people's ability to voice their opinions in institutions that enable the exercise of power, recognizing citizenry as the origin of and the justification for public authority.

According to Freedom House, nearly 40 years ago more than half of the world was ruled by one form of autocracy or another, and many millions lived under outright totalitarianism.[21] The majority now live in democratic States. In 2010, the number of electoral democracies stood at 115. However, a total of 47 countries are deemed not free, representing 24% of the world's polities and 35% of the global population. Using regional criteria, in Western Europe

---

18   Regarding the participation of women, about one in five countries have a quota imposed by law or a Constitution reserving a percentage of parliamentary seats for women, contributing to a rise in the women's share from 11% in 1975 to 19% in 2010. (Human Development Report 2010, *The Real Wealth of Nations: Pathways to Human Development*, United Nations Development Programme—UNDP, New York, 2010.)

19   The lack of a voice is a problem afflicting refugees and migrants who no longer live in their countries of origin and are unable to participate politically in their countries of residence.

20   See Norberto Bobbio, *Democracy and Dictatorship: The Nature and Limits of State Power*, trans. Peter Kennealy and Minneapolis (University of Minnesota Press, 1989). Formal processes of democracy have proliferated at a national level, as illustrated by pioneering initiatives in Brazil, such as the participatory budget formulation process.

21   The share of countries designated as free increased from 31% in 1980 to 45% in 2000, and the proportion of countries designated as not free declined from 37% in 1980 to 25% in 2000. A free country demands free institutions, free minds, civil liberties and law-based societies. (Freedom House, *Freedom in the World 2011—Annual Survey of Political Rights and Civic Liberties—The Authoritarian Challenge to Democracy*).

96% of the countries are considered free, whereas in the Middle East and North Africa just 6% of countries are considered free and 78% of the countries are considered not free. A free country is one where there is open political competition, a climate of respect for civil liberties, significant independent civic life and independent media. A not free country is one where basic liberties are widely and systematically denied.

At a global level, the principle of participation demands an increase in the role of civil society organizations in policy discussion and decision-making processes. In addition, there is a pressing need to strengthen the participation of developing countries in international economic decision-making and norm-setting.[22] As stated by Joseph E. Stiglitz: "We have a system that might be called global governance without global government, one in which a few institutions—the World Bank, the IMF, the WTO—and a few players—the finance, commerce, and trade ministries, closely linked to certain financial and commercial interests—dominate the scene, but in which many of those affected by their decisions are left almost voiceless. It's time to change some of the rules governing the international economic order …".[23]

In this context, the struggle for a new multilateralism is urgent. This would involve reforms in the global financial architecture in order to achieve a new political balance of power, democratizing financial institutions and enhancing their transparency and accountability.[24] The establishment of the G20 (shifting global politics from the old G7 to a new group of emerging powers), demands reform of the voting structures of the Bretton Woods institutions (IMF and World Bank), as well as other initiatives aimed at broadening global governance, democratizing international decision-making arenas and strengthening the voice of the South are worthy of mention. Global challenges cannot be faced without adequate representation for a large proportion of

---

22  See *Analytical Study of the High Commissioner for Human Rights on the Fundamental Principle of Participation and Its Application in the Context of Globalization*, E/CN.4/2005/41, December 23, 2004.

23  Joseph E. Stiglitz, *Globalization and Its Discontents* (New York/London: WW Norton Company, 2003), 21–22.

24  According to Joseph Stiglitz, "We have a chaotic, uncoordinated system of global governance without global government". The author defends a "reform package", including, among other measures: (1) changes in voting structure at the IMF and World Bank, giving more weight to developing countries; (2) changes in representations (who represents each country); (3) adopting principles of representation; (4) increasing transparency (since there is no direct democratic accountability for these institutions); (5) improving accountability; and (6) ensuring better enforcement of the international rule of law, Joseph Stiglitz, *Making Globalization Work* (London: Penguin Books, 2007), 21.

humankind—Africa, Latin America and Asia—at major international forums and decision-making bodies. International order has to be reconceived and reconceptualized. As observed by Andrew Hurrell: "Today's new emerging and regional powers are indispensable members of any viable global order. But the cost of this change is both a far greater degree of heterogeneity in the interests of the major states, as well as an enormous increase in the number of voices demanding to be heard".[25]

Due to the lack of democracy in global governance, it is essential to promote good governance at an international level and effective participation of all countries in international decision-making processes.[26]

## 2.3    *International Cooperation*

Besides social justice and participation, the right to development requires international cooperation as a key dimension.

The right to development demands that globalization be ethical and solidary. In the understanding of Mohammed Bedjaqui: "In reality, the international dimension of the right to development is nothing more than an equitable distribution with regard to global social and economic well-being. This reflects a crucial question of our age, in so far as four fifths of the world's population no longer accept the fact that a fifth of the world's population continues to build its wealth on the basis of the remainder's poverty".[27]

According to the 1986 Declaration, States have the primary responsibility for the creation of national and international conditions favorable to the realization of the right to development and the duty to cooperate in ensuring development and eliminating obstacles to development. States also have the duty to take steps, individually and collectively, to formulate international development policies with a view to facilitating the full realization of the right to development.

Considering that the right to development has both national and international dimensions, it is essential to focus on the joint and external responsibilities of States in the realization of the right to development as a solidarity-based right.

---

25   Andrew Hurrell, *On Global Order: Power, Values and the Constitution of International Society* (Oxford: Oxford University Press, 2009), 7.
26   See Right to Development Criteria and Operational Sub-Criteria, A/HRC/15/WG.2/task force/2.Add.2, February 2, 2010, Annex I.
27   Mohammed Bedjaqui, "The Right to Development", in *International Law: Achievements and Prospects*, ed. M. Bedjaoui (1991), 1182.

The policies of international financial institutions are determined by the same States that have legally binding obligations under the *International Covenant on Economic, Social and Cultural Rights.*[28]

In dealing with the responsibilities of States acting collectively at the global and regional levels for the implementation of the right to development, the following criteria should be considered:[29]

(a) a stable global economic and financial system;
(b) a rule-based, open, predictable and non-discriminatory international trading system;
(c) access to adequate human and financial resources;
(d) access to the benefits of science and technology;
(e) environment of peace and security;
(f) environmental sustainability;
(g) constant improvement in human well-being;
(h) incorporating relevant international human rights standards in formulating development goals;
(i) integrating norms of non-discrimination, participation, access to information and effective complaint and remedy into their policies, systems and programming right across the board, including in project assessment, planning, implementation and evaluation;
(j) promoting good governance at an international level, including promoting the democratization of the system of international governance and promoting effective participation of all countries in international decision-making;
(k) providing for a fair and equitable distribution of the benefits and burdens of development;
(l) strengthening of global financial institutions, improving democratization, transparency and accountability of international financial institutions.

---

28   It is also notable that the *Maastricht Guidelines on Violations of Economic, Social and Cultural Rights* deem a human rights violation of omission "the failure of a State to take into account its international legal obligations in the field of economic, social and cultural rights when entering into bilateral or multilateral agreements with other States, international organizations or multinational corporations".
29   See the report of the High Level Task Force on the implementation of the right to development for the April 2010 session of the Working Group, including the list of criteria, sub-criteria and indicators—A/HRC/15/WG.2/TF/2. Add 2.

In the light of the international rule of law,[30] it is important to identify the extent and degree of the international responsibilities of States in the realization of the right to development, reviewing the traditional human rights doctrine, which endorses as State obligations the duty to respect, protect and fulfill human rights, in order to include the duty to cooperate. Considering that the 1986 Declaration should be perceived as a dynamic and living instrument, there emerges the contemporary challenge of how to strengthen the States' duty to cooperate for the implementation of the right to development in the global arena.

## 3   Right to Development: The Extent of State Duties

Classical doctrine identifies three State obligations in the field of human rights: to respect, protect and implement human rights.

The obligation to respect impedes the State from violating such rights. Regarding the obligation to protect, it falls on the State to avoid and prevent third parties (non-state actors) violating these rights. Finally, the obligation to implement demands that the State adopt measures for the realization of these rights.[31] In Katarina Tomasevski's view: "The obligations to respect, protect and fulfil each contain elements of obligation of conduct and obligation of result. The obligation of conduct requires action reasonably calculated to realize the enjoyment of a particular right. The obligation of result requires States to achieve specific targets to satisfy a detailed substantive standard. ... The obligation to protect includes the State's responsibility to ensure that private entities or individuals, including transnational corporations over which they exercise jurisdiction, do not deprive individuals of their economic, social and cultural rights. States are responsible for violations of economic, social and cultural rights that result from their failure to exercise due diligence in controlling the behavior of such non-state actors".[32]

---

30   For Tom Bingham, "The Rule of Law Requires Compliance by the State with Its Obligations in International Law as in National Law", in *The Rule of Law* (London: Penguin, 2010), 110.

31   In General Comment no. 12, the Committee of Economic, Social and Cultural Rights highlights that the obligation to fulfill can be broken down into the obligation to facilitate, promote and provide.

32   Katarina Tomasevski, "Indicators", in *Economic, Social and Cultural Rights: A Textbook*, 2nd revised edition, eds. Eide, A, C. Krause and A. Rosas (Dordrecht: Martinus Nijhoff Publishers, 2001), 729 and 732. As David Bilchitz points out, "The UN Committee has

With reference to the right to development, as well as the traditional obligations to respect, protect and implement, the obligation to cooperate also stands out. This is because the right to development has solidarity as a founding value, which, in an increasingly global order, invokes the duty of international cooperation. In Article 22, the 1948 Universal Declaration itself enshrines "the right to social security and is entitled to realization, through national effort and international cooperation and in accordance with the organization and resources of each State, of the economic, social and cultural rights indispensable for his dignity and the free development of his personality". The principle of international cooperation is also enshrined in Article 2 of the *International Covenant on Economic, Social and Cultural Rights*: "Each State Party to the present Covenant undertakes to take steps, individually and through *international assistance and cooperation*, especially economic and technical, to the maximum of its available resources, with a view to achieving progressively the full realization of the rights recognized in the present Covenant ..." (emphasis added).

The duty of international cooperation is therefore essential as far as the right to development is concerned.

As well as the obligation to respect, protect, implement and cooperate, the international jurisprudence promoted by the Committee on Economic, Social and Cultural Rights has endorsed the duty of the States to observe a minimum core obligation as far as social rights are concerned. For the Committee: "Minimum core obligations are those obligations to meet the 'minimum essential levels of a right'".

The duty to observe the bare minimum social rights has as its source the greater principle of human dignity, which is a founding, nuclear principle of human rights law, and demands absolute urgency and priority.

Regarding the implementation of social rights, the Committee adopts the following criteria: accessibility; availability; adequateness; quality and cultural acceptability. The Committee has also developed the legal content of social rights (housing—General Comment no. 4; adequate food—General Comment no. 12; health—General Comment no. 14; and education—General Comment no. 13).

Lastly, the reach of the legal obligations resulting from the right to development also includes the principle of the progressive application of social rights.

---

provided various categorizations of the obligations imposed by socio-economic rights on State Parties". In General Comment 3, it recognized the distinction between obligations of conduct and obligations of result. Obligations of conduct require the taking of action "reasonably calculated to realize the enjoyment of a particular right". Obligations of result require "States to achieve specific targets to satisfy a detailed substantive standard. ... socio-economic rights typically impose both obligations of conduct and obligations of result". David Bilchitz, *Poverty and Fundamental Rights: The Justification and Enforcement of Socio-Economic Rights* (Oxford/NY: Oxford University Press, 2007), 183–184.

From them result the principles of non-regression and of the prohibition of government inaction.

General Comment no. 3 by the Committee on Economic, Social and Cultural Rights asserts the obligation of States to adopt measures for the implementation of social rights by means of concrete, deliberate and focused actions in the most effective way possible. Therefore, States have the duty to avoid measures of social regression. For the Committee: "Any retrogressive measures would involve the most careful consideration and would need to be fully justified by reference to the totality of the rights provided for in the Covenant in the context of the full use of the maximum available resources".

It must be mentioned that the *International Covenant on Economic, Social and Cultural Rights* sets out the obligation of the States to recognize and progressively implement the rights declared by it, utilizing the maximum amount of resources possible. The clause of prohibition of social regression in terms of social rights, as well as the prohibition of government inaction or omission, results from the progressive application of economic, social and cultural rights.

Note that there are immediate application measures concerning social rights, as is the case of the prohibition of discrimination clause. As the Limburg Principles highlight: "Some obligations under the Covenant require immediate implementation in full by the State Parties, such as the prohibition of discrimination in Article 2(2) of the Covenant. ... Although the full realization of the rights recognized in the Covenant is to be attained progressively, the application of some rights can be made justiciable immediately while other rights can become justiciable over time".[33]

## 4   Contemporary Challenges of the Right to Development

Considering the key attributes of the right to development from a human rights perspective, its conceptual, legal bases and the extent of State duties, the main challenges to its implementation in the contemporary world order stand out.

---

[33] The Limburg Principles on the implementation of the *International Covenant on Economic, Social and Cultural Rights*, paragraph 22 (UN doc.E/CN.4/1987/17). As Asbjørn Eide observes, "State obligations for economic and social rights were elaborated by a group of experts, convened by the International Commission of Jurists, in Limburg (the Netherlands) in June 1986. The outcome of the meeting is the so-called Limburg Principles, which is the best guide available to state obligations under de CESCR. ... A decade later, experts on economic, social and cultural rights met in Maastricht to adopt a set of guidelines on violations of human rights (*The Maastricht Guidelines on Violations of Economic, Social and Cultural Rights*)", Asbjørn Eide, "Economic, Social and Cultural Rights as Human Rights", in *Economic, Social and Cultural Rights: A Textbook*, 2nd revised edition, eds. Eide, A, C. Krause and A. Rosas (Dordrecht: Martinus Nijhoff Publishers, 2001), 25.

### 4.1 Development of Indicators to Measure the Implementation of the Right to Development

One of the main weaknesses of the international human rights system is related to the difficulty in implementing rights—the so-called "implementation gap". Thus, the challenge of the implementation of the right to development is clear.

The UN High Level Task Force on the implementation of the right to development has made significant efforts to produce indicators and criteria for evaluating and measuring the implementation of the right to development. It recognizes that it is imperative to develop criteria, standards and guidelines for the implementation of the right to development based on a rigorous conceptual and methodological foundation.[34]

For Katarina Tomasevski: "The creation of indicators provides an opportunity to extend the rule of law, and thereby international human rights obligations, to the realm of economics which has thus far remained by and large immune from demands of democratization, accountability and full application of human rights standards. Indicators can be conceptualized on the basis of international human rights treaties because these lay down obligations for governments".[35]

The use of indicators allows the human rights impact assessment to be carried out in relation to the policies, programs and measures adopted by the State. This allows for accountability in relation to the obligations contracted by the State resulting from the right to development in the international and domestic arena. It also promotes the generation of data, statistics and information, which make up a solid base for carrying out a precise diagnosis of the implementation of the right to development.

Adopting indicators means that it is possible to identify advances, backward steps and inaction by public powers in terms of the right to development. It is a precondition for making a precise diagnosis of how public action and inaction are framed in the field of the right to development. It is from a precise diagnosis that it is also possible to identify priorities and strategies aimed at improving the realization of the right to development.

---

34   See report by the UN High Level Task Force on the implementation of the right to development for the April 2010 session of the Working Group, including the attributes of the right to development and the list of criteria, sub-criteria and indicators—A/HRC/15/WG.2/TF/2. Add 2. See also the document "Indicadores de progreso para medición de derechos contemplados en el Protocolo de San Salvador", OEA/Ser.L/XXV.2.1, GT/PSSI/doc.2/11, March 11, 2011.

35   Katarina Tomasevski, "Indicators", in *Economic, Social and Cultural Rights: A Textbook*, 2nd revised edition, eds. Eide, A, C. Krause and A. Rosas (Dordrecht: Martinus Nijhoff Publishers, 2001), 531–532.

The creation of indicators to measure the implementation of the right to development will allow the strengthening of the States' responsibility to respect, protect and implement the right to development. It will contribute to stimulate generation of information by the State, which will allow more precise formulation and evaluation of public policies, thus favoring the incorporation of the human rights perspective into the formulation of such policies.

### 4.2 Adoption of an International Treaty for the Protection of the Right to Development

This proposal has caused politico-ideological polarity and tension among States that favor only the *Declaration on the Right to Development* and States that desire the strengthening of legal protection of the right to development through the adoption of a legally binding instrument (in the form of an international treaty). This debate involves the controversy between the national and international dimensions of the right to development.

In general, developed countries emphasize the national dimension of this right, defending the view that the tutelage of the right to development should be maintained by means of soft law (in this case, with the 1986 Declaration only), without the need to adopt a treaty to this end; whilst developing countries emphasize the international dimension of the right to development, and defend the adoption of a treaty to better protect it.

In this context, those who favor the adoption of a treaty for the protection of the right to development are essentially the Member States of the Non-Aligned Movement (NAM), which includes the G77 countries and China. These are the actors who most actively defend a legally binding convention for the protection of the right to development. However, Canada, the EU and Australia have expressed their resistance and opposition to the proposal. Note that 53 States voted against the convention proposal, including developed countries (all members of the OECD and the EU), whose effort is essential for international cooperation.

However, developed countries emphasize that the majority of Member States of the UN General Assembly favors the adoption of a legally binding instrument, which would strengthen the international dimension of the right to development.

They argue that a binding instrument would signify the crystallization and consolidation of a legal rights regime applicable to the right to development, adding that in the history of the affirmation of human rights at an international level, the first step towards protection has involved the adoption of a declaration and later the adoption of a treaty, which perfects the degree of legal protection of a right. They add that the existence of an international treaty can even have a significant impact in the domestic sphere, providing a special opportunity for setting parameters for the implementation of the right.[36]

### 4.3 Ratification of the Optional Protocol to the International Covenant on Economic, Social and Cultural Rights

One of the greatest gaps in the legal apparatus hindering the monitoring of the right to development by the treaty bodies corresponded to there not being a mechanism through which to petition the protection of economic, social and cultural rights. In the view of Asbjørn Eide: "Social rights refer to rights whose function is to protect and to advance the enjoyment of basic human needs and to ensure the material conditions for a life in dignity".[37]

---

[36] Note that in Article 22, the *African Charter on Human and Peoples' Rights* establishes that "All peoples shall have the right to their economic, social and cultural development with due regard to their freedom and identity and in the equal enjoyment of the common heritage of mankind". In 2010, the African Commission on Human and Peoples' Rights condemned the State of Kenya for the violation of the right to development of the Endorois community, composed of around 60,000 individuals, who had lived for centuries in the region of Lake Bogoria, from where they were removed without any prior consultation or later compensation. For the Commission, "arguments recognizing the right to development requires fulfilling five main criteria: it must be equitable, non-discriminatory, participatory, accountable, and transparent, with equity and choice as important, overarching themes in the right to development. ... The result of development should be the empowerment of the Endorois community. It is not sufficient for the Kenyan Authorities to merely give food aid to the Endorois. The capabilities and choices of the Endorois must improve in order for the right to development be realized" (case no. 276/2003, *Center for Minority Rights Development and Minority Rights Group International on behalf of Endorois community v. Kenya*).

[37] Asbjørn Eide, "Social Rights", in *The Essentials of Human Rights*, eds. Rhona K.M. Smith and Christien van den Anker (London: Hodder Arnold, 2005), 234. For Asbjørn Eide, "Economic, social and cultural rights constitute three interrelated components of a more comprehensive package. The different components also have links to civil and political rights. At the core of social rights is the right to an adequate standard of living. The enjoyment of this right requires, at a minimum, that everyone shall enjoy the necessary subsistence rights—adequate food and nutrition rights, clothing, housing and necessary conditions of care. Closely related to this is the right of families to assistance ... In order to enjoy these social rights, there is also a need to enjoy certain economic rights. These are the right to property, the right to work and the right to social security. ... The notion of cultural rights is more complex. ... cultural rights contain the following elements: the right to take part in cultural life, the right to enjoy the benefits of scientific progress and its applications, the right to benefit from the protection of the moral and material interests resulting from any scientific, literary or artistic production of which the beneficiary is the author, and the freedom indispensable for scientific research and creative activity",

Only on December 10, 2008 was the *Optional Protocol to the International Covenant on Economic, Social and Cultural Rights*[38] finally adopted. It introduced a system of individual petitions, interim measures, inter-State communication and *in locum* investigations in cases of grave and systematic violations of social rights by a Member State. In 1996, the Committee on Economic, Social and Cultural Rights adopted a Protocol project, with the support of countries from Latin America, Africa and Eastern Europe, and facing resistance from the UK, USA, Canada and Australia, among others.

Since 1966, civil and political rights have relied on the mechanism of individual petitions through the adoption of the *Optional Protocol to the International Covenant on Economic, Social and Cultural Rights*, which has strengthened the justiciability of these rights in the global, regional and local spheres. As for social rights, only in 2008 were they able to count on this system, which will positively impact the degree of justiciability of these rights.

The Optional Protocol is an important initiative to break with the unequal protection assigned to civil and political rights, and economic, social and cultural rights in the international sphere.

In the regional systems of human rights protection, the same ambivalence can be observed regarding the diverse manner of treating civil and political rights, and economic, social and cultural rights. In the inter-American system, while civil and political rights were exhaustively enshrined by the 1969 *American Convention on Human Rights*, which in 2015 had 24 Member States, economic, social and cultural rights only came to be enshrined by the *San Salvador Protocol* in 1988 almost 20 years later, the latter had only 16 Member States. The same ambivalence is present in the European system, in which the *European Convention on Human Rights*, which only considers civil and political rights, had 47 Member States in 2015, while the *European Social Charter* only had 27.

For the implementation of the right to development, it is vital to encourage States to ratify the *Optional Protocol to the International Covenant on Economic, Social and Cultural Rights*, which can contribute immensely to the protection, actionability and justiciability of these rights in the international, regional and local spheres.

---

Asbjørn Eide, "Economic, Social and Cultural Rights as Human Rights", in *Economic, Social and Cultural Rights: A Textbook*, 2nd revised edition, eds. Eide, A, C. Krause and A. Rosas (Dordrecht: Martinus Nijhoff Publishers, 2001), 17–18.

38   The *Optional Protocol to the International Covenant on Economic, Social and Cultural Rights* was approved by General Assembly Resolution A/RES/63/117 on December 10, 2008.

## 4.4 International Financial Institutions Reform

Action by international financial institutions—especially with regard to trade, debt and technology transfer—is crucial to the realization of the right to development.

The UN High Level Task Force considers a heavy debt burden as a major obstacle for poor developing countries in meeting their obligations under the *International Covenant on Economic, Social and Cultural Rights*,[39] jeopardizing their right to development. The Task Force observes that the poverty afflicting the least developed countries is exacerbated by an unsustainable debt burden and that the billions of dollars that those countries pay in their debt-servicing obligations divert a large part of the scarce resources from crucial programs of education, health care and infrastructure, severely limiting the prospects for the realization of the right to development. It affirms that a State's obligation to debt had to take sufficiently into account national priorities of human development and poverty reduction, consistent with its human rights obligations and the need to maintain trust in the financing system.[40]

A human rights approach would imply that, under any circumstance, expenditure should not be restricted to the extent that it amounts to violations of the rights to food, health, education, an adequate standard of living and social security. The heavy burden that the current financial and economic crisis is putting on developing countries, especially the poor should also be highlighted.

The World Bank and the International Monetary Fund have operated with diligence to reduce the impact of debt and have introduced innovative programs.[41] The debt-relief initiative is contributing in a significant way to the right to development. However, debt cancellation alone will not be enough for affected developing countries to benefit from the right to development. It must be accompanied by enhanced State capacity, improved governance and respect for human rights, and promotion of equitable growth and the sharing of benefits thereof. An important connection between the right to development

---

[39] In its General Comment no. 2, in Article 22 of the *International Covenant on Economic, Social and Cultural Rights*, the Committee on Economic, Social and Cultural Rights has indicated that "International measures to deal with the debt crisis should take full account of the need to protect economic, social and cultural rights through, inter alia, international cooperation. In many situations, this might point to the need for major debt relief initiatives".

[40] See E/CN.4/2005/WG.18/TF/3, paragraph 63.

[41] See the Heavily Indebted Poor Countries Initiative (HIPC), launched in 1996 by the World Bank and the IMF, and the Multilateral Debt Relief Initiative (MDRI), launched in 2005, to assist HIPCs to reach the MDG (Millennium Development Goals).

and debt-relief initiatives is constituted by non-economic challenges, particularly those relating to issues of political instability, armed conflict and governance, all of which are impediments to the right to development.

The strengthening of global financial institutions, giving developing countries greater voice and representation, improving democratization, transparency and accountability of international financial institutions would also be essential for the realization of the right to development. The policies of the international financial institutions are determined by the same States that have legally binding obligations under the *International Covenant on Economic, Social and Cultural Rights*.[42] The principle of the shared responsibility of debtors and creditors is at the heart of an equitable global financial system. Principles of participation, inclusion, transparency, accountability, the rule of law, equality and non-discrimination must be upheld by both the lender and the borrower. The fact that human rights could permeate macro-economic policy to include fiscal policy, monetary policy and exchange policy is a challenge for international financial agencies. International economic institutions must seriously consider the human dimension of their activities and the sizable impact that economic policies can have on local economies, especially in an increasingly globalized world.[43]

### 4.5  *Promoting International Cooperation*

Thomas Pogge observes that "In 2000, the rich countries spent about USD 4,650 million on development assistance for meeting basic needs abroad while also selling the developing countries an estimated USD 25,438 million in conventional weapons. This represents 69 percent of the entire international trade in conventional weapons. The main sellers of arms are the US, with over 50 percent of sales, then Russia, France, Germany, and the UK".[44]

In this context, it is vital that developed countries invest 0.7% of their GDP in a "Vulnerability Fund" to aid developing countries, thus meeting the

---

42  See the *Maastricht Guidelines on Violations of Economic, Social and Cultural Rights*.
43  Cf. Mary Robinson, "Constructing an International Financial, Trade and Development Architecture: The Human Rights Dimension", Zurich, July 1, 1999, www.unhchr.org. Mary Robinson adds: "To take the example of children again, one economist has noted that 'Trade and exchange rate policies may have a larger impact on children's development than the relative size of the budget allocated to health and education. An incompetent Central Bank can be more harmful to children than an incompetent Ministry of Education'".
44  Thomas Pogge, *World Poverty and Human Rights* (Cambridge: Polity Press, 2002), 219, footnote 30. See also Amartya Sen, *Identity and Violence: The Illusion of Destiny* (New York/London: W.W. Norton & Company, 2006), 97.

commitments made in the Monterrey Conference on Financing for Development—the "Monterrey Consensus", 2002.

Currently, around 80% of the world's population live in developing countries. It is estimated that more than 1.7 billion people live in poverty.[45] A vicious cycle is set in place, in which economic inequality feeds political inequality in the exercise of power at an international level, and vice-versa.

It is essential that international cooperation be conceived of not as mere charity or generosity, but as solidarity, in the sphere of the principle of shared responsibilities in the global order.

### 4.6 *Stimulating Action by Private Actors in the Promotion of Human Rights*

Regarding the private sector, there is also a need to accentuate its social responsibility, especially that of multinational companies, inasmuch as they constitute the great beneficiaries of the globalization process. It suffices to mention that out of the world's 100 greatest economies, 51 are multinational companies and 49 are nation States. For example, it is important to encourage companies to adopt human rights codes relative to commercial activities; to demand commercial sanctions on companies that violate social rights; and to adopt the "Tobin tax" on international financial investments, among other measures.

The panorama of deep financial collapse is demanding the re-invention of the role of the State, greater responsibility by the markets and a new international financial architecture.

It is therefore crucial that the private sector, especially transnational corporations, widen its responsibility in the promotion of human rights, strengthening social, environmental and ethical responsibility.

### 4.7 *Best Practice Consolidation*

For the implementation of the right to development, it is also crucial to identify, exchange and promote best practices, so as to give them a catalyzing effect.

Lastly, we can conclude that the implementation of the right to development involves challenges of a legal, cultural, political and economic nature.

In the legal and cultural sphere, we can envisage that the right to development encompasses a multiplicity of actors that transcends the actors involved in the realization of other human rights.

The right to development requires a rupture with the traditional view inspiring the protective international architecture, in which human rights violations point, on the one hand, to the State (as the violator) and, on the other, to the

---

[45]  Jean-Paul Fitoussi, Amartya Sen and Joseph Sitglitz, *Mismeasuring Our Lives* (New York: Perseo Books, 2011).

singularly considered individual (as the victim). In its complexity, the right to development, in both its national and international dimensions, not only considers the State as violator (but also international institutions and non-state actors) and the individual as victim (but also communities and groups). It is worth saying that the right to development invokes a pattern of conflict different from the classical and traditional pattern that inspires the system of international human rights protection.

In its essence, the right to development translates the right to a national and international environment that ensures the exercise and expansion of individuals' and peoples' human rights, as well as their basic freedoms.

As if such a legal and cultural challenge were not sufficient, there is still a challenge of a more political nature. The process of implementation of the right to development has been characterized by ideological tensions and political ambivalence. The refusal by States to assign the same treatment to economic, social and cultural rights as to civil and political rights stands out. In this sense, the resistance by States to ratify the *Optional Protocol to the International Covenant on Economic, Social and Cultural Rights* and to adopt a convention on the right to development must be mentioned.

A challenge of an economic nature adds to these challenges, considering that the global economic and financial crisis primarily affects the poorer and more vulnerable. Thus, States face the challenge of adopting individual and collective measures and actions for implementing the right to development in the national and international spheres.

In an increasingly complex arena, it is crucial to advance the affirmation of the right to development and global justice in the social, economic and political fields; and to compose a new architecture able to respond to the challenges of the current agenda, of the new power dynamics in the international sphere and in a growing landscape of shared responsibilities.

Demonstrations in different geographical locations denounce settings of extreme inequality and yearn for the same cause: social justice. They reveal the importance of respecting the right to development, focusing on how human beings live and what substantive freedoms they enjoy in each society. These movements have the fight against the violation of the right to development as their major cause and implementation of the right to development as their major claim, based on active, free and meaningful participation.

They reflect how the 1986 *Declaration on the Right to Development* should be perceived as a dynamic and living instrument capable of addressing the contemporary challenge of advancing global democracy and global justice based on international cooperation and the creativity of civil society, considering development as an empowering process.

CHAPTER 3

# The Development Approach of Human Rights

He Zhipeng*

## 1  Introduction

The adoption of the *Declaration on the Right to Development* in 1986 should be regarded as an important event in the history of the development of human rights in the world. The concept of the right to development presented in that Declaration, as well as the presentation of corresponding claims, should be seen as an important step in the improvement and enrichment of human rights theory and practice. Although it is true that the importance of development has been noted in earlier international documents[1] —the United Nations did a great deal for development as well as human rights[2] —development began to be seen as a type of human right only in the text of the *Declaration on the Right to Development*.[3] It is in this document that the glorious vocabulary of human rights was extended to define issues of development. The concept of human rights, as respected and promoted by all nations, was used to describe

---

* He Zhipeng, Professor at Jilin University.
1 For example, Article 55 of the UN Charter (1945) provides: With a view to the creation of conditions of stability and well-being which are necessary for peaceful and friendly relations among nations based on respect for the principle of equal rights and self-determination of peoples, the United Nations shall promote:
    a. higher standards of living, full employment, and conditions of economic and social progress and development;
    b. solutions of international economic, social, health, and related problems; and international cultural and educational cooperation; and
    c. universal respect for, and observance of, human rights and fundamental freedoms for all without distinction as to race, sex, language, or religion.
   Also, Article 2 of United Nations *Declaration on Social Progress and Development* (adopted by the General Assembly on December 11, 1969, GA res. 2542 (XXIV), 24 UN GAOR Supp. (No. 30) at 49, UN Doc. A/7630 (1969)) mentioned:
   Social progress and development shall be founded on respect for the dignity and value of the human person and shall ensure the promotion of human rights and social justice.
   For comments, see A. Sengupta, "On the Theory and Practice of the Right to Development", *Human Rights Quarterly* 24 (2002): 837–889.
2 Ragnar Hallgren, "The UN and the Right to Development", *Peace Research*, 22/23 (1990–1991): 31–41.
3 Article 1 of the *Declaration on the Right to Development* (A/RES/41/128, adopted by the General Assembly on December 4, 1986):

the needs to development. The perspective of human rights was employed to look at the great challenges of development that all states of the world are facing. This concept of development was repeated, renewed, and reemphasized thereafter by a series of international documents. In this short chapter, I will discuss a few ways that the system of human rights and even the world was changed by the notion of development.[4]

## 2  The Development Approach of Human Rights Means a New Vision of Human Rights

There are many aspects of the right to development, including freedom of movement,[5] non-discrimination based on gender,[6] supporting the poor,[7] regional economic and social improvement,[8] filling the digital gap,[9] and acting

---

1. The right to development is an inalienable human right by virtue of which every human person and all peoples are entitled to participate in, contribute to, and enjoy economic, social, cultural and political development, in which all human rights and fundamental freedoms can be fully realized.
2. The human right to development also implies the full realization of the right of peoples to self-determination, which includes, subject to the relevant provisions of both International Covenants on Human Rights, the exercise of their inalienable right to full sovereignty over all their natural wealth and resources.

Article 2 paragraph 1 of the same document:

The human person is the central subject of development and should be the active participant and beneficiary of the right to development.

For discussions on this, see R.N. Kiwanuka, "Developing Rights: The UN Declaration on the Right to Development", *Netherlands International Law Review* 35 (1998): 257–272.

4  As mentioned in the *Vienna Declaration and Programme of Action* (Adopted by the World Conference on Human Rights in Vienna on June 25, 1993): "Democracy, development and respect for human rights and fundamental freedoms are interdependent and mutually reinforcing.… The international community should support the strengthening and promoting of democracy, development and respect for human rights and fundamental freedoms in the entire world".

5  Wilfred Owen, "Immobility: Barrier to Development", *Transportation Journal* 4 (1964): 20–26.

6  Debnarayan Sarker, "Development Theory and Gendered Approach to Development: A Review in the Third World Perspective", *Sociological Bulletin* 55 (2006): 45–66.

7  Bård A. Andreassen, "The Right to Development and Legal Empowerment of the Poor", *The Bangladesh Development Studies* 33 (2010): 311–325.

8  S.R. Osmani, "Realizing the Right to Development in Bangladesh: Progress and Challenges", *The Bangladesh Development Studies* 33 (2010): 25–90; Paul Bomani and Douglas Ensminger, "Tanzania's Road to Development: Bringing Development to the People", *Ekistics* 40 (1975): 111–114; Marcus Power, "The Short Cut to International Development: Representing Africa in 'New Britain'", *Area* 32 (2000): 91–100.

9  V.V. Bhatt, "Harnessing Technology to Development", *Economic and Political Weekly* 17, no. 35 (1982): 69–72; Jacques Richardson, "Communication, a Critical Pathway to Development", *Leonardo* 26 (1993): 347–351.

as an instrument in domestic and international politics.[10] It is also regarded as the basis for other types of individual human rights which predated the term "right to development".[11] Nevertheless, the significance of this new category of human rights is not limited to the above-mentioned aspects. It means that the world may have an expanded landscape of human rights, and that an extended human rights-based dialogue among states and other actors in international relations is possible.[12]

In 1999, Amartya Sen, the economist who won the Nobel Prize in Economics, published the book *Development as Freedom*. The book argues that economic development is closely linked to freedom: political freedom and transparency, freedom of opportunity, and freedom of protection through economic assistance, and that poverty is often associated with lack of freedom.[13] This book also is a profound inspiration for our thinking about human rights, because a shift of perspective often lets us see a different world. For example, to look at development from the perspective of human rights, it is easy to discover that development is not just numbers and charts in various statistics, but must contribute to the ascension of human happiness.[14]

Based on the above-mentioned notion, to look at human rights from the development approach means at least two aspects. The first aspect is that the meaning and scope of human rights are not rigid, but gradually change with the development of society. The second aspect is that development must be seen as a type of human right, whether it is the development of a person, the development of a group, the development of a community, the development of a city, the development of a country, and even the development of a continent, all these should be included in the category of human rights, and none of them

---

10   Bonny Ibhawoh, "The Right to Development: The Politics and Polemics of Power and Resistance", *Human Rights Quarterly* 33 (2011): 76–104.
11   E.g., Benjamin Mason Meier and Ashley M. Fox, "Development as Health: Employing the Collective Right to Development to Achieve the Goals of the Individual Right to Health", *Human Rights Quarterly* 30 (2008): 259–355.
12   Sakiko Fukuda-Parr, "The Right to Development: Reframing a New Discourse for the Twenty-First Century", *Social Research* 79 (2012): 839–864.
13   Amartya Sen, *Development as Freedom* (New York: Oxford University Press, 1999); 2nd ed., 2011.
14   The *Millennium Development Goals* (MDGs) signed by 189 Member States of the UN in September 2000 made human rights an aim and index of development, and further put human rights into the specific requirements of development. For discussions, see Andy Haines and Andrew Cassels, "Can the Millennium Development Goals Be Attained?", *British Medical Journal* 329 (2004): 394–397; Sakiko Fukuda-Parr, "Millennium Development Goals: Why They Matter", *Global Governance* 10 (2004): 395–402; Arlene L. Garces-Ozanne, "The Millennium Development Goals: Does Aid Help?", *The Journal of Developing Areas* 44 (2011): 27–39.

should be omitted. To include development in the scope of the current definition of human rights, and not be limited to the traditional view of human rights defined by freedom, is a positive sign of cultural diversity. This new and inclusive category of human rights not only contributes to the universalization of human rights in the world, but also helps to look at human rights as a whole. In this way, more countries, more peoples, and more cultural types will readily accept human rights. This understanding of human rights will make international and domestic actors treat human rights as a system comprising the desire for good social order in many cultural backgrounds, as well as a system that is conducive to all cultures, all civilizations.

3    The Development Approach of Human Rights Is Conducive to Promoting the Evolution and Deepening of Human Rights Thinking

In terms of values, when the concept of the right to development appeared in the world, a multiple cultural map of human rights emerged. With the continuous advocacy and promotion of the right to development in the international community, non-Western civilizations participated in human rights matters in a broad and deep manner.[15] Non-Western civilizations have tried to provide their own understanding of human rights, and contribute to the theory of human rights.[16] This may also contribute to creating a cross-cultural identification that the traditional culture of human rights tries to include and to tolerate new understandings, new explanations and new elements of human rights. Therefore, a broader range of exchanging human rights ideas and a consensus on human rights institutional issues in the world could be steadily developed, thereby promoting the progress of human rights as a globally recognized vocabulary. We can also understand the fact in this way: as the notion of the right to development was established and consolidated, a broader concept of human rights could be adopted, and the idea of human rights be accepted, recognized and supported by almost all cultures in the world, pushing all countries to work together for a broader and more inclusive scope of human rights.

One positive aspect of placing development within the framework of human rights is that it no longer confines development issues to the international economic system, but to the whole system of human rights. Another positive

---

15   Andrea Cornwall and Celestine Nyamu-Musembi, "Putting the 'Rights-Based Approach' to Development into Perspective", *Third World Quarterly* 25 (2004): 1415–1437.
16   N.J. Udombana, "The Third World and the Right to Development: Agenda for the Next Millennium", *Human Rights Quarterly* 22 (2000): 753–787.

aspect is that, even more importantly, this means an innovation in the human rights tradition, which means a structural remodeling and paradigm shift of human rights ideas from the long and dominant position of human rights thoughts settling in the Western culture as the core, based on the experience of Renaissance, the Reformation, and the Enlightenment.

The thought spectrum of human rights before the ideas of the right to development should be considered as an important achievement of human civilization; it is a great step forward in the sense of the whole world history. It can be seen as the glory of all mankind, a great progress since it represents the wisdom and courage the improvement of human society and human life. But after all, it is quite limited in the temporal and geographical sense. It is only a flower of thought blooming in the flourishing tree of Western cultural ideas. We must bear in mind that there are many types of civilizations and all of them have created significant and useful thinking in human society. Therefore, the traditional human rights ideas cannot ignore the civilizations of other areas in the world and cannot block the continuation of development in human rights. Moreover, the concept of human rights established on the basis of Western thought is concerned more with human freedom, or the negative right of people, that is, it requires the government do as little as possible, not to interfere with people's freedom in social life, especially in speech, elections, religious beliefs. It emphasizes the opportunity of citizens to participate in state governance, and the core of this claim of human rights is to prevent the government and government officers from abusing their power. This can only be said as one aspect of human rights, one field of human rights, one manifestation in human rights, but not the whole picture of human rights. It is wrong to regard this Western style of human rights claims as the only correct version of the world's human rights, the only correct solution for human future.

It is necessary that we analyze and accept new human rights claims, new human rights elements, and even new human rights paradigms from other stages of social development, from other civilizations and cultural fields in the world. Thus, as the emergence of the various claims belong to the so-called "first generation and second generation" of human rights, the creation of the term "right to development" and its acceptance as a new member of the human rights family is of paramount importance for the development of human civilization, and world politics.[17] If the traditional human rights paradigm

---

17   Paul Gready, "Rights-Based Approaches to Development: What Is the Value-Added?", *Development in Practice* 18 (2008): 735–747; Peter Uvin, "From the Right to Development to the Rights-Based Approach: How 'Human Rights' Entered Development", *Development in Practice* 17 (2007): 597–606.

emphasizes the idea of a liberal-based approach to social order and thus seeks an upgraded model of governance, namely to treat people equally, then the updated human rights paradigm calls for a development-oriented governance model, which must be established on the understanding of a widened scope of human rights to gain its justification.[18]

It is undeniable that the traditional concept of human rights has brought benefits to the whole world in the course of historical progress and even within today's political and economic framework. All people in all countries in our human society want to live in a free and safe state. Their human needs, however, are not limited to these factors; people also want to live in a state where the future is promising. Thus, raising the concept of the right to development, and all efforts to achieve this right in the context of domestic policy-making and international political cooperation, is in fact an important manifestation of social progress, cultural integration and the overall development of international society.[19]

It is the expectation of all states and all civilizations in our world today for this right to be turned into reality, into the real life of all people, and to continue to move forward. Therefore, the expansion of human rights, demonstrated by the traditional concept of human rights coupled with the new concept of human rights, will definitely lead to the concept of human rights continuing to develop into a new field, pushing human rights legal regimes to a new and higher degree of progress. This is the ideological inspiration and institutional deepening of the entire human rights spectrum that comes with a series of human rights advocates including the right to development.

## 4 The Development Approach of Human Rights Is Conducive to Correct the Hegemony of Human Rights Based on Single Standards

If we think further, it is not difficult to see that the concept of the right to development is an important manifestation of the rational development of the international community, and when states, multinational corporations and international organizations try to realize and safeguard the right to development

---

18   It is also notable, however, that the traditional Western civilization also includes some elements on the right to development. See John Marangos and Nikos Astroulakis, "The Aristotelian Contribution to Development Ethics", *Journal of Economic Issues* 44 (2010): 551–558.
19   Wade Mansell and Joanne Scott, "Why Bother about a Right to Development?", *Journal of Law and Society* 21 (1994): 171–192.

on a global scale, the world will cooperate in the spirit of solidarity. We can make a judgment that in the perspective of theoretical analysis and cultural comparison, the concept of human rights, such as individualism and individual freedom, or the mainstream view of human rights in the contemporary world is not the whole content of human rights, nor is it the only correct version of human rights. If one sticks to one dimension only and ignores the other dimensions of human rights development, abides by one criterion and neglects other possible criteria of human rights, emphasizes one type and criticizes other types of institutional construction of human rights, it is actually a confinement of human rights development, a major loss to human rights thinking, and a wrong way to perfect the system. That is to say, if we rigidly believe that the notion of human rights must be confined only to the traditional Western political ideology and political practice, and only in this way can the world be in good order, if we stay in the human rights directory which has already constituted a single, authoritative, self-sufficient list so that it cannot contain other new factors, then it is not difficult to infer that there may be a political control in the name of human rights, or political oppression of the different views in international politics.

This is not uncommon in the history of international relations. For example, some states may criticize and even interfere with other states on the grounds of unreasonable and unfair human rights in those places. This is likely to lead to international conflict situations. Such a phenomenon of political intervention, and even use of force under the guise of human rights is not the right way to realize human rights, but rather a political struggle in the name of human rights. And this is not only an embodiment of Western civilization centrism, but also a type of hegemony and power politics stemming from the Western cultural sense of superiority. In the current world of international politics, there is a trend for Western states to use human rights terms to carry out activities such as use of force, occupation of a state, or punish some states by means of embargo. They have created new terms such as "humanitarian intervention" and "responsibility to protect" to justify their stance.

Such ideas and actions are not good, not only bad for the world's direction but also for the promotion of global governance. In recent international affairs, both the subversion of the Libyan government in 2011 and the already internationalized armed conflict in Syria have fully demonstrated that to try to resolve problems in accordance with a single traditional human rights ideology can not only not contribute to world peace and human security, but raises the possibility of bringing the world into a more chaotic abyss; it will by no means help to resolve human rights problems, but raises the potential for human rights flaws to evolve into humanitarian disasters.

Sometimes, states such as China do not agree with such punitive measures, and these disagreements are often described as an attitude against human rights. If a developing approach of human rights may be adopted, human rights does not have just one version; to safeguard the stability of a given society, to assure territorial integrity are also expressions of human rights. When we recognize a range of new types of human rights and collective human rights including the right to the environment, right to development and right to peace, and realize that there are more than only one version of human rights notions and legal systems based on the historical experience of the West, we can easily conclude that human rights have multiple dimensions, multiple levels, and may be expressed and realized by a variety of systems, as well as promoted and developed in different ways. We can say that none of the human rights systems or human rights practices in any country are perfect. So, states should be more open-minded and cooperative in the maintenance and realization of human rights, rather than adopt negative attitudes and activities such as combat, irony, and abuse. In international society, no matter what types of punitive measures are taken, attempts to punish a country's human rights affairs will eventually lead to a reduction in the degree of protection of human rights rather than an increase it. Also, we can have a dialogue on the context of human rights. The difference between Western states and non-Western states is not really the tension of two paradigms of human rights and sovereignty, but rather, the tension of different understandings of human rights. This will help us to achieve comprehensive international politics in a human rights environment, and Western states cannot criticize non-Western states as a group of "bad guys" who oppose human rights.

In this sense, we believe that in international relations concerning human rights, all actors should try to reduce the complacency of a civilization, try to diminish the self-centrism and self-expansion of a certain civilization. All actors should use all means to fully promote the blending of various notions in human rights, the dialogue of different human rights ideas, and cooperate in different human rights regimes, so as to promote the prosperity of the world and its development. Only in this way can we make human rights a matter that is accepted in all states, for all people, and all civilizations; and to make human rights be seen as a wonderful presence in all areas of our planet. On the contrary, if human rights are seen by some states as a means of combating or opposing other countries, and regarded as an excuse or instrument to hit other actors, the possibility that human rights are generally respected and widespread in the world will be reduced. The fate of human rights *per se* is also worth worrying about.

## 5   Conclusion

When the right to development is legally and politically justified, all the world may accept that more elements must be added to the traditional understanding of human rights stemming from Western culture,[20] and thus states may hold discussions on the human rights context concerning issues such as international economic order, international intervention, and domestic political regimes.[21] In general, when we use the human rights approach to address development, we have the opportunity to put many economic development initiatives into the framework of human rights, and thus the legitimacy of human rights is increased, more considerations based on the happiness of people are used to evaluate legal and political institutions.[22] When we use the developing approach to treat issues concerning human rights, we increase tolerance of human beings, widen the spectrum of human rights, and increase the probability that human rights are more widely accepted and endorsed in cross-cultural communications. This will definitely lead to a more healthy and smooth development of human rights in global and domestic politics.

---

20  Wouter Vandenhole, "The Human Right to Development as a Paradox", *Verfassung und Recht in Übersee / Law and Politics in Africa, Asia and Latin America* 36 (2003): 377–404.
21  K.L. Dalal, "Man's Right to Development", *India International Centre Quarterly* 15 (1988): 89–96.
22  Brigitte I. Hamm, "A Human Rights Approach to Development", *Human Rights Quarterly* 23 (2001): 1005–1031; Arjun Sengupta, "Right to Development as a Human Right", *Economic and Political Weekly* 36, no. 27 (Jul. 7–13, 2001): 2527–2536; Noorjahan Bava, "Approaches to Development", *The Indian Journal of Political Science* 42 (1981): 41–57.

CHAPTER 4

# The Relationship between Human Rights and Development: An Analysis of Chinese Scholars' Perspectives and the Practice of the Chinese Government

*Zhang Wei\* and Zhang Aitong\*\**

Human rights, peace and development were the three major tasks undertaken by the United Nations after World War II. Peace is the foundation of the preservation of human rights and promotion of development, which is of universally recognized value. Nevertheless, the issue of the relationship between human rights and development has been long debated between Eastern and Western countries, and between Northern and Southern countries. The vast majority of developing countries believe that their own poverty and backwardness are the long-term consequence of unfair colonial rule, and that developed countries should compensate them. Therefore, they regard development as a kind of collective human right that developing countries should have, and its obligatory source should be developed countries. At the same time, developing countries believe that their own unsatisfactory human rights situation is caused by unfair international standards, and that change needs to be built on the basis of economic development. Without development, how should human rights be discussed? While the Western developed countries believe that human rights are the rights of individuals, and the state cannot become the subject of the right, so the development task cannot be regarded as an international obligation of developed countries to help developing countries. They also uphold the principle of the supremacy of human rights, requiring developing countries to continuously improve the level of protection of human rights, or they would impose economic sanctions in order to force the advancement of the human rights cause in these countries.

---

\* Zhang Wei, Professor at China University of Political Science and Law (CUPL), and Co-Director of the Institute for Human Rights at CUPL
\*\* Zhang Aitong, a postgraduate student of the Institute for Human Rights at China University of Political Science and Law.

In this debate, the reality we are facing now is that despite the increasing economic aggregate of developing countries, the economic gap between the North and the South continues to widen, and the imbalance between developed and developing countries is still significant. Based on the present situation, this chapter introduces the three main perspectives on the relationship between human rights and development, before elaborating on the position of the United Nations on this issue. The third part of this chapter explores the interpretation of the Chinese government of the relationship between human rights and development, and concludes by summarizing the experience of development, identifying pressing issues, and providing a coping strategy.

## 1   Three Main Perspectives on the Relationship between Human Rights and Development

Soon after the concept of human rights came into being, human rights and development were on two separate tracks.[1] People equate development with economic growth and the accumulation of material wealth, while ignoring the vital importance of human beings as a subject of development. With social progress and development, the traditional concept and model of development have been accompanied by many problems, such as the polarization of the rich and the poor, environmental pollution, and social unrest. The emergence of these problems prompted people to rethink and understand the concept of development, and the center of development has been changed from material to human.[2] The relationship between human rights and development, however, is very complex and diverse. There are still wide differences in the understanding of the relationship between human rights and development in different countries, and it is sometimes difficult to summarize them concisely.[3] The following three points of view are relatively prominent.

### 1.1   *Economic and Social Development Is the Basis for the Realization of Human Rights Protection, So Countries Should Develop the Economy First, Then Protect Human Rights*

When there is disagreement on human rights and development objectives, the need for one right may result in the restraint of other rights.[4] The vast majority

---

1   A. Eide, "Human Rights' Requirements for Social and Economic Development", *Foreign Law Review*, no. 4 (1997): 7.
2   Zhang Xiaoling, "On the Relationship Between Human Rights and Development", *Pacific Journal*, no. 11 (2008): 21.
3   J.D. Sethi, "Human Rights and Development", *Human Rights Quarterly* 3, no. 3 (1981): 11.
4   Ibid., 15.

of developing countries believe economic and social development is the basis for the realization of human rights protection, so they believe that countries should develop the economy first, then protect human rights. They believe that human rights are associated with economic development, but one or the other should be prioritized.[5] And they emphasize that the right to subsistence is superior to civil and political rights, which are the primary concerns of Europeans. They also take the view that for any country or nation, the right to subsistence is the most important right of all human rights. It is argued that without the right to subsistence, the other rights would become meaningless.

This view holds that economic development and protection of human rights are prioritized, but they have differing importance, often stressing the former over than the latter. In Third World countries, such as in Asia, Africa and Latin America, political oppression and the deprivation of human rights become the means to expand the private market mechanism and promote monetarism.[6] It obviously violates the law of social development and hinders the development of both society and individuals in society.

### 1.2 Human Rights Are the Prerequisite and Basis for All Aspects of Development; Only by Safeguarding Human Rights Can Economic and Social Development Be Realized

In general, the prevailing view on the relationship between economic and political rights, in particular the relationship between development and human rights, is different in developed and developing countries. Western developed countries mostly meet the above conditions, and thus are better equipped to deal with the contradiction between them.[7] They believe that human rights are the prerequisite and basis for all aspects of development. Human rights are created to prevent the infringement of individual rights by state power.[8] Only by ensuring the realization of universal human rights can economic and social development be achieved. At the same time, they argue that some developing countries prefer to emphasize the protection of economic and social rights, which ignores the level of economic development and the protection of freedom. The result is to criticize governments that supposedly violate the right to freedom.

---

5  Ken Freeman and Gustav Galatz, "The Differences Between European and Chinese Human Rights Concepts", trans. Zhu Ming, *Chinese Journal of European Studies*, no. 2 (2011): 73.
6  J.D. Sethi, "Human Rights and Development", 18.
7  Ibid., 14.
8  Guo Chunzhen, "On the Relationship Between Two Human Rights Preferences and the Positive Orientation of Human Rights in China", *Law Review*, no. 2 (2012): 11.

It is worth considering that the countries that hold this view tend to adhere to the universality of human rights, so when they think that there are human rights violations in other countries, they will criticize without hesitation and regard human rights as political tools for the promotion of values of human rights in the world in order to gain political and economic advantage while securing their national interest. The United States is a typical example of this problem. The United States has long viewed itself as the champion of human rights protection. It has used human rights to attack and suppress socialist countries and developing countries without regard to the historical and economic development of other countries, and it has used human rights as the basis for sanctions against other countries, even using military means to violate sovereign states. History has repeatedly proved that such an approach has not created greater freedom for the people of other countries, but has created a greater human rights catastrophe in the world.

### 1.3 Human Rights and Development Are Interdependent and Complementary, and the Two Cannot Be Simply Separated

This perspective is that economic and social development is the basis for the realization of human rights, and human rights protection counterbalances economic and social development, and plays an important role in promoting it. As Heidemarie Wieczorek-Zeul said: "[d]evelopment policy means protection of human rights. From a philosophical point of view, the two cannot be achieved in isolation".[9] Professor Wang Xigen concluded: "the completely different attitude towards the practice of the right to development originates from different orientations of relationship between human rights and development. They can be summarized into two theoretical models from the global perspective and on the basis of human rights: the view of rights-based development and the view of the right to development". It is necessary to transform the perspective from the right-based approach to the right to development and fully integrate development into human rights.[10] Professor Gong Xianghe explained: "[h]uman rights and development are two wheels of a harmonious society, and they are interdependent and mutually promoted. Human rights are both the target and the means of development, and development is essentially a process

---

9   Heidemarie Wieczorek-Zeul, "Human Rights and Development", *Environmental Policy and Law*, no. 5 (2008): 249.
10  Wang Xigen, "A New Idea of Constructing the Global Legal Mechanism of the Right to Development", *Xinhua Digest*, no. 3 (2009): 16–18. Wang Xigen, *Fazhishehui de jibenrenquanfazhanquanfalvzhidu yanjiu* [*The One of Basic Human Rights in Society with Rule of Law—A Study on Legal System of the Right to Development*] (Beijing: Chinese People's Public Security University Press, 2002).

of expanding human rights".[11] Luo Yanhua also argued: "[t]he combination of human rights and development is the right to development. Development is the fundamental way to realize human rights. Economic development is the prerequisite for the full realization of human rights, and the development of human rights is a gradual and spontaneous process".[12] On the basis of the above two scholars' views, Zhang Xiaoling further pointed out: "[h]uman rights and development are interdependent and complementary".[13] In recent years, this view has been gradually recognized by the international community; the economic structural adjustment policies around human rights implemented by the International Monetary Fund and the World Bank around the world are reflecting the further integration of human rights and development.[14]

But it is noteworthy that human rights cannot be simply integrated into development, and they should be regarded as a measuring standard of development. The guarantee of human rights permeating all areas of society is an important part of development. Human rights are necessary conditions of the rights themselves.[15] Human rights and economic development move forward together, and they interrelate and cannot be separated.

## 2   The Position of the United Nations on the Relationship between Human Rights and Development

One of the purposes of the United Nations is to promote international cooperation for the promotion of economic and social development, and universal respect for and observance of human rights. This chapter explores the position of the United Nations on the relationship between human rights and development, focusing on the evolution of the position of the United Nations on the relationship between human rights and development.

With regard to the evolution of the position of the United Nations on the relationship between human rights and development, there is no definitive

---

11   Gong Xianghe, "Human Rights and Development in the Construction of a Harmonious Society", *Law Science Magazine*, no. 2 (2008): 33.
12   Luo Yanhua, "How to Look at the Relationship Between Human Rights and Development—One of the Focuses of the North-South Human Rights Struggle in the Post-Cold War Era", *World Economics and Politics*, no. 8 (1996): 26.
13   Zhang Xiaoling, "Relationship Between Human Rights and Development", 21.
14   Danilo Türk, "Development and Human Rights", *Studies in Transnational Legal Policy* 26 (1994): 167.
15   John O'Manique, "Human Rights and Development", *Human Rights Quarterly*, no. 14 (1992): 78.

division of the stages among scholars. Nevertheless, by reading a large number of documents of the United Nations and taking into account the views of many experts and scholars, this chapter argues that the evolution of the United Nations on this position can be divided into three stages with significant progress in the field of human rights.

## 2.1 The Early Separation of Human Rights and Development

As early as 1945, the *Charter of the United Nations* had stipulated that one of the purposes of the United Nations is "to achieve international cooperation in solving international problems of an economic, social, cultural, or humanitarian character, and in promoting and encouraging respect for human rights and for fundamental freedoms for all without distinction as to race, sex, language, or religion". But for decades, human rights and development have always been discussed as two distinct issues. Either in theory or in practice, human rights and development were not closely linked. For example, at the United Nations institutional level, the Office of the United Nations High Commissioner for Human Rights (OHCHR), which is under the authority of the Secretary-General of the United Nations, is responsible for coordinating the activities of the United Nations in the field of human rights, while the United Nations Development Programme, as a subsidiary body of the United Nations, is tasked to provide support and help to promote the sustainable development of mankind. The two bodies perform their duties separately, and their contact is not close.

## 2.2 The Reform of "Mainstreaming of Human Rights"

Human rights issues resolve social contradictions, and the purpose of social development is to liberate and develop the individual. Therefore, the protection of human rights clears the obstacles to development and promotes rapid economic and social development. This shows that the mainstreaming of human rights is the inevitable precursor to social development. Without human rights, it is bound to lag behind.

To date, there has been no clear and uniform definition of the mainstreaming of human rights, but changes in the mainstreaming of human rights are reflected in all aspects of the work of the United Nations. At the first World Conference on Human Rights, held in Tehran in 1968, the relationship between human rights and development was heavily valued. In 1969, the United Nations, through the *Declaration on Social Progress and Development*, made it clear that the issue of development should be viewed from a human rights perspective. The Declaration states that "social progress and development shall be founded on respect for the dignity and value of the human person and shall ensure the promotion of human rights and social justice". After the adoption of the

*Declaration on the Right to Development* at the forty-first session of the General Assembly in 1986, the international community began to link the promotion of human rights with development in practice by stating that human beings were the mainstay of development and that every person had the right to participate in, promote and enjoy economic, social, cultural and political development, in which all human rights and fundamental freedoms can be fully realized. In 1993, the World Conference on Human Rights adopted the *Vienna Declaration and Programme of Action*, making it clear that human rights and development were interdependent and mutually reinforcing. In 1997, Secretary-General Kofi Annan, in his report "Renewing the United Nations: A Program for Reform", called on all States to give equal weight to human rights and safe development, and to integrate human rights into all work of the United Nations, that is, to mainstream human rights issues in all the work of the United Nations. "One of the main tasks of the United Nations is to strengthen its human rights program and to integrate it into a wide range of activities of [the] United Nations".[16] The mainstreaming of human rights has been formally and explicitly reflected, and human rights issues have begun to appear as mainstream issues in social, economic, political, cultural and other fields. It began solely in the discussions of experts and scholars, but the shift in the relationship between human rights and development from a fragmented to a converging sense has been reflected in the United Nations, typically in awareness of individual rights of the UNDP and its "human" considerations in the development plan.[17] Such progress has contributed to the development and implementation of all the work of the United Nations and ensures that the three pillars of peace, development and human rights within the United Nations system are interrelated and mutually reinforcing.

But it is worth noting that although advocated by the international community, the mainstreaming of human rights is not well implemented in practice at this stage, the link between human rights and development has not been well reflected.

### 2.3 *Progress from the Millennium Development Goals to the Sustainable Development Goals*

The United Nations Millennium Development Goals (MDGs) is a unanimous plan adopted by all then 191 UN Member States to reduce global poverty by half

---

16    The Fifty-first Session of the United Nations General Assembly, "Renewing the United Nations: A Program for Reform—Report of the Secretary-General", United Nations document, A/51/950 (Chinese version), p. 26, para. 79.

17    David P. Forsythe, "The United Nations, Human Rights and Development", *Human Rights Quarterly*, no. 19 (1997): 345.

(from 1990 levels) by 2015. This plan draws a blueprint for common development for different countries and major development agencies from eight areas, and demands that these countries and institutions go all out to meet the needs of the world's poorest people. The MDGs, however, only apply to the so-called developing countries, and they are only represented by specific economic and social rights, neglecting other important human rights and artificially breaking the interrelated, interdependent objective reality of the human rights.

In line with the MDGs, the United Nations Summit on Sustainable Development was held in New York on September 25, 2015. The then 193 Member States of the United Nations formally adopted 17 Sustainable Development Goals (SDGs) to guide the global development effort from 2015 to 2030 after the MDGs.

Among them, the first and second SDG, "eradicating poverty, eliminating hunger", protect the most basic of human rights, which is the right to subsistence. The realization of this target is particularly important for the majority of the developing countries. To ensure that people fully acquire the food, shelter and other necessities of living they depend on is the prerequisite of all development. The third Goal "good health and well-being" and the sixth Goal "clean water and sanitation" guarantee the right to health, which is compatible with many international conventions and domestic constitutions and laws. There is no doubt that the physical health of individuals is not only a prerequisite for their development, but also a basis for individual development to promote the national and social development. The fourth SDG focuses on "quality education". The right to education is an important part of the *International Covenant on Economic, Social and Cultural Rights*. Good education and access to all areas of expertise are favorable factors for a person's comprehensive and healthy development. The individual can enhance awareness of their rights through various forms of education, and promote their development in and after the process of education. The fifth Goal "gender equality" is compatible with the purposes of the *Convention on the Elimination of All Forms of Racial Discrimination*, and the equality between men and women protects the right to equality of persons. The eighth Goal provides for citizens to obtain "decent jobs and economic growth" and the tenth Goal stipulates "narrowing the gap", which protects citizens' right to development. As the third generation of human rights, the main body of the right to development is the unity of collective rights and individual rights, which is in line with the requirements of the times.[18] The seventh Goal, "clean energy", the ninth Goal "industry, innovation

---

18    He Ying, "Right to Development: Safeguarding the Realization and Development of Human Rights", *Expanding Horizons*, no. 5 (2008): 18.

and basic societies", the eleventh Goal "sustainable cities and communities", the twelfth Goal "responsive consumption and production", the thirteenth Goal "climate action", the fourteenth Goal "sustainable use and conservation of 'underwater organisms'" and the fifteenth Goal "sustainable use and protection of 'terrestrial organisms'" guarantee the right to development of humans and combine human development with a good and sustainable natural environment and social environment so as to achieve mutual promotion. The sixteenth Goal "peace, justice and strong institutions" concerns democratic governance, the rule of law, access to justice and personal security, providing a good social environment for development by promoting civil employment and curbing corruption. Finally, based on national environment, the seventeenth Goal highlights "partnerships for the attainment of goals" and explores the link between the protection of human rights and the promotion of development.

In addition, the theme "measuring human rights for sustainable development" was an important topic for OHCHR in 2016. Under this topic, OHCHR notes that there is a growing recognition that human rights are essential to the achievement of sustainable development.[19] Deliberation on human rights issues should be reflected in all aspects of development.

Analysis of the relationship between human rights and development in the MDGS and SDGS shows that the international community is beginning to recognize the importance of human rights at the MDGS stage, but human rights and development are still fragmented and stipulated in two different sections of the document. While the term "human rights" is not used directly at the SDGS stage, the elaboration of relevant human rights issues shows that human rights principles and standards have been reflected as important elements in a new global framework for development, and the SDGS are also a good interpretation of the relationship between human rights and development. In addition to their broad social, economic and environmental aims, the SDGS not only promise to build "a more peaceful, just and inclusive society free from fear and violence", but also focus on democratic governance, rule of law, access to justice, personal safety and a conducive international environment. Thus, the SDGS cover all human rights, including civil, political, economic, social and cultural rights, in which the right to development is included. In summary, the MDGS mainly aim at development assistance to developing countries, in order to reduce extreme poverty and improve the lives of the world's poorest and

---

19  Office of the United Nations High Commissioner for Human Rights, *Sustainable Development Goals—Human Rights and the 2030 Sustainable Development Agenda*, available on the website of the Office of the United Nations High Commissioner for Human Rights: http://www.ohchr.org/CH/Issues/ MDG/Pages/The 2030Agenda.aspx.

most vulnerable people and meet their basic needs; while the SDGs are global and universal, covering all areas of sustainable development. Seen from the growth model, the MDGs emphasize poverty reduction, the traditional growth model often leading to resource destruction, environmental pollution and social collateral damage in realizing it, while the SDGs are more inclusive, considering economic, social, environmental and individual factors, and conforming to the objective laws of social development.[20]

Progress from the MDGs to SDGs has undoubtedly contributed to the integration of human rights and development and has been further recognized in the international community. The protection of human rights must be reflected in all aspects of the agenda for development. In this regard, the Indian economist Amartya Sen said: "Development should be re-defined, and the development process of social change should be noted. The ultimate goal of development is not the increase in per capita GNP standards, the level of industrialization or urbanization".[21] He affirmed the role of material means for development, but believed that it could serve only as a tool for development and as an instrumental one. The ultimate goal of development is related to quality of life and happiness, and it must be clear that for social individuals, human well-being is the starting point and the foothold of the development. In June 2013, the Sustainable Development Solution Network (SDSN) presented UN Secretary-General Ban Ki-moon with a report named "Action Agenda for Sustainable Development". The report addresses the ten most pressing tasks for the sustainable development of mankind, such as addressing extreme poverty and hunger, ensuring that all children and young people can learn effectively for their livelihoods, and that all people have access to gender equality, social inclusion and human rights, and everyone enjoys the right to health, happiness and clean energy.[22] At the same time, the report stresses that every nation has the right to development, human rights and social inclusiveness, and that the protection of human rights and the promotion of development complement each other in the same process.

The development agenda underpinned by the United Nations, which is based on the principles of sustainable development, has gained increasing recognition and support from the international community. At the same time, in the

---

20  Chen Ying, "United Nations Post-2015 Development Agenda: Progress and Prospects", *Journal of China University of Geosciences* (Social Science Edition), no. 5 (2014): 15.
21  Li Bingyan and Wang Chong, "Amartya Sen's View of Development and Its Enlightenment to China's Scientific Development", *Economist*, no. 2 (2012): 100.
22  Sustainable Development Solution Network, "An Action Agenda for Sustainable Development", accessed November 25, 2016, http://unsdsn.org/resources/publications/an-action-agenda-for-sustainable-development/.

process of achieving the SDGs, the integration of human rights and development is manifested not only at the theoretical level, but also in practice. Starting from the earliest attention focused only in the economic field, human rights issues have gradually infiltrated various disciplines and fields; human rights knowledge has begun to become the process of personnel training in general education.

While the understanding of human rights and development issues has undergone three stages and great progress at the United Nations level, with the emergence of new problems such as food crisis, global economic crisis, climate change, energy crisis and natural disasters, the United Nations development agenda continues to face major challenges, and developing countries are particularly vulnerable to these challenges. In this regard, poverty eradication, employment, development models, the green economy and other core issues have been given a higher priority and importance by the international community and are of common concern to the developed and developing countries.[23] The reason for this is that the eradication of poverty, the resolution of employment and the promotion of development embody the most basic human rights, and the protection of human rights can clear the way for development, which further explains the crucial role of the realization of human rights in the promotion of development.

## 3  The Interpretation by the Chinese Government of the Relationship between Human Rights and Development

This section will focus on the interpretation by the Chinese government of the relationship between human rights and development. In short, from keeping silent about this matter at the early stage, to beginning to explore it after the first White Paper on human rights in 1991, and then to incorporating human rights into the Constitution in 2004, until today, where human rights are discussed at all levels, the understanding by the Chinese government of the relationship between human rights and development has undergone a long and significant evolution. By studying the relevant documents of the Chinese government and the views of relevant experts and scholars, this chapter divides the interpretation by the Chinese government of the relationship between human rights and development into four stages.

---

23  Sun Yiran, "Status and Trends of the United Nations Development Agenda", *Contemporary International Relations*, no. 9 (2012): 42.

## 3.1 From the Early Days of the Founding of the People's Republic of China (PRC) to 1980s: The Separation of Human Rights and Development

At the beginning of the founding of the PRC, the Common Program, which played the role of the provisional constitution, stipulated the fundamental rights and freedoms of citizens, and the people were liberated from the "three big mountains" and became the masters of the country. At the same time, the economy and society developed rapidly. The Constitution of 1954 provided for the basic rights of citizens in fourteen articles. With the coming of the "Great Leap Forward", the "Cultural Revolution" and other special historical periods, however, the basic rights of citizens declined sharply and the national economy retrogressed. Only two provisions of the Constitution of 1975 stipulated the basic rights of citizens, at which point the economy was on the brink of collapse.

It can be seen that the development of the national economy is closely related to the protection of the basic rights of citizens, but the Chinese government at that time did not recognize this point. Human rights and development were in a fragmented state, and economic and social development suffered bottlenecks at this stage.

## 3.2 The White Paper on Human Rights in 1991: A Shift in Perceptions

In 1991, the Chinese government published its first White Paper on human rights, which elaborated China's basic position and policies on human rights issues, introduced a great deal of facts about the fundamental changes in China's human rights situation since the founding of the PRC, and promoted the international community's correct understanding of it. Since then, China has gradually accepted the internationally recognized concept of human rights and its institutional framework, and comprehensively understood the interdependence between human rights and development. Human rights have become a hot topic, the academic research on human rights issues is widespread, and people have realized that human rights are no longer limited to the field of diplomacy in the form of the confrontation between the ideology of China and the West, but reflected in more extensive and more realistic areas in domestic, political and social life.[24]

In 1992, Deng Xiaoping's speech on the southern tour further expanded this notion; laying a foundation for the development of the human rights concept

---

24   Xiao Jinming, "Human Rights Framework and Rights Guarantee System with Chinese Characteristics—Reading the National Human Rights Action Plan (2009–2010)", *Contemporary Law Review*, no. 5 (2009): 22.

in China and the gradual establishment of the human rights protection mechanism. In 2002, the 16th National Congress of the Communist Party of China established "respecting and safeguarding human rights" as an important objective of the Party and the country's development in the new stage and emphasized respecting and safeguarding human rights in the political reform.

### 3.3   Human Rights in the Constitution in 2004: Protection of Basic Civil Rights under the Guidance of the Principle of Universality

In 2004, the Second Session of the Tenth National People's Congress passed the Constitutional Amendment to incorporate "the state respects and preserves human rights" into the Constitution. This demonstrated that the Chinese government had begun to realize that all legislative activities cannot be separated from thinking about human rights issues and began to protect human rights in the form of fundamental law. Since then, the Fourth Plenary Session of the 16th CPC Central Committee regarded "respect and protect human rights, to ensure that the people enjoy a wide range of rights and freedoms" as an important part of improving the ability to govern. In 2006, the Sixth Plenary Session of the 16th CPC Central Committee decided on the basic principles of building a harmonious society, that is, people-oriented first, followed by scientific development. Human rights and development are interacting benignly and developing coordinately; they are interdependent and mutually promoted.

### 3.4   The Stage after the Formulation of the National Action Plan for Human Rights: Further Clarification of the Relationship between Human Rights and Development

In accordance with the principles of the *Vienna Declaration and Programme of Action* adopted by the Vienna World Conference on Human Rights in 1993, the constitutional principle of "the state respects and preserves human rights" and the provisions of the Constitution on "fundamental rights and obligations of citizens", in addition to the *Universal Declaration of Human Rights* and the relevant international human rights conventions, based on the national situation, the Chinese government issued the *National Human Rights Action Plan (2009–2010)* in 2009, and updated the plan in 2012. The *National Human Rights Action Plan (2009–2010)* was the first national plan China has formulated on the theme of human rights. The Action Plan clearly stipulates the objectives and specific measures of the Chinese government in the promotion and protection of human rights.

Among them, the *National Human Rights Action Plan (2009–2010)* pointed out that the Chinese government was people-oriented and safeguarded the rights of the people. The Chinese government implemented the constitutional principles of "the state respects and preserves human rights", and put the protection of the people's rights to subsistence and development in the position of primary importance in the protection of human rights. Based on promoting sound and fast economic and social development, the Chinese government ensured the participation and the rights of equal development of all members of society according to law. The *National Human Rights Action Plan (2012–2015)* was divided into six Chapters that stipulated the economic, social and cultural rights of citizens; civil and political rights; rights of ethnic minorities, women, children, the elderly and the disabled; the education of human rights; the implementation of international human rights treaty obligations; and international human rights exchanges and cooperation, as well as the implementation and monitoring thereof.

In connection with the national economic plan, the national human rights Action Plans fully embody the characteristics of human rights discourse in China and establish a more systematic human rights framework system with Chinese characteristics. It is closely related to the national economic and social development plan, and it is not a single, one-sided view of the improvement of GDP per capita, the level of industrialization and the level of urbanization as the development of economic indicators. It promotes a people-oriented development concept, makes clear the importance of protection of human rights in the realization of economic and social development, and expresses a series of goals regarding the protection of rights in national construction and social development planning.

It is noteworthy, however, that the indivisible relationship between human rights and development remains at the cognitive level, and the integration of human rights and development in practice remains a major problem. President Xi Jinping pointed out at the United Nations Summit on Sustainable Development that the ultimate goal of development is for the people. We should strive for fair, open, comprehensive and innovative development to achieve economic, social and economically coordinated development while eradicating poverty and ensuring people's livelihoods. So far, China has taken a step forward in improving the relationship between human rights and development.

In April 2016, the 23rd meeting of the Central Leading Group for Deepening Reform was held, and Xi Jinping first proposed reform in two directions: development, and fairness and justice. It is noted that the maintenance of social fairness and justice cannot be separated from the protection of basic human rights of citizens. So that citizens have a "sense of gain", that is, in the overall design of the reform, the initiatives of social undertakings, security and improvement of people's livelihood can be truly implemented so that people can achieve what they have expected and it promotes their sense of gain. This confirms once again that the fundamental human rights of the people's livelihood and the protection of citizens' political, economic and cultural life are the key to reform and development. The meeting provided a political orientation for the relationship between human rights and development and it also shows that the interpretation by the Chinese government of the relationship between human rights and development is advancing with the times and in line with the "mainstream" concept of the United Nations.

## 4   Conclusion

To sum up, the protection of human rights can promote economic and social development from two aspects. On the one hand, human rights issues solve fundamental social contradictions, and protect human rights to promote the development of social productive forces. As Professor Gong Xianghe said, productivity is the decisive force to promote social development, and the labor force is the primary factor in productivity, while the change of the labor force depends on the subjective wishes of the workers and the objective situation. Therefore, safeguarding human rights and ensuring the realization of workers' rights in all aspects of political, economic, social and cultural life can play a positive role in promoting the workforce, productivity and ultimately promoting social development.[25] On the other hand, the protection of human rights and private property of citizens, and the implementation of social insurance policies such as medical insurance, can generally improve the living standards of working people, which is conducive to the accumulation of material wealth, and can encourage them to "dare" to consume to some extent, and thus stimulate domestic demand and promote economic development.

As a developing country, China recognizes the importance of keeping pace with the times and adapting to the trend of international social development. In the context of further elaboration of the relationship between human rights and development, the Indian economist Amartya Sen's concept of development has made some contribution to the thinking in relation to Chinese problems. He put forward the theory of poverty of rights, and thought that the reasons for poverty should be expanded from economic factors to politics, law, culture and system. In addition, he put the poverty problem into a comprehensive study of economics, ethics, politics and sociology.[26] This also reminds us

---

25   J.D. Sethi, "Human Rights and Development", 14.
26   Ma Xinwen, "Review of Amartya Sen's Theory and Method of Poverty of Rights", *Social Sciences Abroad*, no. 2 (2008): 69.

that in the process of realizing the integration of human rights and development, China should first consider, but not be confined to, the economic sphere. Human rights and development should be a subject of wider consideration.

The Chinese government and society have begun to understand human rights, think about the relationship between human rights and development, and gradually recognize the interdependence and complementarities of human rights and development. The universal realization of human rights needs to be based on economic and social development, while the healthy and rapid economic and social development cannot be separated from the primary protection of human rights. In addition, the protection of basic human rights is the basis for resolving major social contradictions. It can clear the obstacles to economic development, and improve social development. People's material life and spiritual life will surely promote the realization of human rights. This is the basis for the Chinese government to formulate laws and regulations, relevant policies and development strategies, and it is also the consensus of the current academic circles.

In practice, however, both the real integration of human rights and development, and the formation of the complementary situation of human rights and development, are not easy. China lacks a comprehensive and in-depth study of the relationship between human rights and development. The lack of interdisciplinary thinking capacity and the lack of talent in acquiring the knowledge of human rights, economic management, and social development theory are the core of the problem. This is the sequela left by economists and human rights jurists differentiating their positions at the beginning of the development of human rights. Economists plan for national economic development, but the reality is that these experts mastering the direction of national economic development lack of the knowledge of human rights protection. The lack of integration of human rights awareness and initiatives in social development strategies will hinder not only the development of human rights theory, but also coordinated and sustainable economic and social development to a great extent.

# PART 2

*Environmental Perspective*

CHAPTER 5

# On the Realization of the Right to Development under the Context of Environmental Rights

*Zhang Aining\**

1       Introduction

The right to development is an inalienable human right by virtue of which every human person and all peoples are entitled to participate in, contribute to, and enjoy economic, social, cultural and political development, in which all human rights and fundamental freedoms can be fully realized.[1]

The human right to development also implies the full realization of the right of peoples to self-determination, which includes, subject to the relevant provisions of both International Covenants on Human Rights, the exercise of their inalienable right to full sovereignty over all their natural wealth and resources.[2]

DECLARATION ON THE RIGHT TO DEVELOPMENT, 1986

∵

"Development is a comprehensive economic, social, cultural and political process".[3] Nevertheless, the pursuit of development in the context of environmental rights necessitates greater emphasis on achieving economic development while protecting and preserving the environment in order to realize sustainable development.

While creating unprecedented economic growth and material wealth, mankind has also caused serious damage to the natural environment and thus threatened the future of human beings as a biological species. Catastrophic acid rain, ozone depletion, biodiversity loss, accelerated soil desertification, freshwater resource exhaustion, marine ecological crisis, sharp decrease of forest area, environmental pollution accidents, large-scale ecological damage, water, soil and air pollution by hazardous wastes, etc. As the human race takes pride in the result of development achieved through arduous efforts, they are

---

\*   Zhang Aining, Professor and Director of Center for Human Rights Studies at China Foreign Affairs University.
1   Paragraph 1, Article 1, UN *Declaration on the Right to Development* of 1986.
2   Paragraph 2, Article 1, UN *Declaration on the Right to Development* of 1986.
3   Paragraph 2, Preamble to the UN *Declaration on the Right to Development* of 1986.

"suddenly" brought home to the fact that their hard-won achievements are being eaten up by a progressively worsening environment. It is becoming increasingly clear that the enjoyment of economic development outcomes is inseparable from the state of the environment. A contaminated environment with damaged biodiversity is contradictory to satisfactory living conditions and individual development. Moreover, the worse the environment becomes, the greater the suffering for human beings, in terms of both the right to life and the right to health. All development results can be fully enjoyed only in an appropriate environment, which, if damaged to a certain extent, would make it impossible for their enjoyment and even lead to the total destruction of all civilizations, including the entire human race.

Consideration of these problems has prompted people to pay attention to the relationship between economic development and environmental quality, and that between the model of realization of the right to development and the well-being of the human race.

## 2    Relationship between Development and Environment

Many forms of development are achieved at the cost of the environmental resources upon which they are based. The relationship between environment and development has been a global issue of common concern to the international community since the 1972 United Nations Conference on the Human Environment in Stockholm, and it has also become the focus that society is paying close attention to in China in recent years.

### 2.1    *Development Is the Prerequisite and Priority*

Before the demands for the ebasic necessities of life are satisfied, it would be meaningless to talk about environmental rights, especially for developing countries. The *Declaration of the United Nations Conference on the Human Environment,* adopted at the 1972 United Nations Conference on the Human Environment in Stockholm, states that "Economic and social development is essential for ensuring a favorable living and working environment for man and for creating conditions on the earth that necessary for the improvement of quality of life".[4] It is also pointed out in the Beijing Declaration adopted at the 1991 Ministerial Conference on Environment and Development in Developing Countries that "the right to development in developing countries must

---

4    Principle 8, *Declaration of the United Nations Conference on the Human Environment* (1972).

be fully recognized and measures to protect the global environment should support the economic growth and development of developing countries,[5] which have the right to use their natural resources in accordance with their developmental and environmental objectives and priorities".[6]

## 2.2 Development Leads to Environmental Problems

Resource depletion and environmental pollution often follow social and economic development. In economic and productive activities, development of resources, emissions of soot, dumping of waste, discharge of waste water are inevitable. Without the intervention of appropriate environmental policies, the overall environmental quality or pollution level is likely to be aggravated or exacerbated with increased national income in early stages of economic development.[7] Take Japan for example, which experienced unprecedented economic growth in the 1950s and 1960s, but industrial pollution also worsened. Air pollution from the metallurgical and petrochemical industries led to a high proportion of respiratory diseases among residents in the vicinity of factories. The Itai-itai disease incident in Toyama, the Minamata disease incidents in Niigata and Kumamoto, and the smog incident in Yokkaichi were denounced by the international community as "four major public hazard incidents that shocked the world". The mercury pollution incident discovered in 1956 was called a global scandal of public hazard. In the late 1960s, Japan was known around the world as "island of public hazards".[8] In addition, other developed countries also went through severe environmental damage to some extent in the course of their industrialization. The Maas Valley smog incident in Belgium in 1930, the Los Angeles photochemical smog incident in the United States in 1943 and the Donora smog in the United States in 1948 and the London smog in the United Kingdom in 1952 were also pollution incidents that shocked the world. Now, after 30 years of rapid economic development, China has created a miracle in the history of world economic development and become the world's second largest economy. At the same time, accompanying environmental damage has also risen, as witnessed by various shocking industrial pollution events. In particular, the frequent emergence of large-scale fog and haze in recent years has caused widespread public concern.

---

5  Paragraph 3, *Beijing Ministerial Declaration on Environment and Development* adopted in 1991.
6  Ibid., paragraph 5.
7  Huang Yinglong, "On Environmental Rights and Its Statutory Protection", in *Human Rights Studies*, Vol. 2, ed. Xu Xianming (Shandong People's Publishing House, 2002), 405.
8  Xiao Jianming, *Comparative Environmental Law* (China Procuratorate Press, 2001), 100.

## 2.3 The Final Solution to Environmental Problems Depends on Development

It is recognized in the Stockholm *Declaration of the United Nations Conference on the Human Environment* (1972) that "In developing counties, most of the environment problems are caused by under-development. Therefore, the developing countries must direct their efforts to development, bearing in mind their priorities and the need to safeguard and improve the environment".[9] After more than 40 years, *Human Rights and the Environment* adopted by UN Human Rights Council in 2016 reaffirmed that "the right to development must be fulfilled in order to meet the development and environmental needs of present and future generations equitably".[10]

The realization of environmental rights is closely related to the exploitation of natural resources and the degree of social and economic development. According to the Environmental Kuznets Curve Hypothesis, without the intervention of appropriate environmental policies, the overall environmental quality or pollution level is likely to be aggravated or exacerbated with increased national income in the early stages of economic development. When the national economy attains a high level of development, the environmental quality and pollution level tend to become stable, and gradually ameliorated with increasing national income.[11] The reason is that improved living standards during this period prompt greater demand for a safe, clean, healthy and sustainable environment, and government and enterprises are pressured into taking environmental protection measures. Increased national strength also enables the country to increase investment in dealing with pollution and protecting the environment, making the realization of environmental rights possible.[12] Western Europe, the United States and Japan experienced that in their process of economic development and industrialization. Currently, the serious environmental damage accompanying the rapid economic development in China has prompted a deep reflection on the development models.

---

9   Paragraph 4, *Declaration of the United Nations Conference on the Human Environment* (1972).
10  Preamble to the *Human Rights and the Environment* adopted by the Human Rights Council on March 18, 2016, UN. A/HRC/31/L.10.
11  Huang Yinglong, "On Environmental Rights and Its Statutory Protection", in *Human Rights Studies*, Vol. 2, ed. Xu Xianming (Shandong People's Publishing House, 2002), 405.
12  Take China for example, compared with the investment of environmental pollution control in the Tenth Five-Year Plan, the national investment of environmental pollution treatment was CNY 1,400 billion in the period of Eleventh Five-Year Plan, up by 66.68%, and the investment for the whole thirteenth Five-Year Plan period is expected to reach CNY 6 to 10 trillion. (http://www.h2o-china.com/news/232053.html), accessed February 10, 2017.

The Scientific Outlook of Development was proposed at the Third Plenary Session of the 16th Central Committee of Communist Party of China in 2003 and enshrined in the Party Constitution at the 17th National Congress of the Party. It entails "adhering to people-orientation and establishment of a concept for comprehensive, coordinated and sustainable development, so as to promote comprehensive economic and social development".[13] Here, the sustainable development concept is aimed at prompting harmony between man and nature for coordination between economic development and population, resources and environment and ensuring sustained development from one generation to the next by adhering to civilized development, integrating developed production, well-off life and favorable ecology. With the Scientific Outlook of Development as the guiding ideology, the Chinese economy is now faced with a rare opportunity of upgrading and transforming the growth model for sound economic development. "Low carbon", "green development", "environmental protection", "recycling" and other fashionable expressions are being cherished by the ordinary Chinese and integrated into their attitude towards life.[14]

## 3 Principles of Sustainable Development: The Constraint of Environment over Development

Environmental rights in fact adjust and control the level of enjoyment and the model of realization of the right to development. People were aware of the conflict between the right to development and environmental rights long ago, therefore, while recognizing the need for development, the Stockholm Declaration of 1972 also pointed out that an appropriate balance should be reached between the sovereign rights of states to exploit their own resources and their responsibility to protect the environment from damage, and states that "the developing countries must direct their efforts to development, bearing in mind their priorities and the need to safeguard and improve the environment".[15] The 1992 *Rio Declaration on Environment and Development* further recognized the principle of realizing the right to development to equally meet the developmental

---

13   *Decision of the Central Committee of the Communist Party of China on Questions About Perfecting the Socialist Market Economic System*, 2003.
14   Hua Yi, "What Japan Has Done for Pollution Control—Interview with Japanese Environmental Experts Okazaki Yuta", http://news.sciencenet.cn/htmlnews/2016/12/363998.shtm, accessed February 10, 2017.
15   Paragraph 4, *Declaration of the United Nations Conference on the Human Environment* (1972).

and environmental needs of present and future generations,[16] emphasizing the importance of development for international environmental protection.

It is understandable that economic development is regarded as a priority in countries and regions with backward productive forces. Nevertheless, the right to development should not be pursued at the cost of environmental rights, nor should it be made the justification for large-scale environmental damage. Developing countries should learn lessons from certain mistakes committed by developed countries long ago. It is easy to damage and pollute the environment, but difficult to deal with and recover the damaged environment. In addition, once those non-renewable resources are depleted, extinction of species becomes irreversible. Therefore, environmental damage from economic development should by no means exceed the carrying capacity of the environment or endanger the survival and development of mankind; otherwise, the ultimate goal of development will be lost. In this context, the concept of "sustainable development" aptly encapsulates the balance between environmental rights and economic development.

### 3.1    *Principles of Sustainable Development*

In 1987, the World Commission on Environment and Development defined "sustainable development" in its report entitled "Our Common Future" as follows: "Development that meets the needs of the present without compromising the ability of future generations to meet their own needs".[17]

The two connotations of "sustainable development" are as follows: (1) The development of the present generation of human beings should not damage the natural and ecological basis on which the development of future generations depends. The development and utilization of natural resources must be controlled within a reasonable and appropriate range, in order to maintain their capacity for regeneration and continuous utilization. (2) Development is the goal, and sustainable development means changing the model of development, rather than curbing or restricting it.

The *Rio Declaration on Environment and Development* (1992) further developed the concept of "sustainable development", noting that human beings are at the center of sustainable development issues of universal concern,[18] and

---

16  Principle 3, UN *Rio Declaration on Environment and Development* (1992).
17  World Commission on Environment and Development, *Our Common Future*, trans. Wang Zhijia et al. (Jilin People's Publishing House, 1997), 10.
18  Principle 1, UN *Rio Declaration on Environment and Development* (1992).

that in order to achieve sustainable development, environmental protection should become part of the development process as a whole.[19]

In the jurisprudence of the International Court of Justice on a case concerning the Gabčíkovo–Nagymaros Project (Hungary/Slovakia) in 1997, Judge C.G. Weeramantry stressed in his separate opinion that both the right to development and the right to environmental protection are principles currently forming part of the corpus of international law. They could operate in collision with each other unless there were a principle of international law which indicated how they should be reconciled. That principle is the principle of sustainable development which, according to this opinion, is more than a mere concept, but is itself a recognized principle of contemporary international law.[20] It is also pointed out in the *New Delhi Declaration of Principles of International Law Relating to Sustainable Development*, adopted at the 70th Conference of the International Law Association in 2002, that "sustainable development has now been widely accepted as a global goal and its concept has been fully recognized in a variety of international and domestic laws and regulations, including international treaty laws and national case laws".[21]

In short, the concept of "sustainable development" better expresses the balance between economic development and environmental protection. It has become the primary goal and core value of international environmental protection in the process of economic development. It will be the general guideline for the conduct of states, international organizations, national groups and individuals in the field of environment and development for a long time.

### 3.2   *Intergenerational Equity*

The premise of sustainable development is the self-sustainability of the human species. Therefore, the subject of environmental rights not only applies to the present generation but also future generations as a whole. Development by the current generation should not be accomplished at the cost of future ones through expropriating and debilitating their means of sustainable development as we have only one earth.

The concept of Intergeneration Equity was first put forward by the Vice Chairperson of the American International Law Institute, Professor Edith Brown Weiss. According to the theory, the environment of earth is under

---

19   Ibid., Principle 4.
20   United Nation Publications, *Summaries of Judgement, Advisory Opinions and Orders of the ICJ (1997–2002)*, 9.
21   Paragraph 1, *New Delhi Declaration of Principles of International Law Relating to Sustainable Development* adopted at the 70th Conference of the International Law Association in 2002.

trusteeship for the future generations while the present generation is both entitled to enjoy the same quality of environment as previous ones and responsible for maintaining its status so that it could be passed on to the next generation at a state no less deteriorated than the time it was inherited.[22] Fatma Zohra Ksentini, a special rapporteur of the then Commission on Human Rights, pointed out in her final report on human rights and the environment that all persons have the right to an environment adequate to meet equitably the needs of present generations and that does not impair the rights of future generations to meet equitably their needs.[23] The ICJ refused to exercise jurisdiction to entertain the 1995 Nuclear Tests (*New Zealand v. France*) case on the grounds that the nuclear test was conducted underground rather than in the atmosphere as was in the 1974 case. Judge Weeramantry, in his dissenting opinion, argued that the ICJ has an obligation to protect the rights of future generations: "If a domestic court could act as a trustee for an infant that could not assume his own right, then this court should also regard itself as a fiduciary for the interest of future generation. New Zealand holds that their rights infringed harm not only their present generation but also those who are not yet born. Countries should have a right and obligation to protect these rights".[24] In the 1996 advisory opinion on the Legality of the Threat or Use of Nuclear Weapons, the ICJ pointed out that "the Court cannot conclude definitively whether the threat or use of nuclear weapons would be lawful or unlawful in an extreme circumstance of self-defense, in which the very survival of a State would be at stake".[25] Judge Weeramantry, in his dissenting opinion, stated that "the nuclear weapon irreversibly damaged the rights of future generations".[26] At the 2012 United Nations Conference on Sustainable Development, participating countries renewed their commitment to sustainable development and to ensuring the promotion of an economically, socially and environmentally sustainable future for our planet and for present and future generations.[27]

---

22  Wang Xi, "The Principle of Sustainable Development of International Environment Law", *Law Review*, no. 3 (1998): 96.
23  *Draft Principles on Human Rights and Environment* (1994), ANNEXES of the Final Report prepared by Mrs. Fatma Zohra Ksentini, Special Rapporteur of UN, E/CN.4/Sub.2/1994/9, 23, Principle 4.
24  Edith Brown Weiss, *In Fairness to Future Generation: International Law, Common Patrimony, and Intergeneration Equity*, trans. Wang Jin et al. (Beijing: Law Press, 2000), Preface, 5.
25  UN Publications, *Summaries of Judgement, Advisory Opinions and Orders of the ICJ (1992–1996)*, 94.
26  Ibid., 102.
27  The UN Conference on Sustainable Development, *The Future We Want*, A/CONF.216/L.1, 2012, paragraph 1.

## 3.3   Intra-generational Equity

Intra-generational equity means just and equitable relations within a generation, which means developed and developing countries, and different people within a country, are entitled to the right of an equal development opportunity and a just income distribution.[28]

Globalization has aggravated the gap between the rich and poor,[29] but it is the latter who bear the brunt of contaminated environment caused by globalization and economic growth, contributing to further inequality among nations and social strata. The rich and the powerful are well equipped with economic means and capability to create a reasonably independent healthy and ecologically balanced environment to circumvent air-polluted and arduous areas unlike the poor and vulnerable. Due to a lack of sufficient economic, political or other power, the poor are also subject to discrimination for their lower social status and have no capability in negating the adverse effect brought by arduous environment. They have no choice but to live in the most polluted areas and eat cheap yet contaminated food; *prefer* to work in toxic factories to unemployment; unable to resort to legal means, even when available, to protect their rights. The same logic applies to both individuals and countries.

The earth is a communal space for humankind, a common public resource open to everyone. The use or distribution of any matter on the earth, including those that are put in, should be distributed equally, which should be reflected in the connotation of intra-generational equity. Unfortunately, the concept of intra-generational equity had no representation in international legal documents and practice.[30] Although the *New Delhi Declaration of Principles of International Law Relating to Sustainable Development* discussed the right

---

28  Nico Schrijver, *The Evolution of Sustainable Development in International Law: Inception, Meaning and Status*, trans. Wang Xigen and Huang Haibin (Social Science Academic Press, 2010), 154.

29  In early 2016, Oxfam International pointed out in their research on inequality: the richest 1% has more wealth than the rest of the planet combined. In its report "An Economy for the 99%", in early 2017, it pointed out that the very design of our economies and the principles of our economics have taken us to this extreme, unsustainable and unjust point; new estimates show that just eight men have the same wealth as the poorest half of the world (3.6 billion). The incomes of the poorest 10% of people increased by less than USD 3 a year between 1988 and 2011, while the incomes of the richest 1% increased 182 times as much. The ten biggest companies in the world earn as much in a year as 180 countries' fiscal income. Ref: https://www.oxfam.org/sites/www.oxfam.org/files/file_attachments/bp-economy-for-99-percent-160117-en.pdf, accessed March 18, 2017.

30  Nico Schrijver, *The Evolution of Sustainable Development in International Law: Inception, Meaning and Status*, trans. Wang Xigen and Huang Haibin (Social Science Academic Press, 2010), 154.

of all peoples within the current generation to fair access to the current generation's entitlement to the earth's natural resources,[31] the declaration itself was only a proclamation adopted by the ILA. Not only was the declaration not legally binding, it also had a limited effect in the moral sense, the result of which was that the concept of intra-generational equity is not consistent with the interest of developed countries. For example, on the negotiation of greenhouse gas emissions, developing countries insisted on intra-generational equity. They hold that during a certain period of time, the accumulated emission per capita should be used as a counting unit to allocate total emission quotas for countries based on their population, which was rejected by the developed countries. Not only were the developed countries not willing to let nationals in developing countries enjoy the same quota over greenhouse gas emissions as their own, they were also reluctant to assume their historical emission responsibility. Rather, developed countries hold that emissions should be gradually reduced with countries serving as the unit starting from a certain year.

Historically, the reason why countries became developed was because of their high-speed stride in industry, which would unavoidably give off massive emissions of greenhouse gases. The current level of greenhouse gas intensity in the atmosphere is largely attributable to the unlimited emission by developed countries throughout their hundred-year-long industrialization. Nevertheless, by the time developing countries were striving for economic advancement, they were hampered by the emission-reducing plan of total volume of greenhouse gases put forward by developed countries, one that entirely dismissed historical responsibility, since the 1990s in the name of coping with climate change. If an international responsibility system were established with Emission Reduction as an agenda for negotiation, the gigantic differences between countries' historical emission and per capita emission would be papered over, putting a *de facto* rein on developing countries' total future emissions, and ultimately, their development right.

Based on what had been discussed above, should human rights be universal; should the established right to life, health, fortune, culture and to adequate living standard be realized in a majority of the global populace rather than in a small group of people, intra-generational equity is just and equitable. Conversely, though there is a conflict of interest between developed countries and developing countries and between the rich and the poor in the environment and development, there is no triumph for just one party. Neither environmental pollution nor widespread poverty are separate matters for a particular

---

31   *New Delhi Declaration of Principles of International Law Relating to Sustainable Development*, ILA 70th Conference, 2002.

sovereign state. There is no national border for environmental pollution or climate change, while widespread poverty will inevitably lead to turmoil and a variety of international issues. These problems are not faced by individual states alone, but are common problems that the entire world must face, rendering intra-generational equity a necessity for sustainable development. Even when the concept of intra-generational equity is not embodied in international legal documents and practices, we could still deduce the legitimacy and jurisprudence of it from sovereignty equality, national self-determination as basic principles of international law, equality and non-discrimination as human rights principles and "Everyone is equal before the law" as the general principle of law is recognized widely by different countries' legal institutions.

## 4 Certain Economic Activities with Potentially Significant Threats to the Environment

Countries should cooperate with each other in good faith in some economic activities and major environmental issues that are of the fundamental interest to humankind, regardless of whether there exist relevant legal documents or not. Developed countries should take their responsibilities and avoid the interest-first mentality while developing countries should refrain from adopting a short-termist vision and the pursuit of immediate result.

### 4.1 *The Adverse Impacts of International Trade on Environment*

The liberalization of international trade has improved people's standard of living, but international trade without barriers can cause irreparable damage to the environment, or at least very serious losses, especially for poor and backward countries. The ever-increasing liberalization of international trade leads to increased production which means more resource depletion, thus increased pollution; and a greater volume of trade also means more transport and consequently a degraded environment. In addition, trade liberation also facilitates the transfer of enterprises with negative environmental impacts from certain countries to those with less stringent environmental protection.

Environmental rights demand that international trade fundamentally eliminates trade of products harmful to human health and the ecological environment, for the protection of human beings and the environment. The primary objective of the World Trade Organization (WTO) is trade liberalization, but requirements for environmental protection are included in its objectives in order to avoid the negative impact of trade liberalization on the global environment. It is declared in the Preamble to the 1993 *Agreement Establishing the World*

*Trade Organization* that countries around the world should ensure "the best use of global resources in accordance with the objectives of sustainable development while protecting the environment". The WTO does not specify agreements for dealing with environmental issues, but many of its specific agreements include so-called "Green Clauses" for protecting human life and safety, protecting the health and life of animals and plants and protecting natural resources and the environment. for example, Article 20 paragraphs 2 and 7 of the 1994 *General Agreement on Tariffs and Trade* (GATT), Article 2 paragraph 2 of the 1994 *Agreement on Technical Barriers to Trade* (TBT Agreement), Article 2 and Article 27 paragraph 2 of the *Agreement on Trade-Related Aspects of Intellectual Property Rights* (TRIPS), the *Agreement on the Application of Sanitary and Phytosanitary Measures* (SPS Agreement), the *Agreement on Agricultural* (no reduced subsidies for environmental projects), the *Agreement on Subsidies and Countervailing Measures* (allowing subsidies to enterprises up to 20 percent of their cost for them to get accustomed to newly enacted environmental laws), and Article 14 of the *General Agreement on Trade in Services* (GATS). Aside from the WTO agreements, there are currently more than 200 effective international agreements for dealing with environmental issues,[32] collectively known as multilateral environmental agreements (MEAs), some of them include certain provisions which have impacts on international trade.[33] They include the 1973 *Convention on International Trade in Endangered Species of Wild Fauna and Flora*, the 1987 *Montreal Protocol on Substances that Deplete the Ozone Layer* and its series of subsequent amendments, the 1989 *Basel Convention on the Control of Trans-Boundary Movements or Disposal of Hazardous Wastes and Their Disposal* and the 1998 *Convention on the Prior Informed Consent Procedure for Certain Hazardous Chemicals and Pesticides in International Trade*.

### 4.2 *Environmental Problems Caused by International Investment*

International investment is inevitably changed by the transfer of industries with significant environmental impact from countries with high environmental standards to those with low standards. Some enterprises from developed countries have been known to transfer pollution-intensive industries to developing countries or establish their most dangerous factories in developing countries with the least stringent legal regulation, taking advantage of their insufficient environmental legislation, or lack of statutory restriction or enforcement.

---

32  Bian Yongmin, "The Relationship Between Trade Measures of MEAs & WTO Trade Rules", *Contemporary Law Review* 1 (2010): 152.

33  WTO Secretariat, *Trading into the Future* (Beijing: Law Press, 1999), 84.

Some developing countries have brought in new sources of pollution while introducing investment industries. Due to their weak environmental protection competence, the introduced sources of pollution often cause much greater harm than in developed countries, and in some cases, the pollution can even be disastrous. For example, when the methyl-isocyanate leak broke out in 1984 in the pesticide plant of the United States Union Carbide Corporation in Bhopal, capital city of Madhya Pradesh, toxic gas concentration over the city exceeded by over 1,000 times the standard considered to be safe. The disaster directly claimed 2,500 lives in just two days, 600,000 more injured to varying degrees, and the death toll reached 6,495 people by 1994, with another 40,000 people close to death,[34] becoming the world's most serious pollution incident from a toxic chemical spill. Even today, the cancer instances and child mortality rates among local residents are much higher than other cities in India.[35] According to the Japanese magazine *World Statistics*, in 1991, the 3,353 pollution-intensive foreign-funded enterprises among the total of 11,515 had caused serious damages to the environment and consumers in China.[36]

### 4.3 Environmental Hazards Caused by the Transboundary Movement of Toxic or Hazardous Wastes

Trans-boundary movement of hazardous wastes has become a major environmental concern of the international community since the 1980s. If the legal requirements of waste-producing countries are so stringent as to make domestic disposal very expensive, the wastes may be transported to countries with less stringent laws or less effective supervision in law enforcement. Of course, some countries, especially developing countries, are willing to accept foreign wastes for the sake of remuneration with little consideration for the accompanying dangers. Maritime companies transport wastes from industrialized countries to developing countries willing to receive dangerous substances for payment. It was generally very difficult for developing countries to properly handle imported hazardous wastes due to lack of corresponding technologies and means. Therefore, major incidents of imported wastes polluting the environment of importing countries and endangering the health and safety of local residents were prone to occur. In 1988, the Sub-Commission on Prevention of Discrimination and Protection of Minorities of the UN proposed in its

---

34  "The India Bhopal Poisonous Gas Leaking Incident Shocking the World", accessed January 10, 2017, http://www.people.com.cn/GB/historic/1203/4125.html.
35  Ibid.
36  Institute of Industrial Economics of CASS, *The Report on China's Industrial Development* (Beijing: Economy & Management Publishing House, 2005), 40.

draft resolution "On the Disposal of Hazardous Products and Wastes", submitted to the then United Nations Commission on Human Rights, that governments of states producing toxic and hazardous wastes should ban exports of such wastes to countries lacking the technical capacity for their disposal in an environmentally sound manner and take measures to refrain from jeopardizing human rights and ecosystems of their own countries and other countries of the world.[37] In the same year, the United Nations adopted a regulation in which it urges all states, bearing in mind their respective responsibilities, to take the necessary legal and technical measures in order to halt and prevent the illegal international traffic in, and the dumping and resulting accumulation of, toxic and dangerous products and wastes,[38] and particularly, all states generating toxic and dangerous wastes to make every effort to treat and dispose of them in the country of origin to the maximum extent possible consistent with environmentally sound disposal.[39] Transfer of hazardous wastes to developing countries was further prohibited by the *Basel Convention on the Control of Transboundary Movement of Hazardous Wastes and Their Disposal*, developed under the leadership of the United Nations Environment Program in 1989 and amended at the Conference of the Parties in 1995. Adding a list of wastes banned from export, the Basel Convention was not aimed at entirely prohibiting transboundary movement of hazardous wastes, but controlling their export by imposing payment. The rationale is that the enterprises would voluntarily reduce international movement of hazardous wastes and seek their proper disposal, even if such movement were only charged but not prohibited altogether. It is important that the Basel Convention is a legally binding treaty imposing legal obligations on the States Parties. It has 185 States Parties as of January 30, 2017.

### 4.4 *Potential Threats to the Environment from Extremely Hazardous Activities or Significant Technological Risks*

"Extremely hazardous activities" or "significant technical risks" refer to activities or technologies that are potentially hazardous to the environment and that may produce (and in some cases, have produced) irreparable damage to the environment. They arise with the development of the manufacturing industry, the transport industry, outer space activities and the increased use of dangerous products, as well as certain very dangerous scientific and technical tests,

---

37   Edward Lawson, *Encyclopedia of Human Rights* (Chengdu: Sichuan People's Publishing House, 1997), 1291.
38   UN.A/RES/43/212, paragraph 1.
39   Ibid., paragraph 4.

especially in vivo tests. Notable examples include the explosion of dangerous goods at Binhai New Area in Tianjin, China, in 2015, the leakage of Fukushima Nuclear Power Plan in Japan in 2011, explosion of Chernobyl Nuclear Power Plan in the former Soviet Union in 1986, contamination of the Rhine by toxic materials caused by a warehouse fire in the Sandoz Chemicals of Basel, Switzerland in 1986, dioxin leakage from the ICMESA in Seville, Italy in 1976, the oil spill incident resultant from the *Torrey Canyon* oil tanker running on rocks in the waters of England in 1967, the dumping of methyl mercury by Japan's Kyushu Kumamoto Fertilizer Co. in 1956, etc.

Similarly, new technologies as the main driving force of economic development sometimes entail many risks. The rapid development of biotechnology and major breakthroughs in the utilization of human genes and genetic modification, drug manufacturing based on biological engineering and preparation of bio-immune agents may result in ravaged nature and polluted environment. In particular, various genetically modified organisms (GMOs) may pose potential risks and threats to biological diversity and damage the stability of the ecological environment when released into the environment. The enhanced competence of GMOs in competition against other organisms, resultant from new properties given by scientists may turn them into new dominant species in a region, i.e., invading organisms, accelerating the extinction of local individuals or species originally weak in vitality. In addition, genetically modified organisms may break the boundaries of natural species, thereby disrupting the evolution of biological processes. Now the competition for survival of lives in nature can be said to be in a dynamic equilibrium, which may be transformed into a completely different balance system or may run out of control, once the constraining factors are changed.[40]

## 5   Common But Differentiated Responsibilities: A Practical Model of International Cooperation to Ensure Environmental Targets in Development

International cooperation is the one necessary path for environmental solutions because of the entirety of the global ecosystem and factors contributing to global environment deterioration. In this regard, common but differentiated responsibilities serve as a model of international cooperation for developed

---

40    Gao Chongming and Zhang Aiqin, *15 Lectures in Bioethics* (Beijing: Peking University Press, 2004), 77–78.

and developing countries to work together in environment protection, albeit some developed countries shun away or avoid such a principle.

The principle of common but differentiated responsibilities means environment protection is the common responsibility of all countries with developed ones taking a larger proportion. To grant preferential or favorable treatment to developing countries was already recognized in the International Human Rights Law, the Law of WTO and the International Law of the Sea.[41] The International Environmental Law also employed the phrase "common but differentiated responsibilities" to clarify the different responsibilities of developed and developing countries in global environment protection.[42] The *Vienna Convention for the Protection of the Ozone Layer* (1985) and the *Montreal Protocol on Substances that Deplete the Ozone Layer* (1987) pointed out in their preambles that ozone layer protection should "tak[e] into account the circumstances and particular requirements of developing countries", [43] "acknowledging that special provision is required to meet the needs of developing countries, including the provision of additional financial resources and access to relevant technologies", [44] a *de facto* proposition for developing and developed countries to take up common but differentiated responsibilities in working through the environment protection issue. Since then, common but differentiated responsibilities were incorporated into the 1992 *United Nations Framework Convention on Climate Change*: "In their actions to achieve the objective of the convention and to implement its provisions, the Parties shall be guided, inter alia, by the following: 1. The Parties should protect the climate system for the benefit of present and future generations of humankind, on the basis of equity and in accordance with their common but differentiated responsibilities, and respective capabilities. Accordingly, the developed country Parties should take the lead in combating climate change and the adverse effects thereof. 2. The specific needs and special circumstances of developing country Parties, especially those that are particularly vulnerable to the adverse effects of climate change, and of those Parties, especially developing country Parties, that would have to bear a disproportionate or abnormal burden under the Convention, should be

---

41   *International Covenant on Economic, Social and Cultural Rights*, Article 2, *Convention on the Rights of the Child*, Article 28, *General Agreement on Tariffs and Trade*, Article 18 and Section 4, and the *United Nations Convention on the Law of the Sea* (1982).
42   Nico Schrijver, *The Evolution of Sustainable Development in International Law: Inception, Meaning and Status*, trans. Wang Xigen and Huang Haibin (Beijing: Social Science Academic Press, 2010), 156.
43   Preamble to the *Vienna Convention for the Protection of the Ozone Layer* (1985).
44   Preamble to the *Montreal Protocol on Substances that Deplete the Ozone Layer* (1987).

given full consideration".⁴⁵ The 1992 *Rio Declaration on Environment and Development* not only accepted the concept of common but differentiated responsibilities, but also expanded its application to the entire environmental field: "States shall cooperate in a spirit of global partnership to conserve, protect and restore the health and integrity of the earth's ecosystem. In view of the different contributions to global environmental degradation, States have common but differentiated responsibilities. The developed countries acknowledge the responsibility that they bear in the international pursuit of sustainable development in view of the pressures their societies place on the global environment and of the technologies and financial resources they command".⁴⁶

The principle of common but differentiated responsibilities is based on the following considerations. First, a common responsibility: the earth is the one and only place for humankind to live; a deteriorated living environment would be detrimental to the interest of all countries, making it a common responsibility for the human community to protect the environment. Secondly, a differentiated responsibility: common responsibility does not mean equalitarianism. In terms of equality, Western industrialized countries' development was closely related to severe environment pollution; their ignorance of the environment was a *de facto* subsidy to their hundred-year-long industrialization. Nonetheless, developing countries just starting off on industrialization still need a fairly long time to boost their economy and maintain their current industrial structure. Constrained by the capacity for emissions, which has been used up by developed countries' earlier pollution, developing countries do not have the option of a low-cost development model that would do more harm to environment. Even as developed countries have entered into post-industrialization, their green mountains and blue skies owe their existence partly to the fact that many of their home countries' high energy-consuming and high-polluting industries were transferred to developing countries. The technology developed countries originated would turn into manufacturing in developing countries, whose cheap products that were massively consumed by developed countries came at the price of environment pollution.⁴⁷ Therefore, developed

---

45  Article 3, Clauses 1, 2, the *United Nations Framework Convention on Climate Change* (1992).
46  Principle 7, the UN *Rio Declaration on Environment and Development* (1992).
47  From 1990 to 2008, the developed country signatories to the *Kyoto Protocol* hit a plateau in carbon emissions, while those of the developing countries doubled. The reason lies in the transference of carbon emissions from developed countries to developing countries. Carbon-concentrated commodities were produced in developing countries and consumed in developing countries. Statistics show that between 1990 and 2008, developed countries transferred 16 billion tonnes of carbon emissions to developing countries through trade accumulation, a number that overtook the reduced emission amount by themselves.

countries should take more responsibilities in the global environment protection cause and offer developing countries financial and technological assistance, a move that is not out of generosity or boon, but of an environment indebtedness that they should have paid off in the first place. Developing countries, in choosing to follow an environmentally friendly development model, have a moral and legal right to seek compensation from developed countries for the opportunity cost they must pay for development. Moreover, considering the reality, developing countries' lack of financial and technological support has rendered them unable to adopt the same level of environment protection measures as that of the developed countries that are well positioned with capital and technology to assume a larger portion of responsibilities in finding a solution to the global environmental issue. Besides, it is only when the developed countries take a substantive share that the global environmental protection could bear practical result. In order to ensure success in global environmental protection, developed countries have a special responsibility to provide financial and technological assistance to developing countries.

## 6 Conclusion

The traditional view of development sees the dependence of human well-being only on development, but ignores an obvious fact, that is, development does not necessarily lead to human security and well-being. On the contrary, in certain parts of the world or in some cases, it has become one of the major threats for personal life, health and safety.[48] "The well-being of the people should be the supreme law (*Salus populi sumprema lex*)".[49] Now we have the profound understanding that "as the subject of development, people should be active

---

(Guan Jiang, "Pollution Heaven and Its Neighbors", *People's Daily*, accessed December 24, 2016, http://www.qstheory.cn/gj/gj/201207/t20120724_171836.html.).

[48] Some economic activities have become major threats for indigenous peoples. Gas and oil companies, loggers, miners and entrepreneurs are viewed by indigenous groups as "ghosts of death" for the toxic legacy they can leave behind and which can poison rivers and forests considered as a source of life for these communities. These indigenous groups have developed their own health care and food gathering systems, but which are fragile and easily threatened by damage to the ecosystems wherein they live. All too often contact with outsiders results in the transfer of disease, resulting in epidemics since the indigenous peoples have no immunities to what are common and treatable diseases elsewhere. ("Indigenous Peoples Living in Voluntary Isolation", accessed February 19, 2017, http://www.un.org/events/tenstories/06/story.asp?storyID=200).

[49] John Locke, *The Treaties of Government*, Vol. 2 (Beijing: The Commercial Press, 1964), 100.

participants in and beneficiaries of the right to development".[50] Development must be people-oriented, people should be placed at the center of development, and development should be a means rather than an end. Economic development should take human well-being as its ultimate goal, in other words, it should be aimed at higher security and greater happiness, and the practice of pursuing development at the expense of human safety and happiness should be avoided. Admittedly, at certain stages of economic development, there may be tensions between development and environment: rapid economic development inevitably leads to the emergence of environmental problems, while stringent environmental protection may restrict economic development in the short term.[51] Seen from the developing perspective, however, development and the environment should be the unity of opposites and mutually complementary. Development will bring the final solution to environmental issues; in turn, a sound environment facilitates sustainable economic development. Seen from the ultimate goal, both development and the environment are means rather than ends, serving human well-being.

---

50   Article 2, the UN *Declaration on the Right to Development* of 1986.
51   Li Yanfang, "On the Right to Environment and Its Relationship with the Right to Subsistence and the Right to Development", *The Journal of Renmin University of China* 5 (2000): 100.

CHAPTER 6

# Role of Rural Regulations in Environmental Protection and Green Development

*Findings from Wendou Village in Qiandongnan Miao and Dong Minority Autonomous Prefecture Pinghe County Hekou Township in Guizhou Province*

Gao Qicai*

1        Introduction**

The basic spirit of the *Declaration on the Right to Development*, adopted by the 41st session of the UN General Assembly on December 4, 1986, stipulated that for the right to development and for a people-oriented process of development: "States should encourage popular participation in all spheres as an important factor in development and in the full realization of all human rights" pursuant to the Article 8(2) of *Declaration on the Right to Development*. *Transforming Our World: The 2030 Agenda for Sustainable Development* which was passed at the UN Sustainable Development Summit on September 25–27, 2015 in New York, pointed out that "We are determined to ensure that all human beings can fulfil their potential in dignity and equality and in a healthy environment … We are determined to protect the planet from degradation, including through sustainable consumption and production, sustainably managing its natural resources and taking urgent action on climate change, so that it can support the needs of the present and future generations". The widespread involvement in social actions involving environmental protection, green development and sustainable development by means of rural regulations under the principle of a people-oriented process in Wendou in Qiandongnan Miao and Dong Minority Autonomous Prefecture Pinghe County Hekou Township in GuiZhou

---

\*    Gao Qicai, Professor at Tsinghua University Law School. Special thanks to Allegra Midgette (Ph.D. Candidate at the Graduate School of Education at UC Berkeley) for making corrections to the English draft.
\*\*  This chapter is phased research of the 2015 Ministerial-level Program "Empirical Research About the Rural Regulations' Positive Role in Social Governance" presided by Gao Qicai entrusted by China Law Society (Program Number CLS (2015) ZDWT 22). It is also phased research of "Rural Regulations' Function during the Process of Promoting Rule of Law" of Tsinghua University's sociology science independent research (Project Number: 2015THZWWH 01).

Province is unique and conforms to the basic spirit of the *Declaration on the Right to Development*.

Wendou's history traces back to the end of Yuan Dynasty and the beginning of the Ming Dynasty. It was initially a series of impoverished settlements before Emperor Shunzhi of the Qing Dynasty joined forces with Emperor Kangxi through an agreement to pay taxes. The two sub-areas, Shangzhai, originally part of Liping Prefecture, and Xiazhai, belonging to the Zhenyuan Prefecture during the Qing Dynasty, merged in 1914, to become part of the Jingping Prefecture. Wendou, which had been part of Shangzhai, Xiazhai and Hebian Village, was established after the foundation of the People's Republic of China (PRC). Wendou merged into Hekou Township in 1992 and Shangzhai and Xiazhai merged once again in 2008. Under the Key Village Construction Policy in 2014, another small village, Jiachi, joined Wendou, which then consisted of 15 village teams, 527 households with a population of 2,369 people, 99% of which are ethnically Miao.

The thriving of the wood industry in Wendou during the Ming and Qing Dynasties pushed the gradual formulation of the custom of contractual industrial management—many agreements carved in stone were made. The long history of an honest way of life and social stability, the beautiful environment with green hills and clean streams and the lushness of the bamboo forests, all benefited from the tradition of customary agreements. Thirty tree species and 700 green and mighty ancient trees including the Chinese yew, ginkgo biloba, nanmu and other key state protective plants have been preserved because villagers in Wendou have stringently abided by their forest protection agreements for the past 300 years. In 2010, Wendou was selected as "China's Landscape Village" because of its mountains and verdant landscape and the existence of a long history and culture of harmonious coexistence between nature and people.

Based on lessons learned from previous rural regulations and the pointing out of crucial contemporary issues, Wendou revised and recompiled rural regulations and developed a new *Agreement of Village Self-Governance* (hereafter "the Agreement").[1] The Agreement inherited native customary laws[2] and traditions including comprehensive content related to environmental protection and green development.

---

1 This is the rural regulations of Wendou made in September 2015, entitled "Wendou Rural Regulations", including Wendou Rural Regulations, the Agreement of Self-Governance, etc. I view them as a whole, called the *Agreement of Village Self-Governance*.
2 The customary law in this chapter is not involved in state law. It is restricted to regulations independent of state law and made by social authorities and social organizations, the sum of social regulations with certain compulsory ones. See particularly in Gao Qicai, *Pandect of China's Customary Law*, revised edition (Beijing: China Legal Publishing House, 2008), 3.

To gain a comprehensive understanding of the positive role played by rural regulations in environmental protection, green development, and sustainable development practices, we undertook field investigations on October 1, 2015 and February 23, 2016. From our visits to Wendou we learned about the villager's feelings concerning their ecological environment, participated in their annual October Tree-Worship Festival, viewed the ancient environmental protection stele, consulted Wendou's rural regulations, interviewed the villagers and their local leaders, and as a result had first-hand experience of the function that Wendou's rural agreements and regulations served in environmental protection.

## 2 "The Ancient Environmental Protection Steles" and Environmental Protection and Green Development

Wendou has a long history of self-governance by rural regulations. For example, villagers made a rural regulation to prevent objectionable practices such as the practice in 1773 during the Qing Dynasty of parents being able to force their offspring to accept arranged marriages and ask for money from the marriage. Six prominent families in Wendou made a rural regulation to prevent access to their village by pestilential livestock, also in 1773.

Addressing the issue of environmental protection and green development, villagers built a "Stele of Six Points for Prohibition" in winter of 1773. The inscription on the stele states:

- Ban: Trees, near or far, are all what we need to live by. Cutting down trees is banned, violators will be fined 0.5kg of silver.
- Ban: Crumbled stone stairs before the gate of every family need to be repaired by the family themselves. Violators will be fined 0.25kg of silver. The public can use this penalty to repair the stairs for the family. Leave this ban to pass on to later generations.
- Ban: Lumbering and gleaning is forbidden on the tea oil mountain during any season, violators will be fined 0.25kg of silver.
- Ban: Any family which allows their livestock to stray into Dragon Footsteps will be fined 0.125kg of silver.
- Ban: Pestilential cows and pigs are forbidden access to the village to avoid wicked people butchering them, violators will be turned over to the court to be dealt with.
- Ban: Leading ducks to the river according to seasonal regularity. Women are not allowed to break vegetation, violators will be fined 0.125kg of silver.

There is another stone stele on forest management beside the "Stele of Six Points for Prohibition" established 12 years later. Specific provisions relating to management of forests near Wendou are included in this stele's inscription: "This stele aims to protect the forest of our village, livestock are forbidden to stray here. It helps to preserve the glorious landscape of China".[3]

The two steles are true environmental protection steles. These bans and regulations gradually became rural customs which served as a binding force on social actions by Wendou villagers and had an obvious function in local environmental protection. It could be said that Wendou Village is surrounded by ancient towering trees to this day because of these regulations.

To carry out the rural regulations, villagers of Wendou created a festival called the Tree-Worship Festival with some customs.[4] The villagers cherish trees, protect trees, worship trees as gods, wish happiness for trees, pray to trees. On every Tree-Worship Day, villagers will take Chinese incense, yellow papers and sacrificial offerings to worship trees and pray for their family's safety. For example, villagers in Wendou perform a ceremony during the Tree-Worship Festival together in a *fang* (a kind of family unit). Every *fang* places an altar before Wendou's ancient taxus chinensis tree. People of all ages, male and female, celebrate together. The number of participants makes a spectacular scene with a solemn atmosphere. Many paper-cut talismans are pasted on trees, the writings on the talisman are greetings and prayers. The festival has become a very important environmental protection activity. It serves as an effective mechanism and platform for educating villagers on the value of environmental protection, and as an activity to pass on and strengthen rural regulations.

Wendou Village has many other regulations and customs related to trees. Since as early as the Qing Dynasty, there has been a file recording "marry a wife and mend a road, give birth to a baby and plant a tree", introduced by the director of the village neighborhood committee.[5] Parents plant an evergreen tree when a baby is born, cherishing the wish that the child grows up as healthy as an evergreen tree, along with the tree they planted. Some children see their evergreen tree as their godfather or godmother, believing, as their parents do, that the tree will bless them. Many faded red papers pasted on the roots of

---

3 Yi Wuhong, a Wendou villager recounted that a geography scholar visited Wendou and found that the geographical shape seemed like a phoenix, it needed the amount of trees to be its feather, so that it could fly high. After that, the custom of loving trees, planting trees and protecting trees was handed down. Interview Record of Yi Wuhong, February 23, 2016.
4 The Tree-Worship Festival of Wendou is held in March and October every year. Villagers plant trees in March and worship trees in October. A small sacrifice is made every year, a large sacrifice every three years.
5 Qiu Cunshuang and Wu Yurui, "Wendou Miaozhai jixing" [A Travel Report of Wendou Miao Village], *Guizhou Daily*, May 16, 2014.

trees and burned paper-cut talismans remain on trees. Small trees with trunks thinner than a wrist are marked by grassy objects as symbols of protection.

Influenced by these ecological concepts, Wendou villagers put concentrate on forest protection. For example, one business man from Guangdong Province was willing to buy 20 taxus chinensis trees for CNY 1,000,000. The villagers refused: "It's impossible for us to harm our descendants for temporary benefits. We will not sell these trees even if you pay CNY 10,000,000!" Furthermore, when a new road was built in Wendou in 2010, villagers put a bend in the road to bypass the taxus chinensis trees.[6]

During special periods, the villagers work together to protect the ecological environment and to sustain green development. For example, collective action was taken by the villagers to protect their ancient trees and prevent them being frozen by snow and ice when it snowed during the Spring Festival of 2008. They laid straw around the trees to keep them warm and break up the ice. "We built contemporary wooden ledges beside every ancient tree, young men climbed on the ledges and broke the ice and snow with wooden sticks to reduce the weight on the trees. Villagers bound straw around the trunk of an ancient ginkgo tree that was more than 700 years old". A villager called Jiang Meiyue said that "If a domestic animal dies, we can raise another one. If a house is destroyed, we can build again. However, destruction of ancient trees will be irrevocable". Under the protection of villagers, more than 700 ancient trees have been saved.[7]

Villagers share the knowledge of environmental protection regulations with their offspring in daily life. Even though Jiang Jinlan is only a third-grade primary school student, she already knows to "protect trees in the village". According to the Chairman of Wendou primary school, Jiang Lihui, teachers usually explain the inscription on the stele and the Agreement to students "to cultivate good habits of environmental protection and tree preservation".[8]

Through the long-term influence of rural regulations, villagers in Wendou have cultivated a strong sense of environmental protection. All members participate in environmental protection and actively obey the Agreement in order to maintain their village's beauty, preserve the historically and culturally significant mountains and clear waters, sustain development, and guarantee the peace and safety of their village.

---

6  Ibid.
7  Wang Yuanbai, "Jinping Wendou village: sanbai nian 'lifa shehui'" ["Rite and Law Society" for Three Hundred Years of Jinping Wendou Village], *Guiyang Daily*, January 6, 2010.
8  Ibid.

## 3  Agreement of Village Self-Governance and Environmental Protection and Green Development

Following the traditions of rural regulations, making agreements to protect the environment by discussion and practice became an established mechanism in Wendou. For example, Wendou established an Ecological Benefits Foundation, ensuring that anyone who plants a ginkgo, taxus chinensis or camphor tree will be offered a reward of CNY 50. This incentive led to an increase of more than 900 trees in Wendou.[9]

Actions violating the Agreement are punished by the villagers. The following two cases demonstrate this.

Case 1: Jiang Tianxiu, who was approaching 60 years old, accidentally caused a forest fire when burning weeds in her field one morning in April 2014. More than 3 *mu* (one *mu* equaling 0.165 acres) of forest had burned. The next day she was punished according to the Agreement: (1) fined CNY 150; (2) ordered to pay CNY 20 to each villager who took part in fighting the fire, a total of CNY 460 for 23 participants. She paid the money immediately.[10]

Case 2: Jiang Dongshu, who was 35 years old, set off the fire alarm when his family was cooking at midday in May 2012. Villagers came to fight the fire as soon as they saw the smoke. He was punished according the Agreement: (1) fined CNY 50; (2) participated in night patrol which involved making an announcement to others that the "weather is dry and be careful of candles and fire" from 7pm to 9pm for a month. He accepted the punishment.[11]

Violators take the punishment seriously and learn lessons from it. Other villagers have also learnt from accidents and understand how to prevent fire, obey the regulations and protect the forest.

Following self-governing traditions, the Agreement, which was passed during the villagers' representatives meeting, signed by the heads of households, implemented by the village committee and the Agreement executive team starting from September 11, 2015, contains direct and indirect regulations and the definite obligations of villagers and the committee on environmental protection.

Article 5 of the Agreement states the obligations of villagers to protect the environment: "to protect our community by creating a beautiful environment. Do not cut down scenic trees at the two borders of our village. Do not enter

---

9   Qiu Cunshuang and Wu Yurui, "Wendou Miaozhai jixing" [A Travel Report of Wendou Miao Village], *Guizhou Daily*, May 16, 2014.
10  Interview with Jiang Gengsheng, October 1, 2015.
11  Ibid.

into Dragon mountain to cut down dry and dead trees. Do not burn things in the mountains. Both adults and children are forbidden to make carvings in the trees. Violators will be fined between CNY 50 and CNY 10,000. Unlicensed lumber is forbidden, violators will be reported to the relevant authorities and be fined between CNY 50 and CNY 500".

Article 9 of the Agreement states: "No open flames. Persons making fires in the hills or fields without the permission of the village committee will be fined between CNY 50 and CNY 100. People who cause fire alarms or start fires must pay CNY 50 to each fire fighter besides being punished by the law".

The Agreement values fire prevention in its contents. Article 10 states "Bringing combustible and explosive materials into the village and households is strictly prohibited. Depositing combustible and explosive materials such as petrol, diesel oil, straw, wood veneer, saw timber, firecrackers, etc. into households and the village is strictly prohibited". Article 11 declares "Building planning violation, parking vehicles chaotically and huddling things randomly is strictly prohibited. Villagers should follow village planning rules to build houses, livestock sheds and toilets. Do not appropriate collective farmland. Do not occupy or block traffic and fire lanes. Do not connect to the electricity mains without permission. Violators will be fined between CNY 100 and CNY 1,000".

The Agreement also has requirements regarding fire-fighting equipment and fire water supply to prevent fire and protect the forest. Article 13 of the Agreement states "To protect fire-fighting equipment, improper covering materials must be moved. Borrowing fire-fighting equipment without permission and blocking the fire water supply is prohibited, violators will be fined between CNY 100 and CNY 200 besides requiring rehabilitation". Article 14 reads "Drinking water supply is secondary to the fire water supply, and the fire water reservoir must be full of water. Anyone who gets water from the reservoir without permission will be fined between CNY 100 and CNY 500".

The Agreement has comprehensive and detailed requirements relating to environmental protection. Article 27 of the Agreement states "All families should plant trees and flowers around their house, all vegetable gardens should be fenced in". Article 36 states "All families should foster the concept of becoming better off through diligent work, taking care of the plants in their fields and hill lands. Anyone who leaves land uncultivated will be fined 500 RMB".

The Agreement has effective mechanisms to ensure that all the environmental protection provisions are obeyed by villagers by regulating the Village Committee's obligations in its text:

(1) The executive institution: The Village Committee is responsible for modifying and completing the Agreement. The Agreement will be enforced after being signed by all families. The Village Committee is responsible

for organizing the Agreement executive team composed of a patriarch and village representatives, in total 26 members.[12] The Agreement executive team chaired by the Village Mediation Commission Director has the power to enforce the Agreement.

(2) A routine work system should be established. The Village Committee is responsible for increasing investment in fire prevention equipment. The fire water supply reservoir and fire hydrants are subjected to inspections twice per month, ensuring the fire water supply can work in emergencies. The Village Committee should coordinate the contradiction between the supply of irrigation water and fire water. Domestic and public electricity mains need periodic inspections—aging, softening crack damage should be fixed immediately. Connection to the electricity mains without permission is prohibited. The Village Committee should designate a village fire-fighter, create information and educational material about fire prevention, organize "volunteer fire-fighting team" and organize at least monthly fire drills. Strengthening of the fire prevention and fire-fighting neighborhood system joined by ten families, immediate management and rectification should be carried out regularly to prevent fire hazards. Night watchmen should patrol the village at 8pm every night and make announcements to villagers.

(3) Implementing a definite reward and punishment system. Article 12 of the Agreement states "Obey the fire-safety requirements. Storing any explosives, inflammable or similar items beside cooking range stove will be fined CNY 50 as well as an immediate remedy after two official warnings. Anyone setting off a fire alarm will be fined CNY 50 and be assigned night watchman patrol duties for a month, he will also need to write a self-critical report and compensate for losses if a fire occurs. Causing forest fires means fines of CNY 50 per *mu* for hills; CNY 100 per *mu* for woodland; CNY 200 for economic woodland (except liable to criminal law)". Article 35 of the Agreement states "Villagers should treasure collective lands, hills and rivers. Reporting damaging lands and polluting water by other people is encouraged. Destroyer will be fined between CNY 500 and CNY 5,000".

Agreement violators will receive public criticism and be required to perform an immediate remedy. The Village Committee will not provide public and

---

12 During field investigations, Jiang Gengsheng, the CPC's branch secretary told us "The Agreement executive team is made up of clan leaders because every clan leader represents their respective family, which will make the execution fair. And every clan leader wants to join the team because all clans need other clans' help and support when they manage their clan members". Interview with Jiang Gengsheng, October 1, 2015.

administrative services to families who refuse to sign the Agreement or refuse to pay fines. Other violators who refuse to accept the penalty will go before the Agreement Executive Team, depending on the circumstances.

Compared to former village regulations, the Agreement adopted in September 2015 adds the content of environmental protection and village planning. The Agreement was discussed during the villager's representative meeting and signed by nearly all families.[13] The Agreement will be carved on a stele and set up by the river in Wendou.

## 4   Conclusion and Discussion

The historical traditions, basis of concepts, institutional guarantee, social context and social will of Wendou encourage villagers to take part in environmental protection and green development.

Long-standing traditions of environmental protection exist in Wendou. There are strict rural regulations, ordinances and systems. The present *Agreement of Village Self-Governance* is a result of the development of historical customs, showing the importance of environmental protection concepts and good traditions in upholding agreements. All these reflect the strong cultural and social will to treasure the environment. Many of Wendou's rural regulations originate from the ancient steles at the entrance to Wendou. "The rural regulations and the Agreement is another form that ancient steles still function today", says the CPC (Chinese Communist Party) Secretary of Wendou. "Wendou villagers protect the environment according to the requirements of the ancient steles which have a strong binding effect on Wendou people as they always obey the Agreement. Even more important is that it cultivates strong environmental awareness of Wendou villagers over long periods of time".[14]

In their living conditions, daily life and work, villagers in Wendou protect the environment and achieve sustainable development through the implementation of the Agreement.[15] It shows the consciousness of reverence of

---

13  According to the introduction by Jiang Gengsheng, the CPC's branch secretary, there still are 18 households that have not signed the Agreement because all the family members were working away.
14  Wang Yuanbai, "Jinping Wendou village: sanbai nian 'lifa shehui'" ["Rite and Law Society" for Three Hundred Years of Jinping Wendou Village], *Guiyang Daily*, January 6, 2010.
15  Chai Rongyi and Luo Yihang point out that the ethnic minority in southwest China still keeps the whole frame of their natural worship rituals, which are generally worship of natural matters such as heaven, earth, mountains, rivers, animals and plants. Their reverence for the supernatural force forms the harmonious relationship between human and

nature worship and simple ecological consciousness of harmony between man and nature.

Reflecting on the environment every day, Wendou villagers rely on the forests, trees and natural environment. The villagers view the trees, ecology, and environment as objects having life, will and great capacity. Villagers revere the mountains and trees as they are close to them and believe that ritualistic worship will prevent misfortunes, bless them, bring abundant harvests. Influenced by these beliefs, rural regulations protecting trees and the environment thus gradually developed, inherited from the past and obeyed until the present. The environmental protection practice of the Agreement, based on primitive religious ideas, is therefore unpremeditated.

In order to protect the environment and achieve green development, the Agreement fines violators,[16] which is an effective measure to guarantee the execution of the Agreement. The technical means of setting "liquidated damages by agreement" obviously requires strong constraints and requires villagers to obey the Agreement. In the Agreement, the amounts of liquidated damages by agreement, however, fluctuate widely, such as CNY 50 to CNY 100, CNY 50 to CNY 500, CNY 100 to CNY 500, CNY 100 to CNY 1,000, even as high as CNY 50 to CNY 10,000. The amounts of legal liquidated damages of CNY 5,000 and CNY 10,000 are too high for a civil agreement.[17] As for the nature of the Agreement, it is a self-governance and self-educational agreement which should focus on criticism and education, such a high amount of liquidated damages by agreement being not suitable for the civil agreement. Severe penalization has played

---

nature, and the environmental protection idea and natural law. See Chai Rongyi and Luo Yihang, "Xinan shaoshu minzu ziran chongbaizhe shechu de huanbao xiguan faze" [Environmental Protection Customary Law Reflected from Natural Worship by a Minority Group in Southwestern China], *Guizhouminzuyanjiu*,11(2014).

16   Liquidated damages by agreement is a revised form of fine. According to China's state law, village self-governance organizations do not have the right to fine, so the Wendou Agreement uses liquidated damages to substitute the fine to avoid violation of the state law. The villagers, however, consider the liquidated damages and fine to be the same thing.

17   During the investigation, Jiang Gengsheng, the CPC's branch secretary told us that, "The Agreement was reported to our county's Propaganda Bureau, Agricultural Bureau, Rural Construction Bureau and Justice Bureau in record. The County's Justice Bureau thought that our fines were heavy and I argued that if we do not regulate a heavy fine in the Agreement, villagers will tend to violate because they will get benefit without loss if they disobey the Agreement. A small fine is useless to bind the villagers. We will insist on our opinion of the village self-governance. If we change the fine of CNY 10,000 to CNY 100, I think that villagers may tend to violate the Agreement 100 times over. The Justice Bureau did not oppose the Agreement after hearing what I said". Interview with Jiang Gengsheng, October 1, 2015.

an important role in rural regulation in the past, however, it should be changed and improved, keeping pace with current times.

Meanwhile, according to the requirements of the Agreement, villagers who have not signed the Agreement will not receive any benefit from the village committee until they sign the Agreement and pay the penalty according to the Agreement. This will guarantee the enforcement of the Agreement and will achieve the goal of the Agreement—abiding by the regulations and protecting the environmental. But this mandatory requirement runs contrary to equality of negotiation and the principle of free will and is contradictory to the spirit of law. This local practice should be discussed and revised again. The ecological environment is essential for villagers' daily life and agricultural production, thus environmental protection needs villagers' inner recognition. Enforcement measures and institutional decrees will play a negative role in the Agreement process.

The Agreement adopts the strategic pattern of environmental protection, sets up green development mechanisms, investigates and implements strict responsibility for ecological health and environment pollution prevention. The experience of Wendou Village shows the function of the Agreement in environmental and ecological protection. The participation of Wendou villagers in environmental protection generally through rural regulations, especially through the Agreement, gives a socially favorable result, produces great ecological effects, promotes sustainable green development, and provides a feasible approach for local environmental protection.

The report of the Fifth Session of the Eighteenth Central Committee of the Chinese Communist Party (CPC) claimed: "China must adhere to the basic state policy of resource conservation and environmental protection and adhere to sustainable development"; "The Chinese government is committed to promoting harmonious co-existence between humans and nature, building more scientific and reasonable urban structures, agricultural development structures, ecological security structures, promoting the establishment of the green low-carbon and recycling industrial system"; "China must adhere to the basic state policy of resource conservation and environmental protection and adhere to sustainable development. The entire society will be back on a road of civilized development with developed production, affluent life and a sound ecological environment. China's government will promote the establishment of a resource-conserving and environmentally friendly society and build a new pattern of modernization, construction of harmonious development between humans and nature. The construction of a new and beautiful China will make new contributions to global ecological safety". The case of Wendou Village is a fantastic execution of this and provides an excellent example.

CHAPTER 7

# Development and the Environment: The Conflict and Balance in the View of Human Rights Law

*Perspective and Reflection Based on China*

*Li Hongbo**

## 1    Introduction

Throughout human history, the relationship between development and the environment has never been as intense as it is now: on the one hand, due to the existence of large-scale poverty worldwide, developing countries should promote social progress and improve the conditions for human existence through economic growth; on the other hand, tremendous environmental problems such as resource shortages, species extinction, air pollution, soil pollution and water pollution resulting from industrial production directly threaten the survival and sustainable development of mankind.

From the perspective of human rights law, the above predicament may be summarized as the internal tension and conflict between the right to development and the right to the environment. This issue is universal and it is especially obvious and prominent in developing countries such as China. By introducing reform and opening up, China has kept rapid economic growth since the 1980s and basically shaken off poverty. Nevertheless, extensive economic growth is at the cost of environment, which is unsustainable. When the idea of "Prosperous China" is gradually realized, the Chinese government proposes a new goal of "Beautiful China". To accomplish the latter, it is necessary to review the relationship between these two human rights and seek a way to reconcile and balance them.

## 2    The Proposal of the Right to Development and the Right to the Environment

In the history of human rights development, the right to development and the right to the environment both belong to the so-called "third-generation

---

\*   Li Hongbo, Professor of China University of Political Science and Law, Fellow of Center for Human Rights Studies at China Foreign Affairs University.

rights" that first appeared in the 1970s.[1] The arising of these new rights reflects humans' longer-term thinking and deeper concern for their own destinies.

## 2.1    The Proposal of the Right to Development

On the level of domestic law, the right to subsistence, as an explicit legal norm, was first found in the *Weimar Constitution* of Germany in 1919, in which Article 151 of Section V (Economic Life) of Chapter 2 stipulates: "The organization of economic life must conform to the principles of justice to the end that all may be guaranteed a decent standard of living". Since the Second World War, the concept of the right to subsistence has been widely accepted by all countries. On the level of international law, in 1969, the report of the "Justice and Peace" Commission of Algeria, *The Right to Development of Underdeveloped Countries*, put forward the concept of the "right to development" for the first time. In 1977, the United Nations Commission on Human Rights adopted a resolution to include the right to development as a basic human right; in 1979, the Commission on Human Rights reiterated that the right to development is both a state right and an individual right, and that the opportunity for development should be equal for all. In the same year, the United Nations General Assembly adopted Resolution 34/46 reflecting this view. In 1986, the 41st United Nations General Assembly adopted the *Declaration on the Right to Development* which sets out a systematic exposition on the right to development and calls for promoting development of developing countries and promoting the establishment of a new international order. The *Declaration on the Right to Development* points out: "The right to development is an inalienable human right by virtue of which every human person and all peoples are entitled to participate in, contribute to and enjoy economic, social, cultural, and political development, in which all human rights and fundamental freedoms can be fully realized".

The right to development is a fundamental human right, as other human rights would be out of the question without the comprehensive development of states, society and individuals. "In light of its internal characteristics, the right to development is a qualification or capability of humans as individuals, and states and nations as collectives of human, to freely participate and enhance the comprehensive development of the economy, society, culture and politics and enjoy the benefits of development, and is an essential requirement

---

1   The theory of "third-generation human rights" is a human rights theory first proposed by Karel Vasak, a former legal adviser to UNESCO. Third-generation human rights are a response to global interdependence and a product of constant development of national liberation campaigns. Its central ideas include peace, the environment and development.

of all mankind for comprehensive development; in light of its external characteristics, the right to development is a basic human right widely existing in domestic and international communities for the purpose of meeting basic demands."[2]

The proposal on the right to development reflects mankind's requirement for a fairer new international order. Differing from the first-generation and second-generation human rights, the discourse on the right to development is dominated by developing countries, of which the main content is that developing countries should realize comprehensive, balanced, sustainable and green development. Therefore, "the right to development is a product of undeveloped and marginalized subjects of rights striving for discourse power".[3] In reality, it is very difficult to realize the right to development. On the one hand, a relatively established international economic order and pattern, to some extent, limits the opportunities for underdeveloped countries to acquire opportunities for robust development; on the other hand, changes in the natural environment since industrialization have made development more difficult than it was before the 19th century. In other words, the newly emerging right to the environment constitutes another counterweight and constraint with regard to the right to development.

## 2.2   *The Proposal of the Right to the Environment*

Like the right to development, the right to the environment is also a new type human right: "In light of its internal characteristics, the right to the environment is a qualification or capability of humans as individuals and states and nations as collectives of humans to freely enjoy and protect the resources and environment of the earth and promote the harmony between man and nature as well as the sustainable development of society, and is an internal demand of all mankind to live a healthy and fruitful life".[4]

In 1960, a doctor in West Germany appealed to the European Commission on Human Rights that "the dumping of waste in the North Sea" was an infringement of human rights, thus triggering a dispute over whether the right

---

2  Wang Xigen, "Legal Philosophical Analysis of the Meaning of the Right to Development", *Modern Law Science* 6 (2004): 7.
3  Wang Xigen and Tu Shaobin, "The Right to Development: A Post-Modern Legal Interpretation", *Law and Social Development* 6 (2005): 56.
4  Hou Huaixia, "On the Right to Environment in Human Rights Laws", *The Journal of Suzhou University (Philosophy and Social Sciences)* 3 (2009): 36.

to the environment should be added to the list of human rights in Europe.[5] Since the connection of human rights to environmental problems in the 1972 Stockholm Conference on Environment and Development, more and more people tend to deem the right to the environment as a human right. Later, the right to the environment as a human right was confirmed by a series of international law documents. The *African Charter on Human and Peoples' Rights* declares: "All peoples shall have the right to a general satisfactory environment favorable to their development". The first principle in the Stockholm *Declaration of the United Nations Conference on the Human Environment* reads: "Man has the fundamental right to freedom, equality and adequate conditions of life, in an environment of a quality that permits a life of dignity and well-being, and he bears a solemn responsibility to protect and improve the environment for present and future generations". In addition, exposition of the right to the environment is found in other statements such as the *Declaration on Social Progress and Development* and the *Nairobi Declaration*. Article 11 of the *International Covenant on Economic, Social, and Cultural Rights* adopted in 1966 also declares: "States of the present Covenant recognize the right of everyone to an adequate standard of living for himself and his family, including adequate food, clothing and housing, and to the continuous improvement of living conditions".

There used to be theoretical criticism and questioning as to whether the right to the environment is an independent human right. With the continuous deterioration of the environment, however, more and more people have come to accept the right to the environment and have begun to recognize its status as an independent human right. "The right to the environment requires no harm to the environment as an important standard, which is absent in other rights and also a constraint over other rights. As far as this point is concerned, the right to the environment can't be covered by any other rights".[6] The right to the environment, like other human rights, is a rights system, in which its contents consist of multiple sub-rights, including citizens' right to use, understand and participate in the environment as well as the right to request related departments for protection when the environment is being harmed.[7]

---

5　Li Yanfang, "On the Right to Environment and Its Relationship with the Right to Subsistence and the Right to Development", *The Journal of Renmin University of China* 5 (2000): 96.
6　Lü Zhongmnei, "The Citizens' Right to Environment: A Revisit", *Chinese Journal of Law* 6 (2000): 133.
7　Ibid., 135–139.

## 3 The Conflict between the Right to Development and the Right to the Environment

In today's world, the internal conflict between the right to development and the right to the environment is very obvious. "The opposition between the environment and development is reflected as follows: rapid economic development will inevitably lead to environmental problems and the strict protection of the environment constrains economic development in the short term".[8] Human beings pursue a rich, decent, and dignified life, and to realize this purpose, they will inevitably require more water, lumber, minerals, oil and natural gas from nature. If human demands are controlled within an appropriate extent and within a scope that nature can afford, human development and natural harmony can co-exist. This harmony will inevitably face damage if the reasonable extent of consumption is surpassed.

Compared with earlier time periods, developing countries today are confronted with unprecedented conflict between the right to development and the right to the environment, and its resulting crises. The conflict between the right to development and the right to the environment has become a severe practical problem that developing countries must face.

First, the conflict between the right to development and the right to the environment is a problem concerning man and nature. Though the subjects of rights are humans, and the right to development is for mankind, the goal of the right to the environment is the protection of the environment and ecology. "The right to the environment, as a human institution, also plays its role by acting on humans or units formed by humans. The difference is that behind the relationship among humans, the relationship between humans and nature is implied. The right to the environment, after acting on humans, must affect the relationship between man and nature through these humans".[9] The relationship between man and nature has become increasingly intense since the Industrial Revolution, and the internal conflict between the right to development and the right to the environment has also begun to stand out. The development of the capitalist industrial system has rapidly increased the demands of capital for natural resources, while technological progress makes it possible to exploit natural resources on a large scale. Large machines can empty a mine

---

[8] Li Yanfang, "On the Right to Environment and Its Relationship with the Right to Subsistence and the Right to Development", *The Journal of Renmin University of China* 5 (2000): 100.

[9] Xu Xiangmin, "On the Right to Environment: From the Perspective of Historical Periods of Human Rights Development", *China Social Sciences* 4 (2004): 134.

overnight, while international railways and huge container ships can transport raw materials and goods to places all over the world. With economic and technological development, population increases sharply and consumerism constantly stimulates people's desire for occupation and consumption. All these directly lead to the exacerbation of environmental problems.

Secondly, the conflict between the right to development and the right to the environment is a problem concerning the relationship between contemporary people and future generations. There is an issue of inter-generational justice for the enjoyment of both the right to development and the right to the environment, but there is also some difference in that the right to development is more pertinent to the present, while the right to the environment lays more stress on the future. In face of the global crisis in resources and the environment, American philosopher Rawls proposed a new theory of justice as early as 1972. He holds that the next generation should enjoy at least the same resource and environmental basis as the current generation, which marks the proposal of the inter-generational justice of resources and the environment.

"The inter-generational justice of resources and the environment is the primary and most basic concept of inter-generational justice, and its basic meaning is: human society develops in a state of generational continuation; social members of the current generation, as a whole, jointly own the natural resources on earth and jointly enjoy an environment suitable for subsistence; in specific periods, the current generation is also the manager and custodian of the earth's environment for future generations; this endows the current generation with an obligation to protect the earth and also grants the current generation the right to enjoy the resources and environment of the earth. In short, each generation equally enjoys the right to resources and the environment; the quality of the environment left from one generation to the next should not be worse than the quality of the environment inherited from the previous generation, and the resources available for development left by one generation to the next should not be fewer than those inherited form the previous generation; meanwhile, each generation should not sacrifice its opportunity for developing the economy and improving wellbeing in order to preserve resources and the environment for the next generation".[10]

The earth, resources and the opportunity of subsistence belong to all mankind, not only those currently living, but also future generations. If the current generation exhausts resources and pollutes the environment for its own development, the next generation will lose their development opportunity and pay

---

10  Cheng Wei, "Inter-Generation Justice of Resources and Environment and Its Realization", *Academic Exchange* 6 (2009): 41.

the price for the development of the earlier generation, which is a serious infringement of the next generation's right to development.

Thirdly, the conflict between the right to development and the right to the environment is a global issue. On the one hand, tension between the environment and development is not caused by one country or one group, and all countries and all of mankind should bear the responsibility. After the Second World War, capitalist countries laid one-sided emphasis on economic development, neglected environmental protection and caused serious environmental pollution and resource shortages. When developing countries started to take the path of development, the global environmental problems they faced were very serious. There was not much room for carbon emission, their ability to rapidly develop the economy was lost and their ability to balance economic development and environmental protection was reduced. Even today, developed countries have not eliminated or reduced carbon emissions, but use the already established unfair international economic order to transfer carbon emission to developing countries. Developed countries invent patents, while production and manufacturing are taken on by developing countries. When Europeans and Americans consume a large number of cheap commodities produced in China and India, they are not justified in blaming environmental deterioration and climate change exclusively on developing countries. Although there is a conflict of interest between developed countries and developing countries in the environment and development, there is no victory belonging to just one party. Neither environmental pollution nor widespread poverty are separate matters for a particular sovereign state. There is no national border for environmental pollution or climate change, while widespread poverty will inevitably lead to turmoil and trigger refugee crises and terrorism. These problems are common problems that the whole world must face.

In summary, economic growth *per se* is not an end, and economic development must be in harmony with the natural environment. The *Declaration on the Right to Development* clearly states that development is a multi-dimensional comprehensive process and its purpose is "the active, free and meaningful participation of the entire population and of all individuals in development" and in "the fair distribution of the benefits resulting therefrom", and the constant improvement of the well-being of the entire population and of all individuals.[11] As the *Declaration of the United Nations Conference on the Human Environment* also points out: "In our time, man's capability to transform his surroundings, if used wisely, can bring to all peoples the benefits of development and the opportunity to enhance quality of life. Wrongly or heedlessly

---

11 The United Nations, *Declaration on the Right to Development*, Resolution 41/128 adopted by the United Nations General Assembly (December 4, 1986).

applied, the same power can do incalculable harm to human beings and the human environment". Development would almost become mingled, and the natural environment would suffer from serious pollution and directly threaten human survival. Therefore, the present world and generation must face up to the tension and conflict between the right to development and the right to the environment and must seek the right solution to this crisis; otherwise, mankind will have no future.

## 4  A Path to Sustainable Development: Balance of the Right to Development and the Right to the Environment

Currently facing a world with a polarization of wealth and a seriously polluted earth, and in the face of the unprecedented conflict between the right to development and the right to the environment, the Community of Shared Future should break away from the old pattern of thinking and development, take a new path of sustainable development and realize the harmony of the right to development and the right to environment.

The idea of setting the right to development against the right to the environment is wrong, as we should neither seek development at the expense of the environment nor stop development to protect the environment. "The relationship between the right to the environment and the right to development is a unity of opposites. The opposition between the environment and development is reflected as follows: rapid economic development will inevitably lead to environmental problems, while strict protection of the environment constrains economic development within a short period of time. On the whole, however, the environment and development are unitary, which is reflected as: development leads to environmental problems, while the solution of environmental problems ultimately depends on development".[12] In fact, there is not only conflict and tension, but also the possibility of coordination and accommodation in the relationship between the right to the environment and the right to development.

On the one hand, from a technological perspective, the solution of environmental problems should depend on economic development and technological progress. There is a close relationship between poverty and environmental deterioration; therefore, without the security of a certain economic basis, environmental protection would be meaningless, just like a tree without roots. Meanwhile, environmental problems are complicated, scientific and technological,

---

12  Hou Huaixia, "On the Right to Environment in Human Rights Laws", *The Journal of Suzhou University (Philosophy and Social Sciences)* 3 (2009): 36.

requiring science and technology to be a major problem-solving measure. Without scientific and technological progress and without comprehensive progress in machinery equipment and instruments promoted by scientific and technological progress and development, it would be impossible to resolve environmental problems.

On the other hand, from a social perspective, the solution of environmental problems ultimately relies on the establishment of societal awareness of ecological civilization, and requires people's transformation of their lifestyles, which should be based on development. Only through development can people enjoy a good life, receive a good education, acquire information about science and change their outlook and action patterns to meet the standards of modern civilization and ecology. As the *Vienna Declaration and Programme of Action* points out: "The existence of widespread extreme poverty inhibits the full and effective enjoyment of human rights. Its immediate alleviation and eventual elimination must remain a high priority for the international community".

To realize the harmony of the right to development and the right to the environment, and to realize the development and progress of human society while maintaining healthy ecology, the world should take the following actions.

First, the international community represented by the United Nations should adopt united actions and make responsible arrangements and farsighted planning for major problems concerning human destiny. In 2015, the United Nations' Summit on Sustainable Development was held at the UN Headquarters in New York, and adopted *Transforming Our World: The 2030 Agenda for Sustainable Development*, which points out that we should "ensure that all human beings can fulfil their potential in dignity and equality and in a healthy environment ... We are determined to protect the planet from degradation, including through sustainable consumption and production, sustainably managing its natural resources and taking urgent action on climate change, so that it can support the needs of present and future generations ... We envisage a world in which every country enjoys sustained, inclusive and sustainable economic growth and decent work for all. A world in which consumption and production patterns and use of all natural resources—from air to land, from rivers, lake and aquifers to oceans and seas—are sustainable". To this end, international organizations represented by the United Nations, in the formulation of international laws and rules, must reasonably allocate the obligations and responsibilities of developed countries and developing countries, and realize the balance of development and the environment with fair, reasonable and feasible international law and order. "In terms of the theory and practice of international law conducive to development, to ensure the fulfilment of the right to development, we must admit the fact of inequality of development between developing countries and developed countries and that developed countries must give care to establishing an asymmetrical relationship of rights and obligations between developed countries and developing countries, that is, a system in which developed countries grant special treatment to developing countries such as preferential and non-reciprocal treatment which does not require developing countries to fulfil equal obligations".[13]

Secondly, developed countries must take on their own responsibilities in this process. As far as the environment is concerned, developed countries have compelling responsibilities. The environmental problem is a global problem, and so is the problem of development. No country can avoid these problems. "The right to development is an important measure for human society to realize its own equal and harmonious development, while to truly realize the right to development is the end of social progress and historical development. The right to development entails the basic values of freedom, harmony and equality, and to improve and develop national sovereignty, and to promote the harmonious and balanced development of all countries in the world, especially developing countries, is the contemporary value target of the right to development".[14] Therefore, developed countries must play an active role in the realization of sustainable development. On the one hand, developed countries should welcome the development of underdeveloped countries, instead of being on guard against such development. They should also provide necessary assistance to the development of developing countries and jointly participate in actions to eliminate poverty; on the other hand, developed countries should actively guide and promote environmental protection, and while assuming their own responsibility for reducing carbon emission, they should also help developing countries with their advantages in technology, capital and management.

Thirdly, developing countries must change their models of development, realize green and economic development and take a path to sustainable development. In China, the Fifth Plenary Session of Eighteenth CPC National Congress established five major ideas of development: "innovation, coordination, green development, opening-up and sharing". "Green development" means to promote the harmonious co-existence of man and nature, develop a new pattern of modernized construction with harmonious development of man and nature, promote the construction of a beautiful China and make new contributions to global ecological safety. For China to realize "green development", we

---

13   Wang Xigen, "Jurisprudential Analysis of the Right to Development", *Journal of Legal Studies* 4 (1999): 24.
14   Ibid., 19.

should resolve problems in three aspects. First, we should establish a system and mechanism for green development. We should promote the development of low-carbon circular development, establish a clean, low-carbon, safe and efficient modern energy system. We should comprehensively, safely and efficiently use resources, establish an outlook of saving, intensive and circular use of resources, establish and improve a system of initial allocation of the right to use energy, the right to use water, emission rights and carbon emission rights, and promote the development of a diligent and frugal social custom. Secondly, we should implement strict accountability and punishment for actions of environmental pollution. We should step up efforts in environmental governance, and center on improving environmental quality, implement the strictest environmental protection system, further implement action plans for preventing and treating air, water and soil pollution, and implement the vertical management system of environmental protection institutions below the provincial level for supervision, monitoring and law enforcement. Thirdly, we should implement ecological protection. We should focus on the strategy of giving priority to conservation and natural rehabilitation, implement ecological protection and rehabilitation projects for mountains, waters, fields and lakes, conduct large-scale actions to afforest our land, improve the natural forest protection system and conduct environmental protection for our bays. To implement the decision of the central government and realize green development, the newest *National Human Rights Action Plan (2016–2020)* explicitly points out that on the one hand: "we should generally improve the people's living standards and quality of life; improve the public service system and upgrade the level of service equalization; make full efforts to implement poverty alleviation programs and realize poverty alleviation of the entire poverty-stricken population based on current standards"; on the other hand, we should "implement the strictest environmental protection system, develop an environmental governance system with joint governance by the government, enterprises and the public, focus on resolving prominent environmental problems such as air, water and soil problems, and realize the overall improvement of environmental quality".[15]

## 5 Conclusion

As the largest developing country in the world, China's position is that the right to subsistence and the right to development are primary human rights, and

---

15  The State Council Information Office of P.R.C., *National Human Rights Action Plan* (2016–2020), September 30, 2016.

that without the right to subsistence and the right to development, all other human rights would be out of the question. At present, China has formed a path to development with its own characteristics. Through economic reform, productivity has been emancipated, tremendous progress of the Chinese society has been promoted and the overall improvement of human rights in China has been realized. Extensive economic growth, however, has caused serious environmental problems and ecological cost in some places. Currently, on the basis of summarizing historical experiences and lessons, China is conducting the adjustment and transformation of economic structures and development mode. The world should take an optimistic and welcome posture toward such efforts. After all, the realization of the dream of "Beautiful China" with green mountains and clear water will not only provide conditions for the great rejuvenation of the Chinese nation but also bring benefits to the world.

CHAPTER 8

# Legal Research on Carbon Emission Rights from the Perspective of a Right to Development

*He Miao*[*]

## 1   Academic Debates on the Relationship between a Right to Development and Carbon Emission

Climate warming was first proposed by scientists. In 1872, Fourier, a physicist in France, proposed that carbon dioxide might absorb solar energy; in 1896, Arrhenius, a physicist in Sweden, called Fourier's theory the "greenhouse effect", and Arrhenius first proposed that carbon dioxide caused by human activities would have significant effects on climate change.[1]

The international community was initially unconcerned by climate change, not only because "climate change-related effects have a range of direct and indirect implications for the effective enjoyment of human rights",[2] but also because climate change-related effects would threaten the interests of future generations. Since then, a heated debate on carbon emissions has begun. There are two main ideas. The first is "carbon emission is a right", actually "the definition of a carbon emission right is established on an 'atmospheric environmental capacity theory', and this theory is the object of this right".[3] A carbon emission right refers to the fact that in order to survive and develop, right holders have a legal right to emit greenhouse gases. Essentially, this right means

---

[*]   He Miao, Lecturer and Post-Doctorate Researcher of Law School at Wuhan University, Wuhan, China.
[1]   Han Ying, *Research on International Issue of Climate Change* (Hangzhou: Zhejiang University Publisher, 2012), 4.
[2]   High Level Expert Meeting on the New Future of Human Rights and Environment: Moving the Global Agenda Forward, "… Most recently, the Human Rights Council in its Resolution 7/23 of March 2008 and Resolution 10/4 of March 2009 focused specifically on human rights and climate change, noting that climate change-related effects have a range of direct and indirect implications for the effective enjoyment of human rights …", for detailed information, please see http://www.unep.org/environmentalgovernance/Events/HumanRightsandEnvironment/tabid/2046/language/en-US/Default.aspx, accessed March 22, 2015.
[3]   Wu Jian, *Pollution Rights Trading: A Creative Management System on the Environmental Capacity* (Beijing: Zhongguo Renmin Publisher, 2005), 88.

right holders could gain a right to use a certain amount of the atmospheric environment and natural resources.[4] Specifically, some scholars[5] recognized "a carbon emission right is a right to development". In the context of the *United Nations Framework Convention on Climate Change* (hereinafter UNFCCC), a carbon emission right has changed from a natural right to a legal right.[6] Undoubtedly, the allocation of carbon emission rights should pay more attention to the requirements of a right to development after the *Kyoto Protocol* was issued. The second idea is "carbon emission is a duty", "essentially, the reduction of greenhouse gas emissions evolved into a conflict between the degree of international duties and developmental costs that developed countries should bear and that how much developing countries need to undertake".[7] If we analyze this merely from historical facts and as moral duties, these two ideas lack enough credibility and possibility to execute. Carbon emissions should be recognized as a unity of rights and duties. In the era of globalization, it is necessary to realize the unification between a carbon emission right and a carbon emission duty. "A carbon emission right is a basic human right; a carbon emission right is a part of a right to live, this means that the scope of a carbon emission right directly determines a person's living space. No carbon emission, no life".[8] "If climate change restricts the effort for development, and some persons have a vastly better situation than other people, there is something wrong with the idea that both those who are very well off and those who are very poor can have the same right to development".[9] Of course, if both economic and technical conditions permit, we could promote development of clean energy to reduce carbon emissions. To develop some new type of clean energy is a developmental tendency for the future. Most countries, however, especially developing countries, lack the economic basis and the related technical skills to fully develop clean energy in a short period of time. At present, a carbon emission right, to

---

4  Han Liang, *Legal Studies on International Trade for a Greenhouse Gas Emission Right* (Beijing: China Legal Publishing House, 2009), 29.
5  Eric A. Posner and Cass R. Sunstein, "Climate Change Justice", *Georgetown Law Journal* 96 (2007–2008): 1603; Bryan A. Green, "Lessons from the Montreal Protocol: Guidance for the Next International Climate Change Agreement", *Environmental Law* 39 (2009): 281.
6  Wang Mingyuan, "On Real Right and Right to Development Features of a Carbon Emission Right", last modified May 18, 2011, accessed January 3, 2013, http://www.civillaw.com.cn/article/default.asp?id=53024.
7  Wang Junfeng, "International Liabilities and International Duties of Developed Countries in Greenhous Gas Reduction", *International Technical and Economic Research* 10, no. 3 (2007).
8  "Game on Restricting China in the Context of Carbon Emission", last modified January 1, 2010, accessed January 18, 2013, http://www.360doc.com/content/10/0101/21/9144_12461704.shtml.
9  Lars Lofquist, "Climate Change, Justice and the Right to Development", *Journal of Global Ethics* 7, no. 3 (2011): 251–260.

some extent, refers to each country's international duties, especially environmental duties. The essential issue is how to better balance environmental duties at the international level and poverty reduction at the national level. "A right to development is a basic human right for all individuals and communities who are qualified to freely participate in, promote and enjoy all kinds of interests that benefit from economic, policy, cultural and social aspects at both national and international levels".[10] A right to development results in poverty reduction at the national level. Therefore, for a country, a right to development means to promote economic, policy, environmental and cultural aspects; regarding an individual, a right to development is a cornerstone to enjoy other rights, including economic, social and cultural rights. A carbon emission right means a right to development of countries or communities, on the condition that economic growth and carbon emission have a close relationship.

In order to clarify the relationship between the right to development and the carbon emission right, some basic principles and legal models will be discussed below.

## 2 Basic Principles of the Relationship between Right to Development and Carbon Emission

### 2.1 *Common Principle*

The common principle means that in order to safeguard the common interests approved by all mankind, international society as a whole enjoys the same rights and bears the same duties. Some international treaties have approved this, for instance, the preface to the *Antarctic Treaty* (1959)[11] states "Recognizing that it is in the interest of all mankind that Antarctica shall continue forever to be used exclusively for peaceful purposes ..."; the preface to the *Outer Space Treaty* (1967)[12] states "Recognizing the common interest of all mankind in the progress of the exploration and use of outer space for peaceful purposes ...". According to the "common but differentiated principle" provided by the

---

10   Wang Xigen, *Basic Rights in a Society Ruled by Law: Research of the Legal System Concerning a Right to Development* (Beijing: Chinese People's Public Security University Press, 2002), 61.
11   The *Antarctic Treaty* was signed in Washington on December 1, 1959 by the twelve countries whose scientists had been active in and around Antarctica during the International Geophysical Year (IGY) of 1957–58. It entered into force in 1961 and has since been acceded to by many other nations. http://www.ats.aq/e/ats.htm, accessed June 18, 2016.
12   The *Outer Space Treaty* was opened for signature at Moscow, London, and Washington on January 27, 1967. http://history.nasa.gov/1967treaty.html, accessed June 18, 2016.

UNFCCC, China has emphasized that all mankind lives on the same earth, and to protect the earth is the duty of all mankind. The common principle consists of common approval, common participation and common duties.

### 2.1.1 Natural Communality

The blue earth and green environment belong to all mankind. In 1972, the *Declaration of the United Nations Conference on the Human Environment* stated "The protection and improvement of the human environment is a major issue which affects the well-being of peoples and economic development throughout the world; it is the urgent desire of the peoples of the whole world and the duty of all Governments".[13]

### 2.1.2 Communality of Rights

Climate change restricts the right to development, not everyone has enough rights and abilities to improve their own life. According to the *Charter of the United Nations*,[14] the International Bill of Human Rights and other international legal documents, a right to the environment refers to the fact that everyone should enjoy a free, equal and basic right to life. Articles 3, 4, 10 of the *Kyoto Protocol*[15] mention "common" several times, therefore, both developed and developing countries have the common right to the environment and the common right to development. From another perspective, a carbon emission right can actually be regarded as a right to destroy the environment to a certain degree, specifically, the right to use a certain part of the atmospheric environment capacity. That is to say, everyone enjoys the same right to emit some greenhouse gases to meet the needs of their own survival and development.

---

13   The *Declaration of the United Nations Conference on the Human Environment* was adopted on June 16, 1972 by the United Nations Conference on the Human Environment at the 21st plenary meeting as the first document in the international environmental law to recognize the right to a healthy environment. http://www.unep.org/Documents.Multilingual/Default.asp?documentid=97&articleid=1503, accessed June 18, 2016.

14   The *Charter of the United Nations* (also known as the UN Charter) of 1945 is the foundational treaty of the United Nations, an intergovernmental organization. It was signed at the San Francisco War Memorial and Performing Arts Centre in San Francisco, United States, on June 26, 1945, by 50 of the 51 original member countries. It entered into force on October 24, 1945, after being ratified by the original five permanent members of the Security Council and a majority of the other signatories.

15   The *Kyoto Protocol* is an international treaty which extends the 1992 *United Nations Framework Convention on Climate Change* (UNFCCC) that commits State Parties to reduce greenhouse gas emissions, based on the premise that global warming exists and man-made $CO_2$ emissions have caused it.

### 2.1.3 Rights and Duties Are Equal

It is common knowledge that everyone has the right to a healthy environment, at the same time, everyone has the duty to protect the environment. Rights and duties are equal. A carbon emission right can be regarded as a part of a right to live and a right to development. Just as a carbon emission right also can be regarded as giving an individual or a country the right to destroy the environment to some degree, equally, an individual or a country needs to bear the same duty to protect the environment.

## 2.2 *Difference Principle*

The "common but differentiated principle" was born in the *Declaration of the United Nations Conference on the Human Environment* (1972).[16] According to Principle 7 of the *Rio Declaration on Environment and Development* (1992): "In view of the different contributions to global environmental degradation, States have common but differentiated responsibilities ...".[17] The "common but differentiated principle" applies to all developed countries and developing countries. First, this Principle clearly establishes the common responsibility of States for the protection of the global environment. Secondly, it recognizes broad distinctions between States, whether on the basis of economic development or consumption levels.[18] Therefore, States shall follow the "common but differentiated principle", however different economic developmental levels, emissions per capita per unit GDP, historical cumulative emissions, and possible carbon leakage during international trade should be considered.

---

16   The *Declaration of the United Nations Conference on the Human Environment* was adopted on June 16, 1972 by the United Nations Conference on the Human Environment at the 21st plenary meeting as the first document in the international environmental law to recognize the right to a healthy environment. http://www.unep.org/Documents.Multilingual/Default.asp?documentid=97&articleid=1503, accessed June 18, 2016.

17   Detail information see Principle 7, *Rio Declaration on Environment and Development*, 1992, available at http://www.unep.org/Documents.Multilingual/Default.asp?DocumentID=78&ArticleID=1163. "According to Principle 7: States shall co-operate in a spirit of global partnership to conserve, protect and restore the health and integrity of the earth's ecosystem. In view of the different contributions to global environmental degradation, States have common but differentiated responsibilities. Developed countries acknowledge the responsibility that they bear in the international pursuit of sustainable development in view of the pressures their societies place on the global environment and of the technologies and financial resources they command".

18   Siobhan McInerney-Lankford et al., "Human Rights and Climate Change: A Review of the International Legal Dimensions", *A World Bank Study*, accessed June 18, 2016, http://siteresources.worldbank.org/INTLAWJUSTICE/Resources/HumanRightsAndClimateChange.pdf.

Developed countries shall bear the main duty for emission reduction. The allocation of carbon emission quotas are affected by different factors.

### 2.2.1 Speed Differences

Speed differences for carbon emissions between developed and developing countries should be appropriately considered. Each State, without exception, would have its per capita carbon emission peak during its developmental process. The right to development and emission reduction cannot reach a balance within a short time, and developing countries should not be asked to take on the burden of emission reduction that goes beyond their development stage, responsibility and capabilities.[19] It is undeniable that the current developmental speed of some developing countries is higher than some developed countries; however, most developing countries with a poor foundation began to develop late; current carbon emission levels cannot be used as the only reason to restrict carbon emission and the right to development for them. At present, the main task of developing countries is to ensure the right to development and to reduce poverty.

### 2.2.2 Indicators Differences

It is unfair to control carbon emissions for developed countries and developing countries according to the same indicator. First, indicators can be divided between "survival indicators" and "production indicators" (or "luxury indicators"), the "survival indicator" safeguards the basic survival needs of human beings, and the "production indicator" satisfies the needs of enjoying life. From the perspectives of social welfare and sustainable development, the "survival indicator" is superior to "production indicator". In other words, carbon emissions usually consist of two main parts; one part is the carbon that needs to be emitted to maintain basic life, the other is the carbon emission that is needed for economic development. That is to say, the allocation of carbon emissions needs to consider meeting the requirements of these two parts, especially the first part.[20] To maintain basic life for citizens is the basic responsibility of States. "If all (including future generations) have a basic right to have survival emissions, then the costs associated with achieving those necessary reductions from current emissions must be assigned on the basis of historical luxury

---

19 "China Setting Carbon Emission Targets Is Welcomed by the World", last modified November 27, 2009, accessed December 12, 2012, http://env.people.com.cn/GB/10468245.html.
20 Albert Mumma and David Hodas, "Designing a Global Post—Kyoto Climate Change Protocol that Advances Human Development", *Georgetown International Environmental Law Review* 20 (2007–2008): 635.

and not survival emissions (as the latter cannot serve as the basic for liability) and must grant nations and persons entitlement (to which no future liability attaches) to some basic minimum per capita level of emissions".[21] Essentially, "in examining a nation's historical and current emissions, such a right requires that we distinguish between survival and luxury emissions, ... by this distinction, survival emissions clearly warrant the status of a basic right ..., but luxury emissions do not so clearly qualify for the sort of protection ...".[22] Some carbon emissions in China are survival emissions, for instance, people in the north must use heating in cold winters; however, some developing countries, such as India and Brazil, would not emit the same level of carbon for heating.

Secondly, indicators can be divided into "total indicators" and "per capita indicators". As mentioned above, a carbon emission right is an individual's basic right. In 2011, Friedman Muller, who was working at the German Science and Political Foundation, pointed out that "the only definition for all of us in the world to reach an agreement is the 'per capita indicator', the reason is that everyone has the same right to emit some carbon to our environment".[23] Professor Yoichi Kaya also emphasized the importance of the "per capita indicator".[24]

### 2.2.3 Timing Differences

Before industrialization, the amount of greenhouse gas emissions per capita in each State was similar. After industrialization, the amount of greenhouse gas emissions per capita in different States varied, largely depending on the developmental level of industrialization in the different States.[25] Scientific studies have shown that greenhouse gases stay in the atmospherefor approximately 300 years.[26] From 1850 until 2004, the total amount of carbon dioxide emitted by eight developed countries (Russia, France, the United States, Japan, the United Kingdom, Germany, Italy and Canada) constituted 61% of all carbon

---

21  Steve Vanderheiden, "Climate Change, Environmental Rights, and Emissions Shares", in *Political Theory and Global Climate Change*, ed. Steve Vanderheiden (Massachusetts Institute of Technology), 43–65.
22  Ibid.
23  http://blog.sciencenet.cn/blog-502444-518740.html, accessed January 5, 2013.
24  Yoichi Kaya, "Impact of Carbon Dioxide Emission on GNP Growth: Interpretation of Proposed Scenarios" (paper presented at the Energy and Industry Subgroup, Response Strategies Working Group, IPCC, Paris, 1989).
25  Wang Junfeng, "International Liabilities and International Duties of Developed Countries in Greenhous Gas Reduction", *International Technical and Economic Research* 10, no. 3 (2007).
26  Ji Yushan and Zhao Hongliang, "International Carbon Game in the Context of Safeguarding the Right to Development in China: The Controversy Between Economic Growth and Climate Change", *Economic Theoretical Frontiers and Focus* 6 (2011).

dioxide emitted in the world. However, the total amount of carbon dioxide emitted by five developing countries (China, India, Brazil, South Africa, Mexico) accounted for 13% of all the carbon dioxide emitted in the world.[27] According to the statistics from scientific research led by Ding Zhongli, Vice-Dean at the Chinese Academy of Social Sciences, all developed countries have reached a peak of carbon emissions per capita, for instance the United States reached its peak in 1973; the United Kingdom in 1971; and Germany and France in 1979.[28] More importantly, these States were in a rapid growth period, for instance, from 1901 until 1910, the average growth rate of carbon dioxide emissions per capita in the United States was 5.04%; from 1947 until 1959, the average growth rate in Germany was 9.89%; from 1960 until 1970, the average growth rate in Japan was 11.98%.[29] Obviously, all developed countries were in a rapid growth period of carbon dioxide emissions per capita, the main differences being the growth rates and the time of peak emissions.

Undoubtedly, there are timing differences between developed countries and developing countries. That is to say, with the development of the industrialization, developing countries would follow developed countries in entering into a rapid growth period of carbon dioxide emissions. As mentioned above, existing carbon dioxide into the atmosphere was mainly "contributed" by developed countries. The developing countries are the victims of these "contributions".[30] Thus, developed countries should bear a greater burden for carbon emission reduction. What is more, compared with developing countries, developed countries have greater necessary funding and technology skills to realize carbon emission reduction. They even could benefit from transferring technology skills on how to reduce carbon emissions to developing countries.[31] If we do not consider all these factors, simply asking all States bear the same burden to reduce carbon emissions is unfair.

---

27  Zhang Zhiqiang et al., "Evaluation Index and Quantitative Analysis on Greenhouse Gas", *Geography Journal* 7 (2010).
28  "Academicians Talking About Global Carbon Emission Rights Allocation: Insisting on Fairness and Justice and Safeguarding the Right to Development of China", last modified February 9, 2010, accessed January 4, 2013, Xinhua News: http://news.xinhuanet.com/politics/2010-02/09/content_12960394.htm.
29  Ibid.
30  Richard Tol, "Estimates of the Damage Costs of Climate Change", *Environmental & Resource Economics* 21 (2002): 135.
31  Former chief economist Stern in the World Bank thought that investment in the environmental technology field, such as low carbon, would promote economic growth in the EU.

Some scholars[32] in China have proposed that it is necessary to consider the allocation of carbon emissions per capita from a historical perspective. Based on this, some scholars[33] have emphasized "two convergence principles". The first convergence principle means that in 2100, States' per capita carbon emission should be the same; the second convergence principle refers to the fact that from 1990 (when climate change received world-wide attention) until 2100, the historical cumulative emission in States should be the same.[34] These "two convergence principles" pay greater attention to historical cumulative emissions, and this could help developing countries have more time to realize their right to development.

#### 2.2.4 Duties Differences

As discussed above, carbon emissions should be considered in terms of the "survival indicator", the "production indicator", the "total indicator" and the "per capita indicator". "Indeed, the reason underlying the 'common but differentiated principle' is to 'favor' one group over another taking into account certain disparities that exist in international society".[35] What we should not ignore is that the allocation of carbon emissions should consider population pressure in States. Comparatively speaking, some developing countries' current carbon emissions have risen quickly, however, if we consider population pressure and poverty reduction in these countries, they need to bear a lower burden for reducing carbon emissions. For instance, despite being home to 40% of the planet's population, China and India have together contributed only 9% of the total accumulated anthropogenic greenhouse gases, compared with over 30% by the US (with less than 5% of world population).[36] "By a standard of strict liability (i.e. making no distinction between survival and luxury emissions), the US should bear 30% of total remedial costs, with China and India bearing a combined 9%".[37]

---

32   E.g. Chen Wenying and Wu Zongxin, "Historical Responsibility for Climate Change and Carbon Emissions Quota Allocation", *China Environmental Science* 18 (1998).
33   E.g. Wang Mingyuan, "On Real Right and Right to Development Features of a Carbon Emission Right", last modified May 18, 2011, accessed January 3, 2013, http://www.civillaw.com.cn/article/default.asp?id=53024.
34   Ibid.
35   Sumudu Atapattu, "Climate Change, Equity and Differentiated Responsibilities: Does the Present Climate Regime Favor Developing Countries?" (paper presented at the Conference on "Climate Law in Developing Countries Post-2012: North and South Perspectives", IUCN Law Academy, University of Ottawa, Canada, September 26–28, 2008).
36   See note 21.
37   Ibid.

If we examine differences in duties from the perspective of capacity of States, "capacity in this context means having the financial resources to deal with the climate problem without sacrificing necessities".[38] According to Article 3 of the UNFCCC, the parties to the Convention shall be guided by several principles: the Parties should protect the climate system for the benefit of present and future generations of humankind on the basis of equity and in accordance with their common but differentiated responsibilities and respective capabilities.[39] For instance, it would not be fair or realistic to ask a developing country, where per capita gross national product is less than USD 100, to reduce carbon emissions, for the reason that the primary task in this country would be to feed its own people, the secondary task being meeting its possible international duties and responsibilities. Furthermore, the *Bali Action Plan* (BAP) in the *Bali Road Map*[40] emphasized that in technology development and transfer, nations should consider how to facilitate the transfer of clean and renewable energy technologies from industrialized nations to developing countries.[41] Regarding financial resources and investment, the *Bali Action Plan* states that financial and technical support for capacity-building in the assessment of costs of adaptation in developing countries aid in determining their financial needs.[42] All these pay special attention to capacity-building for developing countries.

Therefore, international cooperation must follow the principle of common but differentiated responsibilities, whereby action demanded of countries is differentiated according to their contribution to causing unsustainable development and their capacity to respond to it. This translates to developed countries taking on greater commitments and supporting poor countries by

---

38  Sivan Kartha et al., "The Bali Roadmap and North-South Cooperation: The Right to Development in a Climate-Constrained World", *European Review of Energy Markets* 3, no. 2 (2009), accessed January 10, 2013, http://www.eeinstitute.org/european-review-of-energy-market/EREM_8-_Article_Kartha-_Kjellen-_Baer_-amp__Athanasiou.pdf.

39  Article 3.1, 1771 UNTS 107, signed on 9 May 1992, entered into force on March 21, 1994, available at http://www.unfccc.de/.

40  The 2007 Bali Climate Change Conference culminated in the adoption of the *Bali Road Map*, which consists of a number of forward-looking decisions that represent the various tracks that are essential to reaching a secure climate future. The *Bali Road Map* includes the *Bali Action Plan*, which charts the course for a new negotiating process designed to tackle climate change, with the aim of completing this by 2009, along with a number of other decisions and resolutions. More information see http://unfccc.int/key_documents/bali_road_map/items/6447.php, accessed June 19, 2016.

41  Ibid.

42  Ibid.

providing assistance such as finance and technology to enable them implement their own sustainable development commitments.[43]

### 2.3  *Principle of Justice*

The principle of justice can also be thought of as the "who is benefited, who is compensator" principle. This principle emphasizes the fact that all human beings in the world enjoy an equal right to use all natural resources on the earth; future generations can enjoy the right to inherit; justice among species; justice among different States and regions.

Benito Muller [44] and Michael Richards [45] have proposed that the principle of justice in developed countries is established on the principle of cost and benefits; however, the principle of justice in developing countries refers to an equal right to use natural resources and an equal opportunity for development. The principle of justice not only refers to judicial interpersonal relationship, justice and species; but also intra- and inter-generational equity, more importantly, it emphasizes both fairness of result and justice during the whole process.[46] The right to development belongs to an individual, a State, a nation; it could be an individual right or a collective right. Based on equality and justice, the right to development combines formal justice and real justice to empower an individual or a State to enjoy real and specific interests.[47] The right to development actually includes the right to have an equal opportunity to development and a right to enjoy benefit-sharing.[48] As discussed above, a carbon emission right is a part of the right to development, it should follow the principle of justice.

From a historical perspective, people living in developed countries enjoy the material wealth created by their predecessors, according to the "polluter-pays principle", the current generation has a duty to pay for their material

---

43  More information see http://rio20.net/wp-content/uploads/2012/02/DRAFT_Reforming-international-susdev-governance-a-rights-based-agenda1.pdf, accessed April 13, 2012.
44  B. Muller, *Equity in Climate Change: The Great Divide* (Oxford: Oxford Institute for Energy Studies, 1989).
45  Michael Richards, *Poverty Reduction, Equity and Climate Change: Global Governance Synergies or Contradictions?* (London: Overseas Development Institute, 2003).
46  Zhuang Guiyang and Chen Ying, *International Climate Regime and China* (Beijing: World Affairs Press, 2005).
47  Wang Xigen and Tu Shaobin, "An Exposition on the Right to Development: From the Perspective of Postmodern Jurisprudence", *Law and Social Development* 6 (2005).
48  Wang Xigen, *Basic Rights in a Society Ruled by Law: Research of the Legal System Concerning a Right to Development* (Beijing: Chinese People's Public Security University Press, 2002), 61.

wealth, that is to reduce carbon dioxide.[49] Compared with a historical perspective, regional unfairness is obvious. One main way to reduce carbon dioxide in developed countries is to transfer secondary industries to developing countries, at the same time carbon emissions may also be transferred from developed countries to developing countries.[50] Nowadays, people living in developed countries enjoy products made by secondary industries. Should people living in developing countries pay for the carbon emissions? For instance, "one big reason for China's fast growth in carbon emissions is that it has become the 'world's factory', or more precisely, the 'factory owned by the world'. Many companies, including some of the most environmentally toxic ones, are subcontractors or direct sub-units of multi-national corporations from the US, Europe and Japan. They are churning out more and cheaper consumer goods for Western consumers, while most of the profits are amassed by multinational corporations that control the brands and distribution channels. In essence, China is a kitchen, while the West is the dining room".[51] It is unfair to ask for people in developing countries pay for the carbon emissions. Therefore, we cannot simply judge carbon emissions from a region or a country, we need to look at where these consumers are. Consumers must bear the main burden to pay for carbon emissions.

## 3       Models for Rule of Law on the Relationship between a Right to Development and Carbon Emission

### 3.1     *Legislative Model*

Legislation is the basis for enforcement; whether the legislation is good or not is directly related to the effect of law enforcement.[52] There are two distinctive points of view on legislation for dealing with the relationship between the right to development and carbon emissions.

---

49   Ji Yushan and Zhao Hongliang, "International Carbon Game in the Context of Safeguarding the Right to Development in China: The Controversy Between Economic Growth and Climate Change", *Economic Theoretical Frontiers and Focus* 6 (2011).

50   Wang Junfeng, "International Liabilities and International Duties of Developed Countries in Greenhous Gas Reduction", *International Technical and Economic Research* 10, no. 3 (2007).

51   Dale Wen Jiajun, "Climate Change and China: Technology, Market and Beyond: A Report for Focus on the Global South", accessed March 20, 2016, http://www.ifg.org/pdf/occasional_paper6-climate_change_and_china.pdf.

52   Gu Anliang, *Legislation* (Beijing: Law Press, 1993), 54.

### 3.1.1 International Law Oriented

The *Kyoto Protocol*[53] built a legal basis for carbon dioxide and carbon emissions trading. The *Copenhagen Accord*[54] endorsed the continuation of the *Kyoto Protocol*. Western developed countries stress that climate change is one of the greatest challenges and emphasize the strong political will to urgently combat climate change in accordance with the principle of common but differentiated responsibilities and respective capabilities. Based on these, developed countries ask that all States in the world bear the burden for reducing carbon emissions. Developing countries, however, insist on the principle of common but differentiated responsibilities and argue that historical developmental levels, per capita carbon emission, and regional unfairness should be taken into account. After 2011, a meaningful Second Commitment Period of the *Kyoto Protocol* began. Yet, without national legal support, it cannot really be put into practice and the related commitment would still be on paper. The realization of a carbon emission right and carbon emissions trading need the support at both international and national levels. Regarding support at national level, domestic law at the national level cannot be ignored.

### 3.1.2 Domestic Law Oriented

Taking the United States as an example, although the United States itself did not join the *Kyoto Protocol*, some states of the United States issued bills on emission reduction and emissions trading, for instance, *No. 32 California Global Warming Solution* issued by California state. Furthermore, on June 26, 2009, the *Waxman-Markey Climate Bill* was promoted by Present Obama and passed through the House of Representatives. This Bill aimed to establish a national emissions trading system to commit the US to a 4% cut in emissions by 2020 from 1990 levels. It is, however, unrealistic that any State, whether a developed or developing country, could extend its domestic law to other States or use its domestic law to solve international issues or disputes.

---

53  The *Kyoto Protocol* is an international treaty which extends the 1992 *United Nations Framework Convention on Climate Change* (UNFCCC) that commits State Parties to reduce greenhouse gas emissions, based on the premise that global warming exists and man-made $CO_2$ emissions have caused it.

54  The *Copenhagen Accord*, drafted by, on the one hand, the United States and on the other, a united position of less-developed countries (China, India, South Africa, and Brazil), is not legally binding and does not commit countries to agree to a binding successor to the *Kyoto Protocol*, whose round ended in 2012. For more information see http://unfccc.int/meetings/copenhagen_dec_2009/items/5262.php, accessed March 20, 2016.

### 3.1.3 Soft Law Oriented

As mentioned above, most international environmental treaties on climate change and carbon emissions have some features of soft law. For instance, the *Kyoto Protocol* is an international agreement linked to the *United Nations Framework Convention on Climate Change*, which commits its Parties by setting internationally binding emission reduction targets. Recognizing that developed countries are principally responsible for the current high levels of greenhouse gases in the atmosphere as a result of more than 150 years of industrial activity, the Protocol places a heavier burden on developed nations under the principle of "common but differentiated responsibilities".[55] According to this principle, developing countries do not have a legally binding duty. The *Copenhagen Accord* addressed the need to establish a comprehensive adaptation program, including international support and emphasized the duty of developing countries, however this is not a legally binding treaty. Thus, how to actively and effectively stimulate all the related countries to put the program into practice is a key issue.

### 3.1.4 Hard Law Oriented

As discussed, *Copenhagen Accord* is merely a political declaration without broad consensus. This shows that global climate change negotiations have become increasingly fragmented; States would resolve climate change and carbon emissions issues on the condition that they get maximum developmental interests. Taking China as an example, in order to reduce carbon emissions and develop a low-carbon economy, China has promulgated some political measures[56] and issued a series of domestic laws and regulations, such as the *Coal Law*, the *Electricity Law*, the *Energy Conservation Law*, the *Law on Renewable Energy* and the *Law on the Promotion of Recycling Economy*. Nevertheless, these political measures, laws and regulations pay more attention to the use of coercive administrative measures and neglect the subjective will of market dealers. Similarly, in order to establish a comprehensive carbon trading quota system, the US Senate proposed a *Low-Carbon Economy Act* in July 2007. It aimed to stimulate enterprises to accelerate technological innovation and to research carbon capture and storage by providing subsidies. In 2004, Germany issued the *Renewable Energy Law* to increase the use of clean energy electricity from

---

55   For more information see http://unfccc.int/kyoto_protocol/items/2830.php, accessed March 12, 2016.

56   For instance, "Measures for Operation and Management of Clean Development Mechanism Projects" was issued in 2005 and amended on August 15, 2011. It laid a good foundation for establishing the carbon trading system.

12% in 2004 to 25%–30% in 2020. The German Government plans to allocate EUR 700 million per year for the construction of energy-saving systems in existing public buildings. It is obvious that developed countries mainly depend on hard law to lead all parties to actively participate in carbon emission reduction.

3.1.5     Following the Two Basic Principles

In order to effectively protect the right to development of all countries in the world, we need a new perspective to examine State responsibilities and to build an international order. The ultimate goal is to maximize the benefits for all mankind, to optimize the use of the earth's resources and to realize the fairness of State responsibilities. We shall insist on (1) interaction between international law and domestic law, oriented to domestic law; (2) unification of soft law and hard law, oriented to hard law.

(1) Interaction between international law and domestic law, oriented to domestic law

In the current context, developed countries, with the largest accumulated amount of carbon emissions, are still in charge of making rules concerning carbon trading and carbon tax systems. The realization of international law largely depends upon the implementation of domestic law. Domestic law provides strong legal support for the international convention on climate change, to some degree it also reserves the right to choose, the right to explain and the right to flexibly apply according to the current domestic situation. Article 4.7 of the *United Nations Framework Convention on Climate Change* states that "The extent to which developing country Parties will effectively implement their commitments under the Convention will depend on the effective implementation by the developed country Parties of their commitments under the Convention related to financial resources and transfer of technology and will take fully into account that economic and social development and poverty eradication are the first and overriding priorities of the developing country Parties".

It is necessary for each State to establish a solid legal basis and legal system to clarify each party's rights and duties as soon as possible, based on the common principles, the principle of differentiation and the principle of fairness. There is also a need for each State to gradually regulate its domestic system for a low carbon economy and improve the carbon emissions trading market. As for developing countries, they must have more discourse at the international level. According to the constraints of international law treaties, based on its own actual situation, each State must establish a practical system to respond to carbon emissions. On June 4, 2007, the Chinese Government formulated the *China National Climate Change Program*, which requires all Parties to develop, implement, publish and regularly update national programs for responding to climate change. The revised *Law of the People's Republic of China on Energy Conservation*, which came into force on April 1, 2008, was the first and major law on carbon emissions in China. Subsequently, on June 30, 2008, the Provincial Response Plan for Climate Change project was officially launched in Beijing.[57] It is noted that China's *Twelfth Five-Year Plan to Control Greenhouse Gas Emissions* and the *Interim Measures on Carbon Emissions Trading* had been issued, and that these could make a great contribution to the establishment of a national carbon emissions trading market.

In addition, climate change is a global issue, which cannot merely be resolved by a country or a legislative agency. To resolve the issues of climate change largely relies on the interaction between international law and domestic law, oriented to domestic law. The rational use of international law can balance various disputes caused by carbon emissions. For instance, the widely internationally adopted "common but differentiated responsibilities" principle can better balance the various demands of different countries in international negotiations on climate change and carbon allocation. In order to reduce carbon emissions, developing countries had to learn or buy new technologies for carbon emission reduction from developed countries. Nonetheless, almost all international cooperation is achieved by different types of international treaties. Once international disputes arise, international law would play a major role in peacefully resolving disputes and clarifying the relevant rights and duties for all countries. The ultimate implementation of international law, however, largely depends on the formulation and implementation of domestic law.

(2) Unification with soft law and hard law, oriented to hard law

Regarding the relationship between the right to development and the carbon emission right, we shall unify soft law and hard law, oriented to hard law, "on the one hand, in order to take into account the interests of a wide range of community members, hard law sometimes has to sacrifice the interests of a small number of community members; on the other hand, with a purpose of maintaining the stability of legal rules, hard law has to give up the possible fairness and justice in some certain condition".[58] As discussed, hard law has worldwide applicability, and climate change is a global issue with great differences in different regions. This means that it is difficult for hard law to accurately

---

57 Wang Youling, "China Formally Launched the Provincial Climate Change Program", last modified June 30, 2008, accessed January 15, 2013, Xinhua Net: http://news.xinhuanet.com/newscenter/2008-06/30/content_8466654.htm.
58 Jiang Mingan, "Soft Law and Some Issues in Soft Law", *China Legal Science* 2 (2006).

judge real situations in different regions, which may result in regional inequity. Nevertheless, comparatively speaking, soft law is more flexible in resolving difficulties to achieve real and concrete justice. The *United Nations Framework Convention on Climate Change* signed in 1992, reached two consensuses: first, most global greenhouse gas comes from developed countries, but global greenhouse gas emissions from developing countries would gradually increase. Secondly, the fairness principle and the "common but differentiate responsibilities" principle are keys to resolving this problem between developed and developing countries. Based on these consensuses, the Convention requires developed countries to take the lead in reducing emissions, while there is no clear requirement for developing countries. This declaratory international treaty does not clearly clarify rights and duties, which is often regarded as a "soft law". Once this "soft law" is adopted, however, a possible method and consultation mechanism would be made.

Notably, some Regulations, Directives and Decisions with the purpose of promoting energy conservation and emission reduction in the EU environmental laws are basically policy-oriented legislation. On the one hand, these Regulations, Directives and Decisions can meet the various requirements of countries in the EU; on the other hand, they are more flexible in efficiently resolving specific environmental issues. Therefore, in order to safeguard the equal carbon emission interests of each State and realize the equal right to development in developing countries, soft law and hard law are indispensable. Hard law plays a major role in strictly clarifying individual responsibilities, social responsibilities and States' responsibilities.

### 3.2  *Responsibility Model*

The legal responsibility system of the right to development can be divided into:

(1) States' responsibility: Article 3.1 of the *Declaration on the Right to Development* states that "States have the primary responsibility for the creation of national and international conditions favorable to the realization of the right to development".[59] Article 8 states that "States should undertake, at the national level, all necessary measures for the realization of the right to development and shall ensure, inter alia, equality of opportunity for all in their access to basic resources, education, health services, food, housing, employment and the fair distribution of income. Effective measures should be undertaken to ensure that women have an active role in the development process.

---

59  The *Declaration on the Right to Development*, A/RES/41/128, December 4, 1986, accessed May 15, 2013, http://www.un.org/documents/ga/res/41/a41r128.htm.

Appropriate economic and social reforms should be carried out with a view to eradiating all social injustices".[60]

(2) International responsibility: "Essentially, safeguarding the right to development must ensure that States are the actors in the international community and establish a national protection system for the right to development".[61]

The requirements of the carbon emission right typically reflect the requirements of the right to development for States' responsibility (taking all necessary measures to protect people's basic needs for survival and production) and international responsibility (undertaking the responsibilities for climate change and international environmental pollution). From the vertical perspective, the responsibility model of carbon emission can be divided into: (1) producers' complete responsibility; (2) consumers' complete responsibility; (3) joint responsibility.

### 3.2.1    Producers' Complete Responsibility

According to the principle of "who benefits, who bears", those who directly benefit from production activities should bear the responsibility for carbon emissions. There is no doubt that producers are the main drivers of economic development, at the same time they are the main culprits of environmental pollution and ecological damage. Whether for survival or production, all carbon emissions are from industrial production. For instance, producers should take responsibility for carbon emissions during the phase of energy harvesting and consumption, production processing and transportation. In order to achieve sustainable use of natural resources, it is necessary for producers to minimize the consumption of natural resources and the emission of exhaust gases.

### 3.2.2    Consumers' Complete Responsibility

From the perspective of product consumption, since consumers' demands stimulate production, consumers should be responsible for resource consumption and environmental pollution. Products consumed by human beings and consumer behavior have a close relationship with the ecological environment. Similarly, carbon emissions have a close relationship with the ecological environment. Some scholars have examined carbon emissions from international trade processes, "estimating 7%–14% carbon emission in 1997–2003 in

---

60  Ibid.
61  Wang Xigen, *Basic Rights in a Society Ruled by Law: Research of the Legal System Concerning a Right to Development* (Beijing: Chinese People's Public Security University Press, 2002), 263.

China resulting from the exports to the US".[62] From this perspective, consumers receive the largest benefits, therefore consumers should bear the primary responsibility for carbon emissions.

### 3.2.3 Joint Responsibility

Joint responsibility means that producers and consumers at all stages should share responsibility for environmental impacts, and they would have the same interests. This proposes that "(1) every stage in the supply chain would be influenced by producers and consumers. All participants in the supply chain need to have an opportunity to voice their opinions; (2) the capture of carbon footprint and the clarification of responsibility for carbon emissions refers to the entire process of production, this stimulates the conversation between producers and consumers".[63] This meets the requirements of the Ten-year Framework of the Plan of Sustainable Consumption and Production Patterns and Goal 12 of *Transforming Our World: The Agenda for Sustainable Development in 2030*:[64] adopting sustainable consumption and production patterns. These requirements may be realized at the national level, however it lacks compulsion and an independent third party to monitor these requirements at the international level. What is more, how to bridge the gap between the national level and the international level is a key question. This is the main difficulty in really promoting international cooperation. As for the relationship between the right to development and carbon emissions, a right to development in developing countries means that residents in developing countries could consume more carbon-containing products to meet the increasing requirements of welfare and development, but without paying an additional cost in the coming period. It is necessary for developed countries to reduce carbon emissions by improving technological skills. Joint responsibility calls for consumers and producers at all stages in both developing and developed countries to share the responsibility, this takes efficiency and fairness into account.

### 3.3 *Judicial Relief Model*

As for a model for the rule of law on the relationship between the right to development and carbon emissions, only using the legislative model and the

---

62  B. Shui and R.C. Harriss, "The Role of $CO_2$ Embodiment in US-China Trade", *Energy Policy* 34 (2006): 4063–4068.
63  Qin Changcai and Huang Zexiang, "Theory and Practice on the Liability Mode of Carbon Emission", *Finance & Economics* 7 (2012): 118–124.
64  *Transforming Our World: The Agenda for Sustainable Development in 2030*, last modified January 13, 2016, accessed June 23, 2016, http://www.fmprc.gov.cn/web/ziliao_674904/zt_674979/dnzt_674981/xzxzt/xpjdmgjxgsfw_684149/zl/t1331382.shtml.

responsibility model cannot make any effective and practical sense without the judicial relief model. In other words, if there is any infringement to the right to development, judicial relief is indispensable. The judicial relief model contains three levels: an international, a regional and a domestic level.

### 3.3.1 International Relief

The *International Covenant on Civil and Political Rights*, adopted in 1966, points out that citizens' civil and political rights can be sued,[65] while the implementation mechanism of the *International Covenant on Economic, Social and Cultural Rights* only includes a national reporting system without any appeals system. Although the UN has established a judicial relief system for the right to development, there is still a need to clarify how to put the judicial relief system into practice at an international level and a national level. "The infringement of a right to development is mainly because of nonfeasance of the States, for instance, the relevant countries ignore the requirements of the international laws on a right to development".[66] In order to establish a new global international political and economic order, the international community has established some supranational political organizations, economic alliances and non-governmental organizations, such as the EU and the WTO. There is, however, no independent and authoritative organization to monitor the fair and efficient distribution of carbon emissions. This is a key issue that needs to be resolved at the international level.

### 3.3.2 Regional Relief

As discussed above, although there is no independent and authoritative organization to monitor the fair and efficient distribution of carbon emissions at the international level, a comparatively satisfactory legal mechanism has been formed at the regional level. For instance, the Council of the EU formally adopted Directive 2008/101/EC to reduce emissions from the aviation industry to the EU ETS on December 20, 2006. The Directive applies to all flights operated within the EU from January 1, 2012. This means that all flights operated within the EU from more than 2,000 airlines must pay an additional carbon tax. Obviously, this has violated the *Chicago Convention* and the *United Nations Convention on the Law of the Sea*; this also violated the "common but

---

65　See Part IV Article 28 of the *International Covenant on Civil and Political Rights*, adopted and opened for signature, ratification and accession by General Assembly Resolution 2200A (XXI) of December 16, 1966, entry into force on March 23, 1976.
66　Wang Xigen, "Legal Remedy System for the Right to Development", *Modern Law Science* 6 (2007): 14.

differentiated responsibilities" principle of the *United Nations Framework Convention on Climate Change* and the *Kyoto Protocol*.

The main object of the current controversy on international aviation is whether we can predict that the international shipping carbon emission will also be included in the similar dispute? How could developing countries protect their right to development and their own interests under the principle of "common but differentiated responsibilities" in this context? A balanced judicial relief system will help a lot.

### 3.3.3   Domestic Relief

To some degree, the carbon emission right can be regarded as countries' or industries' right to destroy the environment within certain limitations to meet their developmental requirements. "A right to development means that a citizen is able to ask for this right from the State, and the State and the relevant authorities have the responsibility to guarantee citizens' right to development".[67] If the right to development is guaranteed by the domestic mandatory legal norms, a citizen is able to directly or indirectly access the domestic legal system for judicial judgements, as in *Massachusetts v. EPA*.[68] Having lost some land due to global warming, the plaintiff required the US Environmental Protection Agency to assume the obligation to set new standards for car manufacturers to regulate the carbon emissions from new cars. This "milestone" court decision shows citizens have the right to ask governments to fulfill their responsibilities by a domestic relief system if the right to development is guaranteed by domestic law.

"More recently a form of property right in carbon dioxide and other greenhouse gases has been developed under the emissions trading scheme (ETS) pursuant to the 2008 *Climate Change Response (Emissions Trading) Amendment Act*, and formulized 'customary rights orders' were created under the 2004 *Foreshore and Seabed Act*".[69] Companies attempting to generate more carbon emissions than they are allowed by their official permit could buy emission permits from other relevant parties through commercial transactions. At the same time, companies with carbon emission permits than they actually need can sell their extra permits. Thus, the relevant civil litigation and its relief system are particularly important.

---

67   Ibid.
68   See *Massachusetts v. EPA*, 127 S Ct 1438 (2007).
69   David Grinlinton and Prue Taylor, eds., *Property Rights and Sustainability—the Evolution of Property Rights to Meet Ecological Challenges* (Leiden: Martinus Nijhoff Publishers, 2011), 281.

## 4 Conclusion

Both developed and developing countries must survive and develop on the earth. With the failure of the *Kyoto Protocol* in 2012, the "post-Kyoto Protocol" period arrived. The *Paris Agreement* lays a solid foundation for the formulation of a global climate governance pattern after 2020. This Agreement embodies the principle of "common but differentiated responsibilities", formulating a ratcheting lock-in mechanism and addressing all countries (including European countries and the United States) to follow "measurement, reporting and verification" system. This means that developing countries have more flexibility in sharing the relevant responsibilities according to their capacities. Nevertheless, we shall clearly be aware that the global climate issue cannot be resolved just because of this Agreement. "Climate change is a problem ... perhaps humankind's first problem of this kind, where poor and wealthy begin to understand that we all share a small planet and that we are all interdependent".[70] Compared with developing countries, which are restricted by historical development, inequality of resources, uneven distribution of per capita resources and other factors, developed countries have more capacity to overcome the challenges of climate change. "As nicely as a right to development may accord with one's innate sense of justice ..."[71] In this context, it is particularly important and urgent to examine the carbon emission right from the perspective of a right to development and to seek some possible feasible legal mechanisms for developing countries to meet the challenge of climate change. Safeguarding national interests, promoting healthy and orderly economic development, guaranteeing citizens enjoy a greater right to development are the key issues in China.

---

70   Sivan Kartha et al., "The Bali Roadmap and North-South Cooperation: The Right to Development in a Climate-Constrained World", *European Review of Energy Markets* 3, no. 2 (2009).
71   Ibid.

# PART 3

*Empirical Analysis*

CHAPTER 9

# Guidance from the Ground up: Lessons from South Asia for Realizing the Sustainable Development Goals

*Sumudu Atapattu\* and Shyami Puvimanasinghe\*\**

1   **Introduction**

The year 2015 was historic for environmental protection as well as for the future of global development. The international community adopted the 2030 Agenda and Sustainable Development Goals (SDGs)[1] and the Paris Agreement on Climate Change.[2] The concept of sustainable development has taken a long and winding road culminating in the adoption of the SDGs. From a rather rocky start with the adoption of the report "Our Common Future",[3] sustainable development seems to have consolidated its position as a policy goal at both national and international levels and its influence on international environmental law within a short span of time is far-reaching with some even claiming the emergence of a new branch of international law called "International Sustainable Development Law".[4] Despite these remarkable developments, sustainable development and sustainability have remained rather illusive

---

\*   Sumudu Atapattu, Director of Research Centers and International Programs at University of Wisconsin Law School; Lead Counsel for Human Rights, Center for International Sustainable Development Law, Montreal; affiliated faculty, Raoul Wallenberg Institute for Human Rights, Sweden; and formerly, Senior Lecturer, Faculty of Law, University of Colombo, Sri Lanka.
\*\*  Shyami Puvimanasinghe, Human Rights Officer, Office of the United Nations High Commissioner for Human Rights; Senior Research Fellow, Center for International Sustainable Development Law; and formerly, Senior Lecturer, Faculty of Law, University of Colombo, Sri Lanka (The views expressed herein are those of the author and do not necessarily reflect the views of the United Nations).

1   *Transforming Our World: The 2030 Agenda for Sustainable Development*, UN General Assembly, A/RES/70/1, October 21, 2015, available at http://www.un.org/ga/search/view_doc.asp?symbol=A/RES/70/1&Lang=E.
2   Paris Agreement adopted at 21st Conference of Parties (2015), UNFCCC, available at https://unfccc.int/files/meetings/ paris _nov 2015/application/pdf/paris_agreement_english_.pdf.
3   "Our Common Future", Report of the World Commission on Environment and Development (Oxford University Press, 1987).
4   Marie-Claire Cordonier Segger and Ashfaq Khalfan, *Sustainable Development Law: Principles, Practices & Prospects* (Oxford, 2004). The *Rio Declaration on Environment and Development*

concepts—hard to define and hard to achieve. The SDGs in this respect are a welcome and long-overdue development. They provide us with measurable goals and targets, and indicators are also in the making. From the Brundtland report in 1987[5] to the Rio Declaration in 1992[6] and from the *Johannesburg Declaration on Sustainable Development*[7] that added a third pillar to sustainable development[8] in 2002 to the adoption of the SDGs in 2015, the global community took close to three decades to flesh out the parameters of sustainable development.

During this period, judiciaries in several regions also engaged in a similar exercise defining sustainable development and tools to achieve it. In the South Asian region, a particularly vibrant body of jurisprudence evolved in the intervening years, catalyzed by public interest litigation in cases combining human rights, environmental and developmental issues. In this chapter, we propose to discuss selected jurisprudence of the apex courts in South Asia (especially India, Pakistan, Nepal, Bangladesh and Sri Lanka, with a particular focus on Sri Lanka) in relation to sustainable development and what guidance, if any, their jurisprudence offers to the achievement of the SDGs. We will discuss seminal decisions of these judiciaries from *Subhash Kumar v. State of Bihar*[9] in India to *Tikiri Banda Bulankulama v. Secretary, Ministry of Industrial Development*[10] in Sri Lanka. We will discuss the strategies used by both lawyers and judges and what the robust jurisprudence from this region offers to the rest of the world. We will illustrate how public interest law suits moved by civil society action combined with innovation by the legal profession, and a certain degree of judicial activism, can bring about progressive development in the integration of human rights, environment and development issues on the ground, and thereby realize the wisdom of sustainable development—integrating its economic, environmental and social pillars.

---

(1992) calls upon states to cooperate, inter alia, "in the further development of international Law in the field of sustainable development" (Principle 27).

5   "Our Common Future", Report of the World Commission on Environment and Development (Oxford University Press, 1987).

6   Adopted at the United Nations Conference on Environment and Development (1992), available at http://www.un.org/documents/ga/conf151/aconf15126-1annex1.htm.

7   *Johannesburg Declaration on Sustainable Development*, A/CONF.199/20 (2002), available at http://www.un-documents.net/jburgdec.htm.

8   The social pillar was added as a third pillar influenced by the *Copenhagen Declaration on Social Development*, A/CONF.166/9 (1995), available at http://www.un-documents.net/cope-dec.htm.

9   See discussion *infra*.

10  See discussion *infra*.

This chapter is in six parts. Part 2 traces the emergence of sustainable development as a policy goal from the Stockholm *Declaration of the United Nations Conference on the Human Environment* to the SDGS. Part 3 will then elaborate on the social pillar of sustainable development and the evolution of sustainable development from a rather vague concept that emerged from the Brundtland report to a much more robust umbrella concept embodying both substantive and procedural components. In Part 4, we will present some of the jurisprudence developed by the superior courts in South Asia and discuss some seminal cases from the region. We will then consider strategies used, public interest litigation and the integration of human rights, environmental protection and economic development in South Asia in Part 5. We will conclude with some observations and draw on some lessons learned in Part 6.

## 2 Emergence of Sustainable Development: From Stockholm to the SDGS

The Stockholm *Declaration of the United Nations Conference on the Human Environment*[11] that laid the foundation for international environmental law also planted the seeds of sustainable development. Although the Declaration itself makes no specific reference to the term, several provisions refer to the need to balance economic development with environmental protection[12] and the need for integrated and rational planning.[13] The Stockholm Conference and the Declaration were catalysts for a number of efforts and programs on environmental law. The United Nations Environment Program was established in 1973 and many countries adopted environmental laws and established environmental institutions. However, not everything was proceeding smoothly. Developing countries, on the one hand, many of them newly independent, were keen on developing their economies, addressing poverty and raising the living standards of their people. Developed countries, on the other hand, wanted to address the negative consequences of economic development that they were experiencing in the form of environmental pollution. These countries developed without paying any heed to the environment, and developing countries saw this as a ploy to stifle their economic development and as

---

11  *Declaration of the United Nations Conference on the Human Environment* (1972), available at http://www.un-documents.net/unchedec.htm.
12  Ibid., Principle 4.
13  Ibid., Principles 13 and 14.

another form of colonization.[14] They also felt that it was unfair to expect them to forego their development efforts in order to protect the environment for rich countries. This polarization between developed and developing countries after the Stockholm Conference that stifled action relating to environmental protection at the international level was the main reason why the UN General Assembly established the World Commission on Environment and Development (WCED) in 1983. The mandate given to the Commission by the General Assembly was, inter alia, to find ways to reconcile economic development with environmental protection.[15] The WCED issued its report entitled "Our Common Future" in 1987 and proposed sustainable development as a way to reconcile economic development with environmental protection. In a much-quoted paragraph that became both celebrated and critiqued, the WCED defined sustainable development as "development that meets the needs of the present without compromising the ability of future generations to meet their needs".[16] This seemed to have placated both developing and developed countries alike and some scholars contend that it has achieved universal acceptance partly because of its "brilliant ambiguity".[17]

Without doubt, the WCED report had a huge impact on the Rio Conference on Environment and Development, held 20 years after the Stockholm Conference. Instead of trying to refine the definition formulated by the WCED, the Rio Declaration elaborated on its components and identified tools to achieve sustainable development. It also identified linkages with other issues such as international peace and security[18] as well as vulnerable groups.[19] While scholars differ on the exact components, the substantive components comprise the following: the principle of integration, inter- and intra-generational equity principle, sustainable use of natural resources and the right to development.[20]

---

14     See Sumudu Atapattu and Carmen Gonzalez, "The North-South Divide in International Law: Framing the Issues", in *International Environmental Law and the Global South*, eds. Shawkat Alam, Sumudu Atapattu, Carmen Gonzalez and Jona Razzaque (CUP, 2015), p. 1 at 5 (hereinafter Alam et al.).

15     "Our Common Future", p. viii.

16     Ibid., 43.

17     David Hunter, James Salzman and Durwood Zaelke, *International Environmental Law and Policy* (5th ed., 2015, Foundation Press), 169 (hereinafter, Hunter et al.).

18     The Rio Declaration in 1992, Principles 24 and 25.

19     Ibid., Principles 20 (women), 21 (youth), 22 (indigenous peoples) and 23 (people under oppression, domination and occupation).

20     This section draws from author Sumudu Atapattu's essay "Paris Agreement and Human Rights: Is Sustainable Development the 'New Human Right'?", *Journal of Human Rights and Environment* 9:1 (2018), 68; See Hunter et al., *International Environmental Law and Policy*, 169.

The procedural component comprises obligations vis-à-vis other states (co-operation, exchange of information, notification of and providing assistance during emergencies, and negotiation in good faith) and those vis-à-vis citizens (provision of information, public participation and access to remedies). The procedural obligations vis-à-vis citizens overlap with international human rights law and are now entrenched in international environmental law.[21] Of the substantive components, the principle of integration, sustainable use of natural resources, and the inter- and intra-generational equity principle are also accepted principles. While the status of the right to development[22] has been rather controversial and support for it is divided along North–South lines,[23] the Rio Declaration recognizes unequivocally, that "The right to development should be fulfilled so as to meet equitably the developmental and environmental needs of present and future generations".[24] Birnie et al. point out that none of these components is new "but the Rio Declaration brings them together in a more systematic form than hitherto"[25] and the procedural components have never before secured such "widespread support" from the international community.[26]

Despite the rather ambiguous nature of sustainable development and the criticisms against it,[27] it is clear that most of the components that comprise

---

21  These are referred to as "access rights" or three pillars of environmental democracy, see Hunter et al., *International Environmental Law and Policy*, 1357.
22  *Declaration on the Right to Development* (1986), available at http://www.un.org/documents/ga/res/41/a41r128.htm.
23  See Sumudu Atapattu and Michelle Toering Sanders, "Development, Environment, and Globalization: Perspectives from North and South. The Dichotomy Between Developed and Developing Countries", Foreword, *McGill International Journal of Sustainable Development Law and Policy* 2:2 (2006): 83.
24  Principle 3, Rio Declaration and Article 11, 1993 *Vienna Declaration and Programme of Action* (A/CONF.157/24, Part I).
25  See Patricia Birnie, Alan Boyle and Catherine Redgwell, *International Law & the Environment* (3rd ed., 2009), 116 (hereinafter, Birnie et al.).
26  Ibid.
27  Sustainable development has attracted attention, both positive and negative. See generally, Michael Redclift and Delyse Springett eds., *Routledge International Handbook of Sustainable Development* (Routledge, 2015); Alan Boyle and David Freestone eds., *International Law and Sustainable Development* (Oxford University Press, 1999); FAO, *Law and Sustainable Development Since Rio* (2002); Richard Revesz, Philippe Sands and Richard Stewart eds., *Environmental Law, the Economy and Sustainable Development* (Cambridge University Press, 2000); Christina Voigt, *Sustainable Development as a Principle of International Law* (Martinus Nijhoff, 2008); European Commission, *The Law of Sustainable Development: General Principles* (2000); Ileana Porras, *The Rio Declaration: A New Basis for International Cooperation in Greening International Law* (Philippe Sands, ed., New Press, 1994), 20; Sumudu Atapattu, *Emerging Principles of International Environmental Law* (Transnational, 2006), Chapter 2.

the umbrella impose coherent obligations on states.[28] As Birnie et al. point out: "the most potentially far-reaching aspect of sustainable development is that for the first time it makes a state's management of its own domestic environment a matter of international concern in a systematic way".[29] Moreover, it has potential implications for the future development of other areas of law such as international human rights law.[30] Nonetheless, many uncertainties remain which could have a direct bearing on whether sustainable development can be considered a legal principle.[31] If it is intended to hold states accountable for achieving sustainability at the international and national level, then we need clear criteria to measure such compliance.[32]

Perhaps the SDGs can fill this void.[33] As noted by Birnie et al.:

> Although it is possible to identify the main elements of the concept of sustainable development, it is far from certain what their specific normative implications are, or indeed, how they relate to each other, or to human rights law and international economic law ... international law cannot be applied in a fragmented way, and sustainable development has no more claim to priority than any other element.[34]

Other scholars have questioned the connection between norms arising in different areas of international law that sustainable development raises, such as environmental, economic and social/human rights fields.[35] Is there a hierarchy? Achieving coherence is necessary but the challenge has been how to balance competing norms. Some scholars substitute the social pillar with

---

28   See Birnie et al., *International Law & the Environment*, 124.
29   Ibid.
30   Ibid., 125.
31   See Vaughn Lowe, "Sustainable Development and Unsustainable Arguments", in *International Law and Sustainable Development: Past Achievements and Future Challenges*, eds. Alan Boyle and David Freestone (Oxford University Press, 1999), 19, and Philippe Sands, *Principles of International Environmental Law* (2nd ed., Cambridge University Press, 2003), 252.
32   Birnie et al., *International Law & the Environment*, 125.
33   *Transforming Our World: The 2030 Agenda for Sustainable Development* (2015), UN General Assembly, A/RES/70/1, October 21, 2015, available at http://www.un.org/ga/search/view_doc.asp?symbol=A/RES/70/1&Lang=E.
34   Birnie et al., *International Law & the Environment*, 125.
35   Philippe Sands, "Sustainable Development: Treaty, Custom and the Cross-fertilization of International Law", in *International Law and Sustainable Development*, eds. Alan Boyle and David Freestone (Oxford University Press, 1999), 39.

international human rights law and consider that of the three pillars, international environmental law forms the central pillar but sustainable development needs support from the other two pillars—international human rights law and international economic law.[36] Yet others consider international sustainable development law to be "at the intersection of three principal fields of international law, each of which contribute to sustainable development"[37]—international economic law (comprising international trade law, international investment law and international competition law), international social law (comprising international human rights law, international humanitarian law, international labor law and other international social development agreements) and international environmental law.[38] This, however, is a very wide interpretation of international sustainable development law.

The *New Delhi Declaration of Principles of International Law Relating to Sustainable Development*[39] adopted by the International Law Association in 2002 further elaborates on sustainable development. It notes that the realization of economic, social, cultural, civil and political rights and people's rights "is central to the pursuance of sustainable development".[40] It further provides that sustainable development involves a comprehensive and integrated approach to economic, social and political processes, thus endorsing and expanding on the principle of integration discussed above. It identifies seven principles as forming part of sustainable development: (a) the duty of states to ensure sustainable use of natural resources; (b) the principle of equity and the eradication of poverty; (c) the principle of common but differentiated responsibilities; (d) the principle of the precautionary approach to human health, natural resources and ecosystems; (e) the principle of public participation and access to information and justice; (f) the principle of good governance; and (g) the principle of integration and interrelationship, in particular in relation to human rights and social, economic and environmental objectives.[41] The precautionary

---

36   Dominic McGoldrick, "Sustainable Development and Human Rights: An Integrated Conception", *International and Comparative Law Quarterly* 45 (1996): 796–797. Cf. Neil Dawe and Kenneth Ryan, "The Faulty Three-Legged-Stool Model of Sustainable Development", *Conservation Biology* 17 (2003): 1458, who critique the depiction of sustainable development as a three-legged stool.
37   Marie-Claire Cordonier Segger and Ashfaq Khalfan, *Sustainable Development Law: Principles, Practices & Prospects* (Oxford University Press, 2004), 51.
38   Ibid., Chapter 4.
39   Resolution 3/2002, *New Delhi Declaration of Principles of International Law Relating to Sustainable Development*, adopted by the International Law Association in 2002 (Hereinafter ILA Declaration), available at http://cisdl.org/tribunals/pdf/NewDelhiDeclaration.pdf.
40   Ibid., Preamble, ILA Declaration.
41   Ibid.

principle and the common but differentiated responsibility principle as well as good governance can be considered as tools necessary to achieve sustainable development, rather than components of it. These principles comprise both substantive and procedural elements as discussed earlier.

The ILA Declaration affirmed that sustainable development is for all states, not just for developing countries:

> Emphasizing that sustainable development is a matter of common concern both to developing and industrialized countries and that, as such, it should be integrated into all relevant fields of policy in order to realize the goals of environmental protection, development and respect for human rights, emphasizing the critical relevance of gender dimension in all these areas and recognizing the need to ensure practical and effective implementation.[42]

By endorsing that sustainable development is a common concern,[43] the ILA Declaration recognized sustainable development as an *erga omnes* obligation as unsustainable developmental practices by one country can have implications for the international community as issues such as climate change and ozone depletion have shown us. Moreover, it recognized that the principle of integration "reflects the interdependence of social, economic, financial, environmental and human rights aspects of principles and rules of international law relating to sustainable development as well as of the interdependence of the needs of current and future generations of humankind".[44] This suggests that all aspects of sustainable development should be given equal weight including the rights of future generations.

As noted before, both inter- and intra-generational equity form part of sustainable development. While the intra-generational equity principle applies to the economic and social pillar, the inter-generational equity principle applies to the environmental pillar. All but five of the SDGs[45] relate to the social pillar[46] combined with the economic pillar, while SDG 7 addresses energy and Goals 12–15 pertain to the environment combined with the economic pillar.

---

42  Ibid.
43  See Friedrich Soltau, "Common Concern of Humankind", in *The Oxford Handbook of International Climate Change Law*, "Our Common Future", 202.
44  ILA Declaration, Principle 7.1.
45  *Transforming Our World: The 2030 Agenda for Sustainable Development*.
46  These include ending poverty, ending hunger, healthy lives, quality education, gender equality, clean water and sanitation, access to modern energy, decent work, reducing inequality, sustainable cities, promoting access to justice and peaceful inclusive societies.

## 3   From Two to Three Pillars: Economic, Environmental and Social

The binary nature of sustainable development changed at the World Summit for Social Development when a third pillar was added to sustainable development:[47]

> We are deeply convinced that economic development, social development and environmental protection are interdependent and mutually reinforcing components of sustainable development, which is the framework for our efforts to achieve a higher quality of life for all people. Equitable social development that recognizes empowering of the poor to utilize environmental resources sustainably is a necessary foundation for sustainable development. We also recognize that broad-based and sustained economic growth in the context of sustainable development is necessary to sustain social development and social justice.

This Declaration clearly influenced the *Johannesburg Declaration on Sustainable Development* in 2002[48] at which the world leaders affirmed: "we assume a collective responsibility to advance and strengthen the interdependent and mutually reinforcing pillars of sustainable development—economic development, social development and environmental protection—at the local, national, regional and global levels".[49] While the Copenhagen Summit added the social pillar to sustainable development, Agenda 21 adopted at UNCED recognized the importance of social development. It recognized the need to combat poverty, address consumption patterns, protect health and promote sustainable human settlements, within the social and economic dimensions of sustainable development.[50]

Thus, sustainable development now comprises three pillars and requires balancing them all. If balancing two pillars was already difficult, balancing three pillars has become quite a challenge for states. But what does social development mean? This third pillar remains under-theorized[51] but seems to encompass basic needs of people in terms of access to food, water, healthcare,

---

47   *Copenhagen Declaration on Social Development*, A/CONF.166/9 (1995), available at http://www.un-documents.net/cope-dec.htm.
48   *Johannesburg Declaration on Sustainable Development.*
49   Ibid., paragraph 5.
50   Earth Summit Agenda 21, United Nations Programme of Action from Rio (1992), available at https://sustainabledevelopment.un.org/content/documents/Agenda21.pdf.
51   Carmen Gonzalez, "Environmental Justice, Human Rights and the Global South", *Santa Clara Journal of International Law* 13 (2015): 151.

shelter and education.[52] The social pillar intersects with human rights and many of the basic needs are expressed in rights language.[53] The Copenhagen Declaration sheds some light on these questions.

According to the Copenhagen Declaration, social development and social justice cannot be achieved in the absence of respect for all human rights and fundamental freedoms. This reflects the intertwined relationship between social justice, human rights and social development. The Declaration further notes that poverty, unemployment and social exclusion represent profound social problems that affect every country.[54] It endorses the inter-generational equity principle and incorporates Principle 1 of the Rio Declaration almost verbatim.[55]

The commitments made by states are insightful and shed light on the social pillar. These include: creating an economic, political, social, cultural and legal environment that will enable people to achieve social development; eradicating poverty; promoting the goal of full employment and enabling men and women to attain sustainable livelihoods; promoting social integration by fostering societies that are stable, safe and just based on the promotion and protection of all human rights, equality and non-discrimination; promoting full respect for human dignity and achieving equality and equity between men and women; and promoting and attaining the goals of universal and equitable access to quality education, and the highest attainable standard of physical and mental health. Clearly, protecting and promoting human rights especially economic, social and cultural rights, achieving gender equality, promoting participation, eradicating poverty and achieving universal education come within the ambit of social development. Environmental justice is recognized as encompassing distributive justice, corrective justice, remedial justice and social justice[56] and also overlaps with the social pillar. Thus, analyzing the Paris Agreement within this context makes it clear that human rights, at least to the extent they fall within the social pillar of sustainable development, should inform the commitments that states made—whether voluntary or not—under the Paris Agreement.

---

52   See *Copenhagen Declaration on Social Development*.
53   See Knox, "Human Rights, Environmental Protection and Sustainable Development Goals", *Washington International Law Journal* 24 (2015): 517–518, who argues that while SDGs set out many worthwhile goals, "the targets often do not contain language that is concrete and focused enough to effectively promote human rights or environmental protection".
54   Paragraph 2, *Copenhagen Declaration on Social Development*.
55   Ibid., paragraph 8.
56   Robert Kuehn, "A Taxonomy of Environmental Justice", 30 ELR 10681 (2000).

Sustainable development is said to embrace the "triple bottom line approach to human wellbeing".[57] It aims for a combination of economic development, environmental sustainability and social inclusion. While there is no consensus on how to balance these three objectives or what the tradeoffs or synergies across the objectives should be, "a shared focus on economic, environmental, and social goals is a hallmark of sustainable development and represents a broad consensus on which the world can build".[58] Social inclusion comprises principles such as non-discrimination, gender equality and participation. While states have the "sovereign right to exploit their own resources pursuant to their own environmental and developmental policies",[59] this right is neither absolute nor limitless. It "cannot lawfully be exercised without regard for the detrimental impact on human rights or the environment".[60] If sustainable development resembles a three-legged stool, it is necessary to give equal weight to each leg (environmental protection, economic development and social development) to ensure that the stool (sustainable development) is stable. However, this depiction of sustainable development has been heavily criticized on the basis that it once again places humanity *outside* the environment and fails to encourage us to recognize our place within the biosphere:[61]

> [i]t perpetuates an even older myth that the environment is something apart from humanity, humanity's economy, and its social well-being. We do not discuss whether sustainable development itself is an oxymoronic concept. We do assume that sustainable development represents a real change in the way humans choose to live so that the viability and subsistence of all living species and their places are ensured.[62]

This observation deserves more in-depth analysis than can be given in this chapter. It acknowledges that "humanity can have neither an economy nor social well-being without the environment. Thus, the environment is not and cannot be a leg of the sustainable development stool. It is the *floor* upon which the stool, or any sustainable development model, must stand. It is the foundation of any economy and social well-being that humanity is fortunate

---

57 Jeffrey Sachs, "From Millennium Development Goals to Sustainable Development Goals", in *Viewpoint* Vol 379, June 9, (2012), 2206.
58 Ibid.
59 Principle 2, Rio Declaration.
60 See Birnie et al., *International Law & the Environment* (3rd ed., 2009), 115.
61 See Neil Dawe and Kenneth Ryan, "The Faulty Three-Legged-Stool Model of Sustainable Development".
62 Ibid.

enough to achieve".[63] As humanity and the economy cannot survive without the ecosystem services provided by nature,[64] a robust environment must be the foundation of all development activities. Critics question whether we will ever understand our place on the planet and choose to live within the limits set by the biosphere. Perhaps we can do it but not by relying on the three-legged stool model "because it continues to place us outside those limits. And while we may be able to think outside the limits, we cannot live outside the limits".[65] Our current neo-liberal economic model with its emphasis on the free market is ill-suited to achieve sustainable development. Relying on the system that caused the problem to fix the problem is shortsighted, to say the least.

Although dominant global thinking and action do not reflect this, there is some awareness of the important role played by nature and of the fact that humankind is only one species among millions. The *World Charter for Nature* adopted by the UN General Assembly in 1982 to mark the tenth anniversary of the Stockholm Conference recognized that "mankind is a part of nature and life depends on the uninterrupted functioning of natural systems".[66] It further notes that "civilization is rooted in nature, which has shaped human culture and influenced all artistic and scientific achievements, and living in harmony with nature gives man the best opportunities for the development of his creativity and for rest and recreation". This remarkable document, forgotten for most part by states and others alike, indicates that humanity and the global economy cannot be sustained without a robust and healthy environment. It also debunks the three-legged stool depiction of sustainable development and identifies nature as the floor or foundation upon which both humanity and the economy flourish. This model of sustainable development forces us to look at nature and environmental protection differently. Rather than thinking of sustainable development as being supported by three separate pillars, environmental protection becomes the foundation and the most important aspect of sustainable development. Not only does this reflect common sense, but rather, our very survival may depend on this reorientation.

Rather than being hung up on the definition of sustainable development or sustainability, the SDGs have provided us with an opportunity to actually

---

63  Ibid., 1459.
64  See Hunter et al., *International Environmental Law and Policy*, 169.
65  Ibid.
66  Preamble, *World Charter for Nature* (1982), available at http://www.un.org/documents/ga/res/37/a37r007.htm.

*achieve* it. For the first time we have the right to development discourse merging with the sustainable development discourse. This is important for several reasons, including the fact that the 1986 UN *Declaration on the Right to Development*[67] defines development as "a comprehensive economic, social, cultural and political process, which aims at the constant improvement of the well-being of the entire population and of all individuals on the basis of their active, free and meaningful participation in development and in the fair distribution of benefits resulting therefrom"; and that this right has since been recognized as integral to sustainable development. Paragraph 10 of the 2030 Agenda states, inter alia, that it is informed by the *Declaration on the Right to Development*; and paragraph 35 states, among other things, that the Agenda recognizes the need to build peaceful, just and inclusive societies that provide equal access to justice and that are based on respect for human rights (including the right to development), on effective rule of law and good governance at all levels and on transparent, effective and accountable institutions. Paragraph 11 reaffirms the outcomes of all major UN conferences and summits which have laid the foundation for sustainable development, including the *Rio Declaration on Environment and Development*; the World Summit on Sustainable Development; the World Summit for Social Development; and "The Future We Want"—Rio + 20, while paragraph 12 reaffirms all the principles of the Rio Declaration.

Going forward, the right to development and sustainable development must be implemented in tandem, in a mutually reinforcing manner. Despite being developed in one forum—the UN—and despite the right to development being integral to sustainable development, they have hitherto developed on separate tracks, ignoring their obvious synergies. We now have these two frameworks merging in the context of the SDGs. The 2030 Agenda extends the development agenda to all countries which have all committed to "work to implement the Agenda within our own countries and at the regional and global levels, taking into account different national realities, capacities and levels of development and respecting national policies and priorities".[68] It is thus up to all sections of the international community at all levels, to proceed together to achieve these 17 Goals and 169 targets. In the next section, we turn to a discussion of how the courts in South Asia have contributed to the development of sustainable development in the region.

---

67 *Declaration on the Right to Development* (1986), available at http://www.un.org/documents/ga/res/41/a41r128.htm.
68 Paragraph 21.

## 4 Sustainable Development Jurisprudence in South Asia—Some Seminal Cases

Sustainable development jurisprudence in South Asia[69] was born out of public interest litigation (PIL), which became popular in the aftermath of the Bhopal disaster of 1984. This involved one of the worst industrial accidents in human history, when 40 tons of the lethal gas methyl isocyanate leaked from a pesticide plant belonging to an Indian subsidiary of Union Carbide, a transnational cooperation based in the USA. Although the ensuing case *In re Union Carbide Corp. Gas Plant Disaster*[70] wherein the Indian government filed suit against the parent company in the USA for compensation for thousands of deaths, injuries and other damage, was settled out of court,[71] this case catalyzed the evolution of PIL in cases involving development, human rights and the environment in the region.

In the early Indian case of *Subhash Kumar v. Bihar and others*,[72] the petitioner filed a public interest lawsuit pleading infringement of the right to life from the pollution of the Bokaro River by the Tata Iron and Steel Company, alleged to have made the water unfit for drinking or irrigation. Upholding this claim, the court construed the right to life to include the right to enjoyment of pollution-free water and air. It stated that if anything endangers or impairs the quality of life, an affected person or *a genuinely interested person* can bring a public interest suit, which involves legal proceedings for vindication or enforcement of fundamental rights of a group or community unable to enforce its rights on account of incapacity, poverty, or ignorance of the law.

The *Dehra Dun* case[73] involved a public interest petition filed by the Rural Litigation and Entitlement Kendra, in the Supreme Court of India. After careful investigation, mostly on its own initiative, the court upheld an order to close several limestone quarries in the Himalayan region of the Dehra Dun district. It emphasized the need to balance the environmental disturbance caused by limestone mining with the need for limestone in industry. To redress the

---

69  Sections 3 and 4 draw substantially from the author Shyami Puvimanasinghe's article "Towards a Jurisprudence of Sustainable Development in South Asia: Litigation in the Public Interest", *Sustainable Development Law and Policy* 10, Issue 1 (Fall 2009): 41.
70  *In re Union Carbide Corp. Gas Plant Disaster*, 634 F. Supp. 842, 844 (S.D.N.Y. 1986) (aff'd as modified); *In re Union Carbide Corp. Gas Plant Disaster*, 809 F.2d 195, 197 (2d Cir. 1987).
71  *Union Carbide Corp. v. Union of India*, A.I.R. 1990 S.C. 273, available at http://www.commonlii.org/cgicommonlii/disp.pl/in/cases/INSC/1989/179.html?query=union+carbide.
72  A.I.R. 1991 S.C. 420 (1991).
73  *Rural Litigation and Entitlement Kendra, Dehra Dun v. Uttar Pradesh & others*, A.I.R. 1988 S.C. 2187, available at http://www.commonlii.org/in/cases/INSC/1985/220.html.

ensuing unemployment, it directed employment of the former mine workers in the local reforestation and soil conservation program.

In *Municipal Council Ratlam v. Vardichand & Others*,[74] the facts arose out of overpopulation, poverty, pollution, ill-planned urbanization, and lack of basic amenities combined with official inaction in part of Ratlam, in Madhya Pradesh. Justice Krishna Iyer confirmed the finding of public nuisance. Citing India's constitutional provisions on social justice and human rights, he said the judiciary must be informed by the broader principle of access to justice, necessitated by the conditions of developing countries. The Sub-Divisional Magistrate Ratlam, acting under the Indian Code of Criminal Procedure, had ordered, by way of affirmative action, the municipality to provide toilets, drainage facilities, access to fresh water, and basic sanitation within a given time and according to certain guidelines. The order was upheld by the Supreme Court which confirmed that a court could compel a statutory body to carry out its duties, in this case under the *Madhya Pradesh Municipalities Act*.[75]

In the later case of *Research Foundation for Science and Technology and Natural Resources Policy v. Union of India et al.*,[76] a public interest suit led to the appointment by the Supreme Court of a Committee to inquire into the issue of hazardous wastes. Numerous other Indian PIL suits include *Akhil v. Secretary A.P. Pollution Control Board W.P.*;[77] *A.P. Pollution Control Board v. Appellate Authority Under Water Act W.P.*;[78] *A.P. Gunnies Merchants Association v. Government of Andhra Pradesh*;[79] *Chinnappa v. Union of India*[80] and *Beena Sarasan v. Kerala Zone Management Authority et al.*[81]

In *Shehla Zia and Others v. WAPDA*[82] in neighboring Pakistan, residents living close to a grid station had alleged that the electromagnetic field created by high voltage transmission lines would pose a serious health hazard. The court upheld the right to life which it interpreted to include a healthy environment, and an adequate standard of living. It construed "life" broadly, to enable not only its sustenance, but also its enjoyment. Noting that energy is essential for

---

74  A.I.R. 1980 S.C. 1622, available at http://www.commonlii.org/in/cases/INSC/1980/138.html.
75  Ibid. The relevant legal provisions were contained in the Code of Criminal Procedure, No. 2 of 1974; India Code Crim. Proc. (1973), Section 133; *Madhya Pradesh Municipalities Act* of 1961, Section 123.
76  No. 657, http://www.elaw.org/node/2192 (S.C. 2005).
77  No. 15490, http://www.elaw.org/node/2020 (Andhra Pradesh H.C. 2001).
78  No. 33493, http://www.elaw.org/node/2524 (Andhra Pradesh H.C. 2001).
79  No. 386, http://www.elaw.org/node/2043 (Andhra Pradesh H.C. 2001).
80  No. 202, http://www.elaw.org/node/2469 (S.C.2002).
81  No. 19547, http://www.elaw.org/node/1892 (Kerala H.C. 2005).
82  P.L.D. 1994 S.C. 693, available at http://www.elaw.org/node/1342.

life, commerce, and industry, the court held that a balance in the form of a policy of sustainable development was required, and appointed a Commissioner to examine the scheme and report back to it. Since the scientific evidence was inconclusive, the court applied the precautionary principle,[83] whereby in the face of threats of serious or irreversible damage, lack of full scientific certainty shall not be used as a reason for postponing cost-effective measures to prevent environmental degradation.

*Bokhari v. Federation of Pakistan*[84] concerned the grounding and collapse of a ship in the port of Karachi in 2003, leading to a major oil-spill, which caused massive environmental damage. In the Supreme Court, the ability of the legal system to respond was found to be totally lacking due to many reasons including lack of preparedness and failure to ratify relevant international conventions. The Court considered the concept of public interest litigation as it had evolved in India and Pakistan, where it was said to be particularly useful because of the realities of poverty, illiteracy, and institutional fragility. In Pakistan, PIL had been used in a wide range of social issues, from environmental pollution to the prevention of exploitation of children. The public interest suit of *Irfan v. Lahore Development Authority*[85] involved air and noise pollution from rickshaws, mini buses and other vehicles and the non-performance of statutory duties by the relevant authorities, charged with ensuring a pollution-free environment for the citizens.

*Bangladesh Environmental Lawyers Association v. Secretary, Ministry of Environment and Forests*,[86] concerned the neglect, misuse, and lack of coordination by governmental authorities in relation to Sonadia Island off the coast of Bangladesh, a precious forest area and rich ecosystem. The authorities were said to be preparing the land for industrial activities which would destroy the environment, including shrimp cultivation, thereby destroying the habitat for fauna and flora, and weakening natural disaster prevention benefits. In *Bangladesh Environmental Lawyers Association v. Bangladesh et al.*,[87] the Supreme Court ordered the closing of ship breaking yards that were operating without environmental clearance and a variety of actions to be taken by the government to prevent future environmental harm.

In the landmark case of *Suray Prasad Sharma Dhungel v. Godavari Marble Industries et al.*[88] in the Himalayan Kingdom of Nepal, the Supreme Court held

---

83   Principle 15, Rio Declaration.
84   2003, available at http://www.elaw.org/node/1848.
85   No. 25084, http://www.elaw.org/node/2390, Lahore H.C. 2003.
86   http://www.elaw.org/node/2452, Writ Petition to Bangl. S.C. Oct. 10, 2003.
87   Bangl. S.C. 2009, available at http://www.elaw.org/node/3747.
88   No. 35, http://www.elaw.org/node/1849 (Nepal S.C. 1995).

that a clean and healthy environment is part of the right to life under the Constitution. It upheld the *locus standi* of non-governmental organizations and individuals working to protect the environment, and directed that environmental protection laws be enacted. In *Sharma et al. v. Nepal Drinking Water Corporation et al.*,[89] the Supreme Court considered the spirit of the country's Constitution and its main objectives. It emphasized the importance of pure drinking water to public health and the responsibility of a welfare state to provide it. Without issuing a writ of *mandamus* to guarantee the right to pure drinking water, as requested by the petitioning public interest lawyer, it alerted the Ministry of Housing and Physical Development to hold the Drinking Water Corporation accountable in complying with its legal obligations under its governing statute.

In *Sharma et al. v. His Majesty's Government Cabinet Secretariat et al.*,[90] the Supreme Court was petitioned to quash a government decision allowing unfettered import of diesel taxis and leaded petrol from India. The court decided that a healthy environment is a prerequisite to the protection of the right to personal freedom under the Constitution and that the state has a primary obligation to protect the right to personal liberty under Article 12(1) by reducing environmental pollution as far as possible. Citing fundamental rights, it stated that the environment cannot be ignored for development and issued a directive to enforce essential measures within a maximum of two years to reduce vehicular pollution in the Kathmandu Valley, known for its historical, cultural, and archaeological significance.

In the island nation of Sri Lanka, the early case of *Keangnam Enterprises Ltd. v. Abeysinghe*[91] arose from a complaint by inhabitants of a village to the Magistrate's Court of Kurunegala regarding the public nuisance from blasting and metal quarrying operations to develop a major road. Excessive noise and vibration from blasting day and night had led to severe damage to people and property, including fear psychosis, hearing loss, drying up of wells, failure of crops, and structural damage to property. The Magistrate granted an injunction restraining the operation of the quarry and a conditional order to remove the nuisance, upon which the company applied for revision to the Court of Appeal. The Keangnam company was found to be operating without an Environmental Protection License under the National Environmental Act, and the court insisted that the company obtain a license.

---

89  No. 2237, http://www.elaw.org/node/1383 (Nepal S.C. 2001).
90  No. 2237, http://www.elaw.org/node/1594 (Nepal S.C. 2003).
91  (1994) 2 Sri L.R. 271 (13 July 1992), available at http://www.commonlii.org//cgi-bin/disp.pl/lk/cases/LKCA/1992/ 18.html? query=keangnam.

*Environmental Foundation Ltd. v. The Land Commissioner et al.*,[92] concerned a lease of state land to a private company to build a tourist hotel in close proximity to an ancient tank and sacred Buddhist temple, and therefore likely to upset the local people and the environment. In spite of the public interest suit questioning the irregularity of the lease, and in contravention of the relevant statutory provisions, the project went through. However, as a result of this case, the authorities were ordered to follow the correct procedure and were compelled to do so by providing notice in the newspaper. This case was the first in Sri Lanka to uphold the standing of a non-governmental organization (NGO) committed to environmental protection, to bring a PIL. It therefore had important implications with respect to access to justice, the role of the judiciary, access to information, public participation in decision-making, and compliance with and implementation of the law.

In *Environmental Foundation Limited et al. v. The Attorney General*,[93] residents of two villages in southern Sri Lanka brought a class action in a fundamental rights petition over serious damage to health and property caused by quarry-blasting operations. They alleged the violation of several constitutional rights, namely: that sovereignty is in the people and is inalienable and includes fundamental rights; that no person shall be subjected to torture or to cruel, inhuman, or degrading treatment; the freedom to engage in any lawful occupation; freedom of movement and of choosing a residence;[94] as well as the Directive Principles of state policy.[95] The case was settled through mediation, and the petitioners obtained relief. The court recognized the possibility of invoking fundamental rights provisions in environment-related cases, and the links between development, human rights and the environment. The first petitioner was an NGO, and the possibility of public interest litigation was also accepted.

In *Environmental Foundation Ltd. v. Ratnasiri Wickremanayake, Minister of Public Administration et al.*,[96] it was unequivocally recognized that public interest litigation could be allowed in suitable cases. In this *certiorari* application,

---

[92] The *Kandalama* case, available at http://www.commonlii.org/lk/cases/LKCA/1992/25.html.

[93] The *Nawimana* case, (1994) 1(1) SAELR 17.

[94] Sri Lanka Constitution Articles 3, 11, 14(1)(g), 14(1)(h), available at http://www.priu.gov.lk/Cons/1978Constitution/ Introduction.htm.

[95] Indian Constitution Art. 48a & 51a(g); Sri Lanka Constitution Art. 27(14) and 28(f); Sri Lanka Constitution Art. 27(4)—the State shall strengthen and broaden the democratic structure of government and the democratic rights of "the People by decentralizing administration and affording all possible opportunities to the People to participate at every level of national life and in government".

[96] 3(4) South Asian Environmental Law Reports 103 (1996), available at http://www.elaw.org/node/1324.

the court explicitly extended *locus standi* to a person who shows a genuine interest in the subject matter, who comes before the court as a public-spirited person, concerned to see that the law is obeyed in the interest of all. In *Deshan Harinda (a minor) et al. v. Ceylon Electricity Board et al.*,[97] a group of minor children filed a fundamental rights application alleging that the noise from a thermal power plant generator exceeded national noise standards and would cause hearing loss and other injuries. Standing was granted for the case to proceed on the basis of a violation of their right to life. Although the Constitution did not expressly provide for the right to life, it was argued that all other rights would be futile without it. The case was eventually settled with an *ex gratia* payment.

In *Gunarathne v. Homagama Pradeshiya Sabha et al.*,[98] the court stated that: "Publicity, transparency and fairness are essential if the goal of sustainable development is to be achieved" and referred to the salient elements of good governance, intrinsic to sustainable development. Going beyond the relevant legal provisions, it asserted that the authorities must notify the neighborhood and hear objections, as well as inform the industrialists and hear their views in deciding whether to issue an Environmental Protection License. It also required that agencies give reasons for their decisions and inform the parties of such reasons, introducing principles of natural justice. In *Lalanath de Silva v. The Minister of Forestry and Environment*,[99] the petitioner argued that the Minister's failure to enact ambient air quality standards resulted in a violation of his right to life, as a citizen. The Supreme Court ordered the enactment of regulations to control air pollution from vehicle emissions in Colombo city, which followed this case.

The landmark case of *Tikiri Banda Bulankulama v. Secretary, Ministry of Industrial Development*[100] concerned a joint venture agreement between the Sri Lankan government and the local subsidiary of a transnational corporation for the mining of phosphate in the North-Central Province. The terms of the mineral investment agreement were highly beneficial to the company with little concern for human rights, the environment and sustainable development, indigenous culture, history, religion and value systems. It was the subject of a public interest suit by the local villagers (including rice and dairy farmers,

---

97  The *Kotte Kids* case (1998), 5(4) South Asian Environmental Law Reports 116.
98  2 Sri LR 11 (April 3, 1998), available at http://www.asianlii.org/lk/cases/LKSC/1998/35.html.
99  The *Air Pollution* case, SC of Sri Lanka, 1998.
100 *Bulankulama & others v. Secretary, Ministry of Industrial Development & others*, 3 Sri L.R. 243 (June 2, 2000), available at http://www.commonlii.org//cgi-bin/disp.pl/lk/cases/LKSC/2000/18.html?query=Bulankulama%20v.%20Secretary.

owners of coconut land, and the incumbent of a Buddhist temple) in the Supreme Court.

The proposed project was to lead to the displacement of over 2,600 families, consisting of around 12,000 persons. The Supreme Court found that at previous rates of extraction, there would perhaps be enough deposits for 1,000 years, but that the proposed agreement would lead to complete exhaustion of phosphate in around 30 years. Stating that fairness to all, including the people of Sri Lanka, was the basic yardstick in doing justice, the court held that there was an imminent infringement of the following fundamental rights of the petitioners, all local residents: equality and equal protection of the law under Article 12(1); freedom to engage in any lawful occupation, trade, business, or enterprise under Article 14(1)(g); and freedom of movement and of choosing a residence within Sri Lanka under Article 14(1)(h). The court cited sustainable development, intergenerational equity, and human development, and analyzed the agreement with reference to principles of international environmental law, including Principles 14 and 21 of the Stockholm Declaration and Principles 1, 2, and 4 of the Rio Declaration. The court stopped the project from proceeding unless and until legal requirements of rational planning including an Environmental Impact Assessment was done. It found that the proposed project would harm health, safety, livelihoods, and cultural heritage. This cultural heritage, the court noted, was not renewable, nor were the historical and archaeological value and the ancient irrigation tanks that were to be destroyed. The decision was based on the view that economic growth is not the sole criterion for measuring human welfare, which went beyond "rupees and cents".

The court relied on international law of sustainable development (in particular the separate opinion of Judge Weeramantry in the ICJ case, *Hungary v. Slovakia*[101]), and the ancient wisdom and local history of conservation, sustainability, and human rights. The company's exemption from submitting its project to an Environmental Impact Assessment was held to be an imminent violation of the equal protection clause. Although the Constitution provides only for civil and political rights to be justiciable, the court adopted a broader interpretation to include socio-economic rights. Natural resources were said to be held in guardianship and public trust by the government for the people.

*Mundy v. Central Environmental Authority and others*[102] concerned several appeals relating to the building of Sri Lanka's first modern highway, the

---

101  Gabcikovo–Nagymaros Project, 1997 I.C.J. 7 (Sept. 25), available at http://www.icj-cij.org/docket/files/92/7375.pdf.
102  (2004), available at http://www.elaw.org/node/1947.

Southern Expressway linking its capital city of Colombo with the Southern city of Matara, an important step in terms of infrastructure development towards enhancing industry, trade, and investment. Protracted litigation opposing the project and its different alternative routes involved allegations of potential damage to human rights including large-scale displacement, and injury to the environment including sensitive ecosystems. The Court of Appeal had upheld the developmental interest, holding that when balancing the competing interests, the conclusion necessarily had to be made in favor of the larger interests of the community, which would benefit immensely from the project. The Court gave highest priority to the public interest in development, then to the environmental damage to wetland ecosystems, and lastly, to the human interests of affected persons. Several persons appealed to the Supreme Court with regard to particular sections of the route which resulted in the taking of their lands with no arrangements for compensation. The Supreme Court varied the order and ordered compensation under the *audi alteram* principle of natural justice and Constitution Article 12(1) on equality and equal protection.

*Weerasekera et al. v. Keangnam Enterprises Ltd.*[103] involved a mining operation which, according to local communities, violated public nuisance law through its noise levels. The Court of Appeal held that possession of a license for the operation did not exempt the Keangnam mining company from public nuisance claims. *Environmental Foundation Ltd. v. Urban Development Authority et al.*,[104] concerned the proposed leasing of the Galle Face Green, a popular seaside promenade in Colombo, by the Urban Development Authority to a private company to build a "mega leisure complex". In a fundamental rights application, the Supreme Court upheld the argument of the petitioner NGO to preserve the island's national heritage for use of the public. It also held that there was an infringement of the right to information by reading Constitution Article 14(1), on the freedom of speech and expression, to encompass a right to information (which at that time, was not provided for in the Constitution). The Court further held that the petitioner's rights to equality under Article 12(1) had been infringed.

Later cases involved for example, unregulated mechanized mining and transport of sand from sand dunes in a wetland ecosystem, without permits under the relevant statutes;[105] activities threatening the coastal zone and its

---

103 (2009), available at http://www.elaw.org/system/files/Metal+Quarry+Balangoda+-+Judgementooo1.pdf.
104 (2005).
105 *Withanage v. Geological Survey and Mines Bureau and Others* (2004), available at http://www.elaw.org/node/1464.

habitats, including destruction of mangroves; coral extraction; destructive fishing methods; coastal pollution and improper constructions.[106] The case of *Center for Environmental Justice v. Ministry of Agriculture, Environment, Irrigation and Mahaweli Development et al.*[107] concerned the protection of a major national park, forming a wetland of international importance under the Ramsar Convention on Wetlands, and alteration of the boundaries of this park by the governmental authorities. It was argued that this alteration would pose a further threat to the ecosystem, already endangered by landfills, aquaculture farms, fisheries, pollution, mining of minerals and clearing of mangroves. The petition argued that the authorities were acting in breach of several international conventions including the Wetlands, Cultural and Natural Heritage and Biodiversity Conventions and the *Bonn Convention on Migratory Species of Wild Animals*, and other instruments including the Johannesburg Declaration, and relevant articles of the Sri Lankan Constitution.

## 5  Strategies Used, Public Interest Litigation and Sustainable Development in South Asia

Following the Bhopal disaster and ensuing struggles in the quest for justice for people and the environment including accountability and remedy to address adverse effects of economic activities, most states in South Asia invoked legislative, constitutional, and judicial mechanisms as strategies in reconciling human rights, environmental protection and economic development,[108] and public interest litigation[109] gradually evolved as an entry point in the pursuit of sustainable development.

As illustrated above, PIL has taken diverse forms, like representative standing, where a concerned person or organization comes forward to take up the cause of poor or otherwise underprivileged persons; and citizen standing,

---

106  Also see *Kottabadu Durage Sriyani Silva v. Chanaka Iddamalgoda* (Sri Lanka Aug. 8, 2003), http://www.elaw.org/node/2487.

107  *Bundala National Park* case (Sri Lanka Court of Appeal 23 Feb. 2006), available at www.elaw.org/node/2070.

108  C.G. Weeramantry, "Private International Law & Public International Law", *Rivista di Diritto Internazionale Private e Processuale* 34 (1998): 313, 324.

109  According to Justice Bhagwathi, a former Chief Justice of India: "Law as I conceive it, is a social auditor and this audit function can be put into action when someone with real public interest ignites the jurisdiction ... public interest litigation is part of the process of participatory justice and standing in civil litigation of that pattern must have liberal reception at the judicial doorsteps". Fertilizer Corp. Kamgar Union, Sindri & others, A.I.R. 1981 S.C. 344, available at http://www.commonlii.org/in/cases/INSC/1980/220.html.

which enables any person to bring a suit as a matter of public interest, as a concerned member of the citizenry. Given the many classifications that divide the social fabric in this region, it seems fair that poor, illiterate, legally illiterate, minority, low caste, and other disadvantaged and underprivileged persons gain access to justice through distortions of traditional doctrines of standing. The test for *locus standi* in these cases has, within limits, been liberalized to accommodate a person with a genuine and sufficient concern, relaxing the need to be an aggrieved person. In addition, class actions allow one suit in the case of multiple plaintiffs and/or defendants, and have been useful in situations where large numbers of people are affected at the same time.

Public nuisance cases often provided the factual context in the pre-environmental era. The case of *Keangnam Enterprises Ltd. v. Abeysinghe*[110] in Sri Lanka, on pollution from quarry blasting coupled with failure on the part of governmental authorities, and the *Ratlam* case in India, on pollution from industry together with neglect of duty by local authorities are examples. In *Ratlam,* the court adopted a holistic approach, making orders for local development and provision of basic needs. Ancient statutes were read in the new light of the social justice orientation of the Indian Constitution, human rights, and concern for the environment. The court commented on the nature of the judicial process, stating that it is not merely adjudicatory, and calling for affirmative action to make the remedy effective. Although the relevant provisions were discretionary in tone, it stated that sometimes discretion could become a duty. The court suggested mobilization of the voluntary services of the local community, known in South Asian societies as *"sramdan",* and the need for the central government to provide more funds to local authorities.

The superior courts of India inspired judicial activism and innovation in the region[111] and PIL gradually became popular also in the lower courts. The resulting body of regional jurisprudence evolved primarily through the agency of citizen action, legal representation in the public interest, and judicial innovation. The judiciary—especially the higher judiciary—have used innovative strategies to uphold and enforce governmental responsibilities and accountability to promote sustainable development. Most of the cases concern local industries, but some also deal with transnational business. This jurisprudence

---

110  *Supra* n. 92.
111  See SACEP/UNEP/NORAD, Report of the Regional Symposium on the Role of the Judiciary in Promoting the Rule of Law in the Area of Sustainable Development (1997); See also SACEP/UNEP/NORAD, Compendium of Summaries of Judicial Decisions in Environment Related Cases, http://www.unescap.org/drpad/vc/document/compendium/(including jurisprudence from the Asia Pacific region); UNEP, *Judges and Environmental Law*, a Handbook for the Sri Lankan judiciary (2009).

should in principle be applicable to both global and local business, provided that transnational corporations can also be subject to domestic law in host states.

Enhanced sensitivity and concerted action in civil society, the legal profession, and the judiciary helped to create an expanded notion of access to justice. The wider civic space that this entails, specifically, with regard to enlarging the class of persons who can sue, tends to have positive effects on promoting good governance and safeguarding the public/social/democratic interest. Strategies employed include a shift from adversarial to inquisitorial judicial methods suited to environmental issues, a progressive approach to statutory interpretation, and greater flexibility in processes adopted and redress granted. Judges in these cases have adopted a more inquisitorial and active role. In the *Dehra Dun* case in India, for example, the judges virtually directed the investigation and evidence. In the *Nawimana* case in Sri Lanka, what emerged from litigation was a mediated settlement between the parties laying down the terms and conditions for quarry mining, which received judicial assent. *Aruna Rodrigues v. Union of India* concerned litigation on genetically modified organisms in which the Supreme Court placed tight restrictions on GMO crop testing, such as prescribing safe distances for test crops from other farms and requiring confirmation that no crop contamination had occurred.[112]

Judicial intervention has served to scrutinize governmental and private sector activities and abate administrative apathy.[113] Significant strategies include the creative and pro-active use of Directive Principles of State Policy in national constitutions, judicial recognition of a right to a healthy environment,[114] and the interpretation of an adequate standard of living to include an adequate quality of life and environment. Directive Principles are intended to provide guidance to laws, policies and governance, and are not justiciable/legally enforceable. In India, however, they have been used to create a range of new rights not enshrined in the Constitution as legally enforceable rights.

In Sri Lanka too, the Directive Principles have been used as guides to interpretation. The island's domestic jurisprudence is closely linked to relevant international law. Sri Lanka's 1978 Constitution in its chapter on Directive

---

112   Available at http://www.envfor.nic.in/divisions/csurv/geac/writ_petition.htm.

113   For example, the *Ratlam* and *Keangnam* cases in India and Sri Lanka, see discussion *supra*.

114   For example, the *Dehra Dun* case, see discussion *supra*; *Mehta v. Union of India and others* (*Shriram Gas leak* case), A.I.R. 1988 S.C. 1086, available at http://www.commonlii.org/in/cases/INSC/1987/262.html (India); *Ms. Shehla Zia & others v. WAPDA*, *supra*; *Mohiuddin Farooque v. Bangladesh*, 48 D.L.R. (1996) H.C.D. 438, available at http://www.worldlii.org/cgi-bin/disp.pl/int/cases/ICHRL/1996/45.html?query=farooque.

Principles of State Policy and Fundamental Duties, includes Article 27(2) whereby the state has pledged to establish a democratic socialist society, the objectives of which include paragraph (e), the equitable distribution among all citizens of the material resources of the community and the social product, so as best to sub-serve the common good. Article 27(14) asserts that the state shall protect, preserve and improve the environment for the benefit of the community. Under Article 28(f), it is the duty of every person to protect nature and conserve its riches. Although Article 29 states that the Directive Principles are not justiciable,[115] the courts have recognized these principles, which they have read in the light of principles of international law. They have thus aided the domestic incorporation of international law, and facilitated the infiltration of international sustainable development law into the domestic legal system. Broad, purposive interpretations of the Directive Principles have served to advance human rights and socio-economic justice.

PIL has been useful in balancing development, environment, and human rights in Sri Lanka.[116] In the region as a whole, several cases have proceeded on the basis that, as pointed out by Justice Matthew in *Kesavananda Bharthai v. State of Kerala*, the scope of human rights is not static and its contents must be guided by the experience and context of each generation. Most cases have involved executive or administrative action and, frequently, business activities. When major administrative decisions concern natural resources and other important issues of public interest, there is usually little room for the public to question these decisions, to be informed of the implications, and to ensure accountability. Decisions are at times made behind closed doors, with little or no disclosure. Meaningful public participation, including a voice for groups which are often not actively engaged in decision-making—such as women, youth, children, minorities and indigenous peoples—is key to sustainable development.

Several environmental cases have been based in constitutional law including fundamental rights, administrative law, public nuisance, and the public

---

115 Available at http://www.priu.gov.lk/Cons/1978Constitution/Chapter_06_Amd.html.
116 See Sumudu Atapattu, *Environmental Rights and Human Rights in Sri Lanka: State of Human Rights*, ed. Law & Society Trust (1997), 149; Shyami Puvimanasinghe, "Development, Environment and the Human Dimension: Reflections on the Role of Law and Policy in the Third World, with Particular Reference to South Asia", *Sri Lanka Journal of International Law* 12 (2000): 35, 40; Public Interest Litigation, "Human Rights and the Environment in the Experience of Sri Lanka", in *International Law and Sustainable Development, Principles and Practice*, eds. Nico Schrijver and Friedl Weiss (2005), 653; and "Towards a Jurisprudence of Sustainable Development in South Asia: Litigation in the Public Interest", *Sustainable Development Law and Policy* 10, Issue 1 (Fall 2009): 41.

trust doctrine. The question of *locus standi* usually arises in writ applications, which are particularly useful in invalidating unlawful action by governmental bodies through a writ of *certiorari,* and compelling them to carry out their statutory duties, through a writ of *mandamus*,[117] respectively. These cases are filed against relevant governmental authorities, pleading for writs as the government is the guardian of natural resources on behalf of present and future generations. Judicial measures in the region have *inter alia* liberalized *locus standi* to include any person genuinely concerned for the environment,[118] placed a public trust obligation on states over natural resources,[119] imposed absolute liability for accidents arising from ultra-hazardous activities,[120] applied the polluter pays and precautionary principles,[121] and promoted good governance and sustainable development.[122]

## 6 Conclusion—Some Lessons Learned

In the South Asian region as a whole, public interest litigation has been useful in injecting a more informed, participatory, and transparent approach to the process of development, and to governmental and private sector actions involving public resources. It has enhanced civic space through giving voice to persons who would otherwise go unheard. PIL enables many stakeholders to participate in the development process, as envisaged in both the right to development and sustainable development. PIL has brought forth an element of accountability in development and governance, towards a more inclusive, equitable and sustainable development, and created greater possibilities for the portrayal of a human face in development. As a tool, PIL has provided a

---

117   For example, *Withanage v. Director Coast Conservation*, CA Application no. 551/2005 of 7 April 2005.
118   See, for example, *M.C. Mehta v. Union of India & others*, see discussion *supra*; the *Kandalama* case, see discussion *supra*.
119   *M.C. Mehta v. Kamal Nath & others*, (1997) 1 S.C.C. 388, available at http://ielrc.org/content/e0216.pdf.
120   In the *Shriram Gasleak* case, the ideas of cost internalization, polluter pays, and absolute liability long preceded the *Rio Declaration*. Another case in point is *Indian Council for Enviro-Legal Action v. Union of India and others*, A.I.R. 1996 S.C. 1446, available at htp://www.commonlii.org/in/cases/INSC/1996/244.html.
121   *Vellore Citizens' Welfare v. Union of India*, (1996) 5 S.C.C. 647, available at http://www.commonlii.org/in/cases/INSC/1996/1027.html.
122   *Gunaratne v. Homagama Pradeshiya Sabha & others*, (1998) 2 Sri LR 11 (3 April 1998), available at http://www.asianlii.org/lk/cases/LKSC/1998/35.html.

viable mechanism to implement sustainable development principles through integrating and reconciling multiple interests.

The South Asian jurisprudence catalyzed by PIL provides lessons learned in practice and experience, towards implementing Principle 10 of the Rio Declaration, as well as SDG 16. Principle 10 of Rio states:

> Environmental issues are best handled with the participation of all concerned citizens, at the relevant level. At the national level, each individual shall have appropriate access to information concerning the environment that is held by public authorities, including information on hazardous materials and activities in their communities, and the opportunity to participate in decision-making processes. States shall facilitate and encourage public awareness and participation by making information widely available. Effective access to judicial and administrative proceedings, including redress and remedy, shall be provided.

SDG 16 aims to promote peaceful and inclusive societies for sustainable development, provide access to justice for all and build effective, accountable and inclusive institutions at all levels. It includes targets to promote the rule of law and ensure equal access to justice for all; develop effective, accountable and transparent institutions at all levels; ensure responsive, inclusive, participatory and representative decision-making; ensure public access to information and protect fundamental freedoms, in accordance with national legislation and international agreements; and promote and enforce non-discriminatory laws and policies for sustainable development.

It goes without saying that realizing sustainable development is a *sine qua non* to realizing the SDGs. Realizing sustainable development requires that all human rights, including labor rights and the right to development, are integral to the development process, which most importantly should avoid crossing the threshold of nature's limits. The above discussion presents guidance from the ground up, through the lived experiences of individuals, communities and peoples in South Asia, one of the world's most impoverished regions, grappling with issues of development, environmental degradation and human rights abuse. Like in many other developing regions, the daily challenges faced in seeking sustainable development and realizing the SDGs calls for a delicate balance. Public interest litigation provides one possible entry point in finding that balance.

CHAPTER 10

# China's Theoretical Innovation and Practical Contribution to the Right to Development

*In Commemoration of the Thirtieth Anniversary of the United Nations Declaration on the Right to Development*

*Wang Xigen\**

The right to development is one of the greatest contributions of developing countries to the human rights system. As the largest developing country in the world, China has been conducting persistent and beneficial explorations in the development of the concept of the right to development, idea optimization and practical protection. The year 1986, when the *Declaration on the Right to Development* was adopted, saw the beginning of reform and opening-up in China. Through development practices over 30 years, great progress has been made in poverty alleviation, food safety, medical care, social security, education equality, and so on. China is the first country to complete the poverty alleviation goal in the *United Nations Millennium Declaration*,[1] and an active advocating and practicing country for *Transforming Our World: The 2030 Agenda for Sustainable Development*.[2] Constantly resolving difficult problems in human rights and development and bravely conducting theoretical innovation, China has gradually developed a discourse system on the right to development with Chinese characteristics, and formed unique modes of practice, which are mainly summarized as the following basic conclusions.

---

\* Wang Xigen, Yangtze Scholar Distinguished Professor and Dean of Law School of Huazhong University of Science and Technology; The Ph.D. Supervisor of "2011 Plan of China" - Collaborative Innovation Center of Judicial Civilization; Director of the Institute of Human Rights Law in Huazhong University of Science and Technology in China; The Chair of Academic Board of the Institute of Human Rights in Wuhan University. Email: fxywxg@whu.edu.cn.

1 According to the poverty standard of the World Bank of USD 1.25 a day (PPP in 2005), the poor population in the world amounted to 1.938 billion in 1981, and was reduced to 1.212 billion in 2010, a reduction of 726 million in the world. In the same period, the poor population in China was reduced from 835 million to 157 million (2009), with a reduction of 678 million. 93.3% of the poverty reduction comes from China. (Poverty Relief Office of the State Council, "China's Contribution to Poverty Alleviation in the world", accessed June 17, 2016, http://news.xinhuanet.com/politics/2014-10/11/c_127086679.htm).

2 UN, *Transforming Our World: The 2030 Agenda for Sustainable Development*, October 21, 2015, A/RES/70/1.

## 1 Orientation: The Right to Development Is a Primary Basic Human Right

There are different views as to which human right is the most important in the human rights system. Some hold that citizens' personal freedom is the most basic right; some hold that political right should rank top; and others believe that there is no priority in human rights, as human rights in any form are equally important. The key to the existence of such different views is the existence of different values. Comrade Deng Xiaoping posed the question long ago: "What are human rights? The first point is, how many people's human rights? Human rights of the minority or the majority, or all people in a State?"[3] To resolve people's problems in clothing, food, living and transportation is the most important human right. "In China, the right to subsistence and the right to development are the most fundamental and important human rights".[4] "To maintain and promote people's right to subsistence and the right to development is always the most important issue for China in terms of human rights".[5] The right to development and the right to subsistence have together become the primary human rights in the human rights system for the following reasons. The first is the political basis. "China advocates the mutual respect of national sovereignty, and gives priority to maintaining the right to subsistence and the right to development of peoples in developing countries".[6] In today's world with the polarization of the poor and the rich, social and economic development in many developing countries is slow, and one-third of the people in developing countries live beneath the poverty line. Only when the extremely adverse influence of the unfair and unreasonable old international political and economic orders on development is eliminated and a fair, reasonable new international relationship order is established can active conditions be created for the common development of all mankind. "For peoples in the developing countries, the most urgent human right issue is still the right to subsistence

---

3   Deng Xiaoping, *Selected of Deng Xiaoping*, Vol. 3 (Beijing: People's Press, 1993), 125.
4   Jiang Zemin, *Selected of Jiang Zemin*, Vol. 2 (Beijing: People's Press, 2006), 52.
5   The State Council Information Office of P.R.C., "China's Human Rights Conditions 1991", *The Bulletin of the State Council of the People's Republic of China* 39 (1991): 1348–1391.
6   "Since 1981, China has participated in each meeting of the government expert team for the drafting of the *Declaration on the Right to Development* by the United Nations Human Rights Committee, and actively proposed opinions until the adoption of the *Declaration on the Right to Development* in 1986 at the 41st United Nations General Assembly. China also actively supports taking the problem of the right to development as a separate topic to be deliberated in the Human Rights Committee. China has always been a co-sponsor for the resolution of problems concerning the right to development in the Human Rights Committee". (Ibid.).

and the right to economic, social and cultural development. Therefore, the right to development should be prioritized".[7] The second is the historical basis. China is the country with the largest population in the world, with relatively poor per capita resources and unbalanced development. Like other developing countries, China was subject to foreign invasion, plundering and oppression for a long time; and after the Second World War, China was contained by the "Cold War" thoughts, and its economic and social development were seriously blocked. "To enjoy the right to subsistence and the right to development has historically become the most urgent demand of Chinese people". The third is the theoretical basis. Fairness and justice are core social values. To comprehensively and equally enjoy the right to development meets the distributive justice principle and is in the basic interest of all people in China. The fourth is the realistic basis. Since reform and opening-up, "the Chinese government has been prioritizing the solution to people's problems with the right to subsistence and the right to development" and vigorously developing the economy. The miracle of becoming the country with the highest average annual growth rate of the national economies has been created, and people's living standard has been greatly improved. Practice has proved that "China prioritizes the right to subsistence and the right to development, comprehensively improve the conditions of human rights under the conditions of reform, development and stability ... The achievements made are also recognized by the world".[8] Of course, to stress the priority of the right to development is not to deny the importance of other human rights. On the contrary, while stressing the right to subsistence and the right to development, China regards the protection of citizens' political, economic, social and cultural rights as human rights goals not to be neglected, because all types of human rights and their specific forms are interdependent and inseparable. This is a "path promoting and developing human rights truly meeting the national conditions in China",[9] which is of critical importance to comprehensively respecting and protecting human rights.

## 2    In Terms of Nature: The Right to Development Is an Essential Requirement of Socialism

On the one hand, a unprecedented basic positive conclusion is drawn that to realize all people's equal right to development through common prosperity is

---

7   Ibid.
8   The State Council Information Office of P.R.C., "The Progress in China's Human Rights Case 1995", *The Bulletin of the State Council of the People's Republic of China* 32 (1995): 1318–1342.
9   The State Council Information Office of P.R.C., "50 Years of Human Rights Development in China 2000", *The Bulletin of the State Council of the People's Republic of China* 10 (2000): 14–26.

the essential characteristic of socialism, the relationship between common development and socialism is apparent, and common prosperity and equal development are taken as the essence and core of the basic political system in China. This is original both in the history of the international communist movement and the history of human rights. Comrade Deng Xiaoping observed: "The nature of socialism is to liberate productivity, develop productivity, eliminate exploitation, get rid of polarization, and finally realize common prosperity".[10] Common prosperity means fair distribution of the results of development, everyone enjoying the results of development from socialism and sharing the benefits of reform, opening-up and economic development. We all know that interests are the substantive contents of rights, and rights are the externalization or forms of expressing interests. The interests and values manifested by common prosperity reflect the attribute of the right to development, and in essence are reflected as people's right to development.

On the other hand, the relationship between the right to development and poverty is apparent from the negative side. It is clear that poverty is the biggest obstacle to the right to development, with the internal correlation between poverty and development, and human rights reflected at the height of institutional nature from a pioneering approach. First is the relationship between poverty and common prosperity. "Socialism is not to let the minority become rich and the majority stay poor. It is not like that. The greatest advantage of socialism is common prosperity, which reflects the nature of socialism".[11] Secondly, the relationship between poverty and development. The objective of development is poverty alleviation. "To practice socialism, we must develop productivity, as poverty is not socialism". "First, we must get rid of poverty".[12] "China should resolve the poverty problem of one billion people, and the development problem of one billion people".[13] "Poverty is not socialism, nor is too slow development socialism".[14] Thirdly, the relationship between poverty and people's livelihood. "Socialism should eliminate poverty and improve people's living standard".[15] We should effectively improve people's well-being and let the results of development benefit all people more fairly. Finally, the relationship between poverty and rights, especially the right to development. As Comrade Xi Jinping has observed: "We should lay a foundation for poverty

---

10  Deng Xiaoping, *Selected of Deng Xiaoping*, Vol. 3 (Beijing: People's Press, 1993), 373.
11  Ibid., 364.
12  Ibid., 225.
13  Ibid., 229.
14  Ibid., 255.
15  Hu Jintao, *Speech at the Seminar on Provincial and Ministerial Main Leading Cadres Improving Their Capability for Constructing a Socialist Harmonious Society* (Beijing: People's Press, 2005), 12.

alleviation through development", and "to eliminate poverty is the basic right of people in their pursuit of a happy life".[16] The developmental course over 30-plus years has shown that the right to development is a proper meaning of socialism and an inevitable requirement for maximally releasing the values and functions of a social institution so as to finally realize all people's equal right to development.

## 3  In Terms of Strategy: The Right to Development Is Implemented by the Strategy That "Development Is the Primary Task"

Since the launch of the reform and opening-up in 1978, the outlook on development proposed by the leading group centering on Deng Xiaoping, "development is a top priority",[17] has enabled the practices of Chinese people regarding the right to development to enter a new historical period of rapid progress. This outlook on development is of a complete system. The motive force behind development is reform, and we should remove obstacles to development and liberate and develop productivity through the reform of economic and political systems. The condition of development is opening-up, and we should strive the backland to realize better development by opening up and leading development of coastal areas.[18] The method of development is "to lay equal emphasis", mainly including "laying equal emphasis on material civilization and cultural and ideological progress", "laying equal emphasis on economic work and ideological work", and "laying equal emphasis on construction and legal system". The focus of development lies in centering on economic construction and accelerating the development of technology and education. The famous judgments that "technology is the primary productivity", and "respect knowledge and respect talents" have been proposed. In 2002, it was proposed that "we should firmly grasp the primary task of development in governing and rejuvenating the country".[19] Since 2003, a scientific outlook on development centering on people and featuring comprehensive, coordinated and sustainable development has been gradually developed. "The scientific outlook on development aims at the all-round development of people to let the results

---

16  Xi Jinping, "Jointly Eliminate Poverty and Promote Joint Development—A Keynote Speech on the 2015 High-Level Forum on Poverty Alleviation and Development", *People's Daily*, October 16, 2015.
17  Deng Xiaoping, *Selected of Deng Xiaoping*, Vol. 3 (Beijing: People's Press, 1993), 377.
18  Ibid., 277–278.
19  Jiang Zemin, *Selected of Jiang Zemin*, Vol. 3 (Beijing: People's Press, 2006), 538–539.

of development benefit all people".[20] The *Decision of the Central Committee of the Communist Party of China (CPC) on Some Major Issuesvol Concerning the Construction of a Socialist Harmonious Society* adopted by the Sixth Plenary Session of the Sixteenth CPC National Congress on October 11, 2006 pointed out: "To construct a harmonious society, we must stick to the people-oriented principle. We should always take the fundamental interests of the vast majority of people as the starting point and objective of all the work of the Party and the State, to realize, protect and develop the basic interests of the vast majority of people, and constantly meet the growing material and cultural demands of the people. We should realize that development is for the people and depends on the people and the results of development are shared by the people and promote their all-round development". Since the 18th CPC National Congress, in particular, the CPC Central Committee headed by Comrade Xi Jinping has disclosed the profound meaning of development from a new historical starting point by repeatedly stressing that "development is still the primary task of contemporary China",[21] "development is the primary task",[22] "only with development can we eliminate the roots of conflict, only with development can we guarantee the people's basic rights … Seek comprehensive development and make the basis of development more solid. The ultimate purpose of development is for the people".[23]

4  **In Terms of Content, We Should Realize the Right to Development Integrating Economy, Politics, Culture, Society and Ecological Conservation**

The right to development may be broken down into the political right to development, the economic right to development, the social right to development and the cultural right to development. After the proposal of the strategy for sustainable development, the right to sustainable development should also be included. The "five-in-one" construction and development theory has

---

20  Hu Jintao, "Speech at the 12th Academicians' Congress of the Chinese Academy of Science and the 7th Academician's Congress of the Chinese Academic of Engineering (June 2, 2004)", in *Selected Important Literature Since 16th CPC National Congress* (Beijing: Central Party Literature Press, 2008), 113–114.
21  Xi Jinping, "Speech at the Welcoming Dinner Hosted by Local Governments and Friendly Organizations in the United States", *People's Daily*, September 24, 2015.
22  "The Suggestion of the CPC Central Committee on Preparing the 13th Five-Year Plan for National Economy and Social Development", *People's Daily*, November 4, 2015.
23  Xi Jinping, "Toward a Mutually Beneficial Partnership for Sustainable Development— Speech on the UN Sustainable Development Summit", *People's Daily*, September 27, 2015.

overcome the backward outlook on development that equates development to economic growth, but it does not simply copy the right to development in the four aspects of economy, politics, society and culture, as determined in the Preamble and Article 1 of the *Declaration on the Right to Development*. Instead, following the new contemporary trend, the outlook actively plans for and enhances sustainable development. Therefore, this outlook has two significant innovations. First, the development from "four aspects" to "five aspects", with particular emphasis on the coordination and consistency among the five key variables, politics, economy, society, culture and ecological conservation. Secondly, the development from "being scattered" to "integration", that is, focusing on people's interests as the basic end result and sticking to people-centered development. In the five aspects of development, political development is the prerequisite for other developments, constituting the basic starting point and foothold of the right to development; only when people enjoy the political status and legal qualification for mastering state affairs can they participate in the decision-making process of development in an orderly and effective manner and determine their own fate and interest in development. Economic development is key to all other developments and lays a solid foundation for the right to development. "Right can never be higher than the economic structure of society and its cultural development which this determines".[24] To accelerate economic construction, the primary meaning of the right to development is upgrading the level and quality of economic development and meeting people's material demands, which substantially surpasses the theory of property right in the classical outlook on human rights and the theory of economic rights in the modern outlook on human rights. Although Locke proposed the idea of classifying human rights into rights to life, health, freedom and property several hundred years ago, the right to economic development far exceeds the right to property, and the rich and diversified contents and forms of the right to development can protect the right to economic development to a larger extent. We may say that without economic development, any right to development would be meaningless. Social development secures the right to development. China does not adopt the liberal idea of development, nor does it copy the idea of social development of the West, especially the welfare states in Northern Europe. Instead, based on its national conditions, China matter-of-factly explores the theory of social security with Chinese characteristics, which may seen as gradually developing from urban-rural binary opposition

---

24  K. Marx, "Marginal Notes on the Programme of the German Workers' Party", in the chapter "Critique of the Gotha Programme", *Marx & Engels Collected Works*, Vol. 24 (UK: Lawrence & Wishart, 2010), 87.

PRACTICAL CONTRIBUTION TO THE RIGHT TO DEVELOPMENT                 175

based on Hukou[25] to the unified "outlook of social equality".[26] Cultural development is an important component in the right to development. Culture is the value basis for the right to development, while the right to development is rooted in specific culture. Without culture, the right to development would lose soft power. Advanced and open national culture is not only a necessity for gathering the power of development, but also a constituent of the right to development *per se*. Ecological conservation not only directly constrains development but also constitutes a basic element of development and becomes a key to promoting sustainable development. A series of insightful ideas has been developing that center on the relationships between the right to development and carbon emissions, GDP and the right to sustainable development, and the environment and the right to development, which make due contributions to enriching the right to development.

5    In Terms of Concept, It Is Proposed That People Share the Equal Right to Participation and Development

The 17th CPC National Congress, held in 2007, officially included the concept of "the equal right to participation and development"[27] in a conference document at the highest level of the ruling party, and the 18th CPC National Congress held in 2012 re-emphasized "ensur[ing] people's equal right to participation in governance and to development".[28] As Article 1 of the *Declaration on the*

---

25   Wang Feiling, "Renovating the Great Floodgate: The Reform of China's Hukou System", in *One Country, Two Societies: Rural-Urban Inequality in Contemporary China*, ed. Martin King Whyte (Cambridge: Harvard University Press, 2010), 335–364. David Whitehouse, "Chinese Workers and Peasants in Three Phases of Accumulation", paper delivered at the Colloquium on Economy, Society and Nature, sponsored by the Center for Civil Society at the University of KwaZulu-Natal, March 2, 2006.
26   It is mainly manifested as the currently implemented poverty alleviation action plan, free population mobility policy between urban and rural areas, educational equity plan, and social security system of rural-urban integration and so on to break the discrimination of the disadvantaged groups such as farmers, migrant workers, stay-at-home children, and migrant children.
27   Hu Jintao, "Hold High the Great Banner of Socialism with Chinese Characteristics and Strive for New Victories in Building a Moderately Prosperous Society in All Respects"—Report to the Seventeenth National Congress of the Communist Party of China on October 15, 2007, accessed April 1, 2017, http://www.360doc.com/content/12/0208/10/627367_184970473.shtml.
28   Hu Jintao, "Firmly March on the Path of Socialism with Chinese Characteristics and Strive to Complete the Building of a Moderately Prosperous Society in All Respects"—Report to the Eighteenth National Congress of the Communist Party of China on November 8,

*Right to Development* clearly provides, the right to development means every human person and all peoples are entitled to "participate in, contribute to, and enjoy"[29] development. Therefore, the right to development is a unity of the right to participate in development, the right to promote development and the right to share in the results of development. Participation in development is the most basic requirement of enjoying the right to development, and the right to participate in economic life is a basic measure for acquiring the right to development. Hence, to resolve the relationship between various elements of development, we should always stress the all-dimensional participation in all processes of development centering on economic construction and emphasize the extensiveness and democracy of political participation so that people can master their own fate and determine their own interest in development in the effective participation in political decision-making. Promoting development means in-depth and continuous participation in development and is an important guarantee for sustainable enjoyment of the right to development. From the perspective of the right to development, we not only need meaningful and valuable participation but also coherent and interactive participation, as only such participation can effectively promote the right to development and obtain substantive benefits of development. "Active, free and meaningful participation in development" is the "basis" for the entire population and for all individuals to constantly improve their well-being and implement the right to development.[30] Otherwise, the right to development would surely not be truly implemented due to passive, negative or temporary participation.

Besides the right to participate in and promote development, the ultimate significance is to enjoy achievements of development in participation and promotion and realize the justice of the distribution of development benefits. "The fair distribution of benefits resulting therefrom"[31] is the fundamental requirement and material means of implementing the right to development. The basic conclusion that the Communist Party of China has repeatedly confirmed: "making results of development more fairly benefit all the people", correctly answers the relationship between the means and end of development and the relationship between development and the right to development. Development is a prerequisite for the right to development, but development does not necessarily equate to the right to development. Only when we integrate the process and results of development, can the means and end of development

---

2012, accessed April 1, 2017, http://www.chinadaily.com.cn/china/2012cpc/2012-11/18/content_15939493.htm.
29  UN, *Declaration on the Right to Development*, A/RES/41/128.
30  Ibid.
31  Ibid.

be actualized as the right to development. In the final analysis, we should clarify the relationship between development and human rights in theory, define the relationship between efficiency and equality, and construct a basic theory with Chinese characteristics for equitable distribution of the achievements of development.

## 6   In Terms of Principle, We Should Adhere to the People-Centered Orientation of the Right to Development

To replace the classical theory of "popular sovereignty"[32] by the principle of "people as central subjects"[33] is a major theoretical innovation in human rights in China. The original point of the right to development is people, and the subjects of the right to development are also people, that is, people as a whole and each individual forming the people, instead of a part of them or a small number of the elite. All discrimination based on birth, identity or status are against the original intention of the right to development. Article 2 of the *Declaration on the Right to Development* provides: "The human person is the central subject of development and should be the active participant and beneficiary of the right to development".[34] "People" are the key to the issue of the right to development. The Western concept of human rights was developed in the Renaissance and the period of the Bourgeois Revolution. The ideas of "popular sovereignty" or "sovereignty residing in people" put forward by Rousseau played a historic role in progress by laying a foundation for the development of the bourgeois concept of human rights. Nevertheless, natural rights, the social contract and the binary opposition of civil society and political state

---

32   The most famous representatives of the theory of popular sovereignty are Thomas Hobbes (1588–1679), John Locke (1632–1704), Jean-Jacques Rousseau (1712–1778). Its central idea is that legitimacy of rule or law is based on the social contract, namely the consent of the governed. Benjamin Franklin vividly made the conclusion as follows: "In free governments, the rulers are the servants and the people are their superiors and sovereigns". Cf. Benjamin Franklin, *The Political Thought of Benjamin Franklin*, ed. Ralph Ketchum (Hackett Publishing, 2003), 398.

33   "Persisting in the dominant position of the people. The people are the subjects of and source of strength for ruling the country according to the law, … rule of law construction is for the people, relies on the people, benefits the people and protects the people, makes guaranteeing the people's basic rights and interests into a starting point and stopover point, guarantees that the people enjoy broad rights and freedoms". See CCPCC, "CCP Central Committee Decision concerning Several Major Issues in Comprehensively Advancing Governance According to Law", *China Law Translate*, accessed February 3, 2017, http://www.chinalawtranslate.com/fourth-plenum-deci-sion/?lang=en.

34   UN, *Declaration on the Right to Development*, A/RES/41/128.

on which this theory was established are by nature idealistic and empirical, which will inevitably be reduced to elitism and elitist human rights. People orientation was proposed in ancient China more than 2000 years ago,[35] and people-oriented development has evolved to make the idea of people as subjects, which means that people are the subjects of the right to development and people's interest in equal development is a core concern of the right to development. "The 'theory of people as subjects' follows the Marxist tradition and sticks to the idea that equality should not stop at the so-called constitutional status of people as equal participants in state sovereignty in the political field, but must be promoted to all fields of human life including society, economy and culture etc".[36] That is, the multi-dimensional economic, social, cultural and political right to development should be equally enjoyed by all people, and the basic interests of people should be the fundamental aim of all developments.

The CPC Central Committee headed by Comrade Xi Jinping has determined people as subjects as the basic value and objective for state governance, which has been illustrated in a series of resolutions, important speeches and discussions since the 18th CPC National Congress. The Fourth Plenary Session of the 18th CPC National Congress decided to establish "people as subjects" as a basic principle. The Fifth Plenary Session of the 18th CPC National Congress further stressed that "to realize, maintain and develop the fundamental interests of the vast majority of people is the fundamental purpose of development, and we must stick to the people-centered idea of development, and take the enhancement of people's well-being and promotion of people's comprehensive development as the starting point and foothold of development".[37]

## 7 In Terms of Steps, We Should Enhance the Right to Development in the Chinese Dream for the Great Revitalization of the Chinese Nation

The essential objective of the "Chinese Dream" may be summarized as two "centennial" objectives, that is, the objective of "comprehensively building a well-off society on the 100th anniversary of the Communist Party of China" and the "establishment of a rich, democratic, civilized and harmonious

---

35   Guan Zhong, *Guan-zi*, Vol. 2 (Beijing: The Commercial Press, 1936), 8.
36   Xu Junzhong, "The Far-Reaching Significance of Re-Stressing 'People's Position as Subjects'", *Guangming Daily*, April 23, 2016.
37   "The Suggestion of the CPC Central Committee on Preparing the 13th Five-Year Plan for National Economy and Social Development", *People's Daily*, November 4, 2015.

socialist modernized country on the 100th anniversary of the People's Republic of China".[38] Comrade Xi Jinping has observed: "The Chinese Dream, in the final analysis, is a people's dream, which must be realized by closely relying on the people and must keep bringing benefits to the people".[39] Therefore, "human" rights are the basic reliance and ultimate goal on the path of realizing the "Chinese Dream". "Development is a cause involving all people", and "development ... always centers on people and takes people as the starting point and end of all actions for development".[40] Marx and Engels repeatedly stressed the importance and necessity of improving and developing people's capacities, deeming that "everyone's responsibility, mission and task are to comprehensively develop all their capacities"; "everyone is indisputably entitled to develop themselves".[41] Capacities are where rights virtually reside, all human rights are the unity of legal capacity and action capacity, and the acquisition, endowment or generation of capacities are the basic hallmarks and source of the power of human rights. Therefore, we should enable each Chinese person to stand on a stage for self-improvement, serve society and have the opportunities to live a brilliant life and turn their dreams into reality.

In terms of content, the Chinese Dream consists of three major aspects—prosperity, national revitalization and people's happiness. But in the final analysis, the Chinese Dream is for people's happiness and welfare and for the people's right to have a greater "sense of achievement", that is the right to acquire the increasingly fruitful results of reform and development. Therefore, we should "constantly make new progress in ensuring that all our people enjoy their rights to education, employment, medical care, pension, and housing, and constantly protect and develop the basic interests of the vast majority of people".[42]

---

38  Xi Jinping, "To Realize the Great Revitalization of the Chinese Nation Is the Greatest Dream of the Chinese Nation in the Modern Era", in *Xi Jinping about State Governance*, ed. the State Council Information Office of P.R.C., the Party Literature Research Center of the CPC Central Committee, and the China International Publishing Group (Beijing: Foreign Languages Press, 2014), 35–36.

39  Xi Jinping, "Speech Delivered at the First Meeting of the 12th National People's Congress", *People's Daily*, March 18, 2013.

40  Mahtar M'Bow Amadou, *People's Time*, trans. Guo Chunlin and Cha Rongsheng (Beijing: China Translation Corporation, 1986), 97.

41  Karl Marx and Friedrich Engels, *Complete Works of Marx and Engels*, Vol. 2 (Beijing: People's Press, 1960), 330–361.

42  Xi Jinping, "Speech Delivered at the First Meeting of the 12th National People's Congress", *Guangming Daily*, March 18, 2013.

## 8 In Terms of Focus, We Should Construct a Fair Social Security System

"Equality of opportunity for development is a central meaning of the right to development". One basic conclusion of the *Declaration on the Right to Development* is: "The right to development is an inalienable human right and that equality of opportunity for development is a prerogative both of nations and of individuals who make up nations".[43] Therefore, "equality of opportunity" has become a theoretical keynote of the Declaration. China has added new elements to this basis by optimizing "equality of opportunity" to become "social equity", and proposing the construction of a social equity system with equity of rights, equity of opportunities and equity of rules to ensure the realization of the right to development. The report of the 18th CPC National Congress opined: "Lose no time to construct a system playing a major role in ensuring social equity and justice, gradually establish a social equity and security system with right equity, opportunity equity and rule equity as its main contents, strive to create an equitable social environment and ensure people's equal participation and equal right to development".

As far as orientation is concerned, using "the view of social equity" as an important theoretical basis for ensuring the right to development transcends the Western formalist view of human rights that everyone is equal before the law. On the issue of justice, the West has always been in dispute from ancient times to the present. The nature of such a dispute lies in the fact that the difference and connection between equality and equity has not been identified. In fact, equality and equity not only have similarities, but also should be strictly differentiated. Equality, which advocates the equation, equivalence and parity of quantity, is an objective factual judgment; whereas equity should be a subjective value judgment, stressing fairness, justice and reasonableness, instead of simply emphasizing equation. Since the proposal of the objective of constructing a harmonious society in the Fourth Plenary Session of the 16th CPC National Congress, social equity and justice have been placed in a more important position. First, the correlation between equity and the development of people's livelihoods is re-examined and positioned in terms of three characteristics—social nature, state governance and core value. The report of the 18th CPC National Congress proposed that equity and justice are the internal requirements of socialism with Chinese characteristics. On January 7, 2014, President Xi Jinping reiterated at a political and legal work meeting of the CPC Committee that "the critical path to state governance lies in equity and

---

43  UN, *Declaration on the Right to Development*, A/RES/41/128.

integrity"; stressing that "we should take promoting social equity and justice as a core value pursuit and take the guarantee of people's livelihood and employment as a basic goal". "Social equity and justice start from the fundamental interest of the vast majority of people".[44] Therefore, social equity is a core value of development and an essential condition for the right to development.

In systemic terms, equity of rights, equity of opportunities and equity of rules surpass the abstract classification of formal justice and substantial justice. If equality of opportunity is a prerequisite, and equality of rights is an objective, then equity of rules is the key. "On whatever level of development, system is an important guarantee for social equity and justice. We should strive to overcome any violation against equity and justice caused by human factors through innovative institutional arrangements, and guarantee people's equal participation and equal right to development". "While constantly expanding the 'cake', we should also do a good job in sharing the 'cake' ... provide solutions through institutional arrangements, legal norms and policy support".[45]

In terms of scope, the theory of justice for human development is used to replace the theory of social justice or global justice. Rawls' social justice cannot spring from interior affairs of a state to focus on justice in the international community. He came to realize this point in his later years and attempted to change it in the course of constructing a *jus gentium* system, but regrettably failed to realize the change due to the inherent features of his theory. A "decent society" must protect the basic rights of all nationals, but this list of human rights only includes the right to life, the right to freedom, the right to personal property and the right to access formal equality. All nationals should approve this simple list of human rights.[46] In fact, "whether in a free society or a decent society, it will not be very likely to have any result to accept this list of human rights".[47] "Rawls' goal is a realistic Utopia".[48] "Rawls, Blake or Negal has no excuse to exempt cross-border institutional arrangements from the evaluation of social justice".[49] Besides, if the maintenance or reform of justice of

---

44   Xi Jinping, "Effectively Unify Thoughts by the Spirit of the Third Plenary Session of the 18th CPC National Congress", *Truth Seeking* 1 (2014).
45   Ibid.
46   John Rawls, *The Law of Peoples, with the Idea of Public Reason Revisited* (Cambridge, Mass: Harvard University Press, 1999), 65.
47   Thomas W. Pogge, "An Egalitarian Law of Peoples", *Philosophy and Public Affairs* 23, no. 3 (1994): 215.
48   Gillian Brock, "Recent Work on Rawls' Law of Peoples: Critics Versus Defenders (1)", trans. Chen Ke, *Foreign Theoretical Trends* 11 (2010).
49   Thomas Pogge, *Kant, Rawls and Global Justice*, trans. Liu Xin and Xu Xiandong (Shanghai: Shanghai Translation Publishing House, 2010), 529.

international rules and international organizations is lost, global justice would never be realized.

## 9 In Terms of Method, We Should Promote the Right to Development by the Idea and Method of Rule of Law

The rule of law, reform, anti-corruption and good governance are external guarantees for the right to development. The 18th CPC National Congress put forward for the first time that "we should employ thoughts and methods of the rule of law to deepen reform, promote development, resolve conflicts and maintain stability". The Fourth Plenary Session of the 18th CPC National Congress re-emphasized this point, while the Fifth Plenary Session of the 18th CPC National Congress specifically pointed out that "we should promote development by ideas and methods of the rule of law",[50] and separate the promotion of "development" by the rule of law from deepening reform, resolve conflict and maintain stability, which reflect the extreme importance of the rule of law for development and the right to development. Of its internal mechanisms, the first mechanism is based on the scientific proposition that "market economy by nature (should) be rule-of-law economy".[51] To promote economic development, "we must comprehensively promote the construction of a socialist country governed by the rule of law and provide institutionalized solutions for these problems through the rule of law".[52] The second mechanism is derived from the nature of the rule of law with Chinese characteristics, that is, "people are subjects in comprehensive state governance by the rule of law". Adhering to the status of people as their own masters and maintaining the basic requirements of people's interests are the fundamental differences between socialist rule of law and other models of the rule of law. We should "maintain people's rights and interests and enhance people's well-being in the whole course of law-based governance, and make law and its implementation fully reflect people's will";[53] "we should unswervingly enforce the rule of law ...to realize economic development, political transparency, cultural prosperity, social justices and fine ecology, we must better play the guiding and regulating role of the rule of

---

50  "The Suggestion of the CPC Central Committee on Preparing the 13th Five-Year Plan for National Economy and Social Development", *People's Daily*, November 4, 2015.
51  Xi Jinping, *Excerpts of President Xi Jinping's Discussions on Comprehensive State Governance Through Rule of Law* (Beijing: Central Party Literature Press, 2015), 10–115.
52  Ibid., 6.
53  Ibid., 28–29.

law".⁵⁴ In the third mechanism, we should ensure the equal right to development by coordinating the relationship between development and conflict of interests. Given the good overall situation of development, we should eliminate unbalanced, inharmonious and unsustainable problems in development. "To resolve the outstanding problems that people are most concerned with, that is, education, employment, distribution of income, social security, medical care and housing, we need to closely weave a network of laws and strengthen the force of the rule of law".⁵⁵ In the fourth mechanism, we should be grounded on the proposition that "the problem of the rule of law or the rule of man is a basic problem in the history of human politics and civilization", and bypass the "development pit" simply equating development with economic growth.

The course of realizing the right to development is in fact a course in which mankind becomes constantly modernized. "With a comprehensive view of modern history in the world, we can see that no country that has been successfully modernized has not well addressed the problem of the rule of law or the rule of man. On the contrary, although some countries have realized rapid development, they have not successfully entered the threshold of modernization, but sunk in this or that 'pit', leading to the stagnation or retrogression of economic and social development. This situation, to a very large extent, is related to ineffective rule of law".⁵⁶ In the fifth mechanism, we should be grounded on the "four aspects" of: "comprehensively building a well-off society, comprehensively deepening reform, comprehensively governing the State by law, and comprehensively strengthening Party self-discipline". To comprehensively deepen reform is the basic driver in realizing the right to development, to comprehensively govern the State by the rule of law is the basic guarantee for realizing the right to development, to comprehensively build a well-off society is the basic support for the right to development, and to comprehensively strengthen Party self-discipline is the basic guarantee for realizing the right to development. To comprehensively build a well-off society is an important milestone in the course of realizing the right to development. "To realize this goal by 2020, the level of development in our country will need to make great strides. ... Without comprehensively deepening reform, development will lack drive, and the society will lack vitality. Without comprehensive law-based governance, it will be difficult to realize the harmonious development of the society. ... Without comprehensively exercising self-discipline of the Party, we cannot make good

---

54   Ibid., 5.
55   Xi Jinping, *Excerpts of President Xi Jinping's Discussions on Comprehensive State Governance Through Rule of Law* (Beijing: Central Party Literature Press, 2015), 10.
56   Ibid., 12.

use of public power to seek the right to development".[57] Only when "four comprehensive efforts" support, promote and enhance each other can we jointly assume the mission of maximally guaranteeing everyone's right to development.

## 10    In Terms of Ideas, We Should Guide the Right to Development by an Innovative, Coordinated, Green, Open and Sharing Outlook on Development

All human rights are established on a certain theoretical basis. As a new human right, for the right to development to be effectively implemented, we must constantly optimize our idea. The Fifth Plenary Session of the 18th CPC National Congress stated: "To resolve the difficult problems of development, and foster advantages of development, we must firmly establish innovative, coordinated, green, open and sharing ideas of development".[58] The internal connection with the right to development is reflected as follows.

Innovation is the primary driver in realizing the right to development. The move from exogenous to endogenous development is a basic approach for acquiring vitality. Endogenous development means a course for self-sufficiency by using local resources and inherent development without relying "on international financial institutions, transnational corporations and international regulatory agencies dominated by the North".[59] A key reason for the difficulty in realizing true improvement of the right to development of developing countries is that current international economic and political relations make it impossible to acquire independent and self-sufficient innovative development, but that development must firmly rely on the technologies, funds and management experience of developed countries. Innovative development from the perspective of the right to development covers four levels of meaning, as follows.

(1) Innovative orientation of the right to development. In terms of the relationship between innovation and the right to development, it is proposed that

---

57  Xi Jinping, "A Speech in the Seminar of Major Provincial and Ministerial Main Leaders and Cadres on Learning and Implementing the Party's Spirit of the Fourth Plenary Session of the 18th CPC National Congress and Comprehensively Promoting Law-Based Governance", *People's Daily*, February 3, 2015.

58  "The Suggestion of the CPC Central Committee on Preparing the 13th Five-Year Plan for National Economy and Social Development", *People's Daily*, November 4, 2015.

59  Ash Amin, "The Difficult Transition from Informal Economy to Marshallian Industrial District", *Area* 26, no. 1 (1994): 13.

"innovation is placed on the central position of the whole situation of national development", and "to make efforts in innovation is to work on development".[60]

(2) The endogenous drive of the right to development. On the practical route to promoting the right to development by innovation, the most fundamental course is to enhance the ability for independent innovation and take the path for realizing independent and self-sufficient innovation.

(3) The innovation system for the right to development. "We should further implement the strategy of innovation driving development, promoting technological innovation, industrial innovation, enterprise innovation, market innovation, product innovation, business innovation and management innovation, and accelerating the development of an economic system and development mode with innovation as the main guidance and support".[61]

(4) The idea innovation of the right to development. Innovation is not just technological innovation but also requires innovation of theory, system and culture. Currently, as to whether the right to development exists and to its theoretical basis and institutional guarantee, there is serious disagreement and even sharp opposition in the international community. Therefore, to realize the right to development, we should conduct our own theoretical, institutional and cultural innovation as well as fully relying on technology-centered material innovation. To this end, we should construct a recognized basic theoretical system for the right to development, develop a complete policy and law regulatory system for the right to development, and create a culture for the right to development generally accepted by mankind.

Coordination is an internal requirement for realizing the right to development. The right to development is the product of deep integration of subject, time and space, and objest. The theory of equality in Western academic circles,[62] post-modernism[63] and the dependency theory of the Latin-American

---

60 "Xi Jinping's Speech on the Colloquium of Some Main Provincial CPC Party Committee Leaders in Changchun on 17 July 2015", *People's Daily*, July 20, 2015.
61 "Xi Jinping's Speech on the Colloquium of Main CPC Party Leaders in Seven Provinces and Cities in East China", *People's Daily*, May 29, 2015.
62 Wayne P. Pomerleau, "Western Theory of Justice", *Internet Encyclopedia of Philosophy*, accessed May 1, 2017, https://www.iep.utm.edu. In fact, from Aristotle to John Rawls, theories of equality have become more and more complex and multidimensional. Nowadays, the theory of justice has arisen suddenly and spread widely, it aims to "help us understand our world better and what our responsibilities are in it". Cf. Gillian Brock, "Global Justice", *The Stanford Encyclopedia of Philosophy* (Spring 2017 Edition), ed. Edward N. Zalta, accessed May 1, 2017, https://plato.stanford.edu/archives/spr2017/entries/justice-global/.
63 Wang Xigen and Tu Shaobin, "An Exposition on the Right to Development: From the Perspective of Postmodern Jurisprudence", *Legal System and Social Development*, no. 6 (2005): 53–64.

school,[64] among others, include analysis of the gap between development and unequal development, which has also produced certain positive significance to enhance the theorical basis of the right to development. Equal development on which the right to development in China depends may be called a "theory of comprehensive coordination". From the comprehensively coordinated and sustainable scientific outlook on development to the current new outlook of coordination, the contents and degree have been constantly developed and deepened. Not only is importance attached to coordination between urban and rural areas, different regions, economy and society, man and nature, and international and domestic situations, but also deep coordination is conducted inside each group of coordination objects, with stress on "promoting the simultaneous development of new industrialization, IT application, urbanization and agricultural modernization, improving national soft power while enhancing hard power, and with continuous reinforcement of overall development". To "reinforce the coordination of development, we must expand the space of development and strengthen capacity for development in weak areas".[65] This means that we should mainly protect the right to development of those undeveloped subjects who are provided with general protection of all people's right to development, specifically reflected in the following.

(1) Promoting coordinated regional development and realizing regional right to development. Region is originally a geographical concept, instead of a subject of human rights. But the jouney of realizing the right to development in China starts from regional development since reform and opening-up. The construction of special economic zones and open cities, Western development, the rise of Central China, the revitalization of old industrial bases in Northeast China, the creation of urban groups, urban circles and main function areas "create a new pattern of coordinated regional development within the capacity of resources and environment with orderly and free movement of elements, effective constraint of main functions, and equalization of basic public services",[66] so that the sparks of regional development finally spread for the benefits of all people's right to development.

(2) Promoting urban and rural coordinated development and realizing the right to development based on equality of identity, with the focus on protecting

---

64   Walter Rodney, "How Europe Underdeveloped Africa, Beyond Borders: Thinking Critically About Global Issues", *International Journal of African Historical Studies* 7, no. 2 (1997): 788–789.
65   "The Suggestion of the CPC Central Committee on Preparing the 13th Five-Year Plan for National Economy and Social Development", *People's Daily*, November 4, 2015.
66   Ibid.

the equal right to development of farmers, migrant workers, and stay-at-home children.

(3) Promoting the coordinated development of material civilization and cultural progress to effectively protect the right to cultural development. With the development from a civilized ancient country to a large country of culture, a cultural power has laid a solid foundation of culture for the right to development. During this process, the right to cultural development as a sub-set of the right to development has been formed by the interpenetration of the right to development and culture. The equal allocation of public and cultural resources such as culture, education and sports, the unequal special preferential treatment for disadvantaged groups and weak regions are turned into reality by the policy balance of the rule of law and the mandatory intervention of public power.

Green development is a necessary condition for realizing the right to development. The right to development, at the beginning of proposal, includes no mention of sustainable development.[67] As problems in the relationship between man and nature become more and more serious, more and more attention is paid to sustainable development, and optimizing the right to development with sustainable development has been put on the agenda. A new form of the right to development—"the right to sustainable development"[68]— has come into being. The concept of green development has brought a new vitality to the sustainability of the right to development, mainly reflected as follows. First, new concepts of green development have been proposed, such as "ecological conservation", "beautiful China" and "beautiful countryside". President Xi Jinping's explanation of the Suggestions of the CPC Central Committee on Preparing the 13th Five-Year Plan for National Economic and Social

---

67　Article 1 of the *Declaration on the Right to Development* points out, "The right to development is an inalienable human right by virtue of which every human person and all peoples are entitled to participate in, contribute to, and enjoy economic, social, cultural and political development, in which all human rights and fundamental freedoms can be fully realized". This indicates that the concept of the right to development, at that time, only included four dimensions—the economic, social, cultural and political development, and does not include any idea of sustainable development. (UN, *Declaration on the Right to Development*, A/RES/41/128).

68　Wang Xigen, "On the Right to Sustainable Development: Foundation in Legal Philosophy and Legislative Proposals", in *The Role of International Law in Implementing the Right to Development*, ed. Stephen P. Marks, Harvard University & Friedrich Ebert Stiftung. Chateau de Bossey, Geneva, Switzerland, 2008; Wang Xigen, "Greening the Right to Development—Legal Philosophical Basis and Legislative Suggestion of the Right to Sustainable Development", the paper of XXIV World Congress of International Association for Philosophy of Law and Social Philosophy (IVR), Beijing, 2009.

Development mentioned "green" seven times and "sustainable" four times, for the purpose of establishing solid category pillars for greening the right to development. Secondly, new values of green development are disclosed. Following the tradition of "unity of heaven and man",[69] we keep innovating and propose that "a fine ecological environment is the most equal public product and public good benefiting the most people";[70] "environment is people's livelihood" and "blue sky is also happiness".[71] These scientific conclusions profoundly disclose the relationship between ecology and people's livelihood, and point to directions of progress for construction of an ecological civilization oriented by the right to development. Thirdly , the objective of the right to sustainable development is focused on. The Third Plenary Session of the 18th CPC National Congress stresses the use of the strictest rule of law[72] to promote ecological

---

69  The idea of "the unity of heaven and man" was first proposed by Chuang Tzu (369–286 BC). He pointed out in the book *Zhuangzi*, "Man and the Heaven Are One and the Same". [Wang Rongpei, trans., *Zhuangzi* (Chinese-English Edition) (Hunan: Hunan People's Publishing House, 1999), 333.] This idea was developed into a philosophy by Dong Zhongshu (179–104 BC), an ideologist in Han Dynasty and thus formed one of the main sources of Chinese traditional culture.

70  "Xi Jinping's Speech in His Inspection Tour in Hainan from April 8–10, 2013", *People's Daily*, April 11, 2013.

71  "Xi Jinping's Speech When the Jiangxi Delegation Participate in Deliberation on March 6, 2015", *People's Daily*, April 11, 2013.

72  In legislation, China has so far promulgated over 200 laws and regulations on environmental protection. In judicial terms, an environmental litigation system has been established and the "crime of undermining the environment" has been added to the *Criminal Law*. According to the Supreme People's Procuratorate, Tengger Desert, in western China, was awarded "Global 500 Roll of Honor for Environmental Achievement" by the UN, some parts of which were seriously polluted by sewage discharged by the local industrial enterprises. All eight pollution cases were given guilty verdicts by the court. ("The Supreme People's Procuratorate: Guilty Verdicts Were Made on All the Eight Cases of Tengger Desert Pollution", accessed February 4, 2017, Chinanews Net: http://www.rmzxb.com.cn/c/2016-02-25/708455.shtml). In recent years, through amending the *Civil Procedure Law* and the *Environmental Protection Law*, the development of environmental public interest litigation has been promoted. During the ten years from 2005 to 2014, the total number of the nationwide civil environmental public interest litigations accepted by the people's court was 47, with an average annual case number less than five. Nevertheless, in 2015 alone, there were 38 cases accepted by the court. The number of cases accepted has increased significantly. (Gonggu, "An Empirical Analysis of China's Environmental Public Interest litigation in 2015", *Science of Law*, no. 9 (2016): 16–33.) Among these cases, the first public interest litigation case on smog was adjudicated by Dezhou Intermediate People's Court of Shandong on July 20, 2016. The defendant, Zhenhua Company was sentenced to pay the damage caused by excessive pollutant discharge CNY 21,983,600. (Wu Shuguang, "China's First Public Interest Litigation Case on Smog's First Verdict Was Declared", accessed February 4, 2017, Xinhua Net: http://news.xinhuanet.com/2016-07/20/c1119250591.htm.).

conservation, and puts the delineation of ecological conservation red line and strictly prohibiting to cross it as the most important and overriding task for strengthening the construction of a system of ecological conservation. Fourthly, the relationship between the right to development and ecological protection is defined. We should reject approaches that take "the right to carbon as the right to development"[73] and seek development at the cost of sacrificing the environment, and instead take an active part in international actions against climate change, and compose a new chapter of "climate justice".[74]

Opening-up is an external condition for realizing the right to development. Article 4 of the *Declaration on the Right to Development* points out: "1. States have the duty to take steps, individually and collectively, to formulate international development policies with a view to facilitating the full realization of the right to development. 2. Sustained action is required to promote more rapid development of developing countries. As a complement to the efforts of developing countries, effective international cooperation is essential in providing these countries with appropriate means and facilities to foster their comprehensive development".[75] Early on, before the adoption of the Declaration, opening-up was already taken as a State policy in China and played a significant role in the system of institutional support for the right to development.

The opening-up policies followed by China in the course of realizing the right to development have been upgraded to a new version of comprehensive opening-up, including a series of new ideas promoting the right to development through opening-up, as follows.

(1) About "coordinating domestic and international situations". "Improve the awareness and capabilities of domestic and international situations, and improve the quality and level of opening-up".[76]

(2) About the "awareness of the community of shared future". Strengthen global connections through cooperation for development, and "reduce

---

73   Yang Zewei, "The Right to Carbon Emission: A New Right to Development", *America Journal of Climate Change*, 01(2)(2012): 108–116.
74   "Kofi Annan Launches Climate Justice Campaign Track", accessed February 1, 2017, Global Humanitarian Forum: https://blogit.realwire.com/kofi-annan-launches-climate-justice-campaign-track. Wendy Koch, "Study: Climate Change Affects Those Least Responsible", USA Today, March 7, 2011. Wangari Maathai, "Africa Speaks up on Climate Change", accessed February 1, 2017, The Green Political Foundation: https://www.boell.de/de/node/270716.
75   UN, *Declaration on the Right to Development*, A/RES/41/128.
76   "Xi Jinping's Speech on the Opening Ceremony of the Seminar of Major Provincial and Ministerial Leaders and Cadres Learning and Implementing the Spirit of the Fifth Plenary Session of the 18th CPC National Congress on January 18, 2016", *People's Daily*, January 19, 2016.

inequality and disequilibrium of global development so that people in all States can enjoy the benefits from economic growth in the world".[77]

(3) About the "system of international development". Participation, innovation and optimization of the international development system provide excellent "international public products"[78] for realizing the right to development and assuming international obligations.

(4) About "global governance". This concept was not initiated in China, but China gives it a fresh meaning and includes values such as equality, justice, democracy, opening-up, tolerance, peace and development. "We should encourage equal participation and full consultation and maximally enhance the open and inclusive nature of free trade arrangement"; improve "institutional discourse power in global governance",[79] and construct an extensive community of interest.

(5) About "peace and development". The five principles of peaceful coexistence are a great invention in China, which still shine in the field of human development. The acting principles and method for the right to development have been adopted by the Declaration. Article 3 of the Declaration stipulates: "States have the duty to co-operate with each other in ensuring development and eliminating obstacles to development. States should realize their rights and fulfil their duties in such a manner as to promote a new international economic order based on sovereign equality, interdependence, mutual interest and cooperation among all States, as well as to encourage the observance and realization of human rights".[80] Peace and development depend on each other and cannot be separated. War, invasion, turmoil and armed forces do

---

[77] "Xi Jinping's Address on the Summit of the G20 2016 on December 1, 2015", *People's Daily*, December 1, 2015.

[78] "Xi Jinping's Address on the Opening Ceremony of the Asian Infrastructure Investment Bank on January 16, 2016", *People's Daily*, January 17, 2016.

[79] UNDP & CCIEE, "Reconfiguring Global Governance: Effectiveness, Inclusiveness, and China's Global Role", August 29, 2013. Xi Jinping pointed out for the first time in his speech in Brazil that the BRICS countries should develop a closer and more solid partnership to strive for more institutional power and discourse power in global governance for developing countries. Xi pointed out at the Central Conference on Foreign Affairs from November 28–29, 2014 that we should increase the representation and discourse power of China and other developing countries. In the United Nations Sustainable Development Summit 2015, President Xi also pointed out that it is important to increase the representation and the voice of developing countries, and give all countries equal rights to participate in international rule-making. (Du Yifei, "What Are Xi Jinping's Famous Conclusions on Global Governance?", accessed February 1, 2017, People.cn: http://politics.people.com.cn/n/2015/1114/c1001-27816100.html.).

[80] UN, *Declaration on the Right to Development*, A/RES/41/128.

the greatest damage to the right to development. We should promote development by peace and consolidate peace by development.

(6) About "peoples of all States share results of development". Win-win cooperation for mutual benefit is the basic principle of opening-up. Oriented by the global right to equal development and through an innovation mechanism, we should ensure the free, convenient and rapid flow of productive elements in all places worldwide to realize the maximum intersection of all parties' interests and realize the maximum sharing of the right to development.

(7) About "development cooperation". Cooperation is a means for realizing the right to development rather than an end. Unilateralism is not an end to development cooperation, as development cooperation is for the common benefit.

In terms of the method of development cooperation, we are dedicated to realizing the following transformation. First, transition from the reduction or exemption of debts or money assistance and technical assistance in the past to strengthening the construction of development capabilities, to promote the right to development by empowerment. "The international community has a duty to help developing countries grow their capacity and to provide them with support and assistance tailored to their actual needs".[81] Secondly, the transition from the mode of rule of man to the mode of the rule of law featuring good governance by good law. "Promoting development with peace and securing peace through development. A sound external institutional environment is required to sustain development. International financial institutions therefore need to step up the reform of their governance, and multilateral development agencies need to increase their supply of resources".[82] Thirdly, the transition from unilateral development cooperation to multilateral development cooperation. Optimize and expand development partnerships and construct new modes for multi-dimensional development cooperation with the interaction of the five elements of international community guided cooperation, South–North cooperation, South–South cooperation, three-party cooperation and participation in cooperation by such stakeholders as private sectors. Fourthly, the transition from scattered cooperation to coordinated cooperation. "Countries need to step up coordination of their macroeconomic policies to avoid as far as possible negative spillover effects. Regional organizations should accelerate their integration and invigorate their overall competitiveness by exploiting intra-regional complementary advantages. The United Nations must

---

81  Xi Jinping, "Towards a Mutually Beneficial Partnership for Sustainable Development—Speech at the UN Sustainable Development Summit", *People's Daily*, September 27, 2015.
82  Ibid.

continue to fulfill its leadership role".[83] Over the past six decades, China has taken an active part in international cooperation and greatly improved the right to development.[84] In the process of implementing this right, the path should be further broadened.[85]

Sharing is an inevitable result of realizing the right to development. The Fifth Plenary Session of the 18th CPC National Congress stated: "We should stick to shared development. We must stick to the guidelines that development is for the people, development relies on the people, the fruits of development are shared by the people, and more effective institutional arrangements should be made so that all the people can have a stronger sense of acquisition, the drive for development is enhanced, people's solidarity is strengthened, and all people stably march towards the direction of common prosperity". To share the right to development is mainly reflected as follows.

(1) Sharing the right to development among subjects. The essence of sharing is that everyone shares the benefits of development. All peoples and each individual, regardless of their innate or acquired differences, should share the possibility of acquiring the right to development. Qualification sharing, opportunity sharing and sharing of rights and capacity are the essential nature of everyone sharing. "Chinese people jointly share the opportunity for a brilliant life, the opportunity for turning dreams into reality and the opportunity for growing and progressing together with the motherland and time". We should correctly deal with the relationship between overall development and individual development. On the one hand, overall development is the condition

---

83  Ibid.
84  "Over the past six decades, China has provided 166 countries and international organizations with nearly CNY 400 billion worth of development assistance and dispatched over 600,000 aid workers, more than 700 of whom have laid down their precious lives in aiding the development of other countries". (Ibid.).
85  China will establish an assistance fund for South–South cooperation, with an initial pledge of USD 2 billion to support developing countries in their implementation of the Post-2015 Development Agenda, continue to increase investment in the least-developed countries, aiming to attain a level of USD 12 billion by 2030, write off the debt on outstanding intergovernmental interest-free loans due by the end of 2015 owed by designated least-developed countries, landlocked developing countries, and small island developing countries, establish an international development center for studying and exchanging knowledge between countries on the theories and practice of development best suited to their respective national conditions, propose a discussion on establishing a global energy internet to facilitate efforts to meet global power demand with clean and green alternatives, work with other stakeholders to make rapid progress on the implementation of the Belt and Road Initiative, quickly render the Asian Infrastructure Investment Bank and the BRICS New Development Bank operational, and contribute to the economic growth of the developing countries and the well-being of their peoples. (Ibid.).

of individual development. "Only when the country is good and the nation is good will everyone be good".[86] On the other hand, the right to development is the right of each individual. It mainly strengthens the protection of the right to development of women, children, old people, persons with disabilities, and migrant workers.

(2) The right to shared development. Common prosperity is the prerequisite for sharing. On the basis of the right to sharing economic developments, realizing the right of comprehensive development is the basic context of the right to sharing development. "People's yearning for a good life is the goal of our struggle". Sharing the right to development means that people can enjoy "better education, more stable jobs, more satisfactory income, more reliable social security, and a higher level of medical care service, more comfortable living conditions, and a better environment".[87] "Social construction should have joint construction and sharing as a basic principle". "The construction of a housing security and supply system is an inevitable requirement for promoting social equality and justice and guaranteeing that the people share the results of reform and development".[88] "China should firmly implement the strategy of rejuvenating the State by science and education, strive to enable each child to share the opportunity of education, and strive to enable 1.3 billion people to enjoy better and more equal education and acquire the abilities to develop themselves, contribute to society and benefit the people". "Let millions of children share excellent education under the blue sky and change their fate with knowledge".[89]

(3) The right to sharing development by region. The right to sharing development requires that all people are treated and respected equally without differences by region and have an equal sense of acquisition. "Former revolutionary base areas" have drawn the world's attention as a special Chinese term. The right to development of rural areas, especially poverty-stricken areas, has become the "most difficult and heavy task" for China to realize the right to development. "If a well-off life is not developed for rural areas, especially poverty-stricken areas, a well-off society is not built in an all-round manner".[90]

---

86  Xi Jinping, *Excerpts of Statements on the Chinese Dream of Realizing the Great Revitalization of the Chinese Nation* (Beijing: Central Party Literature Press, 2013), 3–4.
87  Xi Jinping, "People's Yearning for a Nice Life Is Our Goal of Struggle", *People's Daily*, December 16, 2012.
88  Xi Jinping, "Accelerate the Construction of Housing Security and Constantly Realize the Goal of People's Housing Security", *People's Daily*, October 31, 2013.
89  "Xi Jinping Sent a Letter to Congratulate the Opening of the International Education IT Application Conference on May 23, 2015", *People's Daily*, May 24, 2015.
90  "Xi Jinping's Speech When Visiting People in Straitened Circumstances in Fuping County, Hebei Province on December 29–30, 2012", *People's Daily*, December 31, 2012.

"To construct a well-off society, no ethnic group can be left out".[91] "Development will not be complete without 'former revolutionary based areas' becoming well-off, especially the alleviation of the poverty of people in these areas".[92] To sum up, adhering to innovative development, coordinated development, green development, open development and sharing development is a comprehensive and in-depth reform concerning the overall situation of development in China, which endows unprecedented rich content and fresh characteristics to the right to development and upgrades the theory of the right to development to a new realm.

### Conclusion and Suggestions

The diversity of human rights culture determines the diversity of methods for realizing human rights. Just as in achieving development, there is no uniform mode for realizing the right to development in the world. The mutual exchange and use for reference of different human rights cultures has created good conditions for the sustainable realization of the right to development. China's practices on the right to development in the past nearly 40 years since the 1980s is in keeping with the adoption and practice processes of the *Declaration on the Right to Development* and can provide certain references for countries around the world to implement their right to development, especially in terms of ideas and practice. In a word, China's experience in realizing the right to development is that the right to development has been put in the mainstream of ideas, principles, strategies, methods and actions in the system of human rights. Thus, we suggest the international community should take the following productive and efficient measures to promote the realization of the right to development.[93]

---

91    "Xi Jinping's Speech When Meeting Cadre and Mass Representatives in Gongshan Dulong Nationality and Nu Nationality Autonomous County of Nujiang Prefecture", *People's Daily*, January 23, 2015.

92    "Xi Jinping's Speech at the Colloquium on Poverty Alleviation in Shanxi, Gansu and Ningxia Revolutionary Area", *People's Daily*, February 17, 2015.

93    The author of this chapter, Professor Wang Xigen, gave a keynote speech on the Suggestions on China's Experiences of Implementing the Right to Development during the 33th Session of UN Human Rights Council, and as the representative of China NGO Network for International Exchanges, Mr. Wang presented "The Proposals to Promote Implementation and Protection of the Right to Development" to UN Human Rights Council. ("Countries Can Learn from China's Development Experience: Academic", accessed June 17, 2016, Xinhua Net: http://news.xinhuanet.com/english/2016-09/21/c_135703681.htm.).

First, as to mainstreaming the right to development, on the basis of full awareness of the urgency of the right to development and its correlation with other human rights, the United Nations should set up a special mechanism for safeguarding the mainstreaming of the right to development according to *Declaration on the Right to Development* and other related resolutions. A consensus in mainstreaming the right to development should be reached by in-depth research and discussions in special conferences. It is suggested to make a resolution on mainstreaming the right to development to confirm its concept, basic principles, strategies and action plans.

Secondly, as to the relationship between the right to development and the 2030 Agenda for Sustainable Development, the United Nations should further research the specific paths, measures, steps, reviews and supervision mechanisms which can integrate the right to development into the Agenda, and to set specific phased goals and tasks according to the 17 Goals of the Agenda. To achieve these goals, it is suggested that the United Nations build a high-level task force on the right to development and enhance the internal coordination of the United Nations system and cooperation among international organizations, states, civil societies and research institutions to carry out targeted research. Governments should establish their own schemes according to different national conditions and current development situations to ensure the schemes are realized in a planned way.

Thirdly, as to the priority of the right to development in human rights systems, livelihood issues, such as poverty, hunger, disease, education, unemployment and so on, should be firmly handled. For this, we need to clarify the prerequisite question of the interdependence between the right to development and civil, political rights and economic, social and cultural rights. One should bear in mind that the 2030 Agenda for Sustainable Development has confirmed the correlation between the right to development and the Agenda. Of particular importance is to ensure enough food, clean drinking water, basic health care, adequate housing, full employment, social security and public services are shared by all people.

Fourthly, as to summarizing and sharing experiences of the right to development, the United Nations and other international organizations should build a platform to share the experience of implementing this right. In other words, on the basis of extensively collecting successful experience and lessons from failures of these practices around the world, we may select typical samples to provide references for the international community to carry out the right to development. Since 1979, China has exercised reform and opening-up, forming models for regional development, poverty reduction, fair education, sustainable development, etc., which have made due contributions to the formation and implementation of the 2030 Agenda for Sustainable Development. In April 2016, China released its *Position Paper on the Implementation of the 2030 Agenda for Sustainable Development*, expounding China's position, proposals and initiatives for the implementation of the Agenda. China placed development at the core of the G20's agenda, a ground-breaking move in the Group's history. Working under the theme of "towards an inclusive and interconnected world economy", the G20 will take up the implementation of the Sustainable Development Agenda as one of its priorities of 2018. We hope to exchange China's experience with every state on the principles of quality and free will.

Last but not least, as to global partnership for development, relevant international organizations, countries, corporations and NGOs should cooperate on investment, trade, finance and intellectual property, mainly to help developing countries ease the debt crisis, provide technical assistance and enhance capacity-building. Therefore, all states are called upon to take effective measures to fulfill official development aid commitments in a complete and timely fashion. To increase efficiency, the existing mechanisms, plans and projects of the United Nations should be integrated and a dialogue platform between civil society and the authority should be built. For example, the function of a Social Forum can also be expanded so that the session can be held two or more times instead of only once a year. The representation of the participants should be improved so that scholars and people from commercial enterprises, the financial sector and NGOs can take part in wide discussions on key problems of the right to development and create documents to submit to the UN system as a decision-making reference. In short, the international community should strengthen global and regional cooperation, optimize schemes and take concerted action, jointly creating a bright future for the right to development instead of leaving anyone behind.

CHAPTER 11

# Practices for Realization of the Right to Development and Experience Sharing in Peru

*Carlos Alberto Aquino Rodriguez**

## 1   Introduction

The United Nations *Declaration on the Right to Development*, adopted by the General Assembly in its Resolution 41/128 of December 4, 1986, states the following in its Article 8, paragraph 1: "States should undertake, at the national level, all necessary measures for the realization of the right to development and shall ensure, inter alia, equality of opportunity for all in their access to basic resources, education, health services, food, housing, employment and the fair distribution of income. Effective measures should be undertaken to ensure that women have an active role in the development process. Appropriate economic and social reforms should be carried out with a view to eradicating all social injustices".[1]

In addition, the United Nations established the Millennium Development Goals to be achieved by 2015 that considered the following among its eight Goals: eradicating extreme poverty and hunger, achieving universal primary education, promoting gender equality and empowering women, and reducing child mortality.[2] Again, in January 2016, the United Nations established the Sustainable Development Goals to be achieved by 2030 that considered the following among its 17 Goals: no poverty, zero hunger, good health and well-being, quality education, gender equality, decent work and economic growth, reduced inequalities.[3]

---

* Carlos Alberto Aquino Rodriguez, Professor of the Faculty of Economics at San Marcos National University of Peru and Coordinator of the Center of Asian Studies. His area of research includes International Trade Theory and Policy, East Asia Economies, Comparative Economic Development of East Asia and Latin America, etc.
1   UN *Declaration on the Right to Development*, accessed May 12, 2017, http://www.un.org/documents/ga/res/41/a41r128.htm.
2   We Can End Poverty, Millennium Development Goals and Beyond 2015: http://www.un.org/millenniumgoals/, accessed May 12, 2017.
3   United Nations Sustainable Development Goals, 17 Goals to Transform Our World: http://www.un.org/sustainabledevelopment/blog/2015/12/sustainable-development-goals-kick-off-with-start-of-new-year/, accessed May 12, 2017.

To that end, states should develop policies that can provide the basic resources mentioned in the first paragraph and that are also the objectives of the United Nations Development Goals. In this chapter, a presentation will be made of the policies that Peru is undertaking regarding the best practices for the realization of the right to development and how this experience can be shared with other countries. Reference will also be made to policies that China undertook and have been regarded as successful in the achievement of access to some of the basic resources mentioned above.

## 2  Peru's Record on Economic Growth

In the last decade Peru can be considered to be one of the fastest growing economies in Latin America. As can be seen from Graph 1, Peru's average growth in the last decade was nearly 5%, and in 2016 it achieved growth of around 4.0%, while the average for Latin America was −1.0%, as shown in Table 1.

Peru's economic growth is due to two factors: first, a strong external demand for its natural resources, as it is a country richly endowed with natural resources (minerals such as copper, iron ore, gold, silver, lead; fishery products; natural gas and oil), and in recent years exports of its agro-industrial goods (grapes, asparagus, avocado, paprika, cacao, mangos, etc.) has also increased; and secondly, there has been a strong growth in investment, both governmental and private (foreign and national), in the provision of infrastructure and investment in mining and energy projects, among others.

Thanks to the strong economic growth achieved in the last 15 years, from 2000 onwards, the poverty rate in Peru has decreased from 54.7% in 2001 to 22.7% in 2014.[4] Poverty reduction has been achieved thanks to its rapid economic growth, which has seen an increase in the average GDP per capita, from a low of around USD 4,000 in 2000 to nearly USD 12,000 in 2015 (on a purchasing power parity basis, as seen in Graph 2), and to certain specific social policies that will be detailed below.

The surest and fastest way to achieve a reduction in poverty and to provide basic resources such as education, health services, food, housing, employment, is for the economy to grow. In this regard, China is probably the best example of a country that has been able to grow very fast and made possible a fast reduction in its poverty rate. According to a report by the United Nations published

---

4  See ECLAC, "Social Panorama of Latin America 2015", Table I A 1.1, p. 47, http://www.cepal.org/en/publications/39964-social-panorama-latin-america-2015.

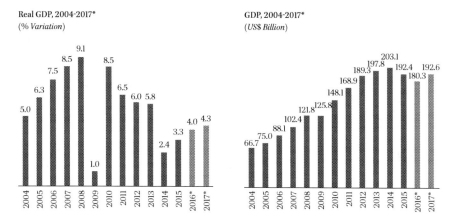

GRAPH 1   Peru GDP Annual Average Variations in % and in Billion Dollars
SOURCE: PROINVERSION PRESENTATION "WHY INVEST IN PERU?",
MARCH 2017

in 2012 entitled "Report Submitted by the Special Rapporteur on the Right to Food, Olivier De Schutter" of a mission to China (from December 15 to 22, 2010), "Domestic food availability has increased from 1,500 calories per capita per day at the start of the 1960s to 3,000 calories per capita per day in 2000. With a population of 1.3 billion and a surface of arable land of 121.7 million hectares, China has 21 per cent of the world's population, 8.5 per cent of the world's total arable land and 6.5 per cent of the world's water reserves".[5] That has meant, as the report states, that "the absolute number of poor fell from 652 million to 135 million between 1981 and 2004".

What is more impressive is that China's economic growth has been consistent since it launched its economic reforms at the end of 1978. From 1979 to 2011, China grew by a yearly average of 10%, and from 2012 it has been growing at an average rate of 7%. That is what a country needs—a stable and continuous economic growth. China can offer a lesson to other countries of how to achieve that, by way of promoting an export-oriented economy that employs an abundant labor force, and policies to promote an increase in production and

---

5  See United Nations General Assembly, Human Right Council, "Report Submitted by the Special Rapporteur on the Right to Food", Olivier De Schutter, Addendum Preliminary Note on the Mission to China (December 15–23, 2010), accessed May 12, 2017, https://documents-dds-ny.un.org/doc/UNDOC/GEN/G11/108/43/PDF/G1110843.pdf?OpenElement.

TABLE 1  Some Economic Indicators for Countries in the Western Hemisphere

Annex Table 1.1.3. Western hemisphere economies: real GDP, consumer prices, current account balance, and unemployment (*Annual percent change, unless noted otherwise*)

| | Real GDP | | | Consumer prices | | | Current account balance | | | Unemployment | | |
|---|---|---|---|---|---|---|---|---|---|---|---|---|
| | | Projections | | | Projections | | | Projections | | | Projections | |
| | 2016 | 2017 | 2018 | 2016 | 2017 | 2018 | 2016 | 2017 | 2018 | 2016 | 2017 | 2018 |
| **North America** | 1.7 | 2.2 | 2.4 | 1.4 | 2.8 | 2.4 | -2.6 | -2.7 | -3.2 | ... | ... | ... |
| United States | 1.6 | 2.3 | 2.5 | 1.3 | 2.7 | 2.4 | -2.6 | -2.7 | -3.3 | 4.9 | 4.7 | 4.6 |
| Canada | 1.4 | 1.9 | 2.0 | 1.4 | 2.0 | 2.1 | -3.3 | -2.9 | -2.7 | 7.0 | 6.9 | 6.8 |
| Mexico | 2.3 | 1.7 | 2.0 | 2.8 | 4.8 | 3.2 | -2.7 | -2.5 | -2.7 | 4.3 | 4.4 | 4.4 |
| Puerto Rico | -1.8 | -3.0 | -2.5 | 0.2 | 1.5 | 0.5 | ... | ... | ... | 11.8 | 12.6 | 12.1 |
| **South America** | -2.7 | 0.6 | 1.8 | ... | ... | ... | -1.9 | -1.9 | -2.1 | ... | ... | ... |
| Brazil | -3.6 | 0.2 | 1.7 | 8.7 | 4.4 | 4.3 | -1.3 | -1.3 | -1.7 | 11.3 | 12.1 | 11.6 |
| Argentina | -2.3 | 2.2 | 2.3 | ... | 25.6 | 18.7 | -2.6 | -2.9 | -3.4 | 8.5 | 7.4 | 7.3 |
| Colombia | 2.0 | 2.3 | 3.0 | 7.5 | 4.5 | 3.2 | -4.4 | -3.6 | -3.3 | 9.2 | 9.5 | 9.3 |
| Venezuela | -18.0 | -7.4 | -4.1 | 254.9 | 720.5 | 2,068.5 | -2.4 | -3.3 | -2.1 | 21.2 | 25.3 | 28.2 |
| Chile | 1.6 | 1.7 | 2.3 | 3.8 | 2.8 | 3.0 | -1.4 | -1.4 | -1.7 | 6.5 | 7.0 | 6.8 |
| Peru | 3.9 | 3.5 | 3.7 | 3.6 | 3.1 | 2.6 | -2.8 | -1.9 | -2.0 | 6.7 | 6.7 | 6.7 |
| Ecuador | -2.2 | -1.6 | -0.3 | 1.7 | 0.3 | 0.6 | 1.1 | 0.9 | -0.1 | 5.2 | 5.7 | 5.8 |
| Bolivia | 4.1 | 4.0 | 3.7 | 3.6 | 4.0 | 5.0 | -5.4 | -3.9 | -2.6 | 4.0 | 4.0 | 4.0 |

| | | | | | | | | | | |
|---|---|---|---|---|---|---|---|---|---|---|
| Uruguay | 1.4 | 1.6 | 2.6 | 9.6 | 7.7 | 7.5 | -1.0 | -1.5 | -1.6 | 7.9 | 7.8 | 7.8 |
| Paraguay | 4.1 | 3.3 | 3.7 | 4.1 | 4.0 | 4.0 | 0.6 | -1.4 | -0.5 | 0.1 | 5.4 | 5.5 |
| **Central America** | 3.8 | 3.9 | 4.1 | 2.1 | 2.8 | 3.5 | -3.0 | -3.1 | -3.2 | ... | ... | ... |
| **Caribbean** | 3.4 | 3.6 | 4.2 | 2.8 | 4.3 | 4.3 | -3.4 | -3.7 | -3.8 | ... | ... | ... |
| *Memorandum* | | | | | | | | | | | | |
| Latin America and the Caribbean | -1.0 | 1.1 | 2.0 | 5.6 | 4.2 | 3.7 | -2.1 | -2.1 | -2.3 | ... | ... | ... |
| East Caribbean Currency Union | 1.9 | 2.4 | 2.3 | -0.2 | 1.7 | 1.6 | -11.7 | -13.8 | -13.8 | ... | ... | ... |

SOURCE: IMF, "WORLD ECONOMIC OUTLOOK", APRIL 2017, PAGE 48.

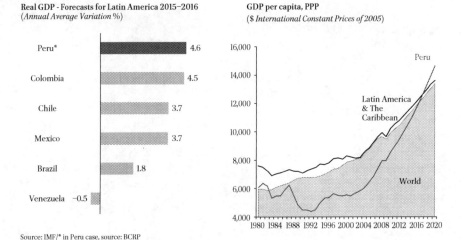

GRAPH 2  Real GDP growth for Peru and some Latin American countries
SOURCE: PROINVERSION PRESENTATION "WHY INVEST IN PERU?",
OCTOBER 2016

productivity in rural areas, by for example establishing a "guaranteed minimum procurement price system for the main grain sorts and agricultural input subsidies, facilitating the flow of resources from industry to agriculture" and in this way improve the lot of farmers, as the report mentioned above states.

In the case of Peru, its economy is still dependent on external demand for its natural resources and as prices of many of these products have decreased from a peak in 2012, the impact was felt in a slowdown of its economic growth. Even so, Peru did not suffer as much as other countries because it does not depend on a few primary goods but has a diversified export basket, and its export markets are also diversified. But Peru's economic structure is still underdeveloped and this need to change to guarantee sustainable economic growth, as seen in China. Also, there is still no consistent policy to improve the lot of farmers, and even if on the one hand the agricultural sector in the coastal area has been modernized and was responsible for the boom in agro-industrial exports mentioned above, on the other hand the agricultural sectors in the Andean and the Amazon regions lack modern machinery for example, and access of products to markets for the farmers is difficult due to the lack of decent roads.

Another question that Peru has to solve is how to give greater value added to the natural resources that it has. What is needed to achieve this is, among other things, the provision of skilled labor so manufacturing facilities can be set up, and the physical infrastructure (seaports, airports, railways and highways) so goods and people can move easily. Provision of information and technology for achieving international competitiveness is also needed. In these things, China's experience gives a very interesting example of how to achieve this, and its experience can be taken into account.

Even so, the reduction in the poverty rate in Peru has also been achieved by the implementation of certain social policies that can be seen as best practices for the realization for the right to development. Poverty cannot be eliminated by economic growth alone; certain public policies should also be in place. The policies that Peru adopted are outlined below.

## 3      Peru Social Policies for Reducing Poverty

Peru adopted certain social policies for reducing poverty and for ensuring access to basic resources, education, health services, food, housing, employment and the fair distribution of income. As has been said, economic growth alone is not enough, because there are people that cannot benefit of the fruits of economic growth, either because they lack certain skills to participate in the labor market, because they live in areas that are difficult to access, or because they have disabilities.

The range of social policies adopted by Peru tried to focus on the groups in need of them. We mention below some of these:

### 3.1    *Health*

Peru's public health system suffers from insufficient funding and many people are left with no access to decent health services if they cannot pay for private care. In order to tackle this issue in 2009 "two public health insurance schemes were established—in addition to public hospitals—to alleviate costs to beneficiaries. The first of them, EsSalud, has a contributory nature and is mandatory for all formal workers, while the second one, SIS, is geared towards the poor and vulnerable population and is, therefore, free of charge".[6]

Even so it is estimated that 30% of people are still not covered by any health insurance. So there is a need to expand the public health system. In this regard the government has been trying to increase the share of public health expenditure relative to the country GDP in recent years, and this has slightly increased from around 4.4% in 1995 to around 5% in 2012.[7]

---

6   Several authors, "Overview of Chilean and Peruvian Social Policies: Impressions from a Study Tour", International Policy Center, Working Paper No. 148, September 2016, p. 5, accessed May 12, 2017, http://www.ipc-undp.org/pub/eng/WP148_Overview_of_Chilean_and_Peruvian_social_policies.pdf.

7   Ibid.

One scheme implemented by Lima city council to make access to a public hospital easier should also be mentioned. The problem with public hospitals is that to receive treatment an appointment is needed beforehand and this can take a long time. So Lima city council created so-called "Hospitales de Solidaridad" (Solidarity Hospitals) which charge PEN 10 (around USD 3) to get an appointment but attention is given immediately. Solidarity Hospitals have allowed many people to get immediate treatment, and the experience has been imitated by other city councils.

### 3.2  Social Security

Peru faces challenges in its social security policy because although on the one hand the working age population is increasing and at the same time is being accompanied by a smaller child population (a reduction that is higher than the proportional increase in the older population) thus creating a demographic dividend, on the other hand the increase in the elderly population in the next decade will create a situation where the social protection network would be financially threatened if the current child population is not large enough to replace the working age population.[8]

Peru has two principal social security schemes with mandatory enrollment and contribution requirements for formally employed workers: one financed by a pay-as-you-earn method, that is, contributors would finance payments for those beneficiaries who had already retired, counting on the guarantee of receiving a fixed pension once they themselves retire, which would be financed by contributions from the working-age population of the following generation;[9] and the other is an individual capitalization system, where people deposit a part of their salary or income in a personal account and when they retire will receive what they have saved.

The problem with these systems is that first, not everyone is enrolled in them, as not everyone has an employment in the formal system; and secondly, the pensions people receive when they retire are not high enough (except for those with a higher income).

So for people who are not employed in the formal sector, or for those whose earnings are so low they cannot save enough money for when they retire, in 2011 the government created a scheme called Pension 65. This scheme gives people older than 65 and living in extreme poverty a bimonthly stipend of PEN 250 (around USD 75). It is estimated that a little more than half a million people (534,000) are now beneficiaries of this program.[10]

---

8   Ibid., 9.
9   Ibid., 11.
10  See "Pensión 65: Bienestar Pero No Más Salud", *"El Comercio" Newspaper*, October 28, 2016, http://elcomercio.pe/sociedad/peru/pension-65-bienestar-no-mas-salud-noticia-1942490?ref=flujo_tags_246627&ft=nota_1&e=titulo.

## 3.3 Education

To encourage children to attend school and to provide them with enough food so they can properly learn, a school feeding program is in existence, called Qali Warma. It provides meals to every child in public school at the primary level. In 2017 it will feed 3,627,723 students in 62,876 schools.[11]

Qali Warma, a Quechua word meaning vigorous child, was created at the end of 2012 to replace the Programa Nacional de Apoyo Alimentario (PRONAA), which itself was created in 1992, and gives children in extreme poverty two meals, breakfast and lunch, and breakfast for other children.

## 3.4 Conditional Cash Transfers

In 2005, Peru's government implemented a new program that gives families living in extreme poverty a periodic cash payment subject to compliance with certain criteria by the families. This program is called "Programa Juntos", and by the end of 2015 there were 814,533 households receiving this benefit, mainly in rural areas, the program benefiting children up to the age of 19 or until they finish the secondary school, and also pregnant women.

Families are given a monthly PEN 100 (around USD 30) but have to comply with certain conditions:[12]

– Families with pregnant and lactating mothers: Mothers must obtain pre- and post-natal care. The focus is to provide adequate vaccination to the mothers, such as tetanus and anti-parasitic shots, as well as health supplements such as folic acid and iron.
– Families with children below the age of five: To avoid malnutrition, children are made to undergo frequent nutritional and health check-ups which guarantee a complete round of vaccinations, iron supplements, vitamin A and parasitic control. These checkups also involve the periodic monitoring of children's height and body weight.
– Families with children between the ages of six and 14, but with incomplete basic schooling: Children in these households are required to attend school for at least 85 per cent of the school year. Given that children belonging to this age group have a higher probability of being involved in child labor due to their poor domestic circumstances, the goal is to provide families with sufficient money so as to allow children to go to school instead of working.

---

11  See the website of Qali Warma: http://www.qaliwarma.gob.pe/?page_id=74, accessed May 15, 2017.
12  See page 25 of the study "Overview of Chilean and Peruvian Social Policies: Impressions from a Study Tour", International Policy Center, Working Paper No. 148, September 2016, http://www.ipc-undp.org/pub/eng/WP148_Overview_of_Chilean_and_Peruvian_social_policies.pdf.

## 4 Conclusions

As can be seen from Peru's experience, certain specific policies have to be adopted to help reduce poverty. These target vulnerable groups such as older persons with no pension system with the Pension 65 program, children in extreme poverty with the Qali Warma school meals program, and the conditional cash payment for families living in extreme poverty with the Programa Juntos.

Perhaps the Programa Juntos conditional cash payment program, said to be one of the most successful public policies implemented by Peru, can serve as example of best practice for the realization of the right to development and can be shared with other countries.

As has been said, economic growth alone will not eliminate poverty or provide basic resources. Specific social policies are needed. Perhaps even China, which has achieved remarkable economic growth since it began economic reforms in 1979, could learn from other countries' experiences with certain public policies, such as those adopted by Peru.

CHAPTER 12

# "Ubuntu-ism" as the Arbiter between Cultural Relativism and Universalism in the Context of the Right to Development

*Mofihli Teleki**

## 1   Introduction

The *Declaration on the Right to Development* (DRD) is a non-binding legal document which has been signed and ratified by world nations. By virtue of the fact that it is a universal legal document, arguments surrounding its application in societies domestically and internationally occur with reference to the law, politics and historical particularity between the North and South nations. These North and South nations often argue for the implementation of the DRD using their respective frame of reference.

Certain frames of arguments regarding the implementation of the DRD often occur with principles where there is a "one size fits all" or by applying the DRD with reference to local principles.[1] Without discarding the one size fits all principle or localized approaches, it is important to re-frame the thinking around the implementing the DRD using other philosophies, other than universalism or cultural relativism.

The concept of Ubuntu is arguably one that could be scrutinized within the context of cultural relativism by virtue of the fact that as a concept or construct it is located within the historical particularity of Africans.[2] Boas' concept of cultural relativism as it appears within the postmodern theories of culture is often misconstrued to reflect linear scenarios of applicability of cultural order thereby objectifying relativism through routinized rhetoric.[3]

---

\*   Mofihli Teleki, Head of Communications at the Commission for Gender Equality (South Africa) and a scholar in the right to development and human rights.
1   Tanja A. Börzel and Thomas Risse, "One Size Fits All! EU Policies for the Promotion of Human Rights, Democracy and the Rule of Law", *Workshop on Democracy Promotion* 4 (2004): 1.
2   Ignasio Malizani Jimu, "Shared Sociability and Humanity", *Journal of Pan African Studies* 9, no. 4 (2016): 404–412.
3   A. Orta, "The Promise of Particularism and the Theology of Culture: Limits and Lessons of 'Neo-Boasianism'", *American Anthropologist*, 106(3) (2004): 475.

It is perhaps the timing and "relevance" of enveloping principles of Boas' theory that could best explain why it is that the notions of cultural relativism are shrouded in linear thought and progression over time. For instance, Brown[4] argues that scholars of relativism,[5] have in the past articulated that the relativist doctrine was appealing to intellectuals who in the past were disillusioned by the aftermath of World War I through which Western cultural superiority was undermined. Through this came an axiom that suggests that each culture should constitute a social order that reproduces itself through enculturation.[6] In light of this, it would seem that the post-World War I epoch along with the challenges that befell the remnants of the war in Western nations, fashioned the notion of enculturation as a result of the destruction caused by the war.

The relevance of scholarship during that period was arguably enticing to those of who sought solutions to the crises caused by the destruction from war as well as the enduring aftermath.

It remains important that, since global and universal nuances of rights are found in several statutes of the African Union (AU) and United Nations (UN), it may be difficult to either ignore or discard human rights obligations in favor of cultural concepts.[7] This means that there could be a symbiotic relationship between cultural concepts such as Ubuntu and certain elements of the right to development. At the same time, the presence of ancient knowledge on these African cultural concepts could function alongside each other, or the cultural concepts could by themselves become enablers to the justification the right to development.

Irrespective of the modal perspective for the justification of the right to development, applying cultural concepts such as Ubuntu in advancing the need for the right to development in Africa cannot always be reduced to a certain level of legitimacy either through the approach of universalism or cultural relativism. The reason for this is that neither cultural relativist thought nor universalism should be antecedents for the relevance of Ubuntu or "Ubuntuism" (or the institutionalization of Ubuntu). I have already pointed out that the

---

4   Michael F. Brown, Regna Darnell, Thomas Hylland Eriksen, Robert M. Hayden, Henrietta L. Moore, Fred Myers, Richard A. Shweder, and Richard Ashby Wilson, "Cultural Relativism 2.0.", *Current Anthropology* 49, no. 3 (2008): 364.
5   Brown et al. (2008, 368) mention students of Boas and refer to Ruth Benedict, Margaret Mead, and Melville Herskovits.
6   Ibid., 364.
7   This refers to *African Charter on Human and Peoples' Rights* (1986, Art. 2) and UN *Declaration on the Granting of Independence to Colonial Countries and Peoples*, General Assembly resolution 1514 (XV) of December 14, 1960.

timing and relevance or even necessity to advance cultural relativism would have varied according to social conditions of a specific era of life.

## 2  Brief Discussion on Fundamentals of Universalism and Cultural Relativism

The contents of this section of the chapter do not attempt to define or redefine universalism and cultural relativism from the current scholarly texts, nor do they attempt to argue for or against either of the principles. I rather make an attempt to illustrate the key fundamentals that give meaning to universalism and cultural relativism as they emerge within the sphere of human rights and within society.

There are those who believe that absolution should not be a key characteristic of either principle, while others believe that there is a symbiotic relationship between universalism and cultural relativism, in that universalist practices could be deemed as relative in the same way that cultural relativism would never offer an absolute answer to the moral agency of most or some cultures. Whether the symbiotic relationship between universalism and cultural relativism are adequate or inadequate is something that requires a much wider debate. The same applies to an attempt to legitimize or assess the adequacy of the relationship between universalism and cultural relativism. So, in this section of chapter the discussion is intended to look into universalism and cultural relativism as doctrines that help to shape the thinking around actualizing either of these concepts, i.e. universalism and cultural relativism.

### 2.1  *Doctrine of Cultural Relativism*
Cultural relativism as a doctrine prescribes that moral behavior of society will be shaped by a culture and if society accepts that culture, the culture will be approved by society and by so doing the actual approval (of that culture) gives credence to cultural actions that society follows.[8] In other words, if society disapproves of a culture, the culture is bound to be immoral and discarded by society, rendering it useless.[9] This could mean that there is a need for a "buy in" from society in order for that particular culture to exist or survive. There seems to be a belief amongst cultural relativists that if human rights are not indigenous to a specific culture, the validity of those rights are then questioned, thus raising a fundamental link between the origins of the value for the

---
8  Seungbae Park, "Defense of Cultural Relativism", *Cultural* 8, no. 1 (2011): 160.
9  Ibid.

culture.¹⁰ Simply put, this points to the belief that the crucial aspect for the acceptance of a culture is justified through discernible values.

Cultural relativism also consists of a set of doctrines that gives society a prescriptive force on how culture is to be advanced.¹¹ The important aspect about cultural relativism in this instance lies in the fact that cultures themselves differ across time and space in a dramatic manner.¹²

When cultures evolve and become fluid, changes within the environment place challenges on certain cultures. The core ideals of cultural relativism do not offer a solution to the clashes and claims made by scholars on how to mediate and mitigate against the conflict that is found in the interpretation of universalism and cultural relativism.¹³ The construct of cultural relativism does not provide a code from which harmony is derived in order to create a balance between conflicting moralities within cultures and outside of those cultures.¹⁴ The negative impact of cultural relativism in this instance concerns the harsh reality of misuse of cultures that are deemed to be naturally good in order to justify human rights abuses within social strata. This is why harmful traditional practices tend to be a problem in countries that follow the doctrines of cultural relativism.¹⁵

## 2.2  *Universalism as a Doctrine*

There seems to be a consensus from various texts on the fact that it is unlikely that cultural relativism can be comparable to universal moral codes.¹⁶

The concept of universalism gives priority over universal disposition and knowledge, compromising other forms of local knowledge (which is deemed non-universal) and by so doing, this actually limits conceptual thinking about the world.¹⁷

Universalism has been a point of discussion from the times of Plato and Aristotle. Xuanmeng mentions that discussions of universalism can be traced back to the time when Kant argued that empiricism was needed to justify why

---

10    Michael E. Goodhart, "Origins and Universality in the Human Rights Debates: Cultural Essentialism and the Challenge of Globalization", *Human Rights Quarterly* 25, no. 4 (2003): 939.
11    Jack Donnelly, "The Relative Universality of Human Rights", *Human Rights Quarterly* 29, no. 2 (2007): 294.
12    Ibid.
13    Seungbae Park, "Defense of Cultural Relativism", 159.
14    Ibid.
15    Jack Donnelly, "Cultural Relativism and Universal Human Rights", *Human Rights Quarterly* 6, no. 4 (1984): 412.
16    Seungbae Park, "Defense of Cultural Relativism", 162.
17    Yu Xuanmeng, "On Universalism", *Academic Monthly* 11 (2008): 9.

something ought to be universal and by so doing Xuanmeng speaks of how mathematics and natural science conform to sameness as a character of universality, as an example.[18]

The key challenge of universalist practices lies in the fact that they tend to exclude non-universal knowledge within society and thus exclude other means of viewing life, values, and ethics that exist outside of the knowledge of universalism.[19] In doing so, "universalism praises the advantage of universal knowledge, takes universal knowledge as the real knowledge or absolute truth[20] ... original meaning of 'knowledge' is broader than that of 'universal knowledge'".[21]

The current theories of universalism in the context of human rights are based on natural law, the notions of justice, moral agency and human capacities, amongst others.

"A perusal of the various universal and regional human rights instruments does yield a number of variations in detail ... no basic philosophical or ideological divergence has appeared which would justify separate regional developments. On the whole, the basic unity of human rights as a universal set of standards has prevailed over cultural relativism and regional fragmentation".[22]

Even though in context of rights, human rights may vary according to conventional wisdom, the rights may also be universal in the same vein, especially if the substantive rights are universal. This means that universalism can be meaningful because it would not serve self-interests of a specific group but would also serve the advancement of rights in a universal manner.[23]

## 3 The Burden of "Thought" Carried by North and South Countries with Regard to the Declaration on the Right to Development

Arguments around the implementation of the DRD have been fraught with divisiveness along the lines of ideology and thought.[24] In societies where cultural relativism is upheld, there is often a strong basis to justify communal

---

18   Ibid.
19   Ibid.
20   Ibid.
21   Ibid.
22   Christoph Schreuer, "Regionalism v. Universalism", *European Journal of International Law* 6 (1995): 485.
23   Jack Donnelly, "Cultural Relativism and Universal Human Rights", 409.
24   Brigitte I. Hamm, "A Human Rights Approach to Development", *Human Rights Quarterly* 23, no. 4 (2001): 1006 and see Michael E. Goodhart, "Origins and Universality in the Human

self-determination as a deterrent to foreign interests and undue interference from the outside world as a threat towards a communal space.[25] The current debates between universalism and cultural relativism revolve around essentialism and it is this essentialism that actually dominates the debates on the concepts of universalism and cultural relativism.[26] This is demonstrated by the fact that in the past three decades there had been a trend where dictators in the non-Western world (South countries) justified their atrocious actions on society using culture, and it is for this reason that universalism never seemed possible to emerge within a political landscape that espouses cultural relativism.[27]

These arguments persist against the backdrop of a history that is important between North and South countries.

Arguments associated with the implementation of the DRD present two frames of thought between North and South countries. North countries carry the burden of being "abusers"[28] of human rights, through colonization, and it is the same setting of colonization which stunted development in non-Western countries.[29] I am referring to the fact that colonization and role of the West, bear much of the blame for the effects of underdevelopment of former colonies. This could perhaps explain why there could be a moral burden on North countries to undo what occurred during colonial times[30] in respect of the destruction caused by the West during colonialism. This is what I refer to as "subsidiary reparations" or the notion that the clauses of the DRD are interpreted to refer to as "secondary reparations" by North countries.

In essence, the application of the DRD, places a far bigger burden on Europe beyond current problems of globalization, from which cross-cultural issues, and movements of world citizens are sometimes sanctioned by international law. This burden is also fueled by national issues versus global or international issues which involve trade, governance, and diplomatic ties to mention a few.[31] It is in this instance that I argue that the thought behind the possible resistance

---

Rights Debates: Cultural Essentialism and the Challenge of Globalization", *Human Rights Quarterly* 25, no. 4 (2003): 938. Christoph Schreuer, "Regionalism v. Universalism", 484.

25   Jack Donnelly, "Cultural Relativism and Universal Human Rights", 410.
26   Michael E. Goodhart, "Origins and Universality in the Human Rights Debates: Cultural Essentialism and the Challenge of Globalization", 940.
27   Jack Donnelly, "The Relative Universality of Human Rights", 282.
28   A case in point being the holocaust and against the Jews by Germany.
29   Sumner B. Twiss, "History, Human Rights, and Globalization", *Journal of Religious Ethics* 32, no. 1 (2004): 40–41.
30   Ibid., 61.
31   Brigitte I. Hamm, "A Human Rights Approach to Development", 1005.

in implementing the DRD (using universalism as a frame of thought) is shaped around the burden that Europe carries as a result of depraved past relations with non-Western countries who were colonized in the past.

The non-Western world or South nations equally carry a burden that emanates from colonial and imperial epoch of history. There are many academics that contend with the notion that indigenous people of the South still grapple with the economic, cultural and spiritual rights which were eroded by the colonial era. For example, Ughi[32] argues that as a consequence of colonialism, "exploitation of natural resources" often led to "indigenous people being violently dispossessed of their ancestral lands—from encroachments to forced evictions of even killings which violates their fundamental human rights". Taking this into account, land, exploitation or plundering of resources are actually an impediment for development in former colonial states. In numerous non-Western states, the issue of land does not appear to be only interpreted and understood for its utilization for commercial gain, but land in South countries provides a spiritual setting in that there is a much deeper spiritual connection between people and land in various ways.[33]

One can mention that cultural rituals tend to be performed in settings that are appropriate for communities.[34] It is for this reason that cultural value would be attached to the rights to land or vice versa. In other instances, land also creates provisions for subsistence and welfare of non-Western countries apart from it also being used for commercial purposes. This is why some scholars claim that arguments on the implementation of the DRD amongst non-Western countries are often advanced with reference to socio-economic rights which are provided by the DRD.[35] So the conceptual arguments amongst non-Western nations on the implementation of the DRD are largely based on elements that give expression to the nuances of economics, the rights to practice culture and self-determination. These fall under the third generation of human rights or the so-called solidarity rights.

---

32  Cristina Ughi, "The 'Right to Development' of Indigenous Peoples: A Critical Approach Through a Comparative Study of Cases Brought Before the Inter-American Court of Human Rights and the African Commission on Human and Peoples' Rights", *The BSIS Journal of International Studies* 9 (2012): 2.
33  Ibid.
34  Ibid., 7.
35  Stephen Marks, "The Human Right to Development: Between Rhetoric and Reality", *Harvard Human Rights Journal* 17 (2004): 147.

Sano[36] argues that the "status of the solidarity rights is not clear, especially the rights to development ... the third-generation rights is connected to grassroots movements, which is hardly completely correct since the right to development, for example, has been promoted by the governments of many developing countries". This could be a cause for concern considering that Article 1 DRD clearly states that "The human right to development also implies the full realization of the right of people to self-determination, which includes, and subject to the relevant provisions of international covenants on human rights, the exercise of their inalienable right to full sovereignty over all their natural wealth and resources". The DRD also provides mechanisms for interaction between the individual and the state in the same way that *Universal Declaration of Human Rights* (UDHR) aims to do the same.[37] Another burden that South countries carry is linked to the fact that:

> Rights talk was, and remains, a defining feature of resistance and liberation movements in developing countries; nationalist and anti-colonial movements framed their demands for self-rule in terms of the everyday constraints that colonial administrations imposed not just on their liberty, but on their livelihoods. In these settings, the right to citizenship was not regarded in the classic liberal sense as something bestowed by a benevolent nation state, together with a bundle of entitlements to which individuals could lay claim. It was seen as something that needed to be fought for, and won, on the basis of prejudice against and the exclusion of the majority of the population, on their exclusion from participation in the decisions that affect their lives and on the basis of the lack of obligation on the part of the state to guarantee certain basic rights.[38]

As a consequence of the burden carried by South countries, it has become difficult to navigate through the prospects of civil rights, and socio-economic development.[39] At the heart of this navigation lies the aspects of good governance within South nations and that there is a burden added to developing nations, especially those that receive a lot of aid from North nations because

---

36   Hans-Otto Sano, "Development and Human Rights: The Necessary, but Partial Integration of Human Rights and Development", *Human Rights Quarterly* 22 (2000): 737.

37   "Article 22 of Universal Declaration of Human Rights", United Nations, accessed 05 September 2018, http://www.un.org/en/universal-declaration-human-rights/.

38   Andrea Cornwall and Celestine Nyamu-Musembi, "Putting the 'Rights-Based Approach' to Development into Perspective", *Third World Quarterly* 25, no. 8 (2004): 1421.

39   Daniel Kaufmann, "Human Rights, Governance, and Development", *Development Outreach* 8, no. 2 (2006): 15.

by implication the added burden is on ensuring that there is accountability through good governance on donor aid that comes from the North countries. The appreciation of the DRD in South countries is used to motivate national priorities using a human rights-based approach.[40]

Marks[41] argues that in order for the DRD to become an implementable tool there requires to be a removal of political obstacles and ensure that there is a shift from political posturing, and rather to create more pragmatic methods that aid governments in the functioning of the DRD. The shift from political posturing could also be extended towards the shift in thought. This ideal is supported by scholars such as Hamm[42] who posits that there is a need to ensure that there is cross-cultural problem solving in relation to how the implementation of the DRD in the Western and non-Western world ought to be undertaken. This may not be difficult to achieve as this has happened before. Sano[43] remarks that several paradigm shifts and frames of thought have occurred in the realm of development research (in the past 30 years since the DRD came into effect) from which a multi-disciplinary and micro-oriented approach to perceiving development had evolved.

Other scholars such as Twiss[44] argue that the consensus on the thought process on the DRD between North and South countries could be achieved by creating a common moral intuition between North and South countries in how they relate to the DRD. This is important to consider especially due to the fact that the very same solidarity rights embraced by South nations should be interpreted to refer to shared responsibility for the advancement of human rights including the right to development.[45]

The outcome of the past and current relationships between North and South countries are arguably shaped by what happened in the past where North countries were seen as abusers or perpetrators;[46] and South countries

---

40   Bonny Ibhawoh, "The Right to Development: The Politics and Polemics of Power and Resistance", *Human Rights Quarterly* 33, no. 1 (2011): 76.
41   Stephen Marks, "The Human Right to Development: Between Rhetoric and Reality", *Harvard Human Rights Journal* 17 (2004): 167.
42   Brigitte I. Hamm, "A Human Rights Approach to Development", 1007.
43   Hans-Otto Sano, "Development and Human Rights: The Necessary, but Partial Integration of Human Rights and Development", 739.
44   Sumner B. Twiss, "History, Human Rights, and Globalization", *Journal of Religious Ethics* 32, no. 1 (2004): 61.
45   Arne Vandenbogaerde, "The Right to Development in International Human Rights Law: A Call for Its Dissolution", *Netherlands Quarterly of Human Rights* 31, no. 2 (2013): 197.
46   Sumner B. Twiss, "History, Human Rights, and Globalization", 41; Stephen Marks, "The Human Right to Development: Between Rhetoric and Reality", 138.

are seen as victims of colonization.[47] This then affects the manner in which North and South countries interpret the use, purpose and aims of the DRD in current times, as I have illustrated in this section of the chapter. This means that it is highly probable that the thought on implementation of the DRD may be argued with a frame of reference that reflects a difficult and irreconcilable past of colonial history.

Recent and current reflections on the issue of colonialism put the North nations under heavy caution of imposition towards South nations and this tends to be foregrounded in the discussions of how universalism and cultural relativism ought to appear in the relationship between North and South nations in the context of human rights.[48]

Cultural relativism is a doctrine that ascribes variations in terms of communal autonomy of societies and self-determination which is driven by moral judgements. And it is this observation that renders the need to ensure that there is a distinction between principles and self-interest actions in that if indeed human rights are afforded to all human beings, then it means that human rights are universal in nature.[49]

The key challenge in unpacking the evolution of cultural relativism in the South countries is that over time, traditional cultures tend to veer off or deviate from international human rights doctrines, slanting more towards traditions of a culture and by so doing lead to instruments of force and arbitrary decisions within specific societies.[50] This happens to be the case even though prior to colonial times, some traditional African cultures had often upheld the nuances of democracy and constitutional governance as was the case in the era. The locus of control here is important. It is for this reason that some non-Western countries that partly uphold cultural relativism and universalism at the same time would ensure that the law is given the locus of control in making sure that traditions do not become harmful. In other words, there is some consideration that the law would inadvertently serve as a guide in terms of the extent to which the traditions do not impact negatively on other rights. This is because constitutional freedoms also have limitations and that there is no abolitionism in the context of rights.

---

47   Makau W. Mutua, "Savages, Victims, and Saviors: The Metaphor of Human Rights", 42 (1) (2001): 202–209.
48   Jack Donnelly, "The Relative Universality of Human Rights", 304.
49   Jack Donnelly, "Cultural Relativism and Universal Human Rights", 400.
50   Ibid., 413.

## 4 Complexities of Cultural Relativism and Universalism in the Right to Development Discourse

### 4.1 *Politics of Cultural Relativism vs Universalism*

There are several challenges associated with cultural relativism and universalism, and these are explored in this section to examine how nuances in cultural relativity and universalism could negate the applicability of human rights within a society.

Spicker[51] argues that particularism as aptly reflected in the study of cultural relativism, puts an emphasis on the suggestion that different moral standards apply to different groups and that universalism is often challenged by communitarian critiques. In this context, Spicker[52] notes that "people are tied to families, communities and localities; these kinds of relationships define the scope of their moral responsibilities … particularism can be qualified by the acceptance of some basic universal principles, but this still implies a presumption in favor of certain discriminatory structures".

Particularism has a direct bearing on the notions of "group identities" within some specific social strata in that cultural identity could involve a network relation of sects in a society.[53]

Mungiu-Pippidi[54] argues that "in a universal society, rules of the game tend to be the same everywhere; in particularistic societies, they tend to be extremely specific for that society only … the two are ideal models, and universalism is not perfect in Western societies nor is particularism consistent across the underdeveloped world". In addition to this consequence of framing thought around universalism, the actual practice and applicability of universalism often ignore history a privileging of sameness "whereas with a particularism worldview, unique circumstances and relationships are more important than abstract rules concerning right or wrong".[55] Taking the latter into account, it could mean that the world view framed in the arguments of particularists would seem to have more depth than the world view of universalists.

---

51  P. Spicker, "Understanding Particularism", *Critical Social Policy* 13 (39) (1994): 5.
52  Ibid.
53  Carlo Trigilia, "Social Capital and Local Development", *European Journal of Social Theory* 4, no. 4 (2001): 427–442.
54  Alina Mungiu-Pippidi, "Deconstructing Balkan Particularism: The Ambiguous Social Capital of Southeastern Europe", *Southeast European and Black Sea Studies* 5, no. 1 (2005): 49–68.
55  C.M. Maugh, "Seeing the World Through Their Eyes: How Peace Corps and Its Volunteer Confront the Universalism/Particularism Continuum", *American Communication Journal* 14, no. 2 (2012): 14–40.

## 4.2 Rights to Development in the Context of Cultural Relativism and Universalism

Maugh[56] argues that even though universalist approaches tend to favor the Western over the non-Western world, there tends to be a sense of reliance by Western nations on particularism when engaging with non-Western countries. Maugh[57] makes this observation using the Peace Corps as a universalist tool from which volunteers from Western countries are bound to internalize particularism when working with non-Western countries. This of course occurs in the context of development, through the agenda of Peace Corps.

In the previous sections of this chapter, I have made mention of the fact that social networks are likely to occur as a result of the particularism, whereby group identity becomes a feature of a particular network of people within a society. This has an impact on the notions of the right to development in that to some extent development could benefit others and exclude the rest within a society, thereby leading to hegemony. On the other hand, social capital which could be given rise to by particularity could imbue a sense of collective good amongst a populace.[58]

What complicates the right to development in a system that upholds particularity is that multiple identities in a multicultural society could lead to political hegemony amongst those who are in the seat of power, and thus using self-development to justify the same hegemony in society.[59] This reality could be best explained with the assertion that suggests that particular knowledge within a society is actually shaped by politics, agendas and policies.[60] In essence there is a close connection between knowledge, information and how that knowledge is controlled by politics and it is in vein that Mungiu-Pippidi[61] observes that "local knowledge is essential to particularistic societies".

Taking into account arguments of elements of cultural relativism and universalism, it would seem that developing countries' positions would arguably be compromised by lack of consensus on the basis of what is suitable for developing countries and their agenda on the right to development.

---

56  Ibid., 20.
57  Ibid.
58  Carlo Trigilia, "Social Capital and Local Development", *European Journal of Social Theory* 4, no. 4 (2001): 433.
59  E. Laclau, "Universalism, Particularism, and the Question of Identity", *October* 61 (1992): 83.
60  J.N. Pieterse, *Development Theory* (Sage, 2010).
61  Alina Mungiu-Pippidi, "Deconstructing Balkan Particularism: The Ambiguous Social Capital of Southeastern Europe", *Southeast European and Black Sea Studies* 5, no. 1 (2005): 50.

Developing countries set their imprint on rights thought in the 1990s, both by making rights more socially oriented and by questioning the focus on the individual that has characterized human rights thought in the West. Human rights thought in the 1990s also increasingly emphasized that the opportunity for individuals and groups to participate in development is a human right. It is true that this is happening as part of what jurists would call "soft law", meaning law that is not binding.[62]

Sano[63] further argues that the discourse of human rights is not only limited to the protection of individuals to create decent living standards for society, thereby depicting human rights as a subject that promotes norms and rules in a just world. It is in this spirit that some scholars such as Lund[64] note that, in infusing the right to development into the global arena, a far deeper understanding of particularism is needed in order for the world to be open-minded about learning certain dynamics about a society or group as opposed to upholding sweeping theoretical generalizations of particularism.

On the other hand, Maugh[65] warns that "universalizing ideal of development encourages less developed nations to act as more developed nations do. Modernization theory holds that both the economic development and the psychology of a people will conform to Western ideals". In essence, development within a universal mode could discard the notions of particularity.

Hamm[66] is, however, optimistic that in light of the challenges of the right to development, either within or outside of nuances of universalism or cultural relativism; there seems to be a movement towards "a more cross-sectoral perspective for problem solving ... where both development policy and human rights are freed from bloc thinking" and it is in this vein that there are possibilities for the advancement of a human rights approach to development.

There are some scholars who propose that the solution in mediating between universalism and cultural relativism could be found by making sure that national issues do not obstruct universal issues for development and to

---

62   Hans-Otto Sano, "Development and Human Rights: The Necessary, but Partial Integration of Human Rights and Development", *Human Rights Quarterly* 22 (2000): 738.
63   Ibid., 741.
64   C. Lund, "Approaching Development an Opinionated Review", *Progress in Development Studies* 10, no. 1 (2010): 20.
65   C.M. Maugh, "Seeing the World Through Their Eyes: How Peace Corps and Its Volunteer Confront the Universalism/Particularism Continuum", *American Communication Journal* 14, no. 2 (2012): 14–40.
66   Brigitte I. Hamm, "A Human Rights Approach to Development", 1008.

ensure that there is universal, regional, elements of governance in the sphere of human rights.[67]

## 5 Brief Description of Ubuntu

### 5.1 *Ubuntu in Brief*

There is no direct or definitive description of "Ubuntu". Apart from several common descriptions of Ubuntu, it is given a meaning in different contexts and scenarios, depending on the subject matter, and dispositions. There are several descriptions of the term Ubuntu, expounded in various schools of thought, in the scholastic disciplines of linguistics, religion, and geography amongst others. Hailey[68] expounds Ubuntu as a word that is commonly found in several Bantu languages of the peoples of Eastern, Central and Southern Africa.[69] Its presence in these languages cuts across Kenya, Mozambique, Malawi, Tanzania, Angola and South Africa. In each of these Bantu languages, there are various cognates of the word Ubuntu as well as its meaning.[70] In all of these languages, the word "Bantu" refers to "people", in the literal sense, whereas "Ubuntu" as a concept is expounded to "human beings" or "humanity".[71]

### 5.2 *The "-ism" of Ubuntu*

It should be noted that within the words universal and cultural relativity, the suffix "-ism" is added to reflect universalism and cultural relativism. What does the "-ism" mean with regard to these principles? The suffix "-ism" is variously used to form *action, doctrines, principles, devotion, condition, practice or state and it also refers to a characteristic or adherence*[72] (Dictionary.com, 2016). Xuanmeng posits that all "-isms" originated from the West, including "universalism"

---

67  Christoph Schreuer, "Regionalism v. Universalism", 499.
68  John Hailey, "Ubuntu: A Literature Review", in *Document* (London: Tutu Foundation, 2008), 23.
69  For example: botho (Sesotho or Setswana), bumuntu (kiSukuma and Kihayi in Tanzania), bomoto (Bobangi in Congo) and gimuntu (kiKongo and giKwese in Angola), umundu (Kikuyu in Kenya), umuntu (Uganda), umunthu (Malawi), vumuntu (xiTsonga and shiTswa in Mozambique).
70  Kithaka Mberia, "Ubuntu: Linguistic Explorations", *International Journal of Scientific Research and Innovative Technology* 2 (2015): 109.
71  Devi Dee Mucina, "Ubuntu Orality as a Living Philosophy", *Journal of Pan African Studies* 6, no. 4 (2013): 21.
72  "Definition of Ism", last modified September 5, 2018, https://www.merriam-webster.com/dictionary/ism.

and "cultural relativism".⁷³ Xuanmeng asserts that "every '-ism' regards a certain theory advocating the priority of something".⁷⁴ So based on the definitions and theory by Xuanmeng, we can deduce that an "-ism" projects advocacy for theories, allowing doctrines to be expound in society, with a view to actualize these doctrines in a social setting.

Taking the above into account for the simple definition of the "-ism", in terms of its applicability to the word "Ubuntu", there are several narratives could be constructed to make reference to Ubuntu as an African epistemological concept (*doctrines*), as an ethic (*adherence*), practice (*communalism*), an adaptable principle⁷⁵(*action*).

The extrapolation of Ubuntu into these aspects, could arguably characterize Ubuntu as a system⁷⁶ of doctrines, ethics, practice and therefore its adaptability could be institutionalized and explored in order to eke out its relevance in current times. There are a number of recent and past settings from which Ubuntu had been used in an institutional forum in order to solve problems of humanity and human rights. One such instance is the Truth and Reconciliation Commission (TRC) process which took place in South Africa in the mid-1990s.⁷⁷ From this process Ubuntu was meant to be a tool from which the ethic of forgiveness, reconciliation and truth telling became the guiding force in an attempt to solve human problems that emanated from human rights violations committed by the apartheid government of South Africa.⁷⁸ The TRC also presented a scenario where Ubuntu was institutionalized, given meaning in the context of human rights.⁷⁹ I deliberately use the term "human rights" alongside the TRC due to the fact that human rights of certain people within a divided apartheid South Africa were violated.⁸⁰ For this reason, Ubuntu was

---

73  Yu Xuanmeng, "On Universalism", *Academic Monthly* 11 (2008): 9.
74  Ibid.
75  Ubuntu has been used in various spheres of African life in different contexts and scenarios, ranging from peace and conflict resolution, the law and as part of the Truth and Reconciliation Commission processes in African states.
76  Wilson J. Rugh, *Linear System Theory*, Vol. 2 (Upper Saddle River, NJ: Prentice Hall, 1996). This follows a systems theory from which there is a cyclical process beginning within Inputs (from community and communalism and inputs given by people within a community), Processing (processing of inputs in for example an extrajudicial inquiry such as the TRC), and Feedback (outcomes of TRC processes for example).
77  Dalene M. Swanson, "Ubuntu: An African Contribution to (Re)search for/with a 'Humble Togetherness'", *Journal of Contemporary Issues in Education* 2, no. 2 (2007): 53–67.
78  Tim Murithi, "A Local Response to the Global Human Rights Standard: The Ubuntu Perspective on Human Dignity", *Globalization, Societies and Education* 5, no. 3 (2007): 277.
79  Ibid.
80  Dalene M. Swanson, "Ubuntu: An African Contribution to (Re)search for/with a 'Humble Togetherness'", 53–67.

extolled for having created peace at a time when South Africa could have been embroiled in a civil war.

From the TRC process in South Africa, Ubuntu probably became the first experiment for applying restorative justice during the post-apartheid era.[81]

The argument that I bring forth at this junction is that there is evidence of Ubuntu as a tool that was institutionalized within the human rights sphere with outcomes that have been explored by several scholars across various disciplines. Be it through its edifices of restorative justice, or the fact that Ubuntu was once a key feature of South Africa's interim Constitution,[82] it is quite clear that Ubuntu as a paradigm has been utilized as a source of the law in South Africa and more specifically in dealing with human rights problems. The mere fact that there are two disciplines attached to the latter assertion means that Ubuntu can be adaptable to various settings. This adaptability is important due to the fact that applicability of the concept actually reflects its flexible characteristic.

## 6  Ubuntu-ism as a Frame of Thought in the Discourse of the Right to Development

### 6.1  *Positioning of Ubuntu amid Universalism and Relativism*

Based on the discussion I have framed in the previous section of this chapter, it would seem that Ubuntu is likely to be perceived to be a cultural concept that is held within the cultural relativism movement rather than a universal principle.[83]

If one were to interrogate Ubuntu along the cultural relativism and universalism perspectives, Ubuntu would arguably not be seen as an aspect that resides within the universalism theory due to its societal characteristics which could be deemed to depict historical particularism of Africans and its advancement of local knowledge.[84]

---

81  M. Nagel, "Ludic Ubuntu: An Appeal Toward Transformative Justice", available at SSRN 2637042, 2014.
82  Yvonne Mokgoro, "Ubuntu and the Law in South Africa", *Buffalo Human Rights Law Review* 4 (1998): 15.
83  E. Laclau, "Universalism, Particularism, and the Question of Identity", *October* 61(1992): 83.
84  Alina Mungiu-Pippidi, "Deconstructing Balkan Particularism: The Ambiguous Social Capital of Southeastern Europe", *Southeast European and Black Sea Studies* 5, no. 1 (2005): 50.

## 6.2 How Has "Ubuntu-ism" Occurred in the Past Spheres of Life Advancing Development and Entitlements (or Rights) in Africa?

The limitations of Ubuntu and it being thrust into cultural relativism creates ironies in the sense that in the past Ubuntu was a key driver of nuances of entitlements, rights and generally rights of human beings.[85] It is my contention that Ubuntu's nuances or principles were actualized through a rights-based approach in the context of development during Africa's historical past; particularly in Southern Africa. In my assessment of how Ubuntu was actualized in the context of rights and development in Southern Africa, I use Lesotho as an example. In doing so, I make reference to the principle of self-determination as one of the key ingredients of the DRD.

To illustrate this, I refer to an example of Ubuntu at play in the context of land rights, agrarian and sustenance as a form of development. In a time of regional wars in Southern Africa through the "Difaqane Wars", the displacement of Southern Africans (as a result of the regional war) gave rise to the need to reconsolidate power, re-form governance in the region, and the King of Lesotho, King Moshoeshoe I, was one such leader who played the role of restoring peace in the region and as such he gave refuge to those people who were displaced by the war.[86]

History scholars of this topic have pointed out that Moshoeshoe created an enabling environment in Lesotho for those who were displaced by the war to be given land for sustenance, along with the entitlement to practice their cultures and languages upon finding refuge in the Kingdom of Lesotho.[87] This meant those who were integrated from foreign tribes and found themselves in Lesotho as refugees were entitled to some of the provisions that are found in the DRD, i.e. the right to self-determination, culture and social rights. Laydevant & Tjokosela[88] note that in the period prior to the wars fought in the region of Southern Africa, Lesotho was able to provide land to the destitute for their own self development and sustenance. Linguistic rights, the rights to self-determination (foreigners residing in Lesotho) are all of the things that are now found within the DRD, e.g. Article 1.1 DRD and Article 1.2 DRD which makes reference to socio-economic rights.

---

85  Tim Murithi, "A Local Response to the Global Human Rights Standard: The Ubuntu Perspective on Human Dignity", *Globalization, Societies and Education* 5, no. 3 (2007): 277.
86  F. Laydevant and MJI Tjokosela, *Histori ea Basotho* (Mazenot Institute, Basutoland, 1965), 24, 25.
87  Max Du Preez, "The Socrates of Africa and His Student: A Model of Pre-Colonial African Leadership", University of Fort Hare, accessed March 20, 2017, http://www.ufh.ac.za/files/max_dupreez.pdf.
88  F. Laydevant and MJI Tjokosela, *Histori ea Basotho*, 25.

Other scholars on the DRD observe that elsewhere in non-Western countries, land rights and the right to self-determination have been part of the way of life for indigenous people of the world by virtue of the fact these rights were important to the spiritual being of non-Western countries.[89] In the case of Lesotho, Moshoeshoe upheld the philosophies of compassion, peace and prosperity for his people and those who were refugees from the war.[90] It is important to note that there is a correlation between these philosophies of compassion, peace and prosperity and common nuances of Ubuntu.[91] It is for this reason that I argue that Ubuntu has had its own place in the development and entitlements of Southern Africans outside of the realm of colonization.

## 6.3 Was Moshoeshoe's Approach in Affording the Right to Development Based on Universalism or Cultural Relativism?

Perry asserts that "the idea of human rights consists of two parts: the premise or every human being is sacred (inviolable, etc.), and the further claim because every human being is sacred (and given all other relevant information), certain choices should be made and certain other rejected; in particular, certain things ought not to be done to any being and certain other things ought to be done for every human being".[92]

Perry[93] believes that the key challenge of human rights is to address part of a societal idea in the midst of contestation on that very same idea within a society. In the context of Lesotho, the idea of nation building after the ravages of a war, was to create peace within the Kingdom. This idea had multiple layers and meanings. Peace meant treating people with respect, compassion, treating others in the same way that one would be treated (equality),[94] with the belief that we are who we are because of others. The philosophical ideals advanced by Moshoeshoe arguably culminated in a rights-based spirit (within his Kingdom) in an indirect manner. In attempting to position this theory in the events of Lesotho during the Difaqane Wars, it is possible to conclude that

---

89  Cristina Ughi, "The 'Right to Development' of Indigenous Peoples: A Critical Approach Through a Comparative Study of Cases Brought Before the Inter-American Court of Human Rights and the African Commission on Human and Peoples Rights", *The BSIS Journal of International Studies*, Vol 9 (2012): 7.

90  Max Du Preez, "The Socrates of Africa and His Student".

91  Mojalefa Koenane and Johannes Lehlohonolo, "Xenophobic Attacks in South Africa-an Ethical Response: Have We Lost the Underlying Spirit of Ubuntu", *International Journal of Science, Commerce and Humanities* 1, no. 6 (2013): 110.

92  Michael J. Perry, "Are Human Rights Universal? The Relativist Challenge and Related Matters", *Human Rights Quarterly* 19, no. 3 (1997): 462.

93  Ibid.

94  Khali Victor Mofuoa, "Paper 8", in *3rd International Conference on Responsible Leadership*, 136.

part of the human rights idea was about self-determination, the right to sustenance and productivity through issuing of land to the landless as a means of compassion (Ubuntu ethic). The notion of sustenance, self-determination and well-being are direct proponents of development. This could mean that in reality, Lesotho's stance on compassionately accepting others who would be offered the same protection as those who were previous settlers in the Kingdom evidences the notion of human rights and right to self-determination. Added to that, the right to enjoy one's cultural existence alongside the right to development was the key feature of King Moshoeshoe's strategy in consolidating power.[95]

The idea that Moshoeshoe sought to build a nation with refugees who share the same entitlements as those who were earlier settlers (of Lesotho), prompts one question. Was Moshoeshoe following or using universalism or cultural relativism as his frame of thought as he was applying Ubuntu in affording the rights to self-determination? It is highly improbable that he would have followed either of those principles. Historians and scholars on this subject make reference to how Moshoeshoe was often consumed by the idea of rebuilding a nation, with peace, stability and good governance.[96] He governed his nation using almost the same tools of a Western and modern democracy[97] and for this, I would argue that he was ahead of his time. Moshoeshoe would not have been part of the contemporary discussions on universalism and cultural relativism, because he died in 1870, about 15 years before the infamous Berlin Conference which sought to institutionalize colonialism.

The common thread between World War II and the Difaqane Wars is that a major consideration was made to reconsolidate power by first making sure that human rights are upheld. Moshoeshoe's rights-based approach to building his country was actually supplemented by applying a few elements of Ubuntu, such as compassion.[98] Scholars have attested to the fact that Moshoeshoe was actually trained to be a leader who practiced some elements of Ubuntu.[99] I would in this instance actually refer to him as an Ubuntu scholar even though no scholar has yet done so. This occurred over a hundred years before the

---

95  Hendrik W. van der Merwe and Odendaal Andries, "Constructive Conflict Intervention in South Africa: Some Lessons", *Clinical Sociology Review* 9, no. 1 (1991): 10.
96  N. Ndebele, "Perspectives on Leadership Challenges in South Africa", *Perspectives in Education* 25, no. 1 (2007): 8.
97  Khali Victor Mofuoa, "The Exemplary Ethical Leadership of King Moshoeshoe of Basotho of Lesotho in the Nineteenth Century Southern Africa", *Journal of Public Administration and Governance* 5, no. 3 (2015): 28.
98  Khali Victor Mofuoa, "Paper 8".
99  Khali Victor Mofuoa, "The Exemplary Ethical Leadership of King Moshoeshoe of Basotho of Lesotho in the Nineteenth Century Southern Africa", 30.

UDHR came into effect in 1948. The UDHR further gave rise to the debates surrounding universalism versus cultural relativism on human rights. So before the DRD was ratified by Member States of the UN, Moshoeshoe had long provided the right to development (through self-determination) without following the universalist or cultural relativist frame of thinking, but arguably using an Ubuntu principle of compassion as a justification for self-determination.

Donnelly states that "Self-determination and sovereignty ground a tolerant relativism based on the mutual recognition of peoples/states in an international community".[100] Cultural relativism is often used as an enabler to self-determination through tolerance which recognizes mutual recognition of states within a global arena.[101] If Moshoeshoe had been alive during the time at which human rights were fashioned in the current conventional form, he would have been hailed as leader who institutionalized Ubuntu in the context of affording the right to development to foreign peoples, giving them land to become productive in society. He would have taken responsibility over scores of people with whom he fought in the Difaqane Wars. This is the same responsibility that North countries were faced with after colonization in Africa.

## 7 Ubuntu-ism as an Arbiter between Cultural Relativism and Universalism in Justifying the Right to Development

In this chapter, I have ascertained that there is connection between universalism and cultural relativism in that at times when universal principles of development are being applied, there is a need to internalize particularity, as an element of cultural relativism in order to understand how development would function within a particular country. This observation remains critical due to the fact that important interactions occur between developed and underdeveloped countries through various means, e.g. investments, foreign direct investment, and foreign aid. The interactions between the West and non-Western countries could be arbitrated by Ubuntu through the three factors I have outlined:

### 7.1 *Inclusivity*
Following the narrative of particularism as an element of cultural relativism, Jimu[102] argues that the danger in the transposition of thought to application of

---

100  Jack Donnelly, "The Relative Universality of Human Rights", *Human Rights Quarterly* 29, no. 2 (2007): 296.
101  Ibid.
102  Ignasio Malizani Jimu, "Shared Sociability and Humanity", *Journal of Pan African Studies* 9, no. 4 (2016): 406.

Ubuntu as a modern phenomenon could continue to instill a sense of exclusivity between Africans and non-Africans in a social setting. This assertion is debatable given that there are concomitant issues of identity between the West and non-Western countries in respect of human rights. I make this assertion having outlined in this chapter that the right to development as well as human rights are actually discernible in Ubuntu principles and practices. For example, the norms pertaining to humanity and humanism are not exclusive or apportioned only to the West but also to non-Western countries.[103] Effectively African countries that are signatory to UN statutes are obliged to adhere to the same principles irrespective of whether these principles are an ethic or a law. It is in this context that I argue that issues that pertain to inclusivity could actually be brought into practice without promoting cultural relativism or universalism but rather using "Ubuntu-ism" as a frame of thought alongside "universalism" and "cultural relativism".

## 7.2   Cross-Cultural Issues

There is an underlying assumption that arguments for or against the right to development are often grounded in whether their applicability is subject to the context of universalism or cultural relativism.[104] Hamm[105] points out that a cross-cultural perspective is needed in navigating the two elements of universalism and cultural relativism in the context of the right to development in order for the world to realize these rights. Perhaps "Ubuntu-ism" could help in being frame of thought that is not only boxed within the cultural relativism perspective but rather as a system that actually bears elements and conditions of Western and non-Western societies in the context of development. In other words, there is a possibility that the adaptable nature of Ubuntu could be the arbiter between "universalism" and "cultural relativism".

## 7.3   Harmony between the Right to Development and Politics

The type of political machinations that have a negative bearing on applying the right to development through hegemony[106] could also be mediated through "Ubuntu-ism". There are some scholars who argue that the ethic of Ubuntu places certain emphasis on responsibility, accountability, and obligations as

---

103   B. Nussbaum, "Ubuntu: Reflections of a South African on Our Common Humanity", *Reflections* 4, no. 4 (2003): 21–26.
104   Peter Uvin, "From the Right to Development to the Rights-Based Approach: How 'Human Rights' Entered Development", *Development in Practice* 17, no. 4–5 (2007): 598.
105   Brigitte I. Hamm, "A Human Rights Approach to Development", *Human Rights Quarterly* 23, no. 4 (2001): 1008.
106   Stephen Marks, "The Human Right to Development: Between Rhetoric and Reality", *Harvard Human Rights Journal* 17 (2004): 141.

ethics within the belief system of Ubuntu.[107] It is in this spirit that it remains plausible that the right to development could be justified through the frame of thought that suggests the need for accountability and responsibilities of governments, and the norms for adherence to the right to development.

## 8    Conclusion

The relevance of Ubuntu could be depicted in the call for it to be the arbiter between the complexities of universalism and cultural relativism as described in this chapter. This then calls for further research on framing "Ubuntu-ism" as a principle that becomes an alternative to universalism and cultural relativism. For that to happen there is a need to re-frame thought and ensure that the thinking becomes applicable to practice.

In illustrating the thought carried by scholars on universalism and cultural relativism, more should be done to find other philosophies that justify the implementation of the right to development. It hoped that when these philosophies are advanced, it should be for the purpose of justifying why it is necessary to implement the right to development as opposed nullifying the right to development and its implementation.

---

[107] Matshidiso Joyce Taole, "Grounding Odl Curriculum in Ubuntu Values", *Open Distance Learning(odl)*: 65.

CHAPTER 13

# The Contribution of the Belt and Road Initiative to the Global Right to Development

*Li Erping\* and Yao Yunsong\*\**

Xi Jinping, the president of China, proposed the Belt and Road Initiative in 2013 to the international community, drawing worldwide attention and responses from many countries. In the meantime, however, some Western countries and media put a label of "Neo-colonialism" on this Initiative. Thus, what are the relations between the Belt and Road Initiative and development, as well as the right to development of the neighboring countries along the route? Is it considered a promoting factor of the UN *Declaration on the Right to Development*? And what type of contributions does the Initiative make to the theory of the right to development? These are the issues that will be explored and discussed in this chapter.

## 1      The Current Situation of Country-Oriented Right to Development

We take the country as a unit to discuss the situation since a state is regarded as one of the main bodies of the right to development. Our objectives are mainly to explore the interdependent relationships between national development and international political and economic order, particularly on issues such as which institutional factors are unfavorable to, or have even impeded, the development of developing countries, and factors can be used or improved to provide more development opportunities and more effective mechanism for developing countries.

First of all, the right to development has become an unquestionable right. Kabe Mbaye, one of the delegates to the then United Nations Commission on Human Rights put forward this concept in his speech on "The Right to

---

\*    Li Erping, Professor at Kunming University of Technology and Science, the syndic of China Society for Human Rights Studies. His major research fields are as follows: International Human Rights Protection, NGOs on Human Rights and Public Policy Analysis. Email: 1638724755@qq.com

\*\*   Yao Yunsong, Professor at Yunnan Normal University.

Development as a Human Right" in 1970, in which he proclaimed that Article 22 of the *African Charter on Human and Peoples' Right* stated: "All peoples shall have the right to their economic, social and cultural development with due regard to their freedom and identity and in the equal enjoyment of the common heritage of mankind. States shall have the duty, individually or collectively, to ensure the exercise of the right to development".[1] The right to development had also been officially approved, and acquired recognition as a right in the document in the 41st session of the UN General Assembly on December 4, 1986. In 1990, the UNDP initiated the concept of the Human Development Index. With further improvement, three indexes, namely Life Expectancy, Adult Literacy Rates and GDP per Capita, have turned out to be highly significant in defining developing countries, as well as in guiding them in their development. The Rio Declaration in 1992 also endeavored to establish a new level of cooperation among governments, major social sectors and ordinary people to promote the right to development. At the same time the *Vienna Declaration and Programme of Action* in 1993 reaffirmed such a right, reiterating that it is a universal and an inseparable right of humans as well as being an "integral part of fundamental human rights". The *Declaration on the Rights of Indigenous Peoples* in 2007 aimed at drawing the attention of the international world to the right to development as well as other rights of the 370 million marginalized indigenous people living in extreme poverty. Thus, the right to development has become an important component of human rights.

Secondly, ever since it was put forward, the right to development has experienced the endless process of being "debated and enriched". There is no doubt that the right to development has not only enriched the content of human rights, but it has also exerted a positive impact on changing unreasonable international economic order. Nevertheless, it has long evoked the argumentation on whether it is an individual right or a collective right, and on how to realize such a right, because the process of development is considered dynamic and connected with many factors and has no fixed model or permanent standard. Chinese scholar Wang Xigen believes that in order to elaborate the concept of the right to development, one basic way is to find a universal rule that fits current development and concurrently represents the past as well as future development and combines special cases with common ones.[2] Furthermore,

---

1 Writing Group, "*Tutorial of International Human Rights Law*", File set Vol. II, ed. Project Team of International Human Rights Law (Beijing: China University of Political and Science Press, 2002), 215.
2 Wang Xigen, "The Definition of the Right to Development in Philosophy of Law", *Modern Law Science,* November 12, 2004, p. 6.

the definition of the right to development has been enriched and developed according to the website on UN human rights affairs. Taking the examples of adaptations in *The Right to Development at a Glance*: "There has been a fierce debate inside and outside the United Nations. On the one hand, owners of the right to development claim that this has a realistic meaning to the development of international human rights (or even an overwhelming position). Yet on the other hand, the sceptics (or the protesters) depreciate it to an inferior position...". However, "We, heads of State and Government, ... are committed to making the right to development a reality for everyone and to freeing the entire human race from suffering shortage".[3]

Thirdly, the obstacles to developing countries realizing the right to development varied with the circumstance of globalization. The unification of the global economy has been accelerating since the 1990s. The communication and connection between states have strengthened and are more convenient, particularly for labor and capital flows. While developing countries embrace more development opportunities, they also face new challenges, as the ways developed countries hinder developing countries have also undergone changes. On the one hand, developing countries still lack self-development ability, especially the least developed countries, though it has long been reaffirmed in the *Declaration on the Right to Development* that "States have the primary responsibility for the creation of national and international conditions favorable to the realization of the right to development". Yet the situation cannot be reversed relying only on the ability of one or a few countries. It was officially confirmed that in 2015 41% of the population living in sub-Saharan Africa are under critical conditions of extreme poverty, which means sub-Saharan Africa is a poverty-stricken area.[4] On the other hand, globalization makes it easier for developed countries to exploit developing and less developed countries. Such exploitation ranges from raw material plundering to the nurturing of the market for product dumping, and from reducing labor costs to the attraction of large number of high-tech talents. And the protection of intellectual property rights under the name of the *Paris Convention for the Protection of Industrial Property* makes such exploitation look "fair". What is concealed is the "hot money", that Wall Street and the London Stock Exchange are to a great extent affecting and even controlling the economic lifeline of developing countries.

---

3  See references: "The Right to Development at a Glance", accessed November 3, 2015, http://www.ohchr.org/en/issues/development/pages/backgroundrtd.aspx; http://www.un.org/en/events/righttodevelopment/pdf/rtd_at_a_glance.pdf.
4  Yu Fangdong, "The International Poverty Line and Current Situation on Global Poverty", *The World of Survey and Research*, no. 5 (2016): 46.

Furthermore, several global issues such as global warming have turned out to be obstacles to developing countries. Some developed countries are not willing to change their luxurious lifestyles and to undertake related legal responsibilities and obligations, instead they require the governments from developing countries, such as China and India, to stop production to decrease carbon emissions, thus sacrificing the development of these countries for a reduced global carbon emissions.

Finally, the emergence of Regional Economy Cooperation Organizations (RECOs) and Free Trade Zones (FTZs) is gradually realizing the right to development. If the third point mentioned above is an obstacle for developing countries, then joining RECOs or FTZs could provide those countries with more chances to realize their right to development to a further degree. The establishment and unification of FTZs since the 1960s forged a model for economic development for countries and regions. Research suggests that, as of 2013, there were over 30 renowned RECOs and FTZs, such as NAFTA, EU, ASEAN 10+1, and more than 1,200 smaller organizations, including 425 organizations established by 15 developed countries (35.4%), and 775 organizations by 67 developing countries (64.6%). The purpose of RECOs is to promote competitiveness of some industries in certain countries or areas through optimizing their advantages in certain resources. In FTZs, tariffs are partially or completely exempted, and storage and processing are permitted in certain areas through the agreement among relevant countries so as to promote the development of local economies and foreign trade. At an earlier stage, RECOs such as the EU, were basically the "club of developed countries and states". Later, a few developing countries also joined to integrate complementary advantages. And in the case of the ASEAN 10+1, the members are mainly developing countries in Southeast Asia. The foundation of the ASEAN 10+1 FTZ both makes this area an economic area with great growth potential, and provides opportunities for each member to enjoy the right to development.

In conclusion, over the past 40 years since the adoption of the Resolution of the *Declaration on the Right to Development* in 1986, the country-oriented right to development is being continuously enriched and improved, and the world economic situation has already gone through great changes. Among its various changes, the most notable is that many developing countries have gained numerous development opportunities from RECOs and FTZs. After over four decades of reform and opening up to the outside world, China has evolved from a developing country to the second largest economy in the world, and it is likely to become the world's number one capital exporting country. The rise of the Chinese economy will definitely provide new materials for the theory of the United Nations right to development, and the Belt and Road Initiative put forward by the Chinese government is a brand new international economic mechanism and will bring a new perspective and approach to both the theory and the practice of the United Nations right to development.

## 2 The Belt and Road Initiative Will Create More Chances for Countries Along the Route

In 2013, the Chinese government revealed the Belt and Road Initiative to the world. This is a new international mechanism following the most-favored nation treatment, WTO and the program of ASEAN 10 + 1. The Belt and Road Initiative will bring huge development opportunities for construction for the countries along the route, promoting and realizing the right to development of developing and extremely poor countries.

As a kind of mechanism to seek complementary resources and win-win cooperation in the international economic system, the Belt and Road Initiative involves developed countries, developing countries and extremely poor countries. Of the 65 countries along the route, no more than ten are developed countries and the rest are developing and poor countries.[5] Of the ten ASEAN countries, only Singapore and Brunei are developed countries, and the rest are developing countries. Among the 18 countries in West Asia, the world's third richest country, Qatar, and Bahrain, Saudi Arabia, Yemen, Oman, United Arab Emirates and Israel are developed countries, the rest are still developing countries. Pakistan, with its per capita income ranking behind 180 countries, is among the least developed. Eight countries in South Asia, including India, Bangladesh and Afghanistan are all developing countries. Among the five Central Asian countries and the seven Commonwealth of Independent States (CIS) countries, Russia can be listed as a developed country, other countries basically belong to developing countries. Sixteen Central and Eastern European countries are developed countries.

The reason for taking developing countries as the main members for the construction of Belt and Road Initiative is not only because they have an urgent need for development, but also because these countries have the potential for development. And all these developing countries and the least developed countries along the route have the following characteristics. First, the standard of living is low, such as in the case of Bangladesh. Secondly, the

---

5  Though there is no specific definition for "developing countries", in 2011 the World Bank classified the world economies into four categories: low-income economies with an average income below USD 1,005, mid-low-income economies with an average income between USD 1,006 to USD 3,975, mid-high-income economies with an average of USD 3,976 to USD 12,275, and high-income economies with an average above USD 12,276. The least developed countries and developing countries usually fall into the first three categories.

level of productivity is low, such as Afghanistan. Thirdly, population growth is rapid and thus creates a heavy financial burden, such as in Pakistan. Fourthly, there exists a relatively high level of unemployment and a lower level of employment, such as in Turkey. Fifthly, the countries depend heavily on agricultural production, such as Laos. Furthermore, the countries have a disadvantaged position in international relations, such as Syria. Finally, the countries have an undeveloped market economy, such as Burma. An underdeveloped market economy is the most essential feature among the above-mentioned characteristics.

Developing and undeveloped countries have been plagued by the above-mentioned characteristics for plenty of years and they are still in urgent need of development in order to eliminate poverty and distress. Moreover, for China, as the world's second-largest economy, the success of its reform and opening up policy over the past years could help countries along the route achieve a win-win solution for the following reasons. First, it is difficult to expect to receive capital investment from the "traditional big economic powers", that they would ever help developing countries since they have already gone through the peak period of "capital expansion". Meanwhile the traditional big economic powers such as the United States, Japan, and European countries such as the United Kingdom, Germany, and France are entering an era of "re-industrialization", industry back-flow and domestic capital demand make it difficult for these countries to invest in developing countries. Secondly, as a capital surplus country, China is urgently seeking capital export. According to statistics from the Chinese Ministry of Commerce, last year China became a net exporter of capital with cumulative non-financial foreign capital output at USD 140 billion in 2015, whereas the amount of China's total overseas direct investment was only USD 2.7 billion in 2002. This means that foreign direct investment by China has increased by more than 40 times over the past ten years. With continuous advancement of the construction of the Belt and Road Initiative, China will soon overtake the United States as the world's largest capital exporter, and the establishment of the Asian Infrastructure Investment Bank will build an excellent platform for capital exportation by China. Thirdly, China has a production overcapacity and capability of massive infra-structure construction. The excess capacity in China is basically consistent with the demands and needs of countries along the route, and China has the ability for the infrastructure construction needed for economic development in the developing countries. For instance, the construction of a Pan-Asian high-speed railway will greatly boost economic development of the Great Mekong Sub-region.

Nevertheless, the Belt and Road Initiative, which will benefit countries along the route, has been severely criticized by some Western media. They believe that the objective of the Chinese government is to implement so-called

"Neo- Colonialism", and the Belt and Road Initiative construction is the Chinese version of the Marshall Plan. Hundreds of years ago, backed by gunboats, Western powers invaded and opened the door to non-Western countries through missionaries, immigration, trading and the notorious slave trade. Today the descendants of the earlier Western colonists link this period of evil history to the Belt and Road Initiative and compare it to the Marshall Plan. This is just a continuation of the cold war mentality of some Western countries. Apparently, the perception of Belt and Road Initiative differs from the Western concept of "Neo-Colonialism". One hundred years ago, China was among the victims of colonization, therefore the Chinese government knows clearly the pain and suffering under Western colonialism. What the Belt and Road Initiative brings to countries along the route will definitely not be "Neo-Colonization", but a win-win cooperation and a mutual benefit for common development rights declared by the United Nations. In addition, the Belt and Road Initiative is not related to any ideology, but a "culture with harmonization" as the foundation of cooperation. The following sections will provide explanations from the perspective of legal philosophy on how the Belt and Road Initiative promotes the right to development of countries along the route.

## 3  The Philosophy of Right Analysis on the Belt and Road Initiative Construction of Countries Along the Route

In 2016, Chinese President Xi Jinping declared on different occasions, including at the Shanghai Cooperation Organization Summit, and Bo'ao Forum for Asia, that "China is willing to expand the overlapping areas of common interest with different countries, promote the construction of new international relations based on cooperation and mutual benefits and facilitate the building of Community of Shared Future, Interest Community for all human beings".[6] The latest speech of Xi Jinping was delivered on August 17, 2016 during the conference to promote the Belt and Road Initiative, and he claimed that "We must stick to the idea of joint discussion, joint construction and sharing, seeking equality and mutual benefit, and stick to the idea of development, which can bring benefit not only to Chinese people, but also to people from countries along the route".[7] The "Fate, Responsibility and Interest Communities" built by

---

6  Zhao Yinping: "Community of Shared Future—the Image of 'Culture of Harmonization' of President Xi", accessed August 8, 2016, Xinhua Net: http://china.huanqiu.com/article/2016-08/9321278.html?from=bdwz.

7  "Xi Calls for Advancing the Belt and Road Initiative", accessed August 8, 2016, Xinhua Press: http://news.xinhuanet.com/fortune/2016-08/18/c_129238325.htm.

practicing mutual respect, mutual development, and win-win cooperation is the starting point of the Belt and Road Initiative, and it is also the purpose and goal of the philosophy of right analysis.

First is the philosophy of rights analysis of the "Responsibility Community". The "responsibility" is a rational agreement made by some facts between two or more sides, or an obligation created by some facts. This rational agreement is also based on the will and freedom of choice from both sides, it is not made by force, cheating or luring by promise of gain. The proposal of the "Responsibility Community" put forward by the Chinese government in the Belt and Road Initiative is a market contract or a rational agreement made by the Chinese government and other governments, thus the market contract or agreement is created by the fact of the Belt and Road Initiative proposed by the Chinese government. If any country wants to take part in the construction of the Belt and Road Initiative, then this country should agree to certain obligations. There is "Responsibility" between "Fact" and "Obligation". As the initiator of the Belt and Road Initiative and the second largest economic state, China is taking the main responsibility, which has been mentioned in *Oppenheim's International Law*, which stipulates that "the responsibility related to a country is not mainly to another country but to the entire international society".[8] In fact, Article 3 of the *Declaration on the Right to Development* declares that States have the duty to cooperate with each other in ensuring development and eliminating obstacles to development. And Article 4 states that as a complement to the effort of developing countries, effective international cooperation is essential in providing these countries with appropriate means and facilities for their comprehensive development.[9] The Belt and Road Initiative and the "Benefit Community" built by countries along the route practices the related terms in the *Declaration on the Right to Development*.

Second is the philosophy of rights analysis of the "Interest Community". The "interest" refers to the material and spiritual needs that human beings use to satisfy their own desires, and as for the common interest, the point is the definition of "common". An organization, a region, a state, or even the entire human society can be regarded as a community. The "common interest" refers to the organization's total benefit or interest that goes beyond any member or individual, and belongs to all members of the organization. The Belt and Road Initiative connects countries along the route with "interest", not only for China, but for countries along the route, and even for the well-being of mankind. The

---

8   Robert Jennings and Arthur Watts, *Oppenheim's International Law*, Vol. I, Part I (Beijing: Encyclopedia of China Publishing House, 1995), 403.
9   Project Team of International Human Rights Law, ed., *Tutorial of International Human Rights Law*, File set Vol. II (Beijing: China University of Political and Science Press, 2002), 72.

common interests of all mankind are abstract, but are concrete from the point of view of philosophy of right—American scholar Bodenheim states "the common interest is neither the sum of the benefits of individual nor the interest of mankind, [but] the sum of the value of things created by a society through cooperation of all members", and "this common interest should be equal to the aspirations of majority in this era".[10] Today, the majority of developing countries are still in poverty due to the unreasonable conventional world economic order. The Belt and Road Initiative meets the common aspirations of countries along the route to develop their economies, this is also the common interest for the majority of the world, as a result an "Interest Community" emerges.

Thirdly, there is the philosophy of rights analysis of the "Community of Shared Future". The word "Future" is supposed to describe human beings, but has been expanded to be used in the field of social sciences to refer to a pattern combined by both constants and variables of things. Shared Future is constant, but opportunity is variable, and things will change after the unification of fate and opportunity. It is generally regarded that "the subject of the right to development is a complex subject covering all states, nations and all people",[11] which means the "complex" formed by people, nations and states can be regarded as the subject of the right to development, but the "complex" formed by different countries cannot. In terms of the content of the Belt and Road Initiative, the "Responsibility Community" can be regarded as "Shared Future", the "Interest Community" as "opportunity", and the unification of "Responsibility Community" and "Interest Community" will create the "Community of Shared Future" which can change things, becoming a developing right "complex" unified by different countries. In sovereign states, national interest is above all else. There are disagreements among countries, but there is also common ground—countries along the route will make a "Community of Shared Future" by applying Chinese "harmony" culture. The idea of a "Community of Shared Future" originated from profound Chinese culture, as President Xi Jinping says: The root of "Community of Shared Future" is "harmony", the core idea of "harmony" means "harmony is precious" "greatness lies in inclusiveness". It pursues the level of "peace and harmony", sticks to the idea that "the whole world is one community", "harmonization of all nations", and particularly stresses the Chinese traditional philosophical thought of "harmony in diversity", and builds the "Community of Shared Future" by practicing Chinese "harmony" culture.

---

10   Edgar Bodenheimer, *Jurisprudence: The Philosophy & Method of the Law*, trans. Deng Zhenglai and Ji Jingwu (Beijing: HuaXia Publishing House, 1987), 301.
11   Wang Xigen, "The Jurisprudential Analysis of the Subject of the Right to Development", *Modern Law Science*, no.1 (2002): 48.

## 4   The Contribution of the Belt and Road Initiative to the Development of the World

Ever since the reform and opening up policy and practice in the 1980s, China has evolved from an undeveloped country to the second largest economy under the leadership of the Chinese Communist Party. The achievements of Chinese economic and social development practice the idea that "States have responsibility to develop, and it is the main body of the right to development" in the *Declaration on the Right to Development*. Now, the ongoing and effective Belt and Road Initiative is not only the embodiment of Chinese economic development and social progress, but also a significant contribution to the world's development and the right to development. This chapter summarizes the contribution of the Belt and Road Initiative to the right to development in the following five points.

First, it is a showcase prioritizing the right to life and development. Human rights are a foreign concept in China, for nearly 40 years from the opening up and reform, human rights have become one of the indicators to measure China's social development and progress. According to China's national conditions, the Chinese government placed economic development and promoting the right to life and development as primary human rights, demonstrating the unity of history and logic of China's human rights development history. When the right to development was put forward in 1970, China was accelerating the construction of its own industrial system. In 1980, the UN General Assembly adopted Resolution 41/128 on the *Declaration on the Right to Development*. The Household Contract Responsibility System in China has made a significant accomplishment, effectively resolving the food and clothing problem in rural areas. In 1993, when the *Vienna Declaration and Programme of Action* once again confirmed the right to development, the world economic integration process accelerated, and China adopted the socialist market economy. Soon China became the largest country attracting foreign investment, products processing and export trading. In 2011, China became the second largest economy in the world. The intention of the Belt and Road Initiative is not only the trickling effect of the Chinese economy, but a wish to share Chinese economic achievement with the rest of the world. It took three decades for China to finish the industrialization process, which took more than 300 years in European capitalist countries. To summarize the successful experiences of China, the most important one is always to adhere to the economic construction as a focus, to put the right to life and development in first place. Only when the economy is developed and the society is stable, can other rights be guaranteed. This is the summary of China's experience and it is also a contribution to both the theory and practice of the right to development, as well as a showcase to other developing countries.

Secondly, the Belt and Road Initiative could realize the right to development of developing countries. The right to development can be divided into three forms, namely *due right, legal right* and *practical right*.[12] Due right is the right written in the declarations, it is the goal. The purpose of legal right is to realize the due right by law. Practical right is the current situation; there is a big gap between practical right and due right. The right to development is a due right written in the *Declaration on the Right to Development*, it is difficult to practice and turn it into a practical right. For the Chinese government, realizing the due right by changing the current situation is the goal of the Belt and Road Initiative. In order to do this, the Chinese government solemnly promises that the Belt and Road Initiative will improve the regional infrastructure and facilitate the formation of safe and efficient land/sea/air transportation network, and put interconnection among relevant countries at a new level. For developing countries, the construction of infrastructure such as road transportation is the foundation of development. "Trade and investment facilitation will be reinforced, high standard free trade area network formed, economic connections tightened, mutual political trust enhanced, cultural communication strengthened". These promises and goals are in line with the current economic and social development of the countries along the route, and thus can optimize and realize the due right.

Thirdly, the right to development is integrated into the responsibilities, rights and interests of the subject countries. The UN, EU, World Bank and some developed countries have tried many ways of helping developing countries, including foreign aid programs, soft loans, talent training and technology transfer. These measures have helped developing countries to some degree, but it is difficult to generate a driving force of internal development. The Belt and Road Initiative emphasizes building a "responsibility community" and "interest community". The development model unified by responsibility, right, and interest will boost the developing process of developing countries. Although the UN has emphasized the participation of states, governments and people, there is no restraint and incentive mechanism, then, all efforts will become "blood transfusions" not "blood producing". What is worth mentioning is that the way to promote the right to development by integrating the responsibility, right and interest is not meant to deny the international humanitarian principles or the responsibility of China as the second largest economy and one of the UN Security Council members. This will never change—seeking a development model by employing relevant factors of responsibility, right and interest is an innovation by China in the right to development.

---

12   Li Buyun, *Three Existing Formations on Human Rights* (Beijing: Academy of Social Science Press, 2010), 54.

Fourthly, the cooperation and win-win right to development initiated by a responsible "big" country. Countries along the route gave positive responses to the Belt and Road Initiative; there is a "initiator" and "cooperator" relationship emerging from the process of "initiate and response". The cooperators' positive response to the initiative and participation makes it possible for China and countries along the route to join their efforts together in the process. The Belt and Road Initiative is not spontaneous market behavior. It is neither a so-called Marshall Plan nor a free trade model between the USA and the United Kingdom from 1846 to 1896, and not to mention "Jungle Law" followed by early European capitalists for overseas colonization and plundering. As the initiator of the Belt and Road Initiative, the Chinese government is trying to avoid the disorderly competition caused by early capitalism, and abandon the capitalist nature of seeking nothing but profits. Instead, through the efforts to connect countries along the route by the tie of "responsibility, right and interest", the initiator and the cooperator share the same responsibility, right and interest, and reach the level of win-win cooperation to promote and realize the right to development of the countries along the route. Win-win cooperation and promoting the right to development is a significant contribution to the right to development of the world made by the Chinese government.

Fifthly, the "Community of Shared Future" of countries is an advanced form to promote the right to development. This a significant contribution that the Belt and Road Initiative makes to the right to development of the world. National "Future" is the greatest expressive form of national interest. In order to maximize national interest, cooperation in competition is important. As a new international economic development, the Belt and Road Initiative will connect the "Shared Future" of countries along the route, build the biggest economic cooperation group in the world. In this cooperation group, the Chinese government will provide the system, designing mutual trust and responsibility, taking it to the level of national "Future". The word "Future" implies a developing pattern, the tendency and rise and decline of things. Setting the "Community of Shared Future" as the core idea of the right to development requires every member in the Belt and Road Initiative to be responsible. The Chinese government connects the Belt and Road Initiative to the shared future of people around the world by adhering to the traditional Chinese cultural idea of "harmony is precious" and "harmony in diversity", maximizing the realization of right to development of countries along the route. Redefining the "Community of Shared Future" creates a new connotation for the *Declaration on the Right to Development*.

CHAPTER 14

# Basic Principles of the Legal System of the Right to Regional Development

*Lyu Ning\* and Wang Xigen\*\**

Coordinated regional development is a systematic project involving enormous work. Its protracted nature, complexity, and arduousness determine that its route choice would rely on the legalization of its process and the authorization of its development patterns. Its development, by placing emphasis on the realization of rights through the practice of coordinated regional development, requires a strong guarantee from the legal system. The basic principles of the legal system of the regional development right are the fundamental and overarching principles and guidelines that should be obeyed while the law decides the connotation of the regional development right, allocates the interests of the regional development parties and deals with conflicts. While making the law, the basic principles directly determine the fundamental properties and content of the legal system, which also set general legal norms for the content of the regional development right and provide guidelines for the relevant specific rules of law. With the background of the rule of law, building a democratic, scientific, standardized and effective legal system of the regional development, first of all, needs clear basic principles for establishing the legal system of regional development right. This is of both practical and theoretical significance for preventing and eliminating internal conflicts and maintaining a harmonious legal system.

## 1 Interest Balancing Principle: Regional Development on the Basis of Balancing the Multiple Interests and Institutional Development

From the view of legislation, the construction of the law system of the regional development right is a process of weighing the benefits. Throughout the history of Western legal philosophy, the connection between law and interest is

---

\* Lyu Ning, Associate Professor at Hunan Normal University, S.J.D of Wuhan University.
\*\* Wang Xigen, Professor of Law School at Huazhong University of Science and Technology; The Chairperson of Academic Board of Human Rights Institute at Wuhan University.

more or less a concern of all law schools, including the Interest School of Law, the Social Engineering Law School and some other schools, which built their theoretical systems based on interest, emphasizing the relevance of law and interest. Jeremy Bentham not only held that the good is happiness in general, but also that each individual always pursues what he believes to be his own happiness. The business of the legislator, therefore, is to produce harmony between public and private interests.[1] Rudolph von Jhering argued that "interests are the basis of rights", emphasizing that the purpose of the law is not only to protect individual interests, but should also seek to balance personal interests and interests of the society. Roscoe Pound believes that interest is "a demand or desire or expectation which human beings, either individually or in groups or associations or relations, seek to satisfy, of which, therefore, the adjustment of human relations and ordering of human behavior through the force of a politically organized society must take account".[2] Multiple differentiation and conflicts of interest in modern society, to some extent, must pass for the expression of interests and meet the legal way, providing evaluation standards for the importance of various interests and for adjusting conflicts of interest between general rules. The subjects of the regional development right include both individual and collective subjects, which determine the diversity of the interests protected by the legal norms of the regional development right. Therefore, we should clarify the importance of the complex interests arising within the region or between different regions. We need to measure the interests in the legislative process, coordinate the conflicts of interests, and maintain the interests balance, in order to ensure the interests of the main subject of the regional development right through the efficient implementation of law. Specifically, the main measurements deal with the following interests.

### 1.1    Overall Interests and Regional Interests

There are mainly two aspects in the course of regional development when measuring overall interests and regional interests. First, importance should be attached to coordination of multiple interests between regional development subjects, including that between countries, that between central and local governments, and that between local governments. The 2005 Report of the Secretary-General of United Nations General Assembly entitled *In Larger Freedom: Towards Development, Security and Human Rights for All* points out that larger freedom can only be advanced by broad, deep and sustained global cooperation among states. Such cooperation is possible if every country's

---

1  Bertrand Russell, *The History of Western Philosophy* (New York: Simon & Schuster, 1945), 775.
2  Roscoe Pound, *Jurisprudence, Volume 3* (Clark: The Lawbook Exchange, Ltd, 2000), 16.

policies take into account not only the needs of its own citizens but also the needs of others. This kind of cooperation not only advances everyone's interests but also recognizes our common humanity.[3] Therefore, overall regional interests should be noted in the legislative process, whose specific measures should be taken as follows: coordinating the interests of different subjects, breaking local barriers, optimizing the allocation of resources, balancing the interests of different subjects, thus promoting common central and local development. Secondly, judging from the development situation of trade and industry, it should be noted that the allocation of industry interests is reasonable and fair. Local government in certain regions should pay more attention to the development of industries with local characteristics, and avoid focusing on one or several types of industry, which may lead to unfair competition and a waste of resources. In the legislative process of regional development, these measures should be taken in order to avoid regional imbalance caused by emphasizing a single industry's development, such as improving legislation for market operation, standardizing behavior of market subjects, thus making it possible to acquire complementary advantages of industries and establish a good competitive mechanism.

### 1.2 *Short-Term Interests and Long-Term Interests*

Coordinated regional development is a systematic project involving an enormous amount of work, which requires continued efforts over several generations. So, in the process of regional development, attention should be paid to long-term interests instead of blind development or repeated construction of short-term interests. Since the implementation of the reform and opening up, China's economy has achieved much. Rapid economic development, however, and extensive economic growth with the characteristics of high input, low output, high consumption and low efficiency has led to wasted resources, which seriously affects sustainable development. According to information provided by the Ministry of Water Resources, the water consumption per CNY 10,000 of industrial added value was 196 cubic meters in 2004, and the proportion of industrial water reuse is approximately 60% to 65%. In developed countries, however, the former is generally below 50 cubic meters, and the latter is 80% to 85% or more.[4] This extensive economic growth has caused

---

3  The Secretary-General at the General Assembly of the United Nations, *In Larger Freedom: Towards Development, Security and Human Rights for All* (A/59/2005, paper presented at the fifty-ninth session of General Assembly of the United Nations, March 21, 2005.).

4  "Water Consumption of CNY 10000 Gross Domestic Product Must Be Reduced by 20% During the Eleventh Five-year Plan", The Ministry of Water Resources, accessed July 31, 2016, http://www.gov.cn/jrzg/2007-02/20/content_531283.htm.

a serious waste of resources and placed a heavy burden on the environment. Therefore, it needs to be changed to intensive economy. In addition, the emphasis placed on economic and political interests has led to a neglect of ecological interests. Waste of resources and environmental deterioration have been two unsettled issues in the process of world economic development. The rights identified and protected by the legal norms of the regional development right are not only based on the interpersonal relationship between political, economic and cultural rights, but also include environmental rights based on the close relationship between man and nature. Therefore, while making the regional development right, we should balance the interests of both relationships, strengthen legislative forecasts, overcome legislative myopia, and expand the temporal and spatial elements of the legal relationship of the right to regional development based on the sustainable development of human beings to deal with the relationship between generations, and to achieve long-term benefits.

### 1.3  *Key Interests and General Interests*

Regional development is a gradual process, and resources are limited and unevenly distributed within a region. It is apparently unrealistic to give equal attention and satisfy all interests in the short term. Thus, in the process of regional development, we should distinguish between the characteristics of different areas or zones and combine them with local resources, dig out their geographical advantages, grasp the key development goals and directions at the present stage, make specific development plans, balance and coordinate core interests and other interests, safeguard by legislation, and achieve the implementation of the regional development right step by step. In 2000, the United Nations General Assembly passed the *United Nations Millennium Declaration*, and intended to put forward eight development goals, 18 measures of specific goals and more than 40 indexes, and highlighted the main direction of development for the millennium.[5] The right to development of regional subjects is achieved through the realization of the specific objectives in the region, which are planned. But it is important to note that in formulating the development laws of the region, we must highlight core interests without neglecting general interests. Core interests and general interests are not distinguished in absolute terms. As the realization and the extent of the right to development change, the content of core interests and general interests may change at different stages

---

5  The Secretary-General at the General Assembly of the United Nations, *Road Map Towards the Implementation of the United Nations Millennium Declaration* (A/56/326, paper presented at the fifty-sixth session of General Assembly of the United Nations, September 6, 2001.).

or even transform into each other. When the preliminary economic rights are realized, to ensure political, cultural, social and other rights will gradually become main interests represented by the law. In addition, in order to ensure the sustainability of development, we should also pay attention to ecological benefits, and turn the focus of the protection of the rights from human society to the realm of man and nature. This means we can discuss the protection of the rights from the perspective of the relationship between man and society and between man and nature.

### 1.4 *Individual and Collective Interests*

The regional development right involves both individual interests and collective interests. Collective interests are not the simple sum of individual interests. Therefore, the achievement of collective interests does not mean achievement of individual interests. These two aspects are relatively independent but closely linked. On the one hand, collective and personal interests are inseparable and influence each other. The situation of the individual development right in a region reflects the degree of security of the collective development right, the implementation of individual rights depends on the realization of collective rights, and the collective development right should be based on individual development. Collective interests will benefit individual interests, and the ultimate beneficiaries of the regional development right will also be individuals. On the other hand, collective and personal interests coexist independently. Each individual as the possessor of the right to development is entitled to pursue their own development rights or benefit from the collective development according to their wishes. Nevertheless, the sum of all individual interests does not equal the collective interest. A collective has its own independent interests, which are a manifestation of the common will of the individuals. A collective has its own interests separate from those of individuals, and it expresses and realizes its interests and needs in a unique and external way.[6] Therefore, the legal norms of the right to regional development should recognize the coexistence of the individual and the collective, and give them equally important statuses in the legal order. It is undesirable to place too much emphasis on individual or collective interests at the cost of the other, which is also a tendency to be avoided when building the legal system of regional development rights.

---

6  Wang Xigen, *Fazhi shehui de jiben renquan—fazhanquan falv zhidu yanjiu* [*Basic Human Rights in Society Governed by Law—Study on the Legal System of Right to Development*] (Beijing: The Chinese People's Public Security University Press, 2002), 64.

## 2  The Principle of Social Equity: On the Form and Substance of Fairness and Fair Implementation

Justice is an interdisciplinary proposition involving ethics, philosophy, political science and law, and it is also a topic that has been debated in the course of human social development. Social justice is different from equality and justice, and "is close to the concept of (social, economic and political) justice on the domestic front and, in the domain of international relations, to the concept of justice and equal rights to participation and democracy in the political, economic and other spheres".[7] From an economic relationship point of view, justice mainly refers to a principle of resource allocation. From a political point of view, justice is an institutional arrangement, and a reasonable basis and criterion to configure rights and obligations. From an ethical point of view, the scope of justice is a combination of "righteousness" and "profit", which is a principle to judge good and evil, right and wrong of social ethics and norms. From a sociological point of view, justice mainly refers to the fair value of a normative social structure and the basic judgment of a certain social structure, a social system, social relations and social phenomena. The regional development right itself contains a fair idea of society. The Preamble of *Declaration on the Right to Development* clearly states: "Development is a comprehensive economic, social, cultural and political process, which aims at the constant improvement of the well-being of the entire population and of all individuals on the basis of their active, free and meaningful participation in the development and the subsequent interests". Justice is the primary virtue of social institutions.[8] At the World Day of Social Justice in 2009, UN Secretary-General Ban Ki-moon sent the message: "Social justice is an underlying principle for peaceful and prosperous coexistence within and among nations. We uphold the principles of social justice when we promote gender equality and the rights of indigenous peoples and migrants. We advance social justice when we remove barriers that people face because of gender, age, race, ethnicity, religion, culture or disability".[9]

Construction and perfection of the right to development of the regional legal system must follow the basic principles of the philosophy of social justice, and judge social phenomena according to the fair value of the existing legal

---

7  The Secretary-General at the General Assembly of the United Nations, *Globalization and Its Impact on the Full Enjoyment of All Human Rights* (A/58/257, paper presented at the fifty-eighth session of General Assembly of the United Nations, August 7, 2003.).
8  John Bordley Rawls, *A Theory of Justice* (New York: Harvard University Press, 1971), 3.
9  UN Secretary-General Ban Ki-moon, "Message on World Day of Social Justice", February 20, 2009, accessed July 19, 2016, http://www.un.org/zh/sg/statements/2009/socialjustice.shtml.

standards of social systems and development structures. Social equity requires a reasonable distribution of benefits for the various stakeholders in the region in the legislative process. The presence of multiple subjects in the region has led to complex interests and needs, coupled with relatively limited resources, which put forward higher requirements for reasonable arrangements for the subjects in the region. Law is a social norm that can acquire reasonable allocation of interests in the guidance of justice and order. The principle of social equity means a full realization of citizens' political, economic and other interests endowed by the society. It means equal rights of the region, equal opportunity to participate in fair developments and equitable sharing of the fruits of development, "ensuring that people enjoy acceptable levels of well-being and a certain equality of opportunity, which is the foundation of global stability and prosperity. Social Justice is not static absolute standards, it is specific and historical".[10] "The Greeks and Romans considered slavery is fair; in 1789, the capitalists advocated the abolition of the feudal system, because it was said to be not fair".[11] So, the idea of eternal fairness not only changes due to location, it even varies from person to person. Social justice should be combined with the situation and characteristics of regional development, should be a reasonable relationship between man and man, man and nature, man and society, which is recognized and accepted by most people in the region under certain historical conditions.

The result of the construction and operation of the legal system that contains the value of social justice is to build a harmonious relationship between the main parties in the region. Under the guidance and guarantee of the law, parties have consciously abided by the values of social justice to make society operate with high efficiency. Each subject in the region shares equal opportunities and receives fair treatment, and is able to maximize their talents through their own efforts. Resources and wealth are allocated according to the social contribution of each member in the community, which can narrow the gap between the rich and the poor, and avoid the natural result of competition, which leads to the strong becoming stronger and the weak weaker. It limits the grasp of the strong on the weak, gives particular attention to socially vulnerable groups, provides for their survival and development conditions and opportunities. The goal of balanced development in the region is not only to achieve intra-generational equity, but also focuses on inter-generational equity, natural justice, etc. It is required to achieve a unified comprehensive development

---

10   Ibid.
11   Karl Heinrich Marx and Friedrich Engels, *Selections (Anthologies) of Marx and Engels* (Vol. 2) (Beijing: People's Publishing House, 1972), 539.

in economic, social, political and cultural aspects, to respect the harmonious development between man and nature, and to share social resources and fruits of development among all subjects within the region.

## 3 Two-Way Adjustment Principle: Through Asymmetric Methods of Rights Guarantee

Subjects of the region should equally enjoy the rights conferred by law. If the legal norms treat the subjects of the region without distinction, such guarantee is not only incomplete, but also incompatible with the requirement of substantive equality. Therefore, legal norms should treat differently the subjects of the region, "that all cases which are equal in the special respect relevant to the kind of treatment which is appropriate in a particular context must be treated equally; that all cases which are unequal in this respect must be treated unequally; that the comparative inequality of the treatment must be proportional to the comparative inequality of the cases".[12] The construction of the legal system of regional development rights should change the traditional practice of parallel protection for the main interests that have real differences in reality, and take the dualism of the legal norms to guarantee the way, that is, under the same legal system, the set of legal norms recognizes the main differences between different subjects in the region and achieve equal rights for regional development rights through an asymmetric mode. In particular, the principle of double specification includes two aspects.

From the perspective of the development level, a region can be divided into developed areas, relatively developed areas and less developed areas. Compared with developed areas, relatively developed areas, especially underdeveloped areas, lag behind in all aspects of life including sharing resources, living conditions, education, and other public resource control. According to World Bank studies: "Africa is not just in poverty. It lags far behind other regions in income, assets (including education and health), control of public resources and access to and utilization of basic services, etc. In addition, there is a general lack of security".[13] If one ignores the different levels of development, the implementation of equal rights and obligations for all relations can only lead to

---

12  A.J.M. Milne, *Human Rights and Human Diversity: An Essay in the Philosophy of Human Rights* (London: The Macmillan Press Ltd, 1986), 47.
13  World Bank, "Can Africa Claim the 21st Century", accessed July 31, 2016, http://web.worldbank.org/WBSITE/EXTERNAL/COUNTRIES/AFRICAEXT/0,,contentMDK:20358914~menuPK:685152~pagePK:146736~piPK:226340~theSitePK:258644,00.html.

material inequalities between the more developed and less developed, thereby to the opposite of equality, contrary to the intention of the right to regional development. So far as debt is concerned, if "the weak", namely "individual poor countries", "become insolvent and offend international financial oligarchies, they may suffer punitive measures taken by the latter", which shows that the debt is not "a simple contractual arrangement between two parties with equal power".[14] In human rights law, "the principle of non-discrimination does not envisage giving equal treatment to everyone in all circumstances", but should take "affirmative action" and implement "special and differential treatment" in some cases for the "poor" and "vulnerable individuals and groups".[15] When the international community provides assistance to the underdeveloped areas, the policy will be made according to the characteristics of those targeted areas and the levels of development. According to the 2005 United Nations Millennium Project "Achieving the Millennium Development Goals: Rural Investment and Enabling Policy", "enhanced programme of debt relief for heavily indebted poor countries (HIPC) and cancellation of official bilateral debt; and more generous ODA for countries committed to poverty reduction".[16] The legal system of the right to regional development should treat differently regions of different levels of development, to give special treatment while setting the rights and obligations. With the double norms of rights and obligations, underdeveloped regions should not have reciprocal obligations, namely, underdeveloped regions should enjoy more rights temporarily, compared with due obligations. Accordingly, developed and less developed regions should have more obligations temporarily, compared with the rights they enjoy. And this asymmetrical set of rights and obligations is aimed at the promotion of common development of all people in developed and relatively developed regions.

From the view of the type of subjects, participants in regional development include not only governments, but also citizens, entities and other social organizations. Regional development is a process of economic, political, social and

---

14   The United Nations Commission on Human Rights, *The Legal Nature of the Right to Development and Enhancement of Its Binding Nature* (E/CN.4/Sub.2/2004/16, paper presented at the fifty-sixth session of the Commission on Human Rights of the United Nations Economic and Social Council, June 1, 2004), 10.

15   The High Commissioner for Human Rights at the United Nations Commission on Human Rights, *Globalization and Its Impact on the Full Enjoyment of Human Rights—Report of the High Commissioner* (E/CN.4/2002/54, paper presented at the fifty-eighth session of the Commission on Human Rights of the United Nations Economic and Social Council, January 15, 2002), 16, 17.

16   IFAD Governing Council, "Achieving the Millennium Development Goals: Rural Investment and Enabling Policy", accessed September 30, 2018, https://rmportal.net/library/content/Rural_Development/e.pdf/view.

cultural development. The process also involves multiple parties. Dominant governments and businesses, civil society organizations and citizens all play an important role.

In the process of regional development, government makes regional economic policies, induces and configures resources at regional level, promotes optimal allocation of resources, promotes regional strategic development, and promotes employment and social justice, in order to improve geographic distribution of economic activities, achieve regional economic development and a harmonious pattern, and maintain a reasonable regional distribution, so as to ensure a sustainable, healthy and stable development of economy and society.[17] Nonetheless, power is inherently expansionary, and so if a power restraint mechanism is lacking, there will be government anomie, for example, corruption, rampant local protectionism, causing obstruction to coordinated regional development. In addition, factors such as the government's decision-making ability and the unpredictable policy environment may also result in wrong decisions by the government, leading to a mismatch between policy measures and goals, between the interests of the regional subjects and the rules of economic development, thus against the inherent requirements of the regional development right. Therefore, there should be legal norms to effectively supervise and control state power, to implement strict administration, and to prevent abuse of power and corruption.

For other market players, development of the region, especially economic development, does not only rely on the government's macro-control, but also relies on the participation and role of the private sector, organizations and individuals. The UN senior panel for the Right to Development emphasized the role of the private sector in the report of the second session conference and acknowledged that the activities of transnational corporations and other enterprises can have a positive impact on the host country's development activities and promote the enjoyment of human rights through creating jobs, bringing a fair and equitable work environment, and promoting economic growth and community development. Meanwhile, the panel also noted that some multinational practices directly or indirectly violated human rights, and reduced basic social, economic and environmental standards.[18] Therefore,

---

17   Deng Hongbing, *Quyu Jingji xue* [*Regional Economics*] (Beijing: Science Press, 2008), 248–256.
18   Stephen Marks, *Report of the High-level Task Force on the Implementation of the Right to Development on Its Second Meeting* (E/CN.4/2005/WG.18/TF/3, paper presented at the seventh session of Working Group on the Right to Development, and the sixty-second session of the Commission on Human Rights of the United Nations Economic and Social Council, December 8, 2005), 17.

while the law controls the behavior of the government, which acts to exercise state power, to protect the rights of citizens, legal entities and other organizations, it also should stipulate the behavior of market players, clarify their rights and obligations, and avoid making market players depart from the rule of law and the connotation of the right to development. "The right to development implies not only the interconnectedness, but also the parity of rights, none to be sacrificed or hegemonized by others".[19] That is, the legal system of the regional development right does not simply grant rights to one government or non-government party and set corresponding obligations for the other, but sets rights and obligations respectively for government and other market parties under a unified legal system, and pays equal attention to standardizing market behavior and government behavior.

4   Principle of Dynamic Power: To Break the Thinking Limitations of the Government in Power, to Promote Positive Actions through Democratic Interactions

Dynamic power means fully ensuring the initiative and efficiency of exercise of power on the basis of public power restriction and supervision, to unify power control and guarantee of exercise of power. It emphasizes building an operational framework for dynamic exercise of power, more than just passively excluding infringement of public authority on the right to development, which urges the government to take responsibility for promoting the realization of the right to development more actively.[20] Power restriction is an inherent requirement of the rule of law and also an internal mechanism for protecting human rights, but only to limit the power is not enough. Achieving development goals requires governments to defend the rule of law, to implement sound economic policies and appropriate public investments, to manage public institutions, to realize democratic participation and protect fundamental human rights. If the government cannot effectively do something positive, economic development will stagnate, and right protection will turn out to be a mere formality. Regional

---

19  The Commission on Human Rights of the United Nations Economic and Social Council, *Mainstreaming the Right to Development into International Trade Law and Policy at the World Trade Organization* (E/CN.4/Sub.2/2004/17, paper presented at the fifty-sixth session of Sub-Commission on the Promotion and Protection of Human Rights of the Commission on Human Rights of the United Nations Economic and Social Council, June 9, 2004), 9.
20  Wang Xigen, "Lun Xibu fazhanquan de falv baozhang" [Study on Legal Protection of the Right to Development in Western Area], *Fazhi yu shehui fazhan* (2002): 16–22.

development consists of primarily government-led projects, but the complexity within the region and the different areas with their own characteristics, such as cross-border river basins, desertification, air pollution and biodiversity, can only be managed by a regional strategy, which poses higher requirements for the efficiency of the government's administrative capacity and exercise of power. At the same time, the complexity and integrity of regional development determines that it is not sufficient only to rely on the unilateral efforts of a local or national government to achieve the right to regional development. The structure and operating method of the power within the region also determines that the realization of the right to regional development should emphasize equality of, consultation and interaction with, and cooperation between the constituent entities. Governments at all levels within the region should conduct dialogues and reach a consensus for political cooperation mechanisms, such as the African Peer Review Mechanism, and provide more regional public goods.[21] All these are inseparable from efficient and democratic operation of power.

In order to realize the right to development in the region, it is necessary to clarify the government's functions and make clear divisions between state power and social power, authority and rights. Under such a premise, power control and guarantee should be combined, emphasizing not only power control, but also the efficiency of exercise of power. Specifically, when it concerns the area development rights legal system, the following points should be noted.

First, clarify the responsibilities and powers of each authority in the area through legislation to ensure that power can be exercised within the range set by law, avoid the abuse of power or absence of power, provide effective legal norms for administration according to law, and provide premise conditions for rule of the law. Set boundaries for the reach of power performance, standards and legal process, so as to prevent the expansion of rights into private areas and rights violations, and avoid wasteful duplication of power operating costs.

Secondly, pay attention to the development of relevant procedural law, and ensure wide participation of the regional subjects through the exercise of power regulated by procedural norms. Modern connotation of the rule of law includes not only traditional forms of the rule of law, but also requirements for the real substance of the rule of law. The legal system of coordinated regional development needs substantive legal norms to determine the boundaries of exercise of power, and it also needs procedural legal norms to standardize the

---

21  IFAD Governing Council, "Achieving the Millennium Development Goals: Rural Investment and Enabling Policy", accessed September 30, 2018, https://rmportal.net/library/content/Rural_Development/e.pdf/view.

form of exercise of power, and guarantee a legal, proper and moderate exercise of power in the process of regional development. The role of procedural law is not only reflected in the effective control of public power, but also in the protection of public participation. Whether it is "due process of law on the United States Constitution", or English law on the "principle of natural justice", both affirm the effect of the procedures on the protection of citizens' right to participate. Involving the public in the process of government decision-making and other processes through legal procedures will contribute to developing a good interaction mechanism between the government and social subjects.

Thirdly, establish a scientific and effective power supervision mechanism. Without such a mechanism, it would eventually be impossible to have legitimate and efficient operation of regional public authority. Good governance, transparency, responsiveness and accountability also require the establishment of a full range of power supervision, especially for the protection of democratic supervision. Supervision of administrative power includes both internal and external oversight. Internal oversight mainly involves superior to subordinate guidance and supervision, as well as supervision for democratic recommendation and administrative functions. External oversight includes judicial supervision, social democratic supervision, etc. Diversification of forms and subjects of supervision makes it necessary, in the process of regional development, to institutionalize and standardize power supervision through making relevant laws and regulations and clarifying oversight functions, forms, procedures and methods, so as to ensure long-lasting supervision.

# PART 4

*Global Order*

CHAPTER 15

# The Declaration on the Right to Development as a First Step towards a Comprehensive Southern Vision on Human Rights

*Tom Zwart**

## 1   Introduction

By adopting the *Declaration on the Right to Development* on December 4, 1986, the UN General Assembly officially recognized the right to development as a human right. For those involved in the campaign to promote the right to development at the international level its adoption was a true highlight.[1] The Declaration not only marks the official recognition of the right to development, but it can also be regarded as the first successful joint action undertaken by the Global South at the international level in the area of human rights.

Thus, the right to development as such was conceptualized by Kéba M'baye, who was a prominent Southern scholar.[2] The drafting and the adoption of the Declaration itself was the fruit of constructive cooperation among Southern states located on different continents.[3] As a result of their coordinated efforts and their numerical majority, they were even able to overcome Northern opposition to the document.[4] The reference to the rights of "peoples" in the Declaration in particular exemplifies the preponderance of Southern philosophy

---

*   Tom Zwart, Professor of Human Rights at Utrecht University and Director of the Cross-Cultural Human Rights Center of Netherland.
1   Personally, I assisted in organizing a high-level conference in The Hague, see International Commission of Jurists, *Development, Human Rights and the Rule of Law*, Report of a Conference Convened by the International Commission of Jurists in The Hague on April 27-May 1, 1981 (Oxford: Pergamon Press, 1981), and I lobbied the government of the Netherlands to cast its vote in favor of the Declaration.
2   Keba M'baye, "Le Droit du Dévelopment comme un Droit de l'Homme", *Revue des Droits de l'Homme* 5 (1972): 503.
3   R.N. Kiwanuka, "Developing Rights: The UN Declaration on the Right to Development", *Netherlands International Law Review* 25 (1988): 257.
4   Khurshid Iqbal, "The Declaration on the Right to Development and Implementation", *Political Perspectives* 1 (2007): 4–5.

and intellectual input during the drafting process.[5] Therefore, the document served as a challenge to and a repudiation of the individual-centered orientation of Northern liberal modernism.[6]

This chapter makes the point that the efforts to get the Declaration adopted should serve as a source of inspiration. It is important to again join Southern forces in the area of human rights to produce another document, this time to lay out a comprehensive Southern vision on human rights. Section 2 will explain why there is a need for such a vision. Section 3 will identify some aspects of the *Universal Declaration of Human Rights* (hereafter: UDHR) which can serve as a support for such a vision. Section 4 will tentatively identify elements which could be included in such a document. Section 5 contains some concluding observations.

In this chapter, a distinction is being made between the North, which consists of Europe and the US, and the South, which comprises Asia, Africa and Latin America.

## 2   The Declaration on the Right to Development as a Source of Inspiration

On several occasions Southern countries have rightly taken issue with the hegemonic Northern view on human rights. Thus, as part of the "Asian values" debate, South East Asian countries have asserted their right to implement universal human rights within their own distinctive social, political and cultural context.[7] African States Parties to the Rome Statute are abandoning the International Criminal Court because it insists on applying Northern retributive justice, while refusing to include the African sense of justice.[8] Southern states should be commended for making their positions known in this way.

However, for three reasons their attempts to impact the international human rights debate are less effective than they could be. First, most of their contributions to the debate amount to critique on the liberal-modernist positions taken by Northern governments, activists and academics. Consequently,

---

5   Bonny Ibhawoh, "The Right to Development: The Politics and Polemics of Power and Resistance", *Human Rights Quarterly* 33 (2011): 85.
6   Bonny Ibhawo, "Right to Development", 86.
7   Leigh Jenco, "Revisiting Asian Values", *Journal of the History of Ideas* 74 (2013): 237; Dian K. Mauzy, "The Human Rights and 'Asian Values' Debate in Southeast Asia: Trying to Clarify the Key Issues", *The Pacific Review* 10 (1997): 210.
8   Kamari M. Clark, Abel S. Knottnerus and Eefje de Volder, eds., *Africa and the ICC, Perceptions of Justice* (Cambridge: Cambridge University Press, 2016).

these Southern comments come across as being defensive, while they leave intact the ability of Northern actors to set the agenda and to frame the issues. Secondly, these Southern interventions are often perceived and portrayed as challenges to the human rights system, rather than the liberal-modernist take on it, and not enough is done to correct that impression. Thirdly, the positions are put forward by individual states and regional groups rather than the Southern community of states as a whole.

These shortcomings could be easily remedied if the community of Southern states would launch a document which lays out a positive vision on human rights, while fitting perfectly within the four corners of the international human rights framework. For the purposes of this chapter this document will be called the *Comprehensive Southern Vision on Human Rights*.

The question could be raised as to whether there is enough similarity between the human rights views of Southern countries to act as a basis for a Comprehensive Southern Vision. It is true that Southern countries do not always show the same voting behavior at the international level regarding human rights issues,[9] but that does not mean that they do not share a common human rights vision. When one reviews the regional documents and the official positions taken by diplomats, such a vision becomes easily discernable. The different elements will be laid out in Section 4.

## 3      Towards a Comprehensive Vision: Relying on the Original Meaning of the UDHR

### 3.1    *Introduction*

The drafters of a Comprehensive Southern Vision have the foundational document of the international human rights regime, the UDHR, to fall back on. The UDHR is often portrayed as an ode to liberal-modernism. However, when the proper rules of interpretation are applied, a different picture emerges, which supports many if not all of the positions on human rights taken by Southern countries.

The interpretation rules relied upon in this chapter are modeled on the *Vienna Convention on the Law of Treaties*. It is true that the UDHR is a General Assembly resolution rather than an interstate agreement, and therefore it declares ambitions rather than creating rights and obligations. However, since the drafters dealt with the contents of the document first and its status second,

---

9  Peter Ferdinand, "Rising Powers at the UN: An Analysis of the Voting Behavior of BRICS in the General Assembly", *Third World Quarterly* 35 (2014): 376.

the UDHR was set up in a treaty-like manner, despite the fact that in the end this status was not accorded to it. In addition, Article 8 of the Vienna Convention relies on a flexible rather than a formal treaty definition, which signals that it can also cover documents other than treaties.

Therefore, applying the rules of interpretation as stated in Articles 31 and 32 of the Vienna Convention by analogy appears justified. These rules give center stage to the terms of the document, its object and purpose, subsequent agreements and subsequent practice, as well as the *travaux préparatoires* or preparatory work.

The object and purpose of the UDHR consists of the goals that motivated the drafting of the text and its adoption. These goals have been reconstructed by an analysis of the text of the UDHR in light of the discussions that took place between the drafters, as reflected in the *travaux préparatoires*.

Due to the grave injustice of colonization, many African and Asian countries were not present at the table when the UDHR was being drafted. Since its adoption these countries have become independent and they have provided their own interpretation of the UDHR in regional documents such as the *African Charter on Human and Peoples' Rights* and the *ASEAN Human Rights Declaration*. The colonial deficit of the negotiating process can be partly solved by giving extra weight to these subsequent agreements.

### 3.2 Object and Purpose: A Spiritual Guide for Humanity

The object and purpose of the UDHR is expressed in the concluding recital of the Preamble, which describes the promotion and observance of the rights contained therein by every individual and every organ of society as its end.[10] Therefore, in the words of the Chilean member of the Drafting Committee, the UDHR was meant as a spiritual guide for humanity:[11] the rights laid out in the UDHR should be brought to life by the people in their relations with other people. This is confirmed in the second recital of the *Vienna Declaration and Programme of Action*, which emphasizes that the human person is not only the prime beneficiary of these rights and freedoms, but should also participate actively in their realization.

The idea that it is mainly up to the people to respect and realize the rights of their fellow human beings is also expressed in other ways in the document. Thus, during the final stages of the drafting process, the title of the UDHR was

---

10  Johannes Morsink, *The Universal Declaration of Human Rights, Origins, Drafting and Intent* (Philadelphia: University of Pennsylvania Press, 1999), 35.
11  William A. Schabas, *The Universal Declaration of Human Rights, The Travaux Préparatoires* (Cambridge: Cambridge University Press, 2013), 719.

changed from "international" to "universal". This was done to shift the focus of the document away from the delegates and nations that did the drafting to the ordinary men, women, and children to whom it was primarily addressed.[12] The drafters were also intent on keeping the document short, so that it could be understood by the common man.[13]

This intention to rely mainly on the people to bring the rights and freedoms of the UDHR to life is the "object and purpose" of the UDHR within the meaning of Article 31 of the Vienna Convention.[14] It acts as the interpretative polestar which can assist in navigating the document. It is both amplified by and provides meaning to other key elements of the UDHR.

Thus, in Article 1 of the UDHR through use of the words "conscience" and "in a spirit of brotherhood" the people are called upon to turn human rights into a reality by doing good to others. In addition, because rights are shaped mainly within horizontal relations, the UDHR emphasizes the importance of duties as corollaries of rights of other members of the community. Moreover, the framers have done their utmost to draft a common document which would appeal to the largest possible group of people, regardless of their philosophical, religious or political outlook. Therefore, they avoided elevating one philosophy above the others in order not to unnecessarily alienate part of the world population.

### 3.3 The UDHR Does Not Represent One Single Philosophy or Worldview

In view of its object and purpose, the delegates were intent on and succeeded in drafting a document which does justice to all civilizations and has the potential of touching the soul of every human being. They went out of their way to turn the UDHR into a "big tent". Although regrettably the representatives from Asian and African countries were small in numbers, they more than made up for that by the high quality and aptness of their contributions, which represented the worldview and the interests of the people of those continents.

Although some of the language used in the UDHR is reminiscent of Enlightenment philosophy,[15] this was not the dominant view among the drafters.

---

12    Johannes Morsink, *The Universal Declaration of Human Rights, Origins, Drafting and Intent*, 324.
13    William A. Schabas, *The Universal Declaration of Human Rights, The Travaux Préparatoires*, 161, 784; Johannes Morsink, *The Universal Declaration of Human Rights, Origins, Drafting and Intent*, 33-34.
14    See Mrs. Roosevelt as quoted by Mary Ann Glendon, *A World Made New, Eleanor Roosevelt and the Universal Declaration of Human Rights* (New York: Random House, 2002).
15    Johannes Morsink, *The Universal Declaration of Human Rights, Origins, Drafting and Intent*, 282.

Morsink argues that most drafters did not share the Enlightenment belief in a single—divine or natural law—source of value.[16] They came from a great variety of ideological and philosophical backgrounds, such as Judeo-Christianity, Marxism, Confucianism, Buddhism, and Islam and they did not think that the rights in the UDHR were the prerogative of any particular philosophy.[17] Therefore, those who only apply an Enlightenment lens run the risk of misreading the document.[18]

The diverse nature of the UDHR is also exemplified by the fact that the human rights provisions of a large number of constitutions from across the world served as its building blocks. They were gathered by the Secretariat, which brought them together is a voluminous document on which the first drafts were based.

It should come as no surprise that these different approaches led to different positions during the discussions. The delegates were very much aware that they had to overcome these differences. Compromises had to be made and pragmatic choices were unavoidable. It was clearly the intention of the drafters, therefore, to reach consensus between these approaches, as repeated calls were made to draft a declaration which would be acceptable to all the participating states.[19] As the Chinese representative Zhang Pengchun indicated, the process was meant to bring together the strong points of different civilizations.

Zhang in particular ensured that the UDHR retained its diverse character. During the discussions, he stressed that a human being at all times has to be conscious of other persons, in whose society he lives,[20] which is encapsulated by the notion of *ren* or "two-man-mindedness".[21] This notion of consciousness of one's fellow man,[22] or human interrelatedness, exemplifies the idea that every person is a social being, whose life gets shape through relationships with other people. The road to personal fulfillment leads through commitment to community as opposed to selfishness and isolation.[23]

---

16  Ibid., 283.
17  Ibid.
18  Ibid.
19  Ibid., 21.
20  Sumner B. Twiss, "Confucian Contributions to the Universal Declaration of Human Rights, a Historical and Philosophical Perspective", in *The World's Religions, A Contemporary Reader*, ed. Arvind Sharma (Minneapolis: Fortress Press, 2011), 110.
21  Ibid., 106; this, of course, is a literal translation of the Chinese character.
22  Johannes Morsink, *The Universal Declaration of Human Rights, Origins, Drafting and Intent*, 297.
23  Wing-Tsit Chan, "The Evolution of the Confucian Concept of Jên", *Philosophy East and West* 4 (1955): 311.

Zhang expressed the view that the UDHR should aim for the humanization of man.[24] Therefore, at Zhang's insistence, *ren* was included in the UDHR and appeared both as "conscience" and as "the spirit of brotherhood" in Article 1.[25] According to Zhang, the notion of brotherhood matched the Chinese concepts of *li*, or propriety, and *ren*, the considerate treatment of others.[26] These Confucian notions have three dimensions: man as a social being; the need to bring about goodness; and the importance of people relying on their inner conviction.

His interventions prevented the Northern perspective from acquiring too dominant a position. Thus, according to Zhang, the aim of including the notion of brotherhood in Article 1 was to prevent the catalogue of rights from becoming a source of selfishness and insularity.[27] By introducing these Confucian notions, Zhang helped prevent the UDHR from becoming a manifestation of self-centeredness.

### 3.4 The Realization of Human Rights Has to Take Place Within Their Local Political, Social and Cultural Context

In view of the fact that the UDHR was meant to be applied first and foremost by the people in their relationships with others, while the document serves both as a reflection and legitimization of diversity, it comes as no surprise that it assumes that human rights need to be implemented within their local political, social and cultural context. Applying human rights in relations with others should be stimulated by an inner drive. This calls for human rights which are embedded, i.e. which match the values and norms of the people on the ground. The importance of the implementation of human rights in a way which resonates with the people is exemplified by the fact that many of the subsequent agreements are of a regional nature, which were meant to give room to the regional social, political and cultural context to the maximum extent possible.

The need to take account of the particular cultural, social and political circumstances has been stated in paragraph 5 of the *Vienna Declaration and Programme of Action*. This provision stresses the importance of national and regional particularities and various historical, cultural and religious backgrounds. The Preamble to the African Charter indicates that the virtues of Africa's historical tradition and the values of its civilization will be taken

---

24   Sumner B. Twiss, "Confucian Contributions to the Universal Declaration of Human Rights", 110.
25   Ibid., 111; Johannes Morsink, *The Universal Declaration of Human Rights, Origins, Drafting and Intent*, 296–302.
26   Sumner B. Twiss, "Confucian Contributions to the Universal Declaration of Human Rights", 111.
27   Ibid., 111–112.

into consideration while applying the document. According to Article 7 of the ASEAN *Human Rights Declaration*, the realization of human rights must be considered in the regional and national context bearing in mind different political, economic, legal, social, cultural, historical and religious backgrounds.

### 3.5 *There Is No Monopoly on Implementation Through Law and Individual Enforceable Rights*

For some time during the negotiations it was unclear whether the document would become a "Manifesto", which would state a number of ambitions, or an "Act of Parliament" which would lay down binding obligations, which had to be implemented.[28] During the final stages the Manifesto format was chosen, which meant that questions regarding implementation would be left to the negotiations on the covenants.

What remains is a reference in the eighth recital of the Preamble to teaching and education, as well as to national and international progressive measures, to promote the rights and freedoms contained in the UDHR as well as to secure their recognition and observance. This essentially leaves states free to choose any measure of implementation they see fit.

A similar picture emerges from the subsequent human rights covenants, which do contain binding obligations and indeed deal with implementation. Their implementation clauses do not prescribe incorporation, relying on law—albeit with a few exceptions—or according individual court enforceable rights. Implementation was left as a discretionary matter to the States Parties, in accordance with public international law. This means that there is no basis, neither in the UDHR nor in subsequent conduct, for assuming a monopoly of implementation through legislative measures.

In addition, associating "rights" in the UDHR with enforceable claims and entitlements should be avoided. Especially in light of the reference to "consciousness" and "in the spirit of brotherhood" in Article 1, legal concepts were not what the drafters had in mind. According to Twiss, the framers identified "priority interests" which were captured in rights language: "the use of this language was not intended to subvert or supplant other cultural idioms at the local level which might be used to guarantee the 'priority interests' represented by international human rights language".[29]

---

28   The two models were distinguished by Geoffrey Wilson, the British member of the Drafting Committee, see William A. Schabas, *The Universal Declaration of Human Rights, The Travaux Préparatoires*, 722.

29   Sumner B. Twiss, "Confucian Ethics, Concept-Clusters and Human Rights", in *Polishing the Chinese Mirror: Essays in Honor of Henry Rosemont, Jr.*, eds. M. Chandler and R. Littlejohn (New York: Global Scholarly Publications, 2007), 55.

## 3.6 Since Rights Are Being Exercised in Relation to Others and Within the Community, They Also Entail Duties

The idea that the UDHR is a "people's charter" which comes to life when people do good to each other, goes hand in hand with the need for duties. The individual is a member of society and he must affirm his right to be a human being by clearly recognizing the duties which were corollaries of his rights.[30] The duty of one person corresponds with the right of the other.[31]

There was widespread support among the delegates for including duties as complements of rights.[32] Thus, this support was not only expressed by the Chinese[33] and the Egyptian representatives,[34] but also by the French,[35] and the Australian representatives.[36] Initially, the UDHR was even referred to as a declaration on rights and duties.[37]

Therefore, it comes as no surprise that Article 29 stipulates that the individual owes duties, both to the community as a whole and to others. The importance of duties is also a common element in regional documents. The African Charter even devotes a separate chapter to duties,[38] while these are also mentioned in Article 6 of the *ASEAN Human Rights Declaration* and Article 32 of the *American Convention on Human Rights*.

## 3.7 Conclusion

The UDHR is a "people's charter" aimed at the promotion and observance of the rights contained therein by every individual and every organ of society. It is an amalgam of different philosophies and worldviews, which is meant to appeal to people from different cultural, political and philosophical backgrounds. The document serves as a platform for multiple human rights approaches, including community-oriented ones like the theory on human interrelatedness laid out by Zhang Pengchun.

The UDHR calls for taking account of the local political, social and cultural context when realizing human rights. There is no basis in the UDHR or in subsequent conduct for the assumption that human rights obligations have

---

30  Johannes Morsink, *The Universal Declaration of Human Rights, Origins, Drafting and Intent*, 247, quoting the Cuban delegate.
31  Ibid., 243–244.
32  Ibid., 248.
33  William A. Schabas, *The Universal Declaration of Human Rights, The Travaux Préparatoires*, 179.
34  Ibid., 198.
35  Ibid., 200–201.
36  Ibid., 21, 105, 179, 201.
37  Ibid., 4, 5, 6, 8, 12, 15, 98.
38  Articles 27–29.

to be implemented through law or individual enforceable rights. Since rights are being exercised in relation to others and within the community, they also entail duties.

This interpretation exercise shows that certain elements were included in the UDHR or played a part in the deliberations, which have since moved into the background. These are exactly the elements which are at the core of Southern human rights thinking. Therefore, it would be very important to include those elements in a comprehensive Southern vision document.

## 4   Towards a Comprehensive Vision: Elements Which Could Be Included

### 4.1   *Introduction*
It will be up to the Southern states themselves to determine what should be included in a Comprehensive Southern Vision. However, based on the UDHR and the common positions taken by Southern actors, a few elements can already be identified.

### 4.2   *Relying on Culture, Customary Law, and Morality*
As the UDHR suggests, statements of human rights should stay as close to the outlook and experiences of the people as possible. This means that the implementation should not rely on formal state law, but on culture, customary law and morality.

China takes the view that while law can play an important role in the implementation of human rights obligations, this role should not be restricted to formal written law, but should also extend to the moral rules which regulate society.[39] At the local level, human rights may be better protected by morality, or by a mix of moral and formal legal rules, than by formal law. As Jie rightly indicates, while the North only relies on legal standards to avoid and redress human rights violations, in China much importance is also attached to moral rules.[40] Chinese people tend to believe that cultivating morality is an effective way to respect and protect rights.

### 4.3   *Emphasizing the Need to Respect Subsidiarity and Non-interference*
As a result of signing up to the international human rights regime, countries can no longer claim to enjoy absolute sovereignty in the area of human rights. However, international human right law still emphasizes the importance of

---

39   Liu Jie, *Human Rights, China Road* (Beijing: China Intercontinental Press, 2014), 31–32.
40   Ibid., 31–32.

subsidiarity, a principle under which it is first and foremost up to the States Parties to deal with human rights issues under their own jurisdiction. This principle has been expressed in Articles 2 of both Covenants. International bodies are only allowed to step in when the states fail to live up to their obligations. In addition, although the States Parties are supposed to live up to the obligations laid out in the instruments, they enjoy full discretion to determine how they want to discharge this duty.

Secondly, as the 1991 *White Paper on Human Rights in China* (hereafter: the White Paper),[41] makes very clear, China opposes the use of human rights by one state as a pretext to force its ideology on another. The international human rights instruments themselves prevent such use of human rights as a "Trojan horse". These instruments do not prescribe a particular philosophy or world view which has to be adopted by States Parties. They are only supposed to live up to their obligations, nothing more, nothing less.[42] Therefore, no support can be found in the instruments themselves for claims that they require the adoption of liberal-modernism by all States Parties. This would fly in the face of the UDHR which was meant by the drafters to be a value "big tent".

### 4.4 Collective Rights Are at Least as Important as Individual Rights

The position that collective human rights are as important as individual ones finds support in the UDHR and its drafting history. Thus, Article 1 of the UDHR stipulates that all human beings are endowed with conscience and should act towards one another in a spirit of brotherhood. As was discussed above, these words were included in Article 1 at the initiative of the Chinese delegate, Zhang Pengchun.

These notions are not only closely related to the Chinese concept of *ren*, but also to its African counterpart *ubuntu*. Since in Africa, power radiates outward from the core political areas and tends to diminish over distance, the state plays only a limited role in the daily lives of many Africans.[43] Therefore the individual/state paradigm, which determines human rights relations in the North, is of less relevance to the African setting. Instead, Africans tend to rely on and to invest in their local community, in particular in their extended family. Rather than pursuing individual self-interest, the African approach is focused on collective survival, and therefore relies on cooperation, interdependence,

---

41  The State Council Information Office of the People's Republic of China, *White Paper on Human Rights in China*, Beijing, 1991, accessed November 2, 2016, http://china.org.cn/e-white/7/index.htm.
42  Tom Zwart, "Using Local Culture to Further the Implementation of International Human Rights: The Receptor Approach", *Human Rights Quarterly* 34 (2012): 546.
43  Jeffrey Herbst, *States and Power in Africa, Comparative Lessons in Authority and Control* (Princeton: Princeton University Press, 2000), 251–272.

and collective responsibility.[44] Individual rights exist within the context of the group and therefore must always be balanced against the collective interest.[45]

### 4.5 The Right to Subsistence and Development as Paramount Rights

In the White Paper, the State Council has made it clear that the rights to subsistence and development are paramount human rights. According to the White Paper, for any country the right to subsistence is the most important of all human rights, without which the other rights cannot exist.[46] Therefore, securing the right to subsistence is China's main priority.

In addition, China also gives precedence to the right of the people to economic, social and cultural development. China emphasizes that, according to the *Declaration on the Right to Development*,[47] this right encompasses both individual and collective rights.[48] Therefore, the right to development also includes a fair and just world economic order, especially from the perspective of developing countries.

### 4.6 The Yin and Yang of Rights and Duties

In the South, rights and duties are regarded as two sides of the same coin.[49] This idea is reinforced by Article 29 of the UDHR, which stipulates that the individual owes duties, both to the community as a whole and to others. The importance of duties is also a common element in regional documents. Thus, they are mentioned in Article 6 of the *ASEAN Human Rights Declaration* and Article 32 of the *American Convention on Human Rights*.

The African Charter devotes a separate chapter to duties.[50] In Africa, entitlements and obligations form the very basis of the kinship system. Each member is supposed to assist the family in operating as an economic and social unit. This assistance is embedded in a framework of interconnected rights

---

44   Josiah A.M. Cobbah, "African Values and the Human Rights Debate: An African Perspective", *Human Rights Quarterly* 9 (1987): 320–324.
45   Lakshman Marasinghe, "Traditional Conceptions of Human Rights in Africa", in *Human Rights and Development in Africa*, eds. Claude E. Welch, Jr. and Ronald I. Meltzer (Albany: State University of New York Press, 1984), 33; Josiah A.M. Cobbah, "African Values and the Human Rights Debate", 320–324.
46   See also Robert Weatherley, *The Discourse of Human Rights in China, Historical and Ideological Perspectives* (Houndmills: Palgrave, 1999), 121.
47   Adopted by the General Assembly of the United Nations on December 4, 1986, A/RES/41/128.
48   See also Sun Pinghua, *Human Rights Protection System in China* (Heidelberg: Springer, 2014), 89.
49   Sun Pinghua, *Human Rights Protection System in China*, 94.
50   Articles 27–29.

and duties.[51] Inherent in the membership of the extended family are certain rights.[52] These rights are complemented by the duties one has towards the members of one's family.

In Northern societies, it is up to the state to assist the infirm and the vulnerable, like elderly people, widows and orphans, through social welfare. Within the African context, by contrast, such assistance is deemed a family matter.[53] It is the responsibility of the family to help out those who have fallen victim to a bad harvest, fire, or theft, to settles disputes between its members, including husbands and wives engaged in domestic battles, and to invest in the education and advancement of its members.[54] In Africa, therefore, duties are not owed to a distant and anonymous state entity, but to relatives who are close, and on whose support one depends in order to survive. Consequently, human rights relations in Africa are more direct, personal and reciprocal, and therefore more horizontal than they are in the North.

### 4.7 *The Dialectics of Universality and Contextuality*

The UDHR was meant to be applied first and foremost by the people in their relationships with others. It also serves both as a reflection and legitimization of diversity. Therefore, it comes as no surprise that the UDHR assumes that human rights need to be implemented within their local political, social and cultural context. The need to give weight to the specific cultural, political and social context of the country concerned has been confirmed in several subsequent agreements, which serve as important tools for the interpretation of the UDHR.

Thus, the requirement to take account of the particular cultural, social and political circumstances has been stated in paragraph 5 of the *Vienna Declaration and Programme of Action*. This provision stresses the importance of national and regional particularities and various historical, cultural and religious backgrounds. The Preamble of the *African Charter on Human and Peoples' Rights* indicates that the virtues of Africa's historical tradition and the values of its civilization will be taken into consideration while applying the document. According to Article 7 of the *ASEAN Human Rights Declaration*, the realization of human rights must be considered in the regional and national context bearing in mind different political, economic, legal, social, cultural, historical and religious backgrounds.

---

51  Josiah A.M. Cobbah, "African Values and the Human Rights Debate", 320–324.
52  Lakshman Marasinghe, "Traditional Conceptions of Human Rights in Africa", 32.
53  Ibid., 34.
54  Ibid., 36.

## 5 Conclusion

The adoption of the *Declaration on the Right to Development* not only marks the official recognition of the right to development, but it can also be regarded as the first successful joint action undertaken by the Global South at the international level in the area of human rights. This chapter makes the point that the time is right to again join Southern forces in the area of human rights to produce another document, this time to lay out a comprehensive Southern vision on human rights. The success of the adoption of the *Declaration on the Right to Development* can serve as a source of inspiration.

Southern states could have a major impact on the human rights debate by launching a *Comprehensive Southern Vision on Human Rights*, which lays out a positive vision on human rights, while fitting perfectly within the four corners of the international human rights framework.

The drafters of a Comprehensive Southern Vision have the foundational document of the international human rights regime, the UDHR, to fall back on. The UDHR is often portrayed as an ode to liberal-modernism. Certain elements were included in the UDHR or played a part in the deliberations, which have since moved into the background. These are exactly the elements which are at the core of Southern human rights thinking. Therefore, it would be very important to include those elements in a Comprehensive Southern Vision document.

It will be up to the Southern states themselves to determine what should be included in a Comprehensive Southern Vision. However, based on the UDHR and the common positions taken, a few elements can already be identified, such as the need to rely on culture, customary law and morality for the implementation of human rights obligations; the importance of respecting subsidiarity and non-interference; the acceptance of the idea that collective rights are at least as important as individual ones; the recognition that the rights to subsistence and development are paramount; the acknowledgement that rights and duties are two sides of the same coin; and the acceptance of the idea that contextual implementation furthers the universality of human rights.

CHAPTER 16

# A Comprehensive and Multidimensional Survey of Law and Development in the 21st Century
*Taking Stock of the New Right to Development*

Zhu Liyu*

1        Law and Development: Then and Now

If we look back at the post-World War II jurisprudential movements in US legal academia, the law and development movement is probably meant to be one of the most policy-driven, knowledge-intensive and far-reaching intellectual activities.[1] In the 1950s and 1960s, the US government and US-based foundations dispatched a large group of development experts and lawyers to Latin America, Africa, and Asia. Their mission was to carry out a set of comprehensive programs for legal modernization. Evidently, the law and development movement was a complicated enterprise, for it attracted a wide range of participants with various backgrounds and disciplines. For that account, there is no unified action logic, single knowledge source, or systemic theoretical framework within the law and development community. As Lawrence Friedman, a leading figure in American law and society scholarship, puts it: "In recent years, intellectuals in the United States have grown more and more aware of the problems of the developing nations. Scholars in many fields and disciplines have turned outward to the world, often quite literally. They have packed their bags and gone abroad partly for their own edification, partly for the advancement of knowledge, and partly for reasons of national policy".[2] In the mid-1970s, the law and development movement gradually faded away.[3]

---

\*   Zhu Liyu, Professor of Law at the School of Law at Renmin University of China, and the Executive Director of Renmin University's Centre for Human Rights Studies. The gist of this chapter was initially presented in Chinese as a preface to a book entitled *Multidimensional Studies of the New Law and Development—An Interdisciplinary Inquiry Toward Comprehensive Development* (published by China Law Press in November 2016).
1   See David M. Trubek, "Law and Development: Then and Now", *American Society of International Law* 90 (1996): 223–226.
2   Lawrence M. Friedman, "On Legal Development", *Rutgers Law Review* 24 (1969): 11.
3   E.g., David M. Trubek and Marc Galanter, "Scholars in Self-Estrangement: Some Reflections on the Crisis in Law and Development Studies in the United States", *Wisconsin Law Review*, no. 4 (1974): 1062–1102; Francis G. Snyder, "The Failure of Law and Development", *Wisconsin*

Fundamentally speaking, the law and development movement, though externally buttressed by a group of development intellectuals, is internally determined by the foreign aid policies of Western capitalist countries. Along this line of thinking, the vicissitudes of the law and development movement are the epitome of Cold War battles. During the late 1970s and the 1980s, the third wave of democratization greatly inspired the consciousness of human rights in Third World countries. What followed was the market-oriented "Washington Consensus" and neoliberalism in the field of international development. Under the powerful force of "global capitalism", the revival of the new law and development movement, quite predictably, seems to be a new epitome of the re-energized Western rule of law promotional industry. Nowadays, post-Cold War law and development, in whatever form it may take, is a "global business" rather than a "jurisprudential movement". As David Trubek expressed:

> All that has changed. Today, most development institutions have identified legal reform as a major area of programmatic concern. If we add up the current "rule of law" portfolios of the World Bank, regional banks, major foundations, the US Agency for International Development (USAID), and other bilateral aid institutions, we can easily identify several billion dollars' worth of assistance funds being spent on law projects, not to mention the local counterpart contributions to such projects. As several of the participants on this panel will testify, the World Bank and USAID have made multimillion-dollar investments in Russia alone. Law and development has emerged from the ashes as big business.[4]

Based on this author's such observations, law and development in the 21st century is moving from a "movement" to a "field". In particular, there is growing evidence that at least four sub-fields of law and development are emerging and/or burgeoning, namely aid-funded law and development policy, policy-driven law and development movement, interdisciplinary-based law and development studies, and science-oriented law and development research.

## 2  Law and Development Policy as Foreign Assistance

As an applied field, law and development is internally driven by the Western legal assistance policy and often internally demanded by newly emerging

---

Law Review (1982); Brian Z. Tamanaha, "The Lessons of Law-and-Development Studies", *The American Journal of International Law* 89, no. 2 (1995).

4  David M. Trubek, "Law and Development: Then and Now", *American Society of International Law* 90 (1996): 223.

nation states since the end of World War II. Dating back to the modern history of economic development, policymakers and economists have advocated three major economic policies for developing countries to achieve rapid catch-up and modernization. In the 1950s and 1960s, a large number of developing countries (especially Latin American countries) widely adopted the import substitution industrialization (ISI). This inward-looking development strategy contains high tariffs, import quotas, foreign exchange control, and other trade protection measures to ensure the preferential development of national industrialization. As a result, developing countries adopted economic planning and administrative directives to control the private sector. In the 1970s and 1980s, a growing number of developing countries (such as "the Four Asian Tigers") turned to export-oriented industrialization. This outward-looking development strategy involves tariff reduction, export subsidies, gradual removal of trade restrictions, and other export stimulation measures. Accordingly, developing countries are required to use free trade policies to further integrate the local private sector with international markets. Since the 1990s, after the dissolution of the Soviet Union and the end of the Cold War, many transition countries, such as Russia and Eastern European countries, have adopted large-scale and radical economic reforms. This market-oriented economic policy seeks to achieve a quick transition from a command economy to a market economy by maintaining macroeconomic stability and promoting trade liberalization, privatization, and institutional reform. If we take a closer look at specific policy claims in the field of rule of law assistance, it is not a coincidence that each legal assistance policy highly correlates with corresponding development orthodoxies in each period.[5]

In concrete terms, legal assistance is a by-product of Western foreign assistance. During the Cold War era, US-based national development aid agencies and IMF-led international financial institutions launched a large number of legal assistance programs in the Third World. Under the influence of arms competition and ideological confrontation, capitalist developed countries sought to assist underdeveloped countries to realize "democracy and human rights through economic assistance", by providing financial, technical and humanitarian assistance. These policy actions rested upon a strategic motive holding that capitalist ideology (especially the liberal democratic rule of law ideas) could be permeated through most Third World countries. As a consequence, donor countries packaged legal assistance as a form of technical assistance, and the underlying logic implied that legal technical assistance was ready to

---

5 See David Kennedy, "The 'Rule of Law', Political Choices, and Development Common Sense", in *The New Law and Economic Development: A Critical Appraisal*, eds. David M. Trubek and Alvaro Santos (Cambridge: Cambridge University Press, 2006), 95–173.

use and politically neutral. To co-opt more Third World countries into the capitalist camp, legal technical assistance was primarily targeted at Latin American, African and Asian countries, regardless of whether the recipient countries were democracies or autocracies.[6] Moreover, the Cold War legal assistance specifically aimed at establishing a set of legal and regulatory frameworks compatible with the policy goals of economic recovery and national reconstruction. Major law reforms related to economic laws (price controls, foreign exchange controls, and tax administration) in the realm of macroeconomics and organic laws (central-local institutional building, fiscal budget, and personnel management) in the field of public law.[7] In essence, the nature, scope, and substance of legal assistance were ultimately determined by the Cold War foreign aid policy.

Since the post-Cold War era, the World Bank-led multilateral development aid agencies have regarded both "markets" and "democracy" as the ultimate agents for development, and further implemented market-oriented rule of law reforms and democratic reforms in a large number of developing countries on a global scale.[8] On the one hand, post-Cold War legal assistance no longer confines itself to legal technical assistance but transforms into rule of law assistance under the banner of democracy assistance. Obviously, Western policymakers and developers not only take rule of law assistance as a technical instrument for development but also as a universal political ideal. In general, democratic assistance incorporates electoral aid, political party building, government development, rule of law aid, civic education, civil society organization building, and media strengthening. Among them, legal reform (creating a legal and regulatory framework for a market economy), justice reform (placing the judiciary at the core of the justice sector), and civil society law reform (enhancing legal empowerment for civil society) are three pillars of rule of law reforms.[9] On the other hand, institution-based rule of law reforms target the judiciary, police, prosecution, correctional institutions, tax administration,

---

6   See generally Thomas Carothers, *Aiding Democracy Abroad: The Learning Curve* (Washington D.C.: Carnegie Endowment for International Peace, 1999), 19–29.
7   See Franz Ballman, "Legal Technical Assistance of the International Monetary Fund to Member Countries Through Economic Development Legislation", *Journal of Law and Economic Development* 3 (1968): 197–199.
8   E.g., Jacques Delisle, "Lex Americana? United States Legal Assistance, American Legal Models, and Legal Change in the Post-Communist World and Beyond", *University of Pennsylvania Journal of International Law* 20, no. 2 (1999): 179–308; Paul Gewirtz, "The US-China Rule of Law Initiative", *William & Mary Bill of Rights Journal* 11, no. 2 (2003): 603–621.
9   Thomas Carothers, *Aiding Democracy Abroad: The Learning Curve* (Washington D.C.: Carnegie Endowment for International Peace, 1999), 85–90.

legal profession and education,[10] while ends-based rule of law reforms focus on: (1) rule of state; (2) equality before the law; (3) law and order; (4) efficient and impartial justice; and (5) protection of human rights.[11] In a nutshell, the basic logic of Western rule of law assistance is: institution-based rule of law leads naturally to ends-based rule of law.

Since the 1990s, rule of law assistance has widely covered transition countries such as Russia and Eastern European countries, failed states and post-conflict societies in the Middle East, Africa, and Asia. Western development aid agencies proclaim that the policy goals for rule of law assistance are to help transition countries achieve dual transformation in both economic and political spheres, and support failed states and post-conflict societies in maintaining peace and social order. As compared to Cold-War legal assistance, rule of law assistance in the post-Cold War era is growing into global rule of law promotional industry. In this sense, law and development policy as foreign assistance equals to the "rule of law aid movement".

## 3  Law and Development Scholarship as Intellectual Movements

As a scholarly field, the first wave of law and development movement, rooted in the American legal academia, arose in the 1950s and had its heyday in the 1960s.[12] A vast array of development experts and scholars from a variety of disciplines asserted that this was an excellent opportunity to spread the advanced legal knowledge of the United States to Third World countries, and further threw themselves into the rule of law promotional enterprise. As the paradigm of the first law and development movement, modernization theory claims that the only viable way for developing countries to realize the evolutionary transition from tradition to modernity is to introduce the Western values and behavior patterns. Therefore, in line with the import substitution industries in the economic sphere, law and development scholars advocated a government-oriented legal development model which prioritized public sector reforms,

---

10   See generally Michael J. Trebilcock and Ronald J. Daniels, *Rule of Law Reform and Development: Charting the Fragile Path of Progress* (Northampton: Edward Elgar Publishing, 2009).

11   See Rachel Kleinfeld, "Competing Definitions of the Rule of Law", in *Promoting the Rule of Law Abroad: In Search of Knowledge*, ed. Thomas Carothers (Washington D.C.: Carnegie Endowment for International Peace, 2006), 33–73.

12   See generally Elliot M. Burg, "Law and Development: A Review of the Literature & a Critique of 'Scholars in Self-Estrangement'", *The American Journal of Comparative Law* 25, no. 3 (1977): 492–530.

that is, governments in Third World countries managed to change stereotypical behavior and inveterate traditions by mobilizing resources and top-down decision-making. In the legal sphere, law and development scholars also initiated reforms on legal education. They appealed to Third World countries to accept law as a tool for social change and lawyers as social architects. Law and development scholars made prior assumptions that cultural reforms could lead to institutional reform and economic legislation to political and social legislation as well. Even if the first law and development movement declined in the mid-1970s,[13] the intellectual enthusiasm of law and development scholars was triggered and their interests were growing.

Since the 1970s, human rights discourse and market fundamentalism have been aroused by the third wave of democratization and deregulation movement. After the demise of the Cold War, the second wave of law and development movement (also known as the "rule of law and development movement") spread rapidly throughout the globe. As the paradigm of the rule of law and development, neoliberalism, in favor of market mechanisms and private property rights, limited government and judicial independence, and equality of opportunity and individual responsibility, supplanted the once-dominant modernization theory. Undergirded by the "Washington Consensus" and its radical programs, law and development scholars proposed a private sector-led and market-oriented legal development model. The core ideas of new law and development orthodoxies embrace legal neoformalism and neoliberal rule of law. The former regards law as a neutral framework for market efficiency,[14] while the latter hails judicial independence. Later, the neoinstitutional rule of law, supported by the UN Millennium Development Goals and neoinstitutional economics, reinforced the neoliberal rule of law and promoted a multifunctional view of law in the late 1990s. Since then, law and development scholars have switched to the notion that law is not only conducive to economic growth but also necessary for social purposes, such as poverty alleviation, fighting corruption, access to justice, affirmative action, environmental protection and peacekeeping.[15] Apparently, today's law and development movement has become a worldwide intellectual activity, and more and more development

---

13  See Francis G. Snyder, "Law and Development in the Light of Dependency Theory", *Law & Society Review* 14, no. 3 (1980): 723–804.

14  See Victoria Nourse and Gregory Shaffer, "Varieties of New Legal Realism: Can a New World Order Prompt a New Legal Theory", *Cornell Law Review* 95, no. 1 (2009): 97.

15  See Kerry Rittich, "The Future of Law and Development: Second Generation Reforms and the Incorporation of the Social", in *The New Law and Economic Development: A Critical Appraisal*, eds. David M. Trubek and Alvaro Santos (Cambridge: Cambridge University Press, 2006), 203–252.

experts and scholars have committed themselves under the rubric of "law and development".

With regard to the intellectual styles of law and development scholarship, John Merryman points out that there are three scholarly inclinations in the first law and development movement, including (1) *action-oriented*: law and development scholars always hurried to bring changes rather than learn the local development of the Third World; (2) *non-theoretical*: law and development scholars ignored theoretical constructions, and focused too much on solving practical problems; (3) *non-quantitative*: law and development scholars seldom applied quantitative methods to their analyses.[16] Today's law and development scholars, however, are making more efforts to obtain academic autonomy, by establishing theoretical foundations of and adding empirical research to their intellectual works.

## 4   Law and Development Studies as Academic Disciplines

When the theoretical foundations of law and development scholarship become solid and institutionalized, it stands to reason that law and development scholarship could be considered as an academic field. In this regard, law and development studies pivot on independent academic thinking and interdisciplinary-based research methods. As is seen in legal academia, a growing number of law and development scholars introduced economics, politics, sociology, anthropology, ethnology, statistics and even cognitive sciences to their specialized fields of study. Hence the knowledge of law and development has significantly broadened and deepened. Up to now, there are generally three dominant themes in the field of law and development studies.

First, "law and economic development" is the core topic of law and development studies. In the long history of economic activity, human beings constantly search for the ultimate answer as to what the root cause of a country's economic development is. As far as we know, development economists have reached a reasonably solid conclusion that economic development is a dynamic function of natural resources, capital accumulation, technological progress, human education and institutional innovation.[17] As modern economies

---

16   See John Henry Merryman, "Comparative Law and Social Change: On the Origins, Style, Decline & Revival of the Law and Development Movement", *The American Journal of Comparative Law* 25, no. 3 (1977): 473–483.
17   See Yujiro Hayami and Yoshihisa Godo, *Development Economics: From the Poverty to the Wealth of Nations* (Oxford: Oxford University Press, 2005), 9–30.

become more diverse and sophisticated, institutions begin to act as a determining factor in the process of economic development. Obviously, this conclusion forms one of the most fundamental theoretical foundations of today's law and development studies. Law and development scholars widely accept the notion that law causes or furthers development. In recent years, they have gradually concentrated on a much more context-sensitive analysis of the role of law in particular societies.[18] As a result, law and development scholars claim that short-term economic growth may rely on regulatory law and planning law in a command economy, while long-term, sustainable economic growth to a large extent hinges on facilitative law and commercial law in a market economy. In general, the study of law and economic development involves three subtopics:

(1) *Law and finance in transition economies*: Law and finance in advanced economies analyzes the positive effects of investor protection rules on mature equity markets,[19] while law and finance in transition economies explores multivariate correlations between shareholder property rights, investor protection rules, trading rules and the economic performance of equity markets in emerging economies.[20]

(2) *Legal origins theories*: Legal origins theory assumes that measured differences in legal rules and regulations across countries matter for economic and social outcomes. To a large extent, legal differences depend heavily on different countries' legal families.[21] In the long run, market-supporting common law solutions will perform better than policy-implementing civil law solutions, especially in mature economies.[22]

---

18   See Kevin E. Davis and Michael J. Trebilcock, "The Relationship Between Law and Development: Optimists Versus Sceptics", *The American Journal of Comparative Law* 56, no. 4 (2008): 895–946.
19   E.g., Rafael La Portal et al., "Legal Determinants of External Finance", *The Journal of Finance* LII, no. 3 (1997): 1131–1150; Rafael La Portal et al., "Law and Finance", *Journal of Political Economy* 106, no. 6 (1998): 1113–1155; Rafael La Portal et al., "Investor Protection and Corporate Governance", *Journal of Financial Economics* 58, no. 1–2 (2000): 3–27.
20   E.g., Katharina Pistor, "Law as a Determinant for Equity Market Development: The Experience of Transition Economies", in *Assessing the Value of Law in Transition Economies*, ed. Peter Murrell (Ann Arbor: University of Michigan Press, 2001), 249–287; Katharina Pistor et al., "Law and Finance in Transition Economies", *Economics of Transition* 8, no. 2 (2000): 325–368.
21   See generally Simon Deakin and Katharina Pistor, eds., *Legal Origin Theory* (Cheltenham: Edward Elgar Pub, 2012).
22   See Rafael La Portal et al., "The Economic Consequences of Legal Origins", *Journal of Economic Literature* 46, no. 2 (2008): 285–332.

(3) *Effects of legal transplantation*: In contrast to origin countries that develop their law internally, transplanted laws may have weaker effects on the economic development of reception countries, because the ways, process, and methods of legal transplantation are much more important determinants of legal effectiveness.[23] Here, it is worth mentioning that most law and development scholars tend to equate "economic development" to "economic growth".

Secondly, "law and political development" is a focal topic of law and development studies. For development political scientists, one of the most widely discussed issues is how to define and realize political development. If we review the modern political process in Third World countries after World War II, political development mostly consists of four conceptual dimensions: political stability, political democracy, political transparency and political efficacy. On the whole, political scientists generally hold that democratization is the touchstone for the modernization of political development, and rule of law mechanisms provide basic institutional frameworks for democratization. Based on this, law and development scholars begin to focus on the relationship between law and political development in general, and rule of law and democracy in particular. Currently, the study of law and political development mainly covers three subtopics:

(1) *International law of development and the right to development*: As the international human rights movement and dependence theory became dominant in the 1970s, law and development scholars (especially those in the non-Western world) attempted to justify the right to development as an emerging third-generation human right. They argue that developing countries could not participate in and benefit from the international economic order without the institutional support of the international law of development.[24]

(2) *Good governance and rule of law*: Since the early 1990s, the World Bank, regional banks and many other Western development aid agencies have advocated a major policy change from state-centered "government" to multi-level "governance", with a special focus on the indispensable role of good governance

---

23   E.g., Daniel Berkowitz et al., "Economic Development, Legality, and the Transplant Effect", *European Economic Review* 47, no. 1 (2003): 165–195; Daniel Berkowitz et al., "The Transplant Effect", *The American Journal of Comparative Law* 51, no. 1 (2003): 163–203.

24   See Ronald Y. Rich, "The Right to Development as an Emerging Human Right", in *Law and Development(Legal Culture 2)*, ed. Anthony Carty (Aldershot: Dartmouth Publishing, 1992), 223–264; see also Jack Donnelly, "In Search of the Unicorn: The Jurisprudence and Politics of the Right to Development", in *Law and Development (Legal Culture 2)*, ed. Anthony Carty (Aldershot: Dartmouth Publishing, 1992), 169–205; Muthucumaraswamy Sornarajah, "The Resurgence of the Right to Development", in *Law and Development in Asia*, eds. Gerald Paul McAlinn and Caslav Pejovic (Abington: Routledge, 2012), 43–67.

in creating a sustainable, participatory, and accountable institutional framework at both the international and domestic levels. Thus, law and development policymakers and scholars search to examine the interconnection between "good governance" (including the rule of law) and "development".[25]

(3) *Anti-corruption law*: As developing countries have always suffered from rampant corruption, law and development scholars have growing confidence in the nexus between the rule of law and the fight against corruption. Their idea is to establish domestic anti-corruption legal systems and/or introduce transnational anti-corruption legal regimes.[26]

Thirdly, "law and social development" is an emerging topic of law and development studies. To a great extent, the study of law and social development is derived from those of law and economic development. In the beginning, law and development scholars used to give undue priority in analyzing the correlation between law and economic growth (such as GDP, GNI, FDI), while failing to explore the role that law should play in economic development (e.g., quality of life, educational and environmental standards). As the wealth gap, illiteracy, prejudices, and environmental pollution have become major social problems for developing countries, more and more law and development scholars adopt a micro perspective and bottom-up approach to dissect the relationship between law and social goodness.[27] In general, three subtopics are mainly concerned with the study of law and social development:

(1) *Law and the disadvantaged groups*: We have learned from past failures that rights-supportive legal reforms are far from sufficient. What's more, law and development policymakers and scholars further accentuate the role of law in empowering and protecting socially disadvantaged groups, such us women, children, the disabled, racial and ethnic minorities, and even LBGT groups.[28]

(2) *Law and labor rights*: In developing countries, labor-intensive industries maximize their profits at the cost of employees' rights. Some law and development scholars argue that international labor law should provide minimum

---

25  About Worldwide Governance Indicators/WGI, available at http://data.worldbank.org/data-catalog/worldwide-governance-indicators.
26  E.g., Kevin Davis, "Does the Globalization of Anti-Corruption Law Help Developing Countries?", New York University Law and Economics Working Papers, Paper 203 (2009); Kevin Davis, "The Prospects for Anti-Corruption Law: Optimists Versus Skeptics", *Hague Journal on the Rule of Law* 4 (2012): 319–336.
27  See Richard Cameron Blake, "The World Bank's Draft Comprehensive Development Framework and the Micro-Paradigm of Law and Development", *Yale Human Rights and Development Journal* 3, no. 1 (2000): 167–172.
28  See Ann Stewart, "The Dilemmas of Law in Women's Development", in Sammy Adelman and Abdul Paliwala, *Law and Crisis in the Third World* (London: Hans Zell Pub, 1993), 219–242.

standards to protect employees' basic rights to income, work safety, and social security.[29]

(3) *Law and alternative dispute resolution*: Developing countries usually lack sufficient judicial resources to meet the needs of all citizens for dispute resolution.[30] As a result, law and development scholars emphasize the advantages of alternative dispute resolution mechanisms over formal enforcement of contracts.

In summary, all these subtopics mentioned above frame the general outline of today's law and development studies. One the one hand, law and development studies have created various subdisciplines in legal academia and covered a wide range of topics encompassing almost every aspect of social concerns. Nevertheless, law and development scholars also lack general theories and interdisciplinary communication in their studies, which in turn leads to *topical fragmentation*. On the other hand, most law and development scholars seem to ignore or devalue the study of "law and cultural development".[31] This *cultural superiority or research incapacity* inherent in the law and development community eventually results in the abandoning of a culturalist approach. Ironically, an array of law and development scholars is now engaging in scientific inquiries of law and development, by adopting a fact-based and indicator-oriented approach.

## 5 Law and Development Research as Social Sciences

Science-oriented law and development research aim to effectively reinforce the accuracy and predictability of law and development policies by using scientific methods and statistical information. After the end of World War II, Western developed countries implemented a series of domestic development policies to resuscitate the economy and enhance social welfare. In the 1960s and 1970s, the US government and local think tanks launched the social indicators movement by using economic and social indicators to guide policymaking and

---

29  See Sammy Adelman, "The International Labor Code and the Exploitation of Female Workers in Export-Processing Zones", in *Law and Crisis in the Third World*, eds. Sammy Adelman and Abdul Paliwala (London: Hans Zell Pub, 1993), 195–218.
30  E.g., Michael Trebilcock and Jing Leng, "The Role of Formal Contract Law and Enforcement in Economic Development", *Virginia Law Review* 92, no. 7 (2006): 1517–1580.
31  E.g., Lan Cao, "Culture Change", *Virginia Journal of International Law* 47, no.2 (2007): 357–412; Amy Cohen, "Thinking with Culture in Law and Development", *Buffalo Law Review* 57, no. 2 (2009): 511–586.

assess policy outcomes.[32] In the mid-1970s, this movement became prevalent in some international organizations and many Western nations, such as the United Kingdom, France, Germany, Netherlands, Canada and Europe. In this sense, the first law and development movement can be considered a product of the US social indicators movement. In the beginnings of law and development research, law and development scholars sought to establish a conceptual framework for legal variables by dividing legal systems into three components: (1) *legal structures*: legal institutions, legal participants, legal procedures, and legal resources; (2) *legal substances*: rules, doctrines, statutes, decrees, and decisions; and (3) *legal cultures*: internal legal culture of professionals (such as lawyers, judges, prosecutors) and external legal culture of the popular masses. Law and development scholars then moved on to empirical comparative analysis between different countries' legal systems, with a particular focus on the laws and institutions in non-Western underdeveloped countries. During these periods, the social indicators movement and the law and development movement were coexistent and mutually reinforcing. In spite of limited data and insufficient resources, early law and development research formed the basic theoretical foundation of the future rule of law assessment movement.

Perhaps, the most flourishing field of today's law and development is law and development research, for science-oriented law and development activities have received strong financial and technical support from both policy circles and academia in recent years. Since the 1990s, international development aid agencies (e.g., the Work Bank, the European Bank for Reconstruction and Development, the Asian Development Bank) and domestic government agencies (e.g., the United States Agency for International Development, the UK Department for International Development, and Global Affairs Canada) have promoted massive rule of law assistance programs in transition countries, failed states and post-conflict societies. Inspired by the early achievements of law and development research, rule of law aid providers stimulated the rise of the global rule of law assessment movement in the mid-1990s. From then on, various rule of law indicators have been designed and applied to evaluate the effectiveness of legal assistance policy, such as the UN Rule of Law Indicators, the World Bank's Worldwide Governance Indicators, and the World Justice Project's Rule of Law Index. By and large, there are three main characteristics of today's rule of law assessment movement:

---

32   See generally Clifford W. Cobb and Craig Rixford, *Lessons Learned from the History of Social Indicators* (Washington: Redefining Progress, 1998), 1–36.

(1) *Systematic quantification*: the quantification of rule of law is based on a solid analytical framework, which is intended to operationalize rule of law variables into coherent and measurable factors.

(2) *Comprehensive data sources*: rule of law data are collected from a large number of household and expert surveys and cross-country assessments of governance.

(3) *World map of rule of law*: rule of law assessment is devoted to measuring, comparing and ranking different countries' rule of law performance, and then predicting and evaluating the policy outcomes of specific rule of law assistance programs.

Law and development research, by its nature, represents an essential form of global diffusion of general legal knowledge. In the international policy circle, there is a growing consensus that science, instead of ideologies, should play a vital role in the process of policymaking. As Joseph Stiglitz forcefully argued: "How can we explain the strong advocacy of a major change in the international economic architecture other than ideology and/or capture by certain special interests? But the strongest antidote to both is science-theory and evidence". From this perspective, the inquiry-oriented rule of law assessment movement concentrates on evidence-based policymaking, while the action-oriented law and development movement strongly relies on policy-based evidence making. Nevertheless, it should be pointed out that today's rule of law assessment movement tends to produce and disseminate three types of legal knowledge:

(1) *General knowledge*: providing meta-narrative theories and across-the-board solutions, disregarding local context and individual cases, such as state-led modernization theory or market-orient neoliberalism, and public sector or private sector-led legal reform.

(2) *Objective knowledge*: claiming that legal knowledge, based on hard facts, is observable, measurable, and reproducible, but different perspectives on and perceptions of laws and legal institutions might be neglected.

(3) *Explicit knowledge*: assuming that legal knowledge is readily codified into indicators and easily transferred across countries, and can be acquired through logical deduction and practical experience.

In reality, the diffusion of law at a global level appears to be a complex and indirect process. In clarifying the impact of legal transplantation on developing countries, William Twining recognized and pinpointed a constant tension between technological, contextual-expressive, and ideological perspectives on law.[33] By the same token, legal knowledge is also likely to be local, subjective,

---

33  See William Twining, "Diffusion of Law: A Global Perspective", *Journal of Legal Pluralism* 36, no. 49 (2004): 1–49.

and tacit in most parts of developing countries. As a consequence, today's law and development research is trying to adjust its scientific methods by switching from "global empiricism" to "local empiricism".[34] The effects of this methodological change, however, remain unknown.

## 6     Retrospect and Prospects: The New Right to Development under the Policy Support of UN Post-2015 Development Agenda

### 6.1    *The Pros and Cons of the Right to Development*

Admittedly, twenty-first century law and development is led by the Global North, and law and development scholars in the Global South are striving to participate in international legal development networks, which are being established to promote North–South dialogue and South–South cooperation in the legal field of international development. To achieve a more fair, open and innovative global legal order, countries in the Global South have the responsibility to make efforts to explore context-sensitive local legal knowledge. Here, the new right to development under the policy support of UN Post-2015 Development Agenda can be considered as a breakthrough point in the future study of law and development, especially for law and development scholars in the Global South.

As is widely acknowledged, the first round of the right to development was a Third World-led human rights movement emerging in the 1970s and 1980s. Although the idea of the right to development remained controversial and lacked consensus, its basic conception emphasized an autonomous and comprehensive development of all states and all peoples, particularly those in the developing countries. On a practical level, the *Declaration for the Establishment of a New International Economic Order* (1974), *Buenos Aires Plan of Action on Technical Cooperation Among Developing Countries* (1978) and *Declaration on the Right to Development* (1986) formed the central sources of the international law of development, which were integrally considered as a rising branch of modern international law during the Cold War era.

On a theoretical level, policymakers and scholars in the Third World generally introduced three representative theories in support of the legitimacy of the right to development:

(1) *The indispensable theory* presupposes that if the state fails to develop, its peoples' basic demands could hardly be fulfilled and protected. And the

---

34   See David M. Trubek, "Scan Globally, Reinvent Locally: Can We Overcome the Barriers to Using the Horizontal Learning Method in Law and Development?", *Nagoya University Journal of Law and Politics*, no. 258 (2014): 11–25.

right to development, conceptually equal to the right of self-determination, acts as an indispensable component and prerequisite of all other types of human rights.

(2) *The generative theory* treats the right to development as a third generation human right, especially in comparison with the first-generation human rights (civil and political rights) and the second-generation human rights (economic, social and cultural rights). In this sense, the right to development, termed a solidarity right, implies international action based on the duty to cooperate.

(3) *The synthesis theory* generally views the right to development as a synthesized combination of all existing individual and collective human rights.

Nonetheless, as the World Bank-led Washington Consensus and neoliberalism became dominant development orthodoxies after the end of the Cold War, the first round of the right to development quickly faded away. Most Western policymakers and scholars sharply suspected or objected to the legitimacy of the right to development. Typically, their arguments against the right to development mainly include five points:
- First, the market economy and trade liberalism based on capitalism outweigh the creation of the right to development.
- Secondly, no states have legal duties and obligations to take progressive measures to protect the right to development.
- Thirdly, most developing countries are in need of development instead of pursuing autonomous development.
- Fourthly, the UN Human Rights Council lacks jurisdiction over matters of trade, international lending and financial policy, activities of transnational corporations, and other aspects of globalization.
- Fifthly, the state-based right to development sharply contradicts the legacy of human rights abuses and mass atrocities committed by some infamous governments in the Global South.

Since the 1990s, the right to development has been widely recognized as a political rhetoric other than an effective legal institution.

## 6.2   *Three Policy Signals of the New Right to Development*

Here, this chapter attempts to propose a research project on the emergence of the new right to development. The basic presupposition of such a new research project is that the revival of the new right to development remains unknown and debatable. Apparently, the right to development persistently lacks effective implementation mechanisms at both the international and domestic levels in the past 20 years, while most policymakers and scholars in the Global South fail to strongly respond to those aforementioned arguments against the right to development posed by the Western world. Nevertheless, some more or less positive policy signals should be highlighted:

First, the new right to development will seek legitimacy from the "international rule of law" in the context of global governance, rather than the "international law of development" in the Cold War era. On August 23, 2004, the UN Security Council articulately defined the concept of the rule of law:

> The "rule of law" is a concept at the very heart of the Organization's mission. It refers to a principle of governance in which all persons, institutions and entities, public and private, including the State itself, are accountable to laws that are publicly promulgated, equally enforced and independently adjudicated, and which are consistent with *international human rights norms and standards*. It requires, as well, measures to ensure adherence to the principles of supremacy of law, equality before the law, accountability to the law, fairness in the application of the law, separation of powers, participation in decision-making, legal certainty, avoidance of arbitrariness and procedural and legal transparency.[35]

Secondly, there is a growing consensus about the relationship between the right to development and the rule of law in the field of international development. For example, the United Nations attached great importance to the role of the right to development and its mutual correlation with the rule of law on November 30, 2012, which could be seen as a symbol of the rise of the new right to development:

> We are convinced that the rule of law and development are strongly inter-related and mutually reinforcing, that the advancement of the rule of law at the national and international levels is essential for sustained and inclusive economic growth, sustainable development, the eradication of poverty and hunger and the full realization of all human rights and fundamental freedoms, including *the right to development*, all of which in turn reinforce the rule of law, and for this reason we are convinced that this interrelationship should be considered in the post-2015 international development agenda.[36]

---

35   The Secretary-General, *Report of the Secretary-General: The Rule of Law and Transitional Justice in Conflict and Post-Conflict Societies*, 4 U.N. Doc. S/2004/616 (August 23, 2004) (emphasis added).

36   The Secretary-General, *The General Assembly: Declaration of the High-level Meeting of the General Assembly on the Rule of Law at the National and International Levels*, 2 U.N. Doc. A/RES/67/1 (November 30, 2012) (emphasis added).

Thirdly, according to UN Post-2015 Development Agenda, the rule of law should play a pivotal role in achieving sustainable development and empowering human rights, while the UN's new development agenda has profound strategic significance in the 30th anniversary of the *Declaration on the Right to Development*.

> Without peace, stability, human rights and effective governance, based on the rule of law—we cannot hope for sustainable development ... The SDGs aim to significantly reduce all forms of violence, and work with governments and communities to find lasting solutions to conflict and insecurity. Strengthening the rule of law and promoting human rights is key to this process, as is reducing the flow of illicit arms and strengthening the participation of developing countries in the institutions of global governance.[37]

The new research project discussed above is guided by three underlying questions: Why is the right to development still necessary in today's international human rights discourse? What will be the most legitimate theory in defining the basic concept of the right to development? How should the rule of law contribute to the realization and protection of the right to development? Most importantly, are there effective implementation mechanisms with stronger enforceability and weaker justiciability? In my opinion, the autonomous development of the state is overemphasized in the first round of the right to development, while the dependent development of most developing countries can partly be ascribed to the unbalanced and unjust international economic order. Therefore, law and development scholars in the Global South will be able to explore and discover the new legitimacy and enforceability of the new right to development, by first addressing three pressing challenges: (1) redefining the concept of the right to development in terms of international human rights norms and standards by using the idea of the international soft law; (2) justifying the legitimacy of the right to development by introducing a new theory with both substantive and procedural concerns; (3) examining the correlation between the realization of the right to development and the rule of law, especially the international rule of law.

---

37  About UN Post-2015 Development Agenda, available at http://www.undp.org/content/undp/en/home/.

CHAPTER 17

# Implementation of the Right to Development by Optimizing WTO Regulations

*From the Perspective of the Doha Development Agenda*

Wang Bei*

## 1 Introduction

As one of the significant frameworks concerning development adopted by the United Nations in 2015, *Transforming Our World: The 2030 Agenda for Sustainable Development* "recognizes the need to build peaceful, just and inclusive societies that provide equal access to justice and that are based on respect for human rights (including the right to development)".[1] In order to achieve development and the right to development, the improvement of the international trading system cannot be neglected. Goal 10.a of the 2030 Agenda calls for the implementation of "the principle of special and differential treatment (SDT) for developing countries, in particular least developed countries, in accordance with World Trade Organization agreements". Moreover, the 2030 Agenda reaffirms the important role of Doha Declaration and Doha Development Agenda in Goal 3.b, Goal 17.10 and Section 68,[2] which indicate that the completion of the Doha Agenda as soon as possible will pave the way to achieve the

---

* Wang Bei, Ph.D. Candidate, Law School at Peking University, LLM from University of Edinburgh, UK.
1 The United Nations, *Transforming Our World: The 2030 Agenda for Sustainable Development*, A/RES/70/1.
2 Goal 3.b of the Agenda indicates that "Support the research and development of vaccines and medicines for the communicable and non-communicable diseases that primarily affect developing countries, provide access to affordable essential medicines and vaccines, in accordance with the *Doha Declaration on the TRIPS Agreement and Public Health*, which affirms the right of developing countries to use to the full the provisions in the *Agreement on Trade-Related Aspects of Intellectual Property Rights* regarding flexibilities to protect public health, and, in particular, provide access to medicines for all". Goal 17.10 provides to "promote a universal, rules-based, open, non-discriminatory and equitable multilateral trading system under the World Trade Organization, including through the conclusion of negotiations under its Doha Development Agenda". Section 68 "call[s] upon all members of the World Trade Organization to redouble their efforts to promptly conclude the negotiations on the Doha Development Agenda". The United Nations, *Transforming Our World: The 2030 Agenda for Sustainable Development*, A/RES/70/1.

SDT-based development with equity and right to development. Nevertheless, hardly any substantive progress has been made between the Doha Round officially commenced in November 2001 and the adoption of the *Bali Ministerial Declaration* on December 7, 2013.[3] Therefore, it is necessary to analyze how to improve the SDT-related provisions in WTO agreements in light of the 2030 Agenda.

With the publication of the *Doha Ministerial Declaration* in 2001,[4] an increasing amount of attention has been drawn to the concern for how to further make developing country Members, especially least developed country (LDC) Members participate more actively in multilateral trade systems. In this process, the significant role of assistance such as SDT given to these Members in need cannot be neglected. SDT is generally a more favorable treatment provided for WTO Members whose economic development is in less advanced stages compared to others. Under these SDT-related provisions, WTO Members are allowed to deviate from general rules and regulations under WTO agreements, such as the most-favored-nation principle, to give developing country Members and LDC Members preferential treatment. Besides, another crucial feature of the provisions is "non-reciprocity"[5] between the donor and the beneficiary, which is quite different from the reciprocal principle that has always been emphasized in international trade. Yet, SDT is not given without conditions. In practice, the developed country Members give SDT to developing country Members or LDC Members only if the latter meet certain non-trade prerequisites. Among all WTO agreements, there are in total 148 provisions concerning SDT.[6] The provisions are categorized into six substantive types: increasing trade opportunities for developing country Members; safeguarding interests of developing country Members; giving flexibility for less-developed countries as to commitments, action, and use of policy instruments; providing extended transitional time periods for developing country Members and LDC Members; offering technical assistance; and providing LDC Members with provisions specially designed to help them.[7] In terms of quantity and variety, it seems that the protection is sufficient and comprehensive enough to provide developing country Members and LDC Members with chances to integrate in international trade. A deeper analysis of the wording and the case law of

---

3  The Ninth WTO Ministerial Conference in Bali, accessed April 20, 2017, https://www.wto.org/english/news_e/news13_e/mc9sum_07dec13_e.htm.
4  Doha Ministerial Conference, *Ministerial Declaration*, WT/MIN(01)/DEC/1 (November 20, 2001).
5  The *General Agreement on Tariffs and Trade* (1994), Part VI.
6  Committee on Trade and Development, *Special and Differential Treatment Provisions in WTO Agreements and Decisions*, WT/COMTD/W/196 (June 14, 2013), 5.
7  Ibid., 3–4.

these provisions will, however, lead to a view that full integration still faces challenges. This essay will examine the current SDT-related WTO provisions from three perspectives in accordance with the mandate made in paragraph 44 of the *Doha Ministerial Declaration* that are "more precise, effective, and operational",[8] and analyze the reasons why these provisions fail to meet the goals set out by the Doha Ministerial Conference, as well as the future intensification and improvement.

## 2    Precision: Rights and Obligations of SDT

### 2.1    *Who Are Eligible to Be Receivers of SDT?*

The terms used to describe receivers in the SDT-related provisions are usually "less-developed contracting parties" and "developing country Members". Some provisions, especially in the category of SDT-related provisions, designed to help LDCs, directly point out that it is the LDC countries that should be the receivers of the SDT. As for the status of being an LDC in the WTO, Article XI:2 of the WTO Agreement clarifies that LDCs are those countries "recognized as such by the United Nations",[9] which gives an explicit definition of this group of countries because the United Nations provides an authoritative list of LDCs subject to regular inclusion, graduation and criteria changes. As for the "less-developed contracting parties" and "developing country Members", however, it is never clear how to correctly construe them. There is no universally recognized criterion to identify a country as a developing country. WTO Members can decide themselves whether they are developing countries or not, which aggravates the ambiguity of the beneficiary under the SDT-related provisions. Undoubtedly, LDCs belong to less-developed contracting parties, but do the so-called "developing countries" also fall within the scope of this norm? Article XVIII(4) of the GATT 1994 defines the receivers as countries "the economy of which can only support low standards of living and is in the early stages of development".[10] The *Ad* notes further explain that "the normal position" rather than "exceptional circumstances" should be taken into account when assessing the term "the economy of which can only support low standards of living", and the phrase "in the early stages of development" also includes "the economies of which are undergoing a process of industrialization to correct an excessive

---

8   The *Doha Ministerial Declaration* (n 4), 9.
9   *Marrakesh Agreement Establishing the World Trade Organization*, Article XI.
10   GATT1994 (n 5), Article XVIII.

dependence on primary production".[11] Although such explanation gives certain distinctiveness to the term "developing country Members", it remains too vague and broad, which still cannot offer criteria for differentiation. Similarly, Article 27.2 of the *Agreement on Subsidies and Countervailing Measures* (SCM Agreement) specifically points out that the countries referred to in Annex VII of the Agreement are entitled to enjoy the treatment.[12] Moreover, paragraph 12 of the Generalized System of Preferences (GSP) scheme implemented a notion of "graduation" in WTO.[13]

In a number of cases related to the use of the SDT provisions, the parties involved have already agreed that the status of being a developing country need not to be challenged due to the self-selection system in WTO. Instead, it is the countries claiming their status as developing countries that need to demonstrate that they are qualified for SDT.[14] Nevertheless, it is difficult to determine what evidence is needed to support the qualification. Although some clarifications as mentioned above exist, they are either not clear enough or supplementary to a specific provision, and thus are not sufficient to solve the problem. It seems that if the issue of eligibility is addressed, it will be easier for both the WTO Members and Dispute Settlement Body (DSB) to deal with SDT-related problems. Thus, it is necessary to clarify LDCs based on certain development criteria proposed by the United Nations and other international organizations. The criteria, such as GDP per capita calculated by the International Monetary Fund,[15] the World Bank,[16] and the United Nations,[17] as well as the Human Development Index (HDI)[18] created by the United Nations Development Programme, can be used to identify eligibility for SDT. As with the list of LDCs created by the United Nations as discussed above, the WTO can also create a list to identify developing countries and implement the mechanism of "graduation" by changing the list regularly. The method of using a list to classify developing countries is not without precedent. As early as 1966, the problem of identifying countries in the Australian *Wavier* case was resolved by referring

---

11  GATT1994 (n 5), *Ad* note of Article XVIII.
12  *Agreement on Subsidies and Countervailing Measures*, Article 27.2, Annex VII.
13  *The Generalized System of Preferences: A Preliminary Analysis of the GSP Schemes in the Quad*, WT/COMTD/W/93 (October 5, 2001), 3.
14  *Republic of Korea—Restrictions on Imports of Beef* (Report of the Panel) (November 7, 1989), 28.
15  International Monetary Fund, "World Economic Outlook: Subdued Demand: Symptoms and Remedies", Washington.
16  World Bank, World Development Indicators Database.
17  United Nations, "National Accounts Statistics: Main Aggregates and Detailed Tables".
18  United Nations Development Programme, "The Human Development Concept".

to an unofficial list of developing countries.[19] Although the list used in this case was informal and lacked any legal effect, it is possible to make a list in the future if the aforementioned clearer criteria are used. Yet, it is difficult to neglect the tension between developing countries and developed countries that can severely hinder negotiations in creating a list. Generally, a more uniform method to determine the criteria for graduation should be adopted by WTO.

### 2.2  What Are the Specific Obligations and Duties of WTO Members?

Obligations in the SDT provisions can be classified as "obligations of conduct" and "obligations of result".[20]

An illustrative example of obligation of conduct is Article 10.1 of the *Agreement on the Application of Sanitary and Phytosanitary Measures* (SPS Agreement) stating that "Members shall take account of special needs" of developing countries and LDCs in the perspectives of preparation and application of SPS measures.[21] The word "shall" indicates that the burden is on WTO Members. Nonetheless, because of the use of the phrase "take account of" and lack of prescription of any result, they only have an obligation of conduct rather than the obligation of the result. Members are considered to assume the obligation if they adopt the course of conduct such as "take account of". In *EC—Approval and Marketing of Biotech Products*, the complainant Argentina argued that the EC's measure is inconsistent with Article 10.1 because it failed to take account of the impact of its import restriction on Argentina's biotech products. The Panel rejected Argentina's argument and reaffirmed that the term "take account of" only requires the Members "to consider" the need rather than entailing any obligation of achieving a real result.[22] In practice, it is difficult to show that a Member has actually disregarded the special needs of developing countries.

"Obligations of result" provisions require Members to achieve certain results without giving any instruction of implementation actions. Article 12.2 of the *Agreement on Technical Barriers to Trade* is a representative example. It provides that "Members shall allow a reasonable interval between the publication …

---

19  Guglielmo Verdirame, "The Definition of Developing Countries Under GATT and Other International Law" (1996) GYIL 178.
20  *Implementation of Special and Differential Treatment Provisions in WTO Agreements and Decisions*, WT/COMTD/W/77/ Rev. 1/Add.2 (December 21, 2001), 4.
21  The SCM Agreement (n 12), Article 10.1.
22  *European Communities—Measures Affecting the Approval and Marketing on Biotech Products* (Report of the Panel) (September 29, 2006), 7.2939.

and its entry into force in order to allow time for ... particular in developing country Members ...". This provision requires Members to ensure that sufficient time is provided between the publication and the entry into force of a regulation, while Members are free to choose what has to be done to achieve this result. It is also ambiguous as to what is a "reasonable interval". Due to the freedom given by the provisions, less-developed countries have made many recommendations and requests regarding the explicit means and current achievement to the Committees on different sectors.[23]

In order to clearly allocate rights and obligations, it is necessary to stipulate what behavior patterns need to be taken and what the legal consequences will be. As for behavior patterns, actions to be taken under the SDT provisions can be classified into three categories, namely should, shall, and shall not. As for legal consequences, the observance of an SDT provision will have a positive outcome, while the violation will yield a negative outcome.

## 3  Effectiveness: Legal Binding Force of SDT

Pursuant to Article 11.2 of the WTO Agreement, SDT-related provisions in both the Agreement itself and other multilateral trade agreements in the Annexes are "binding on all Members". The wording of each provision, however, will largely affect the efficiency and the legally binding force. Provisions containing the world "should" are generally categorized as non-mandatory, while the use of the word "shall" in the provisions make them have a mandatory nature in a strictly legal sense. Yet, because of lack of sufficient description of substantive contents, the mandatory provisions are constantly blamed as "best-endeavor" obligations that offer no means for the developing countries and LDCs to make developed countries keep their commitments.[24] Even the Committee on Trade and Development, that is instructed by the WTO Members by their adoption of the *Decision in Implementation-Related Issues and Concerns*, has recognized that these types of SDT provisions are not necessarily effective because they leave the obligations flexible for WTO Members to assume.[25]

---

23  *Non-Mandatory Special and Differential Treatment Provisions in WTO Agreements and Decisions*, WT/COMTD /W/77/ Rev.1/Add.3 (February 4, 2002), 2.
24  Peter Lichtenbaum, "'Special Treatment' vs. 'Equal Participation': Striking a Balance in the Doha Negotiations", *AUIL Review* (2002): 1003–1014.
25  WT/COMTD/W/77/Rev.1/Add.3 (n 23), 2.

### 3.1 Mandatory in Nature

An illustration of this type of clause is Article XXXVII:1 of the GATT 1994. It states that "the developed contracting parties shall to the fullest extent possible—that is, except when compelling reasons, ...: (a) accord high priority to the reduction and elimination of barriers to products ..." of less-developed countries. It only sets an objective of giving priority on reduction of barriers to importation. Nonetheless, it is very difficult to interpret such provisions as really imposing an obligation on developed country Members, since it has no instruction regarding how to achieve the object.

### 3.2 Non-mandatory

Article XXXVI:2–7 of the GATT 1994 contains non-mandatory SDT provisions. These provisions identify the need for increasing trade opportunities for developing countries and LDCs by stating reasons such as "dependence of many less-developed contracting parties on the exportation" and facilitation of "the rapid expansion of economies of the less-developed contracting parties". Yet, there is no use of the word "shall" and no explicit action prescribed in such provisions. The provisions are more like a preamble of a statute or a treaty. Similar provisions are paragraph 1, 2 of the Enabling Clause,[26] Article 10.2, 10.4 of the SPS Agreement,[27] Article 27.1 of the SCM Agreement,[28] and Article 21 of the DSU.[29] Because of the hortatory characteristic, it seems that it is difficult for these types of SDT provisions to effectively play the role of providing more favorable treatment to less-developed countries.

### 3.3 Problems Occurred in Utilization

The aforementioned poor drafting imposes major obstacles for developing countries and LDCs to utilize SDT provisions in dispute settlements. In a series of cases, developing countries and LDCs raise their main arguments based on the SDT-related provisions, either mandatory in nature or non-mandatory, but they can hardly convince the Panel or the Appellate Body. From the perspective of the DSB, it is also difficult for it to clarify solid instructions from the provisions. According to Article 3.2 of the DSU, the clarification of rules "cannot add to or diminish the rights and obligations provided in the covered

---

26   The *Decision on Differential and More Favorable Treatment, Reciprocity and Fuller Participation of Developing Countries*, L/4903 (November 28, 1979), paragraphs 1, 2.
27   The *WTO Agreement on the Application of Sanitary and Phytosanitary Measures*, Article 10.2, 10.4.
28   The SCM Agreement (n 12), Article 27.1.
29   The *Understanding on Rules and Procedures Governing the Settlement of Disputes*, Article 21.

agreements".³⁰ Nevertheless, faced with the situation of a lack of sufficient information in the SDT provisions, it is unclear what can "add to" or "diminish" the rights and obligations. This gives the judiciary more space for maneuver. Yet, the greater space for maneuver in interpretation does not in practice meet the object of protecting the interests of developing countries and LDCs. The DSB usually has no choice, but is forced to define the criteria in the SDT provisions on an *ad hoc* basis and provides no concrete reason for doing so.

Article 12.10 of the DSU is classified as an "obligation of result" provision, as the provision indicates that the Panel "shall accord sufficient time for the developing country Members to prepare and present its argumentation".³¹ It requires the judiciary to make a decision as to whether or not to allow sufficient time, but does not provide any instruction regarding on what basis the Panel can make such a decision. The "maneuver" renders different results in two cases in which both India and Argentina requested the Panel to grant more time based on Article 12.10 of the DSU. While in *India—Agricultural, Textile and Industrial Products*, the Panel found India's arguments were sufficient to grant a longer time-period,³² the Panel in *Argentina—Imports of Preserved Peaches* rejected Argentina's request because the reasons Argentina gave were not sufficient.³³

Moreover, unpredictability of result is not limited to the utilization of the mandatory SDT provisions but also to the non-mandatory SDT provisions. The different results received from the application of Article 21.2 of the DSU about "reasonable period of time" are examples to illustrate this point. In four cases involving Indonesia as a defending party to respond to its measure affecting the automobile industry, the disputes were all referred to arbitrators to decide "reasonable period of time" in Article 21.3 in accordance with Article 21.2 of the DSU. The arbitrator awarded Indonesia an additional six-month period to adapt its domestic ruling to implement the rulings and recommendations of the judiciary because the reasons provided were deemed sufficient.³⁴ Conversely, in the two cases that Chile was complained about for its taxes on

---

30   The DSU (n 29), Article 3.2.
31   WT/COMTD/W/77/Rev. 1/Add.2 (n 20), 18.
32   *India—Quantitative Restrictions on Imports of Agricultural, Textile and Industrial Products* (Report of the Panel) (April 6, 1999), 5.8–5.10. The case was appealed later. The Appellate Body, however, upheld all the findings of the Panel that were appealed.
33   *Argentina—Definitive Safeguard Measure on Imports of Preserved Peaches* (Report of the Panel) (February 14, 2003), 4.2–4.7.
34   *Indonesia—Certain Measure Affecting the Automobile Industry* (Arbitration under Article 21.3 of the DSU) (December 7, 1998), 24.

alcoholic beverages, the results of the arbitration based on Article 21.3 were negative because the arbitrator did not see the sufficiency of Chile's reasons on difficulties to implement the rulings.[35] Confronted with the aforementioned utilization problems, it is crucial to intensify the function and effectiveness of SDT provisions.

## 4 Operability: Practicability of SDT

Generally, there are two problems impeding the realization of giving more favorable treatment to less-developed countries in practice. The first, as discussed above, is that some SDT provisions are too vague to provide any practical meaning in helping LDCs. Another problem is that some provisions such as the "Enabling Clause" are enforceable to a certain degree. But the value of such provisions has not been exploited due to conditions imposed on the access of less-developed countries. The Generalized System of Preferences, usually referred to as GSP, is a non-reciprocal system designed to promote the interests of the developing countries and LDCs. The concept was developed on the basis of the 1971 Waiver Decision, and eventually became a part of the WTO system after the Contracting Parties' adoption of the *Decision on Differential and More Favorable Treatment, Reciprocity and Fuller Participation of Developing Countries* (the "Enabling Clause") in 1979. Under the system, WTO Members can unilaterally grant non-reciprocal preferences to the LDC Members. A concern, however, that is usually raised by developing country Members is non-trade conditions imposed on accession to the GSP. Many developed countries link preferences with non-trade conditions, such as the fight against drugs, labor standards, intellectual property rights, environmental protection and so on. These eligibility requirements curtail the number of beneficiaries of GSP and are accused of leading to discrimination among receivers. In *EC—Tariff Preferences*, the Appellate Body rejected the Panel's interpretation of the term "non-discriminatory" in footnote 3 of paragraph 2(a) of the "Enabling Clause". Rather than requiring "identical tariff preferences under GSP schemes to be provided to all developing countries without differentiation",[36] the Appellate Body clarified the term as meaning countries with the same "development,

---

35  *Chile—Taxes on Alcoholic Beverages* (Arbitration under Article 21.3 of the DSU) (May 23, 2000), 44, 46.

36  *EC—Conditions for the Granting of Tariff Preferences to Developing Countries* (Report of the Appellate Body) (April 7, 2004), 148.

financial or trade needs" should not be treated differently.[37] It further elaborated three conditions for giving GSP preferences, namely, the "development, financial or trade need" must be evaluated through "an objective standard",[38] a sufficient connection should exist between "the preferential treatment provided" and "the likelihood of alleviating the relevant 'development, financial or trade need'",[39] and the need at issue "can be effectively addressed through tariff preferences".[40] Although the EC claimed that their drug arrangement is available to all identically situated developing countries,[41] it does not have criteria or standards that can be used to ensure developing countries take advantage of the arrangement. Instead, it is the need to tackle illicit drug production and trafficking in beneficiaries that makes the EC provide tariff preferences. Nevertheless, such need can meet none of the aforementioned three requirements to identify a "development, financial or trade need" of developing countries. The US GSP scheme has a similar problem. If its GSP is challenged, the burden is on the US to prove that the alleviation of the need to protect intellectual property rights has a sufficient nexus with tariff preferences, and the need can be addressed effectively by granting tariff preferences. Yet, it cannot be said with certainty that the beneficiaries indeed have such legitimate need or the US can provide sufficient evidence to prove the causal link.[42]

Moreover, in the category of SDT provisions providing transitional time periods, it is questionable whether the time periods stipulated are reasonable for developing country Members and LDC Members to fulfill particular obligations. Although some vagueness existed in Article 10.2 of the SPS Agreement concerning "longer time-frames for compliance", the Doha Ministerial Conference has clarified that the term normally means at least six months.[43] In most provisions, it is quite clear how long the additional time provided for the less-developed Members is. Article 2:2 footnote 5 *Automatic Import Licensing of the Agreement on Import Licensing Procedures* is an example. It provides a developing country Member that "has specific difficulties with the requirement of Article 2:2 subparagraphs (a)(ii) and (a)(iii)" with more time to apply. Though 24 developing country Members invoked the provision, the delay

---

37    Ibid., 165.
38    Ibid., 163.
39    Ibid., 164.
40    Ibid., 165.
41    Ibid., 188.
42    Lorand Bartels, "The WTO Legality of the EU's GSP+ Arrangement", *JIEL* (2007): 879–881.
43    *Implementation-Related Issues and Concerns*, WT/MIN(01)/17 (November 20, 2001), 2.

allowed for all of these countries had already expired.⁴⁴ A concern is whether the explicit stipulations concerning the time periods offer enough additional time. It may still be difficult for these countries with less social and economic resources to fulfill obligations. Some may argue that these provisions also allow less-developed Members to extend time periods. For example, Article 27.4 of the SCM Agreement says "if a developing country Member deems it necessary to apply such subsidies beyond the 8-year period", it still has opportunity to receive an extension. The extension, however, is unpredictable. Under the Article, developing countries can only consult with the Committee about the extension. Issues such as whether the extension will be granted and how long the extension is are up to the Committee based on "all the relevant economic, financial and development needs of the developing country Member in question".⁴⁵ But what are the exact criteria for evaluating "the relevant economic, financial and development needs"?

## 5  Recommendations

The three critical problems undermining the value of the SDT provisions as analyzed above are not mutually exclusive. The ambiguity of SDT provisions leads to a lack of enforceability and further creates operational obstacles. If the ambiguity problem can be resolved, it will be easier to tackle the other two problems. The Committee on Trade and Development has presented two methods to change the non-binding, non-mandatory, and vaguely formulated SDT-related provisions, first, through amendment according to the WTO Agreement, and secondly, through authoritative interpretation of the WTO Agreements.⁴⁶

### 5.1  *Amendment*

Any WTO Member is able to initiate a proposal for an amendment during the regularly held Ministerial Conference. It seems that the first method is relatively easy, however the complicated procedure and the consensus requirement stipulated by Article X of the WTO Agreement make it particularly difficult to be approved. According to Article X: "if consensus is not reached at a meeting of the Ministerial Conference within the established period, the Ministerial

---

44  *Special and Differential Treatment Provisions in WTO Agreements and Decisions*, WT/COMTD/W/196 (June 14, 2013), 55.
45  The SCM Agreement (n 9), Article 27.4.
46  WT/COMTD/W/77/Rev.1/Add.3 (n 23), 3.

Conference shall decide by a two-thirds majority of the Members whether to submit the proposed amendment to the Members for acceptance". SDT provisions are directly related to the interests of each country Member. No matter if it is a developed country or a less-developed country, it is particularly difficult to convince either side to sacrifice more interest in international trade. Although making an amendment is not a shortcut, an attempt to make an amendment regarding SDT provisions should not be given up if such a possibility exists. The Ninth Session of the Ministerial Conference in Bali had also recognized the need to draw up a Protocol of Amendment.[47]

The proposal for an amendment can be designed in accordance with the following four ideas:

(a) The attending parties. Each interest group can elect representatives to participate in negotiations prior to the formal vote on the amendment. Parties attending negotiations should be those who can represent the majority of each interest group. Besides, the function of leading powers to coordinate and to persuade other countries in the world cannot be ignored. Furthermore, an alternative method can be considered before the consensus is reached on the amendment—that is to initiate bilateral agreements containing better SDT provisions between a less-developed country and a developed country or economic entity. Such agreements are designed to overcome the deficiency of huge divergences produced by multilateral systems and reach a consensus within a smaller scope. With increasing influence, the agreement can pave the way for future consensus in the WTO.

(b) The contents of the amendment. The paramount purpose of the amendment is to balance trade protectionism and trade liberalism as well as the interests of each Member. It is undoubtedly important to protect as much as possible the interests of the less-developed countries. It is also of vital importance, however, to pay attention to the interests of developed countries. An amendment that can be accepted by both sides will realize more favorable treatment in SDT provisions without overlooking the interest of developed countries. Whereas developed countries sacrifice their interests in giving SDT to developing countries and LDCs, LDCs should make developed countries profit in other perspectives, such an increase in market access to the products and services from SDT donors, decrease trade deficit and so on. In this sense, SDT should still be based on reciprocal interaction though making clear the allocation of rights and obligations under SDT provisions via that amendment is in accordance with the non-reciprocity principle.

---

47   *Agreement on Trade Facilitation*, WT/MIN(13)/36 (December 11, 2013), 1.

(c) The attitude of each side. A consensus needs to be reached between developed and LDCS. Developed countries should recognize that SDT is not only beneficial for LDCS. Instead, SDT promotes economic resurgence worldwide from a sustainable aspect, of which developed countries can also take advantage. As for LDCS, they should and must realize that enjoying treatment without assuming any responsibility is not conducive to them taking part in increasingly harsh international competition. In a word, without concession made by both developed and LDCS, it is impossible to add enough value to SDT.

(d) The scope of issues. Unlike the agenda set in the Doha Round, future negotiation on SDT should not contain too many issues. The contracting parties during the Doha Ministerial Conference made a decision considering the implementation of SDT provisions—that is "to identify those that Members consider should be made mandatory, and to report to the General Council with clear recommendations for a decision by July 2002".[48] Although mandated Members to comply before a deadline, nothing changed substantially. Even during the subsequent conferences in Bali and Nairobi, consensus has been reached only regarding marginal issues. A more practical method is required in order to resolve the SDT-related problems more effectively. Besides, it seems that it is impractical to incorporate the "single undertaking" principle[49] that has the objective of having Members agree with every issue of a negotiation in the SDT-related negotiations. The correct sequence of processing SDT-related negotiation should go from easy issues to hard issues and from simple issues to complicated issues.

## 5.2 *Interpretation*

In 2014, the General Council adopted the Protocol of Amendment of adding the *Trade Facilitation Agreement* (FTA) to Annex 1A of the WTO Agreement. Three years later, the FTA has finally entered into force through ratification pursuant to Article X:3 of the WTO Agreement. The new agreement mainly addresses the problem of SDT in the perspective of technical assistance and capacity building.[50] Nevertheless, further amendment is still required. It is acknowledged that amendment can only be achieved after a long-term negotiation. A wiser approach to alleviate the problem from a short-term perspective is to increase the effectiveness of SDT provisions via authoritative interpretation. While the binding language such as the term "shall" in the provisions shows a

---

48  WT/MIN(01)/17 (n 43), 8.
49  WTO, "How the Negotiations Are Organized", accessed April 19, 2017, https://www.wto.org/english/tratop_e/dda_e/work_organi_e.htm.
50  WT/MIN(13)/36 (n 47), 21–27.

mandatory obligation for Members, the use of the term "should" indicates the non-mandatory nature from an analytical-jurisprudence perspective. In deciding whether to grant more favorable treatment to LDCs, both the DSB and the arbitrators in the relevant cases reaffirm the necessity to consider the interests of LDCs in these SDT provisions. For example, the arbitrator in determining a "reasonable period of time" in *Chile—Taxes on Alcoholic Beverages* noted "Article 21.2 [of the DSU], whatever else it may signify, usefully enjoins, inter alia, an arbitrator functioning under Article 21.3(c) to be generally mindful of the great difficulties that a developing country Member may, in a particular case, face as it proceeds to implement the recommendations and rulings of the DSB".[51] Although interpretation of WTO agreements cannot reduce or add rights and obligations pursuant to the last sentence of Article 3.2 of the DSU, it is worth noting that Article 3.2 also states that clarification of the covered agreements can be done in light of international law, such as the *Vienna Convention on the Law of Treaties* (VCLT). Based on Article 31 of the VCLT, "a treaty shall be interpreted in good faith in accordance with the ordinary meaning to be given to the terms of the treaty in their context and in the light of its object and purpose". Apparently, literal reading of the SDT provisions cannot meet the very purpose of designing these provisions mainly because of lack of sufficient articulation as mentioned above. In order to assist LDC Members in multilateral trading systems, the adoption of the contextual reading or even the object and purpose reading with more dynamic interpretation is necessary.[52]

### 5.3    Monitoring

Improving the monitoring mechanism of the implementation of SDT provisions is a relatively quick way to mitigate the conflict. Currently, WTO Members have adopted a decision on Monitoring Mechanism on Special and Differential Treatment at the Bali Ministerial Conference, however, the position taken by the Mechanism is rather passive in reviewing the implementation of SDT provisions. Although the Mechanism will operate regularly—twice a year, it can only give recommendations to the relevant WTO body rather than making any decision.[53] In order to make the Monitoring Mechanism more useful, it is necessary to:

---

51    *Chile—Taxes on Alcoholic Beverages* (n 35), 45.
52    Amin Alavi, "On the (Non-)Effectiveness of the World Trade Organization Special and Differential Treatments in the Dispute Settlement Process", *JWT* (2007): 346–347.
53    *Monitoring Mechanism on Special and Differential Treatment*, WT/MIN(13)/45 WT/L/920 (December 11, 2013), 1–2.

(a) Strengthen the effect of monitoring. All SDT donors should be monitored by a powerful and effective agency set specially in the WTO system in order to ensure implementation of the regulations related to the SDT. If a country Member is reluctant to take supervision, the result, either punishment or warning, needs to be clear as well.

(b) Stipulate all the issues related to implementation that will be supervised. The SDT provisions lack precision in terms of action models and responsibilities. If the monitoring system still does not contain detailed regulations, the whole system will remain superficial.

(c) Set up criteria to make an evaluation and review during monitoring. Without an evaluation and review toward the implementation of SDT provisions, the Monitoring Mechanism will not have any practical meaning. The feedback of the evaluation will guide and urge SDT donors to comply with the provisions and avoid making their granting discriminatory for LDCs.

## 6   Conclusion

Integrating development into the WTO is an irreversible tendency. Even though the WTO is not a development organization, it is an intergovernmental trade organization and has a development obligation due to the inextricable connection between trade and development.[54] In order to secure the share of LDCs in international trade, it is significant to establish a more precise, effective, and operational legal system. The contribution of LDCs is indispensable. If developing countries and LDCs do not take a more active role as well as make certain compromises, the issue of development underlined during the Doha Ministerial Conference will still not be able to progress. The key to resolving the development problem is to bridge the non-reciprocity principle and the reciprocity principle and to balance the interests of all parties through amendment, interpretation of WTO agreements and monitoring the implementation of SDT provisions. Without giving up seeking opportunities for international dialogue and cooperation, a multilateral trading system with active participation of LDCs can be achieved through taking these measures step by step. Further, with the achievement of an impartial and inclusive international trading system, the realization of the right to development is not far away.

---

54   Elimma C. Ezeani, *The WTO and Its Development Obligation: Prospects for Global Trade* (Anthem Press, 2010), 16.

# Index

Academic disciplines 277–281
Anti-corruption 280

Belt and Road Initiative 3–4, 233–240

Carbon emission 91, 111, 114–115, 117–138
China 4, 67–71, 104–105, 128, 130–132, 168, 186–196, 233–236, 238–240
Civil and political rights 32, 43, 136
Cultural relativism and universalism
    Doctrine 209–211
    Politics 217–220
Collective rights 64, 127, 245, 267–268

Duties
    State duties 37–39
    International duties 118–119, 123, 126
    Rights and duties 6, 118, 121, 131–133, 265, 268, 270

Environment
    Economic activities with threats 85–89
    Relationship with development 76–79, 109–112
    Rights 79–81, 112–115
    Protection 78–81, 85, 87, 90–104, 108–109, 111–112, 114–115, 120–121, 123, 137, 141, 143–144, 148–152, 157–162

Financial institution 16, 34, 36, 44–45, 184, 191, 273
Foreign assistance 272–275

Green development 79, 94–104
Good governance 19, 35–36, 147–148, 153, 159, 164, 166, 182, 191, 214–215, 225, 253, 279–280

Harmonious society 60–61, 69, 173, 180
Human dignity 38, 150
Human rights
    Approach 30
    Relationship with development 11–12, 58–61, 109–112

    Standards 53–55
    Treaty and documents 12–16, 21–24, 258
Humanity 151–152, 220–221, 227, 243, 260

Individual rights 59, 63–64, 245, 267–268
International cooperation 2–3, 12–17, 23, 27–29, 35–38, 41, 45–47, 61–62, 89–92, 126, 132, 135, 189, 192, 236

National Human Rights Action Plan 69–70, 115
NGOS 196

Peru 197–206

Regional development 186, 195, 211, 241–253
Right to development
    Content 173–175
    Concept 28–29, 39–40, 48–49, 51–54, 79–81, 106, 141–143, 168, 175–177
    Challenges and obstacles 18, 46–47, 49, 67, 129, 287
    Declaration 11–12, 16–18, 20–35, 37, 41, 47–49, 63, 75, 94–95, 106, 111, 133, 153, 168–169, 174–180, 189–190, 194–195, 197, 207, 211, 229–232, 236, 238–240, 246, 257–270, 284, 287
    Implementation 17, 20–21, 24–25, 27, 29, 31, 36–43, 46–47, 178–179, 182–184, 207, 211–216, 228, 246, 264, 288–302
    Orientation 60, 152, 169–170, 177–178, 180, 184, 258
    Principle 31–34, 177–178
    Relationship with human rights 58–61, 109–112
Rule of law 3, 65, 128–137, 182–184, 252, 272–276, 279–283, 286–287

Scholarship 208, 275–277
Sustainable development
    Emergence 143–148
    Goals 21–24, 141–143, 195–198
    Right 187–188

Sustainable development (cont.)
    Path    112–115
    Pillars    149–153
    Principles    79–85
South Asia    154–166
Social equity    180–182, 246–248
Social science    281–284

Technology    36, 44, 92, 113–114, 124, 126–128, 131, 155, 172, 185, 202, 239

Ubuntu-ism    207, 222–223, 226–228

United Nations
    Documents    12–16, 21–24, 63–67, 87–92, 105–108, 130–131, 259–260, 284–287
    Position    61–67

Vienna Declaration    20, 31, 63, 69, 113, 230, 238, 260, 263, 269
Vulnerable groups    4–5, 19, 32, 144, 206, 247

Wendou Village    94–104
WTO Regulation    85–86, 288–302